HELLBLAZER
rise + fall

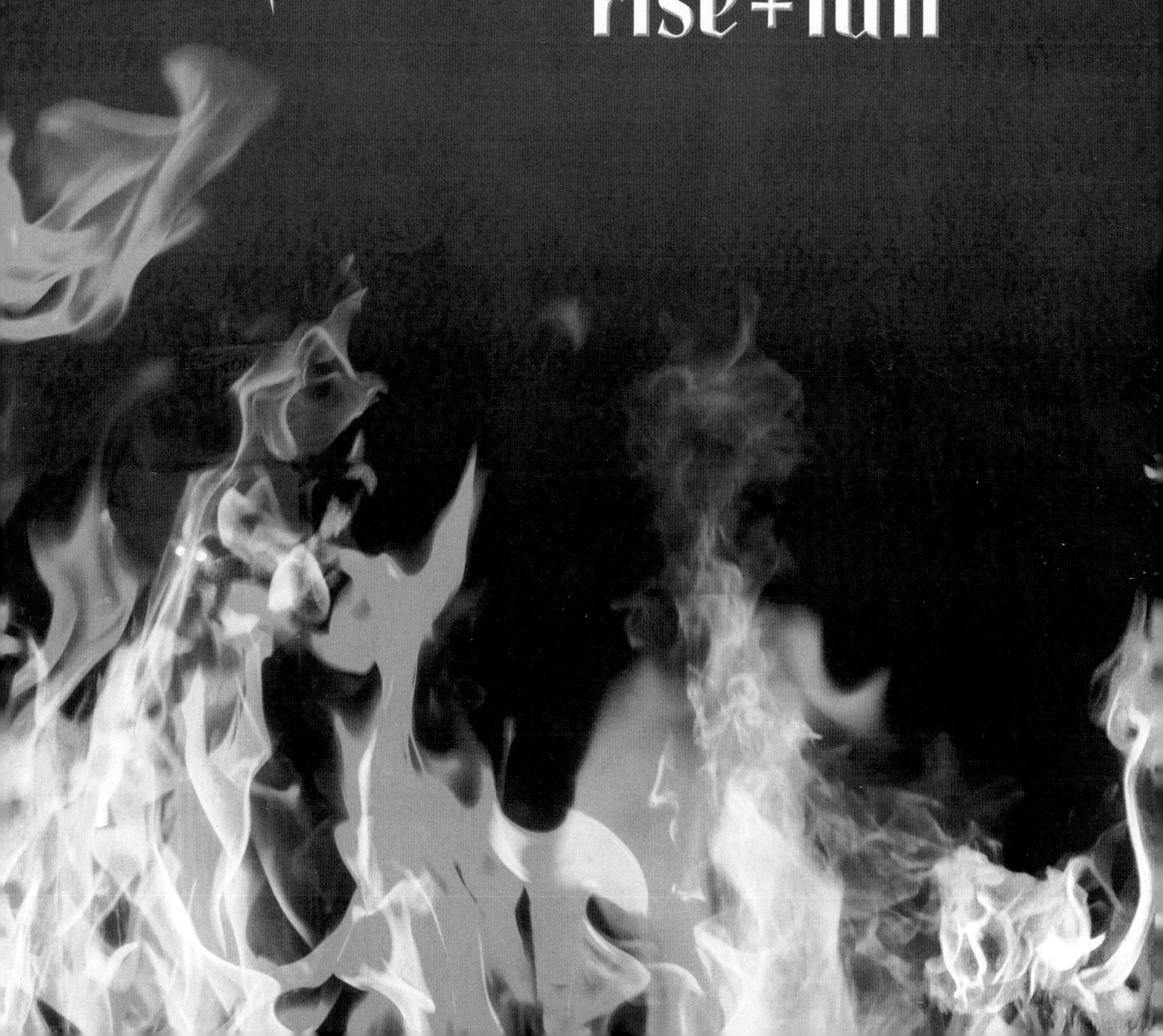

HELLBLAZER
rise + fall

story by
TOM TAYLOR

art by
DARICK ROBERTSON

color by
DIEGO RODRIGUEZ

lettering by
DERON BENNETT

cover art by
DARICK ROBERTSON
and
DIEGO RODRIGUEZ

John Constantine created by
Alan Moore, Steve Bissette, John Totleben,
and Jamie Delano & John Ridgway

ANDY KHOURI EDITOR – ORIGINAL SERIES
AMEDEO TURTURRO EDITOR – ORIGINAL SERIES & COLLECTED EDITION
MAGGIE HOWELL ASSOCIATE EDITOR – ORIGINAL SERIES
STEVE COOK DESIGN DIRECTOR – BOOKS
AMIE BROCKWAY-METCALF PUBLICATION DESIGN
SUZANNAH ROWNTREE PUBLICATION PRODUCTION

MARIE JAVINS EDITOR-IN-CHIEF, DC COMICS

DANIEL CHERRY III SENIOR VP – GENERAL MANAGER
JIM LEE PUBLISHER & CHIEF CREATIVE OFFICER
DON FALLETTI VP – MANUFACTURING OPERATIONS & WORKFLOW MANAGEMENT
LAWRENCE GANEM VP – TALENT SERVICES
ALISON GILL SENIOR VP – MANUFACTURING & OPERATIONS
NICK J. NAPOLITANO VP – MANUFACTURING ADMINISTRATION & DESIGN
NANCY SPEARS VP – REVENUE
MICHELE R. WELLS VP & EXECUTIVE EDITOR, YOUNG READER

HELLBLAZER: RISE AND FALL

Published by DC Comics. Compilation and all new material Copyright © 2021 DC Comics.
All Rights Reserved. Originally published in single magazine form in *Hellblazer: Rise and Fall* 1-3.
Copyright © 2020, 2021 DC Comics. All Rights Reserved. All characters, their distinctive likenesses,
and related elements featured in this publication are trademarks of DC Comics. The stories, characters,
and incidents featured in this publication are entirely fictional. DC Comics does not read or accept
unsolicited submissions of ideas, stories, or artwork. DC – a WarnerMedia Company.

DC Comics, 2900 West Alameda Ave., Burbank, CA 91505
Printed by Transcontinental Interglobe, Beauceville, QC, Canada. 3/19/21.
First Printing.
ISBN: 978-1-77950-466-1

Library of Congress Cataloging-in-Publication Data is available.

PEFC Certified

This product is
from sustainably
managed forests and
controlled sources

PEFC/01-31-106 www.pefc.org

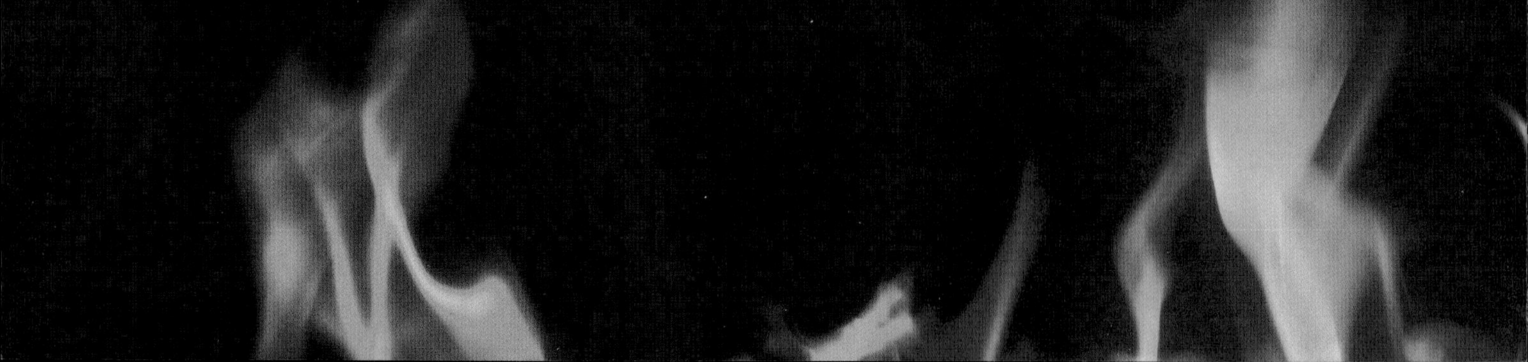

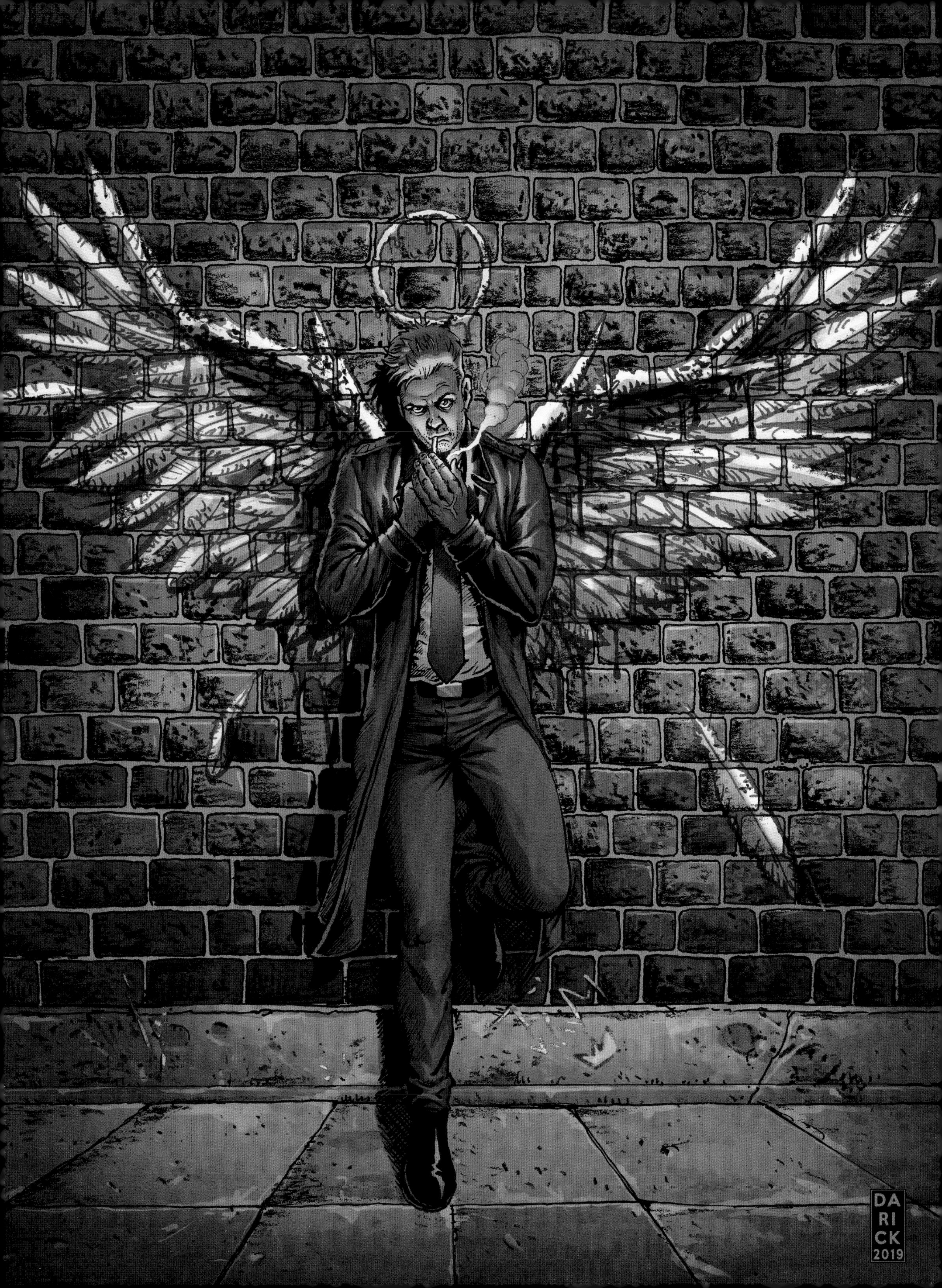
DA
RI
CK
2019

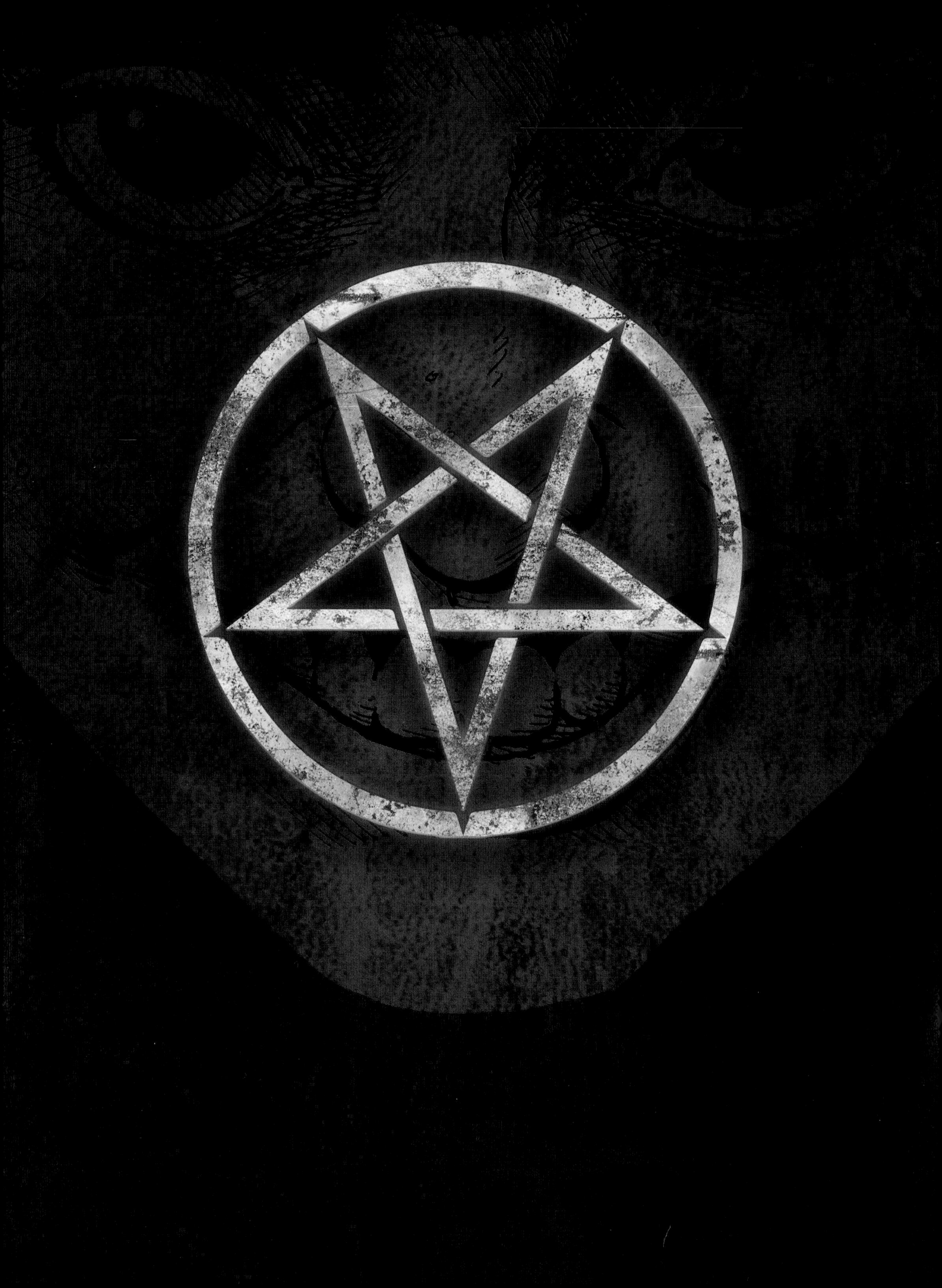

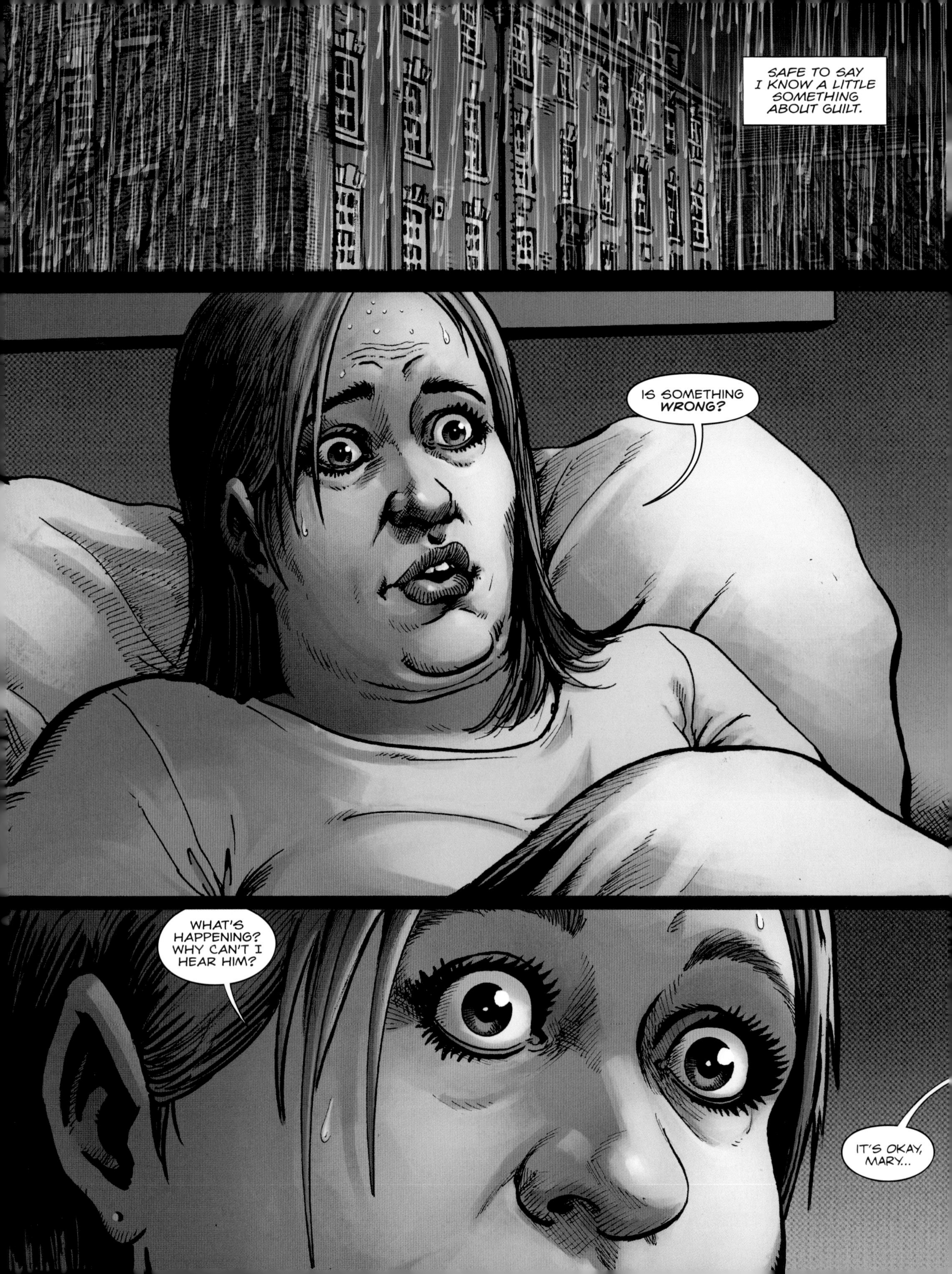
SAFE TO SAY I KNOW A LITTLE SOMETHING ABOUT GUILT.
IS SOMETHING *WRONG?*
WHAT'S HAPPENING? WHY CAN'T I HEAR HIM?
IT'S OKAY, MARY...

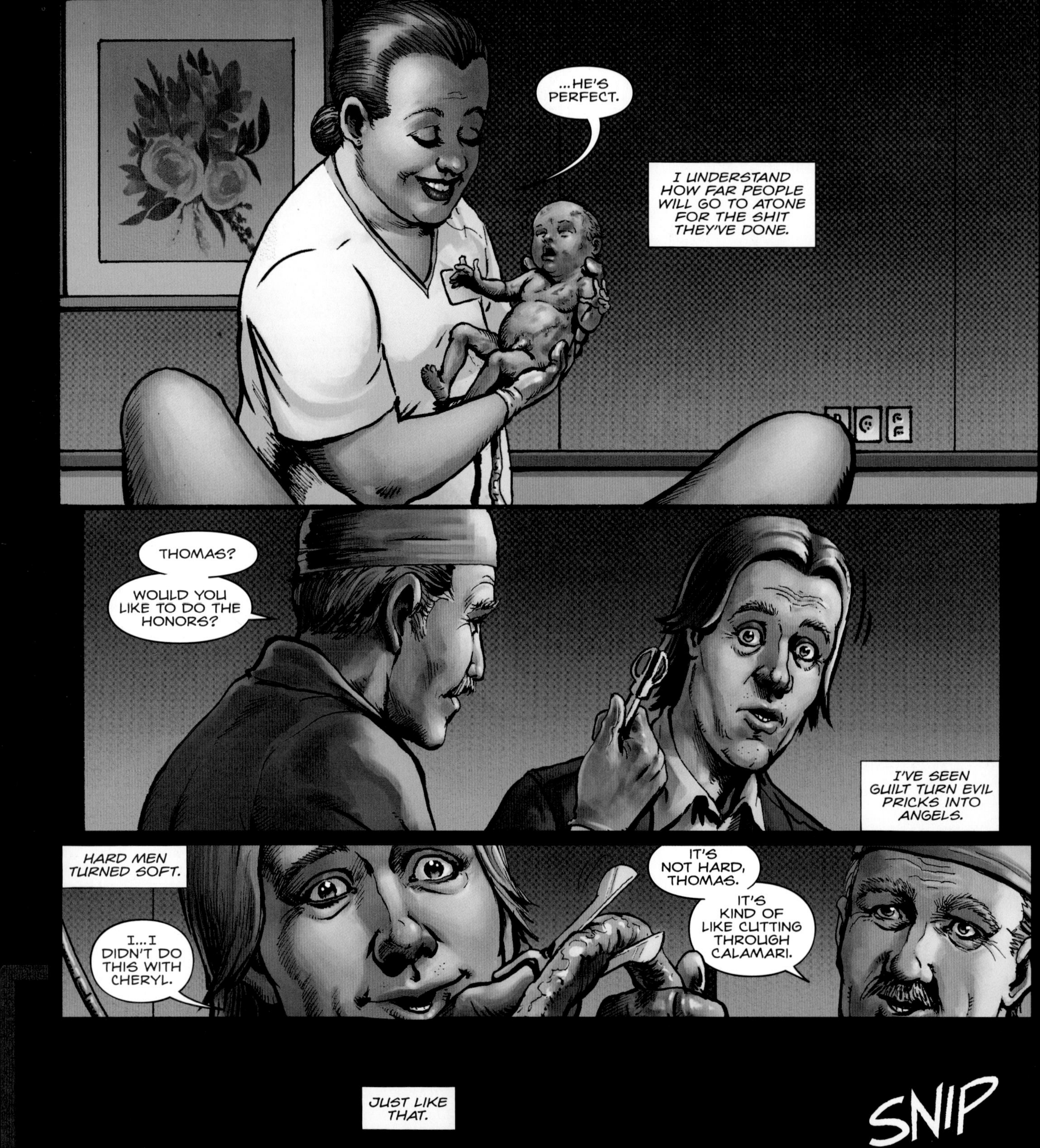
...HE'S PERFECT.
I UNDERSTAND HOW FAR PEOPLE WILL GO TO ATONE FOR THE SHIT THEY'VE DONE.
THOMAS?
WOULD YOU LIKE TO DO THE HONORS?
I'VE SEEN GUILT TURN EVIL PRICKS INTO ANGELS.
HARD MEN TURNED SOFT.
I...I DIDN'T DO THIS WITH CHERYL.
IT'S NOT HARD, THOMAS.
IT'S KIND OF LIKE CUTTING THROUGH CALAMARI.
JUST LIKE THAT.
SNIP

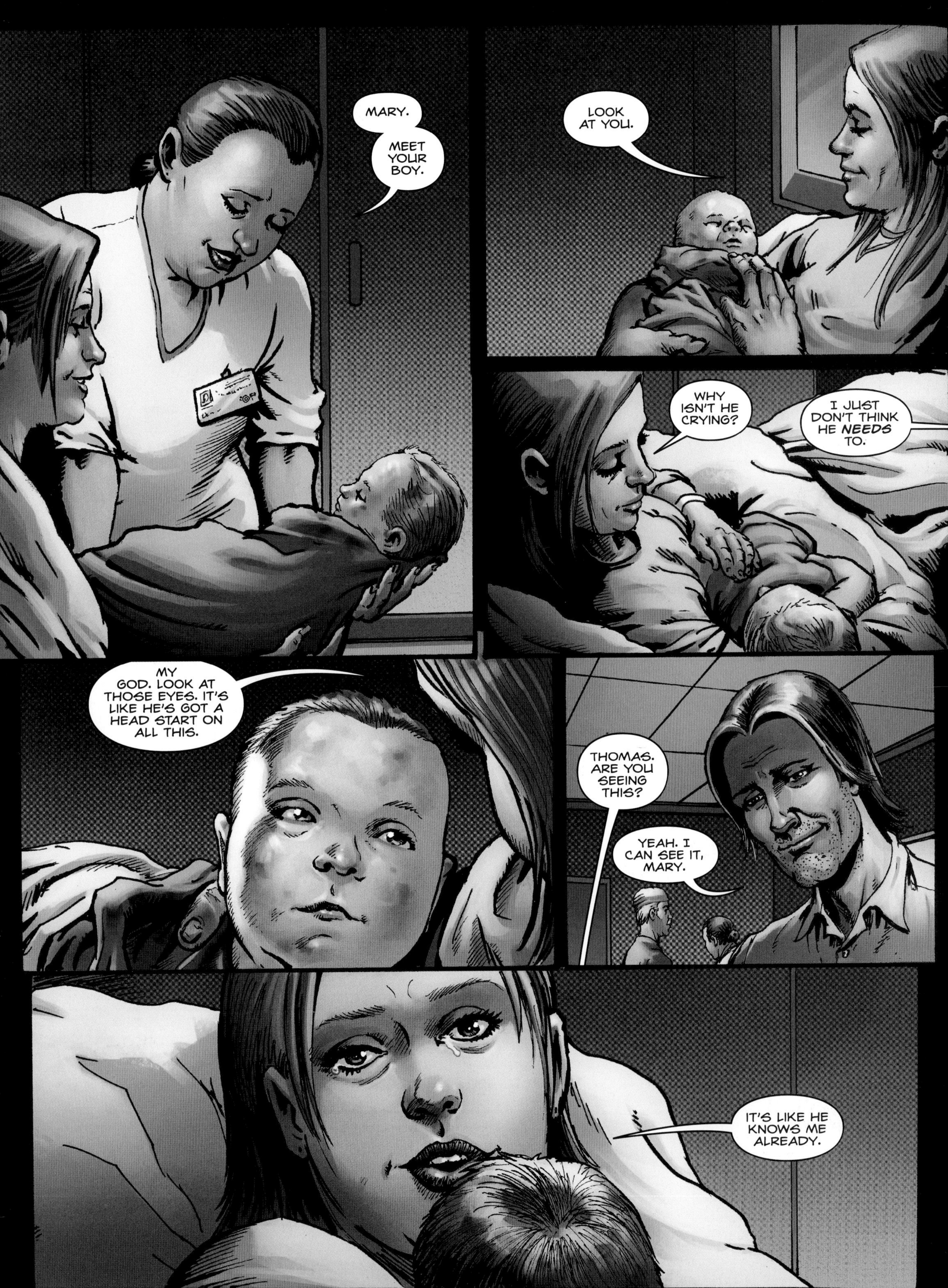
MARY.
MEET YOUR BOY.
LOOK AT YOU.
WHY ISN'T HE CRYING?
I JUST DON'T THINK HE NEEDS TO.
MY GOD. LOOK AT THOSE EYES. IT'S LIKE HE'S GOT A HEAD START ON ALL THIS.
THOMAS. ARE YOU SEEING THIS?
YEAH. I CAN SEE IT, MARY.
IT'S LIKE HE KNOWS ME ALREADY.

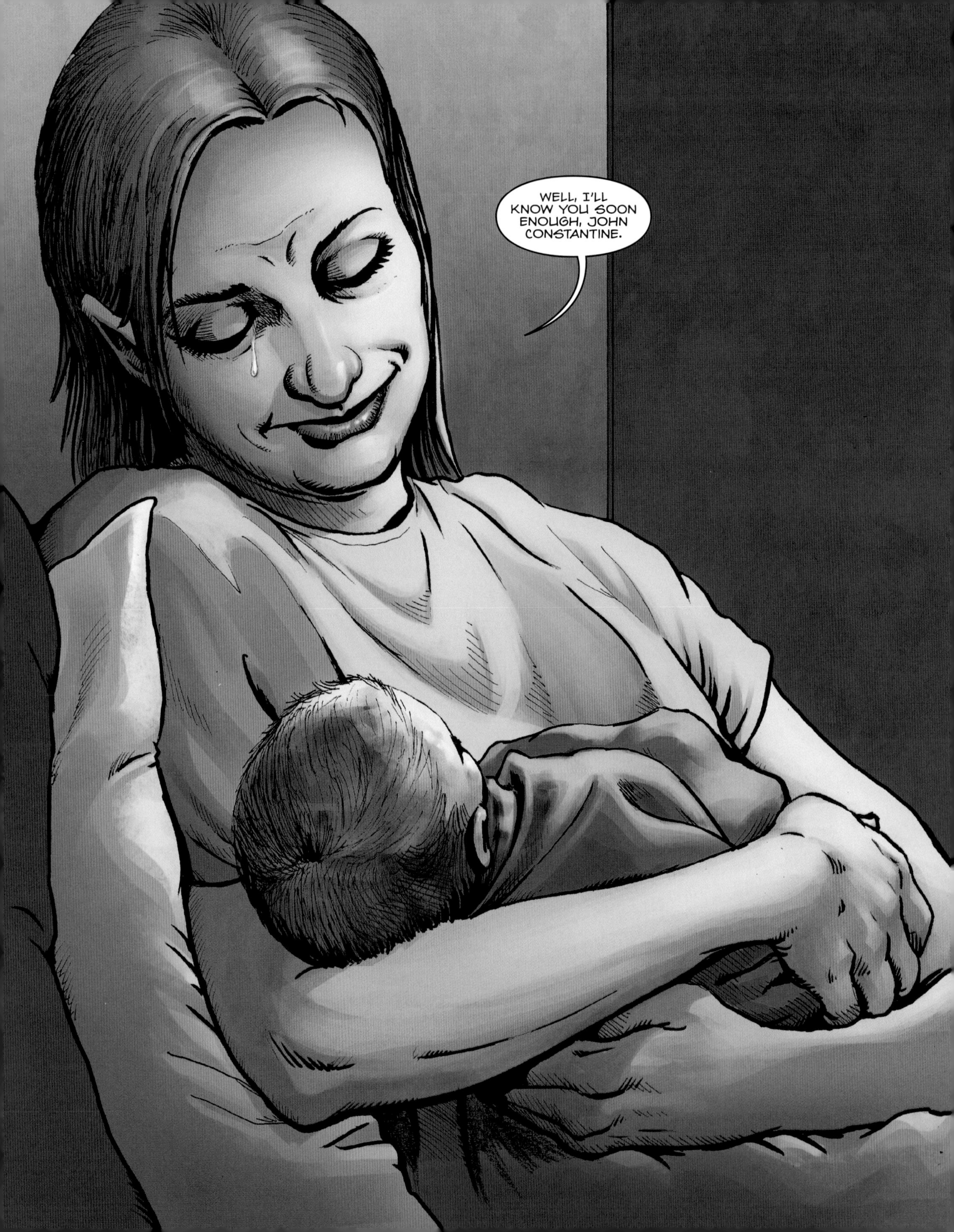
WELL, I'LL KNOW YOU SOON ENOUGH, JOHN CONSTANTINE.

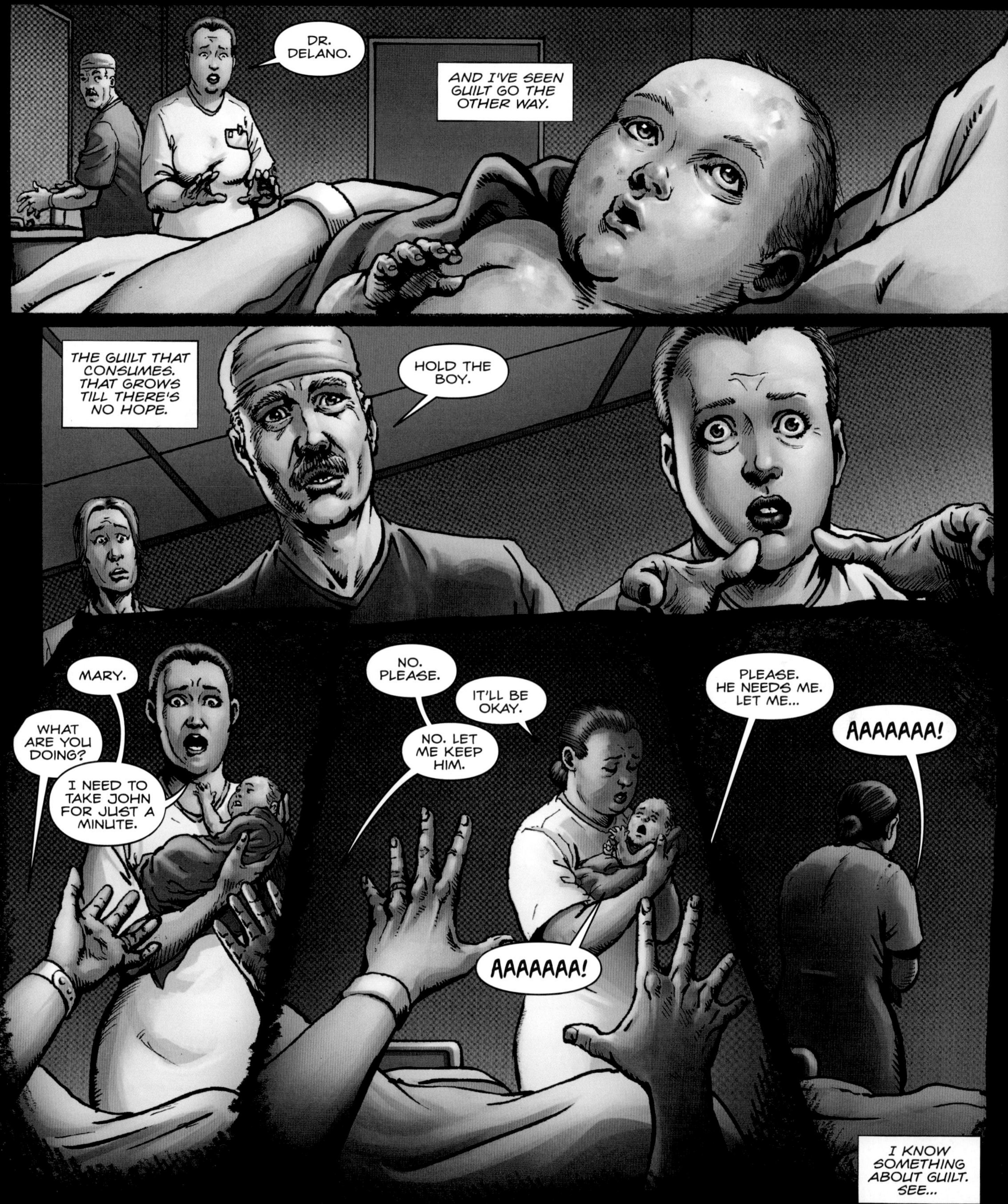
DR. DELANO.
AND I'VE SEEN GUILT GO THE OTHER WAY.
THE GUILT THAT CONSUMES. THAT GROWS TILL THERE'S NO HOPE.
HOLD THE BOY.
MARY.
WHAT ARE YOU DOING?
I NEED TO TAKE JOHN FOR JUST A MINUTE.
NO. PLEASE.
IT'LL BE OKAY.
NO. LET ME KEEP HIM.
AAAAAAA!
PLEASE. HE NEEDS ME. LET ME...
AAAAAAA!
I KNOW SOMETHING ABOUT GUILT. SEE...

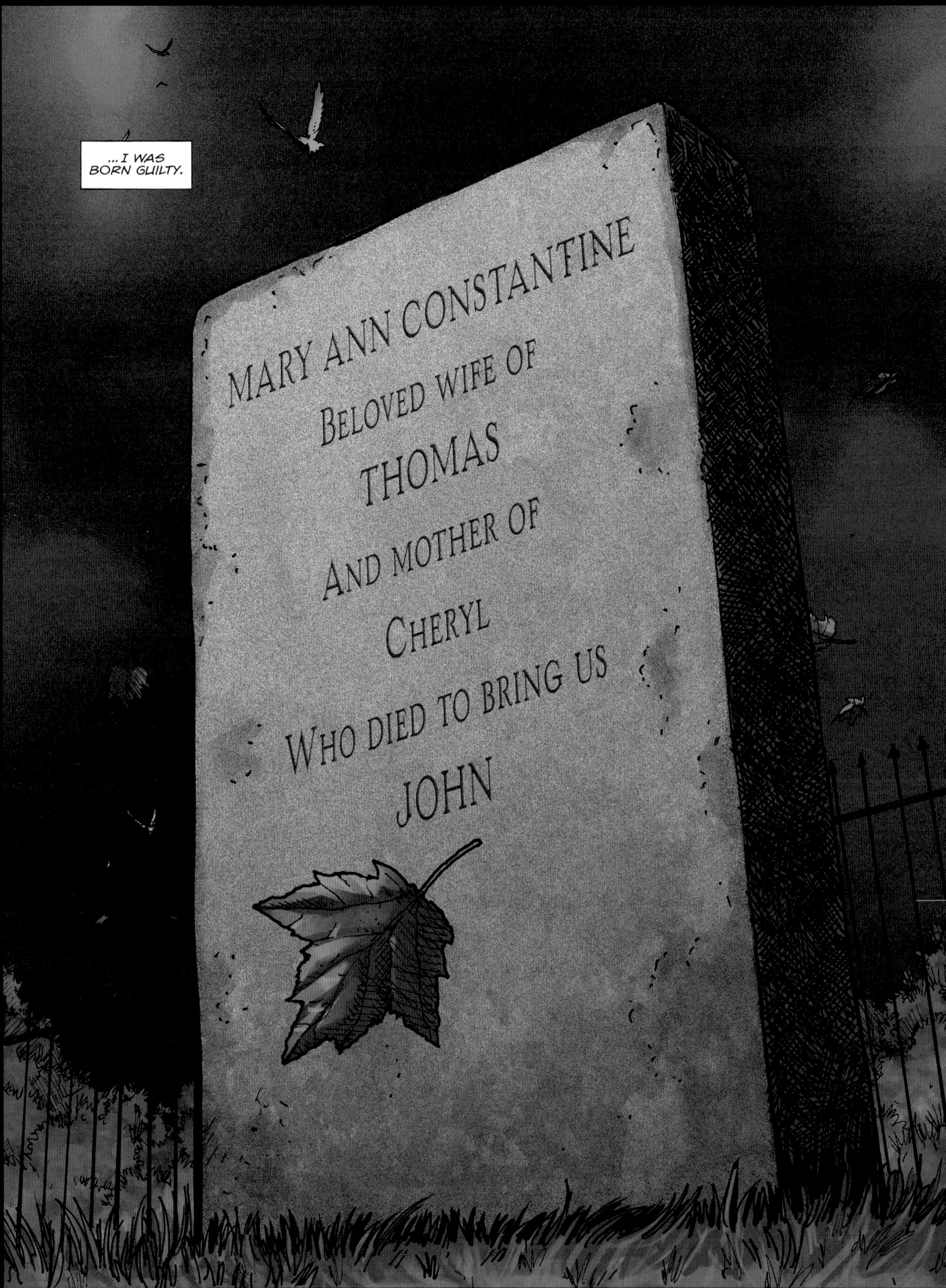
...I WAS BORN GUILTY.
MARY ANN CONSTANTINE
BELOVED WIFE OF
THOMAS
AND MOTHER OF
CHERYL
WHO DIED TO BRING US
JOHN

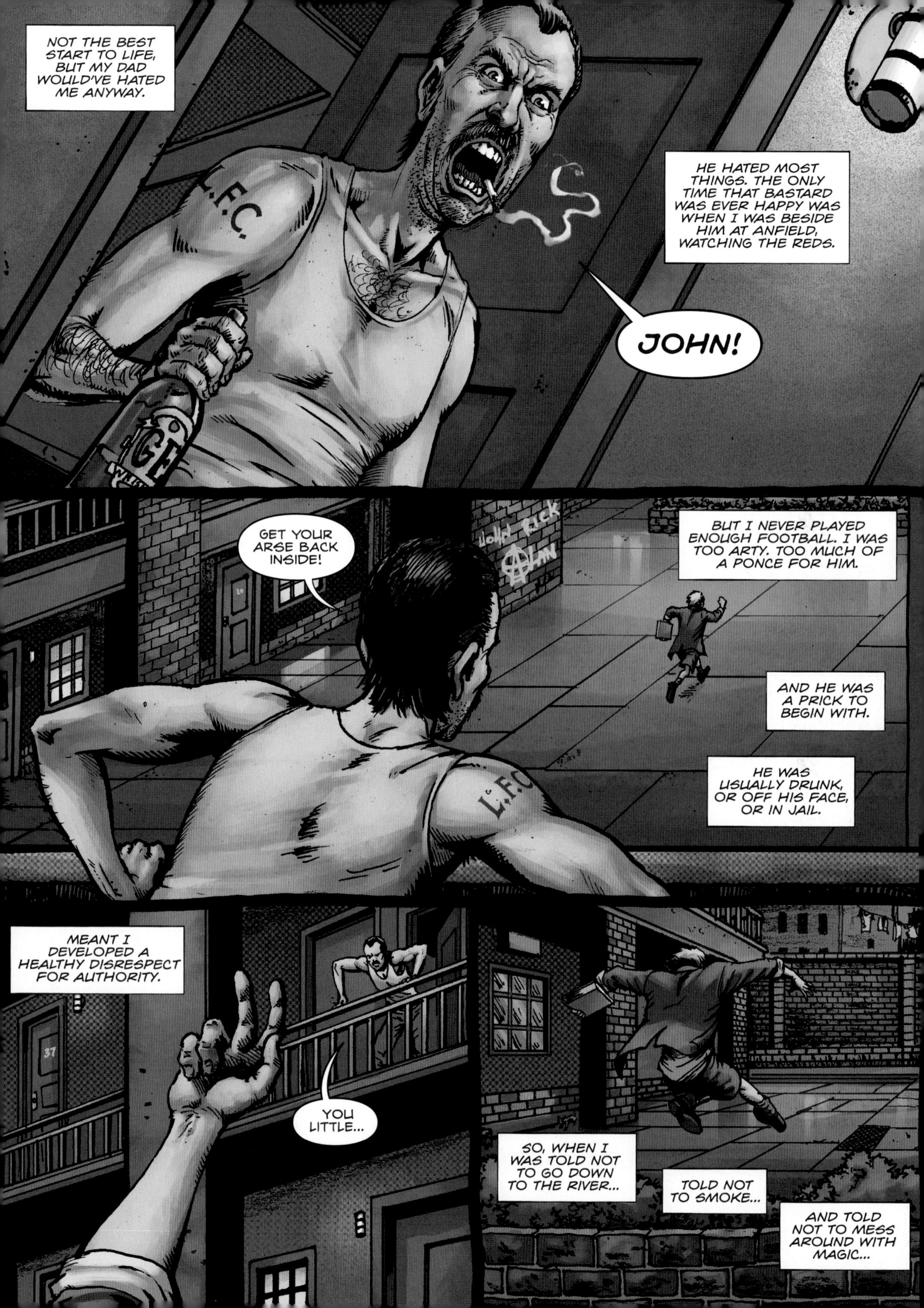
NOT THE BEST START TO LIFE, BUT MY DAD WOULD'VE HATED ME ANYWAY.
HE HATED MOST THINGS. THE ONLY TIME THAT BASTARD WAS EVER HAPPY WAS WHEN I WAS BESIDE HIM AT ANFIELD, WATCHING THE REDS.
JOHN!
GET YOUR ARSE BACK INSIDE!
BUT I NEVER PLAYED ENOUGH FOOTBALL. I WAS TOO ARTY. TOO MUCH OF A PONCE FOR HIM.
AND HE WAS A PRICK TO BEGIN WITH.
HE WAS USUALLY DRUNK, OR OFF HIS FACE, OR IN JAIL.
MEANT I DEVELOPED A HEALTHY DISRESPECT FOR AUTHORITY.
YOU LITTLE...
SO, WHEN I WAS TOLD NOT TO GO DOWN TO THE RIVER...
TOLD NOT TO SMOKE...
AND TOLD NOT TO MESS AROUND WITH MAGIC...

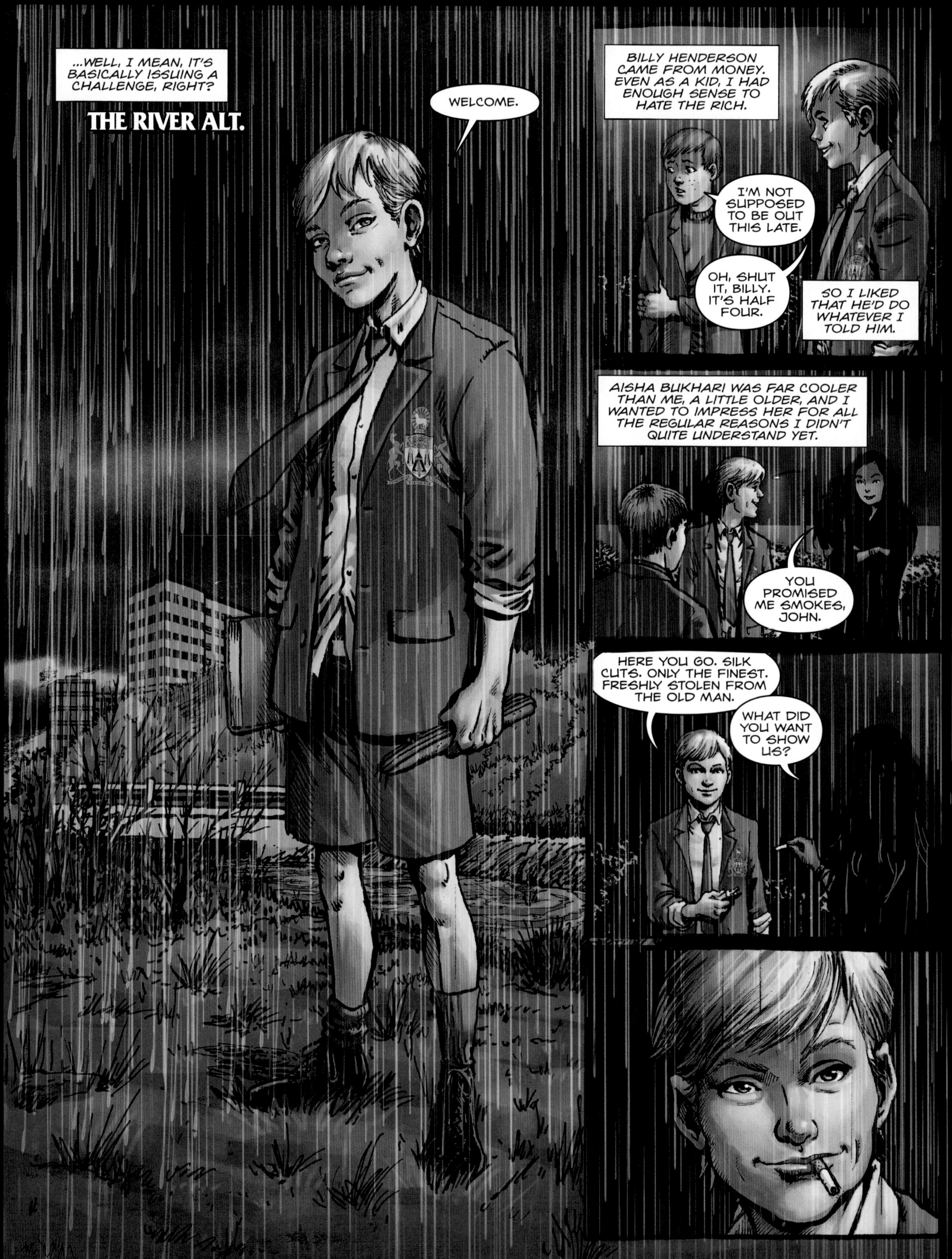

...WELL, I MEAN, IT'S BASICALLY ISSUING A CHALLENGE, RIGHT?
THE RIVER ALT.
WELCOME.
BILLY HENDERSON CAME FROM MONEY. EVEN AS A KID, I HAD ENOUGH SENSE TO HATE THE RICH.
I'M NOT SUPPOSED TO BE OUT THIS LATE.
OH, SHUT IT, BILLY. IT'S HALF FOUR.
SO I LIKED THAT HE'D DO WHATEVER I TOLD HIM.
AISHA BUKHARI WAS FAR COOLER THAN ME, A LITTLE OLDER, AND I WANTED TO IMPRESS HER FOR ALL THE REGULAR REASONS I DIDN'T QUITE UNDERSTAND YET.
YOU PROMISED ME SMOKES, JOHN.
HERE YOU GO. SILK CUTS. ONLY THE FINEST. FRESHLY STOLEN FROM THE OLD MAN.
WHAT DID YOU WANT TO SHOW US?

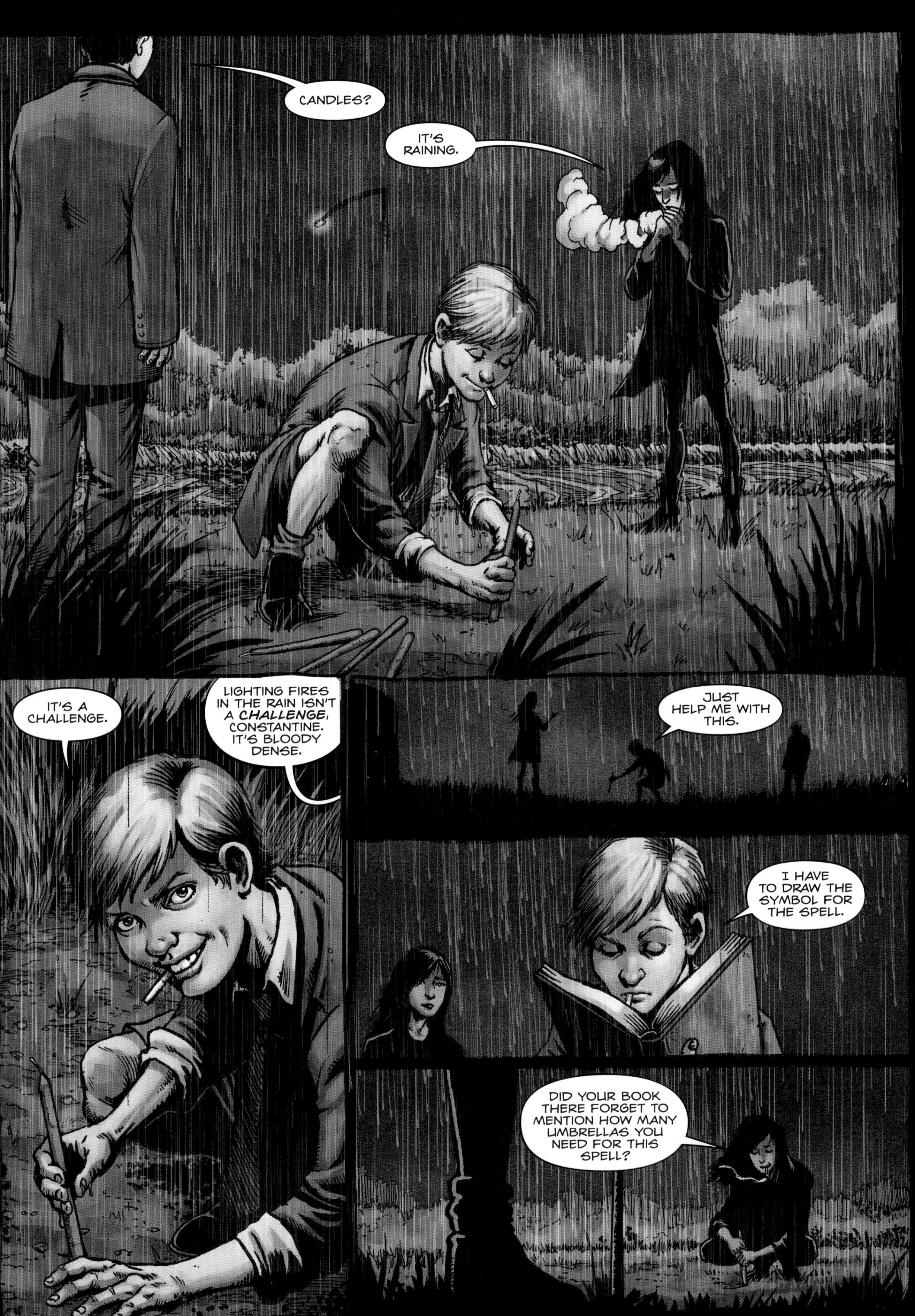
CANDLES?
IT'S RAINING.
IT'S A CHALLENGE.
LIGHTING FIRES IN THE RAIN ISN'T A CHALLENGE, CONSTANTINE. IT'S BLOODY DENSE.
JUST HELP ME WITH THIS.
I HAVE TO DRAW THE SYMBOL FOR THE SPELL.
DID YOUR BOOK THERE FORGET TO MENTION HOW MANY UMBRELLAS YOU NEED FOR THIS SPELL?

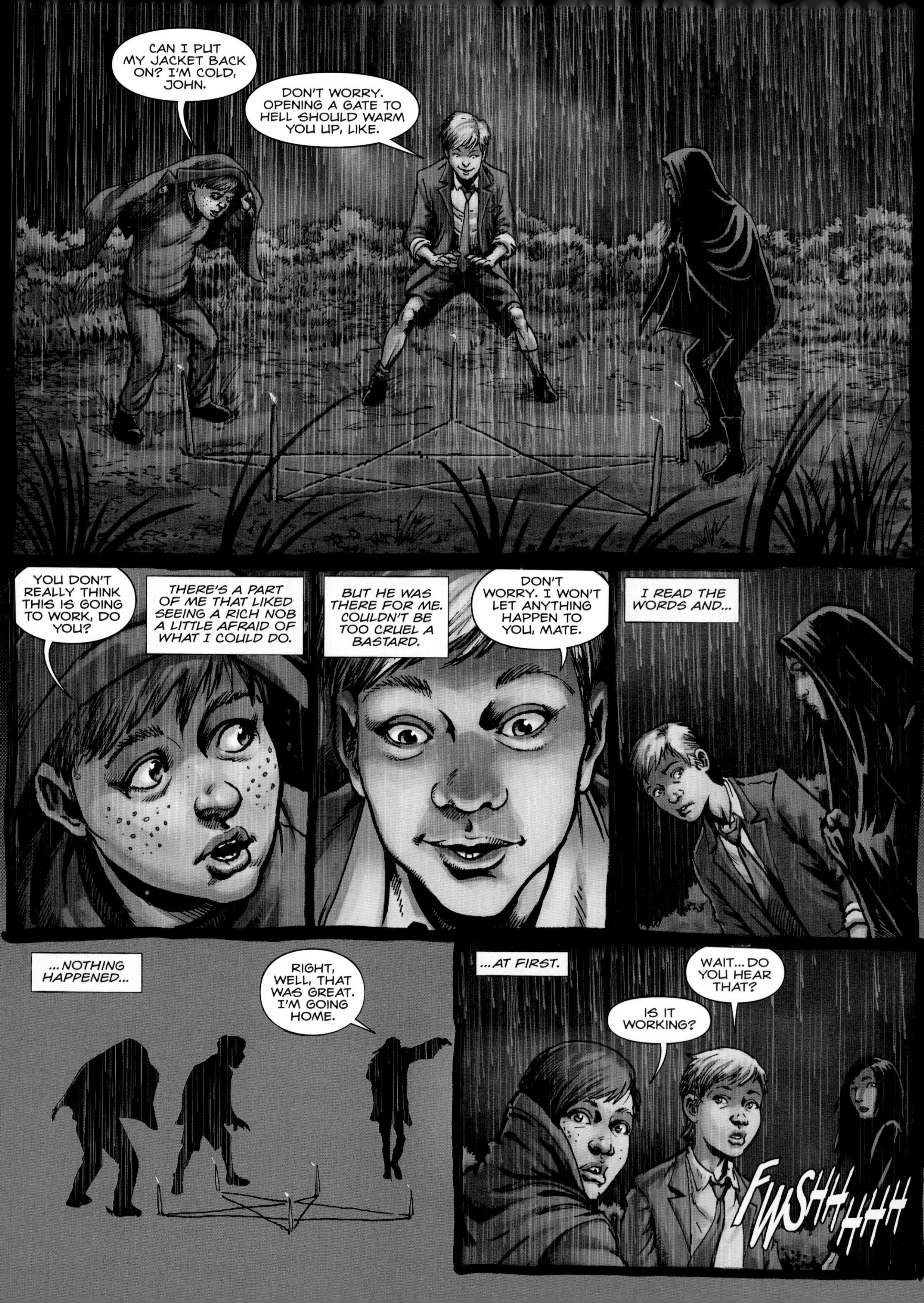
CAN I PUT MY JACKET BACK ON? I'M COLD, JOHN.
DON'T WORRY. OPENING A GATE TO HELL SHOULD WARM YOU UP, LIKE.
YOU DON'T REALLY THINK THIS IS GOING TO WORK, DO YOU?
THERE'S A PART OF ME THAT LIKED SEEING A RICH NOB A LITTLE AFRAID OF WHAT I COULD DO.
BUT HE WAS THERE FOR ME. COULDN'T BE TOO CRUEL A BASTARD.
DON'T WORRY. I WON'T LET ANYTHING HAPPEN TO YOU, MATE.
I READ THE WORDS AND...
...NOTHING HAPPENED...
RIGHT, WELL, THAT WAS GREAT. I'M GOING HOME.
...AT FIRST.
WAIT... DO YOU HEAR THAT?
IS IT WORKING?
FWSHHHHH

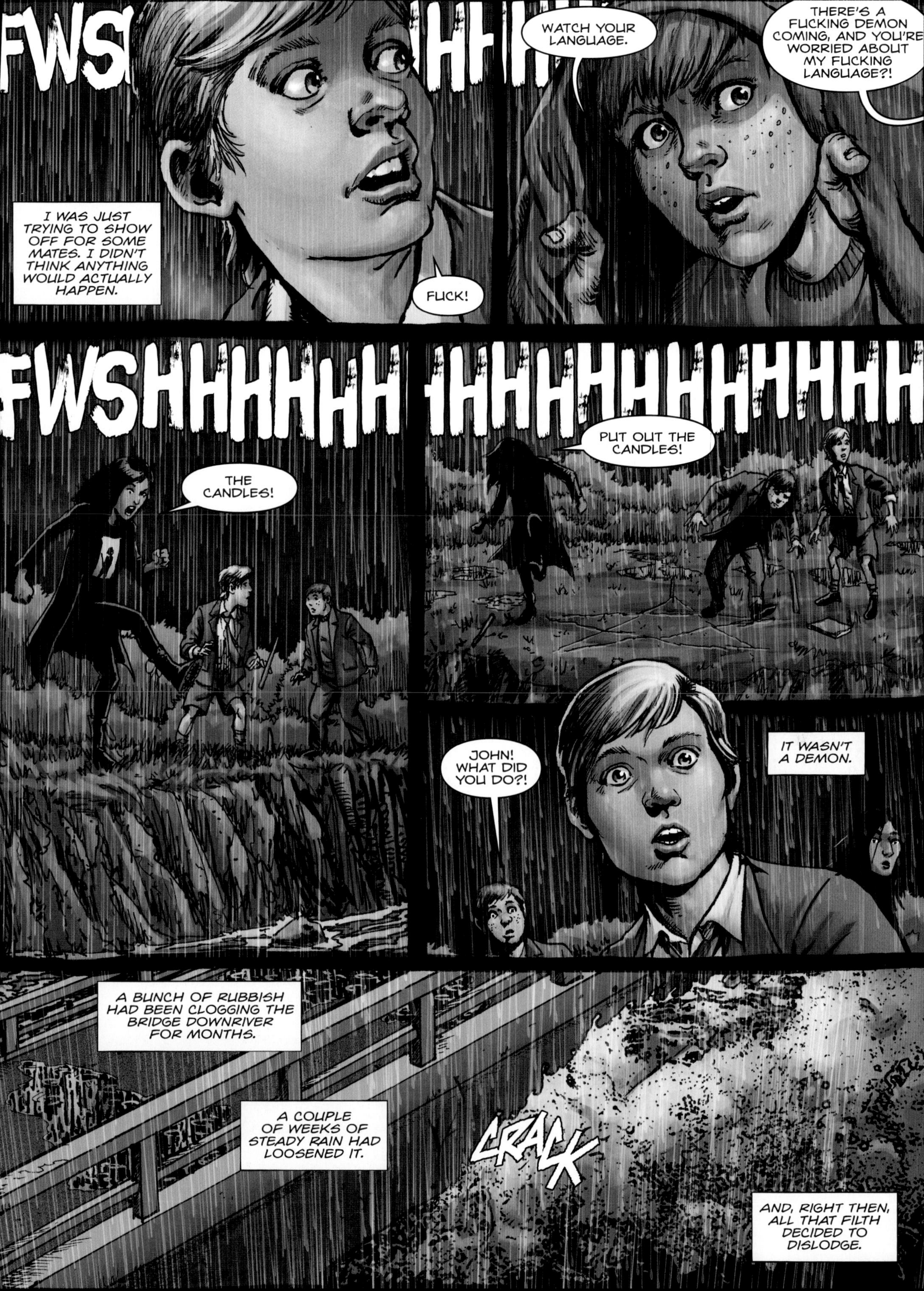
FWSHHHH
I WAS JUST TRYING TO SHOW OFF FOR SOME MATES. I DIDN'T THINK ANYTHING WOULD ACTUALLY HAPPEN.
FUCK!
WATCH YOUR LANGUAGE.
THERE'S A FUCKING DEMON COMING, AND YOU'RE WORRIED ABOUT MY FUCKING LANGUAGE?!
FWSHHHHHH HHHHHHHHHHH
THE CANDLES!
PUT OUT THE CANDLES!
JOHN! WHAT DID YOU DO?!
IT WASN'T A DEMON.
A BUNCH OF RUBBISH HAD BEEN CLOGGING THE BRIDGE DOWNRIVER FOR MONTHS.
A COUPLE OF WEEKS OF STEADY RAIN HAD LOOSENED IT.
CRACK
AND, RIGHT THEN, ALL THAT FILTH DECIDED TO DISLODGE.

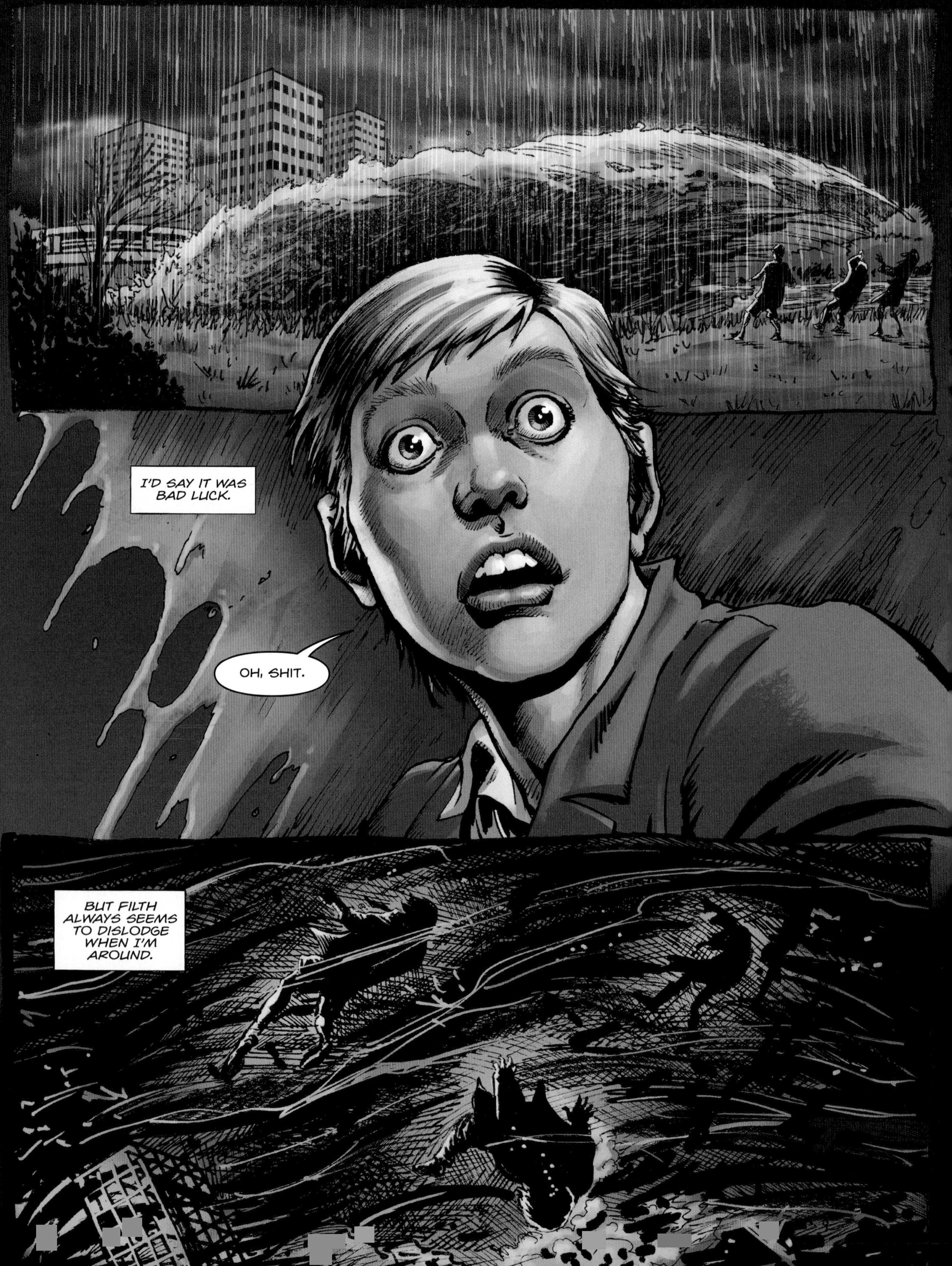
I'D SAY IT WAS BAD LUCK.
OH, SHIT.
BUT FILTH ALWAYS SEEMS TO DISLODGE WHEN I'M AROUND.

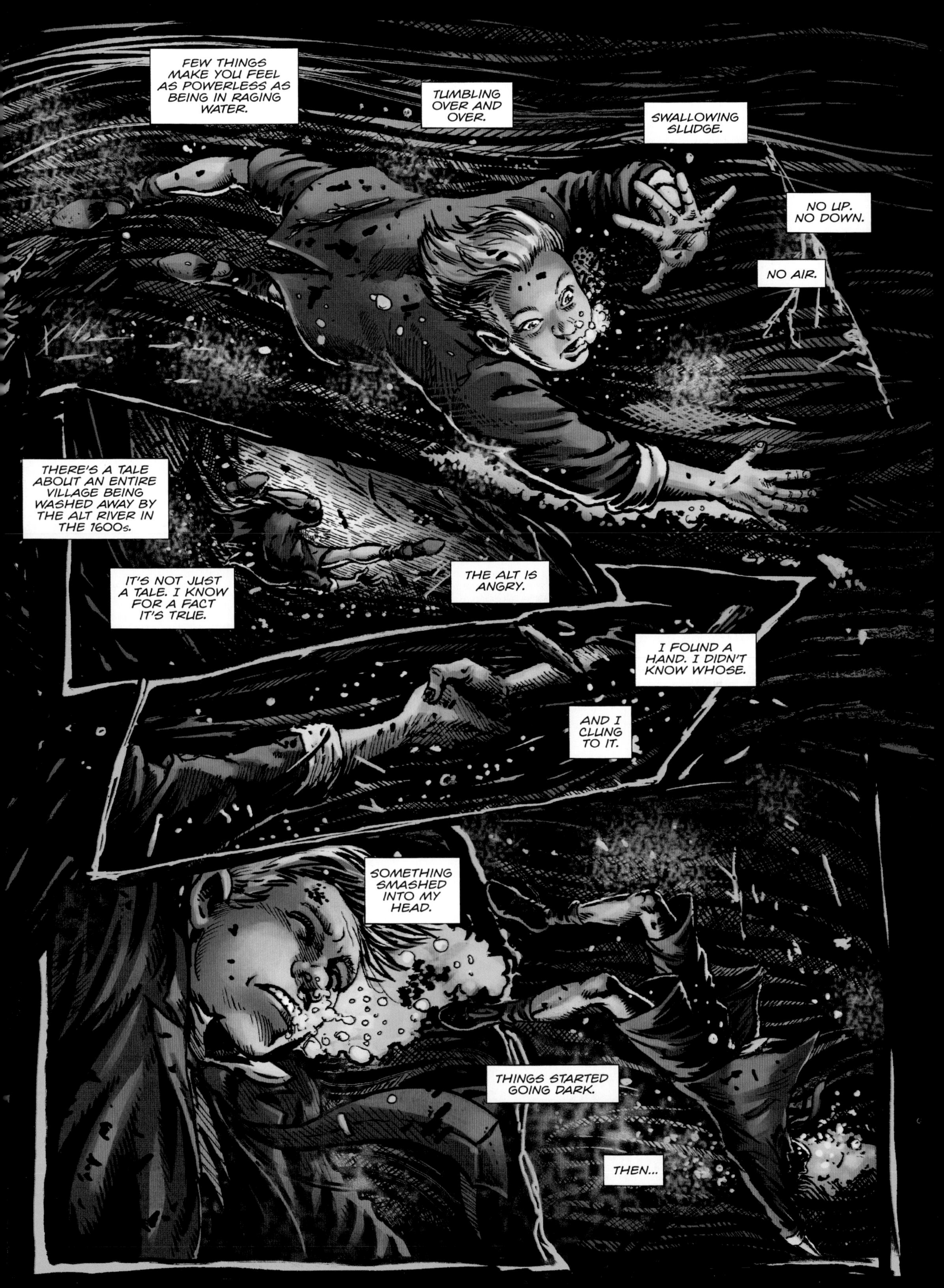
FEW THINGS MAKE YOU FEEL AS POWERLESS AS BEING IN RAGING WATER.
TUMBLING OVER AND OVER.
SWALLOWING SLUDGE.
NO UP. NO DOWN.
NO AIR.
THERE'S A TALE ABOUT AN ENTIRE VILLAGE BEING WASHED AWAY BY THE ALT RIVER IN THE 1600s.
IT'S NOT JUST A TALE. I KNOW FOR A FACT IT'S TRUE.
THE ALT IS ANGRY.
I FOUND A HAND. I DIDN'T KNOW WHOSE.
AND I CLUNG TO IT.
SOMETHING SMASHED INTO MY HEAD.
THINGS STARTED GOING DARK.
THEN...

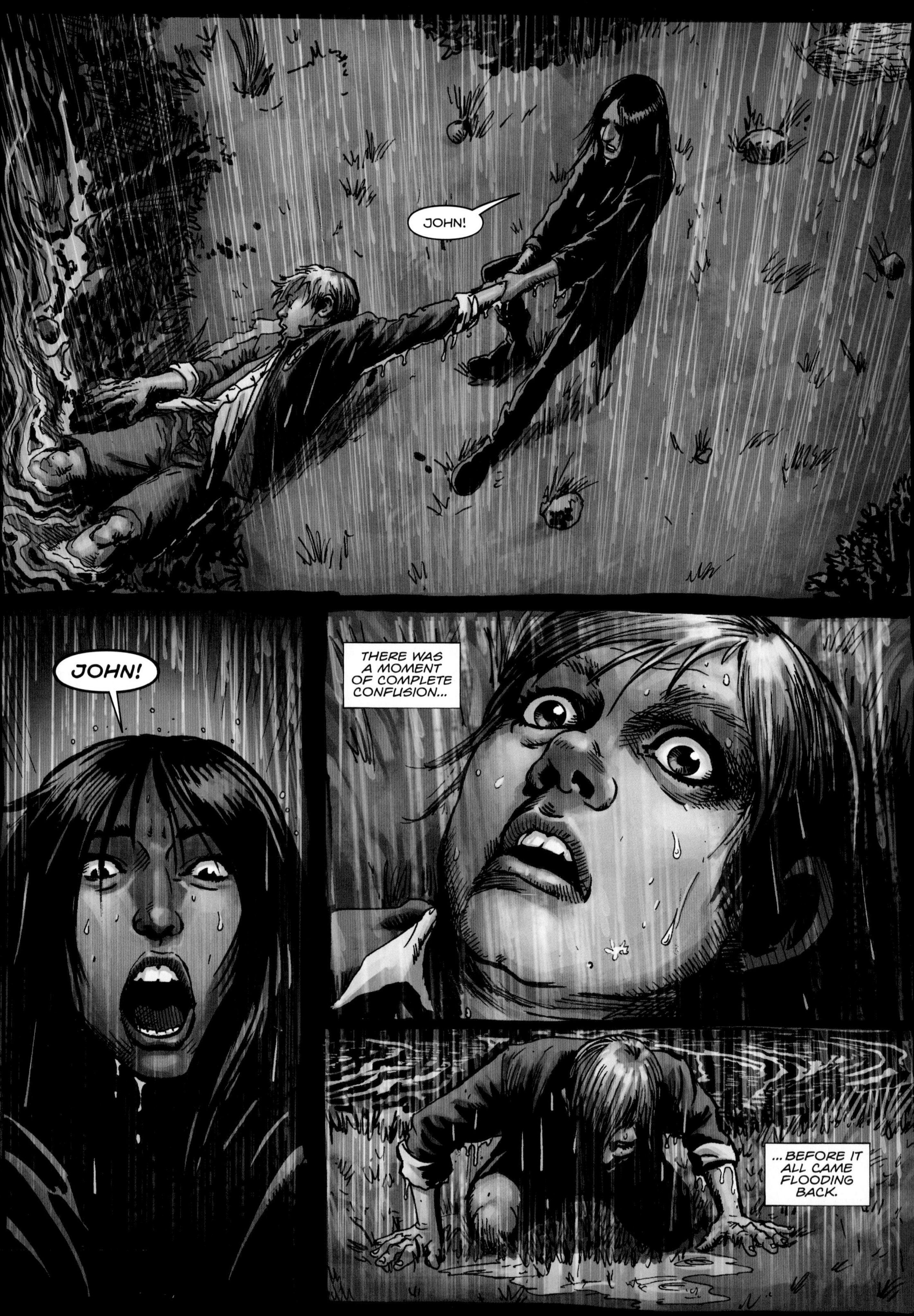
JOHN!
JOHN!
THERE WAS A MOMENT OF COMPLETE CONFUSION...
...BEFORE IT ALL CAME FLOODING BACK.

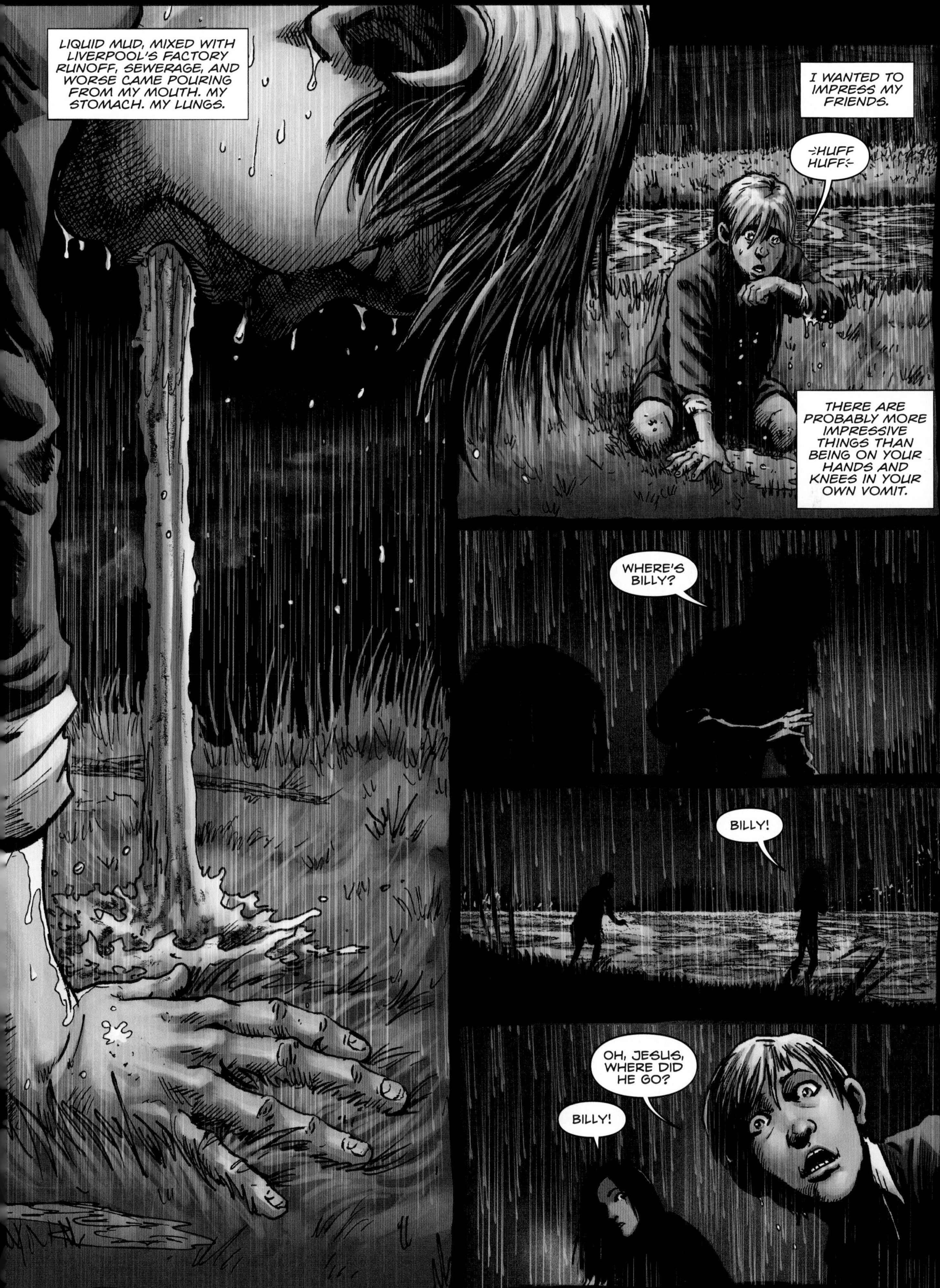
LIQUID MUD, MIXED WITH LIVERPOOL'S FACTORY RUNOFF, SEWERAGE, AND WORSE CAME POURING FROM MY MOUTH. MY STOMACH. MY LUNGS.
I WANTED TO IMPRESS MY FRIENDS.
HUFF HUFF
THERE ARE PROBABLY MORE IMPRESSIVE THINGS THAN BEING ON YOUR HANDS AND KNEES IN YOUR OWN VOMIT.
WHERE'S BILLY?
BILLY!
OH, JESUS, WHERE DID HE GO?
BILLY!

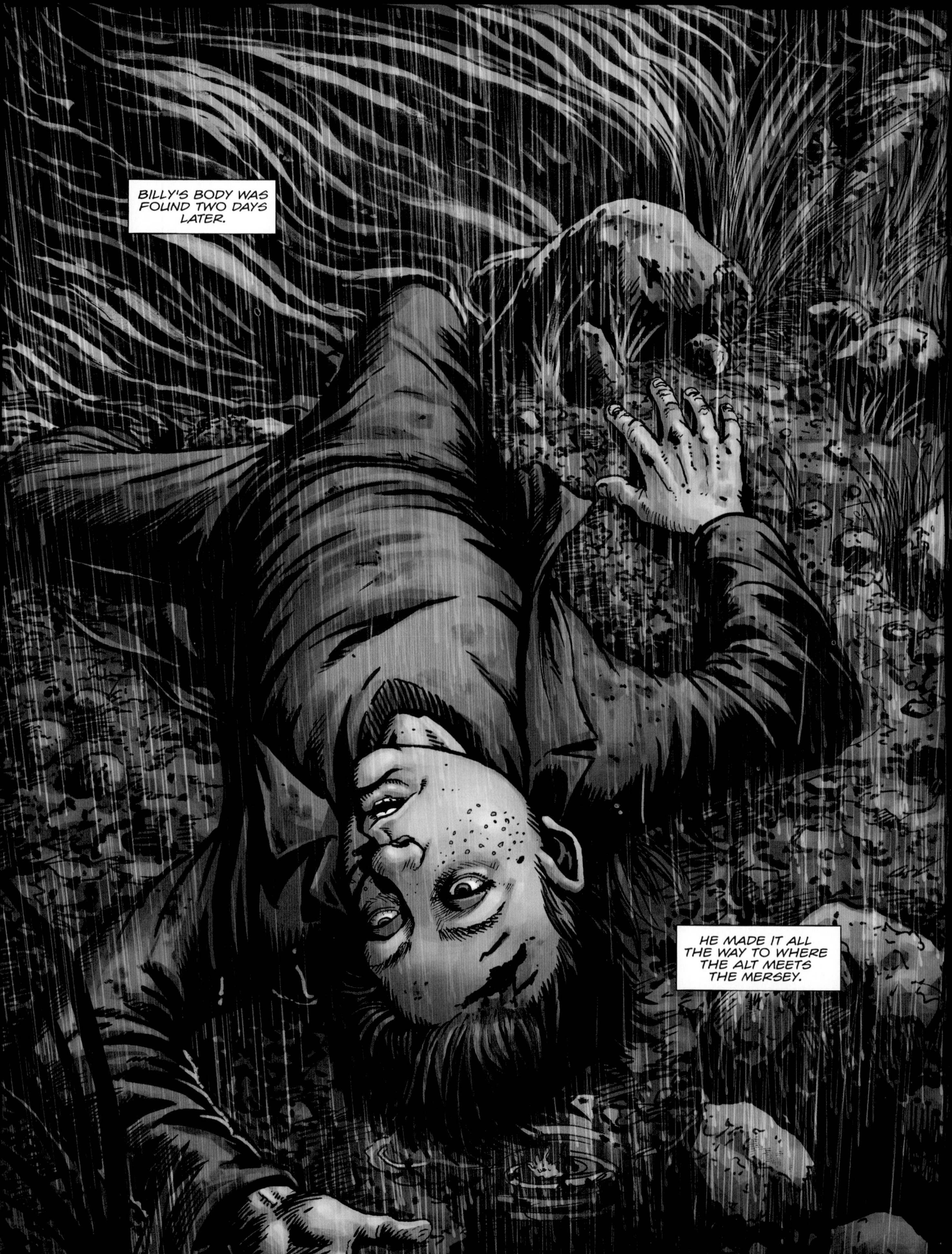
BILLY'S BODY WAS FOUND TWO DAYS LATER.
HE MADE IT ALL THE WAY TO WHERE THE ALT MEETS THE MERSEY.

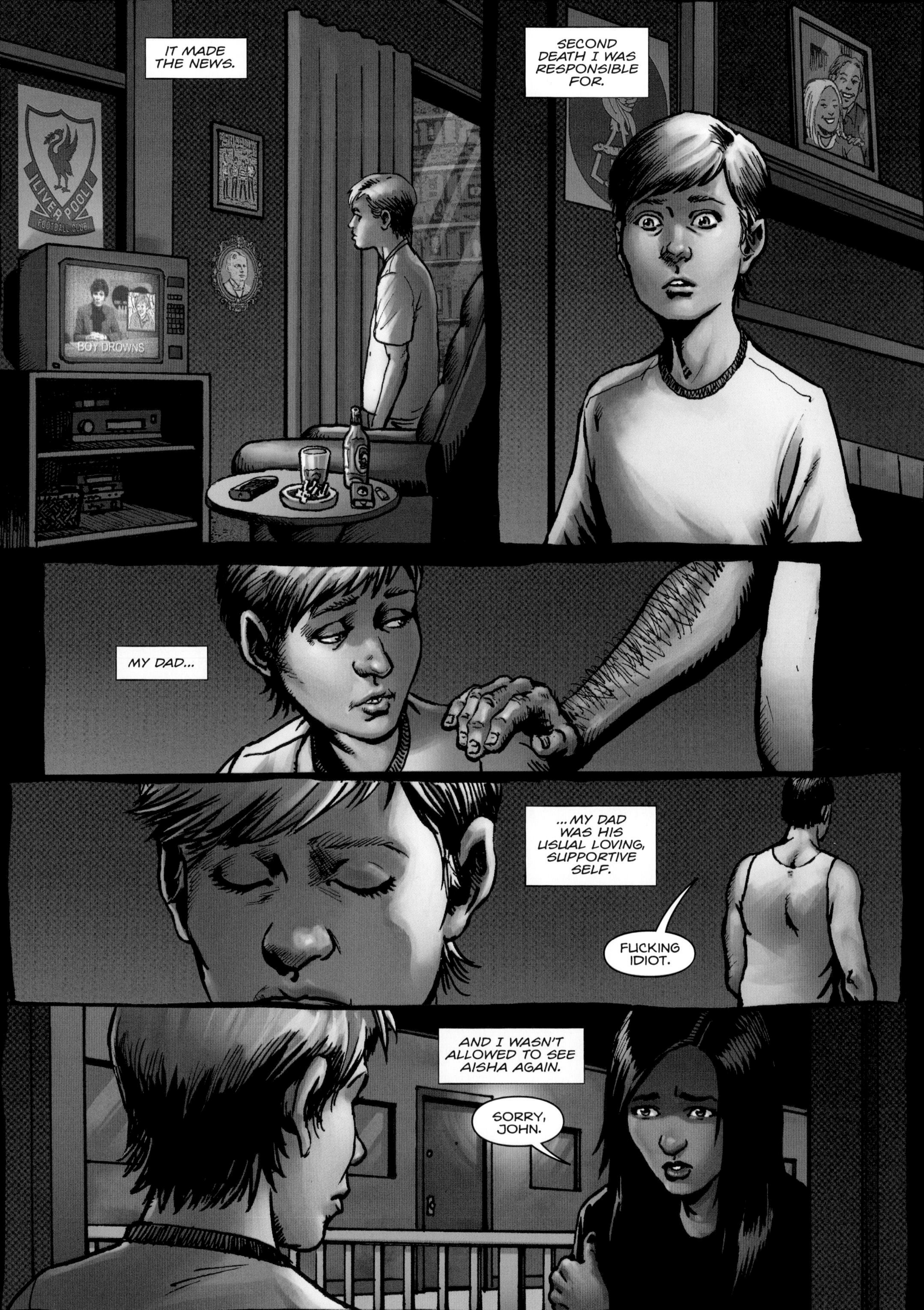
IT MADE THE NEWS.
SECOND DEATH I WAS RESPONSIBLE FOR.
LIVERPOOL FOOTBALL CLUB
BOY DROWNS
MY DAD...
...MY DAD WAS HIS USUAL LOVING, SUPPORTIVE SELF.
FUCKING IDIOT.
AND I WASN'T ALLOWED TO SEE AISHA AGAIN.
SORRY, JOHN.

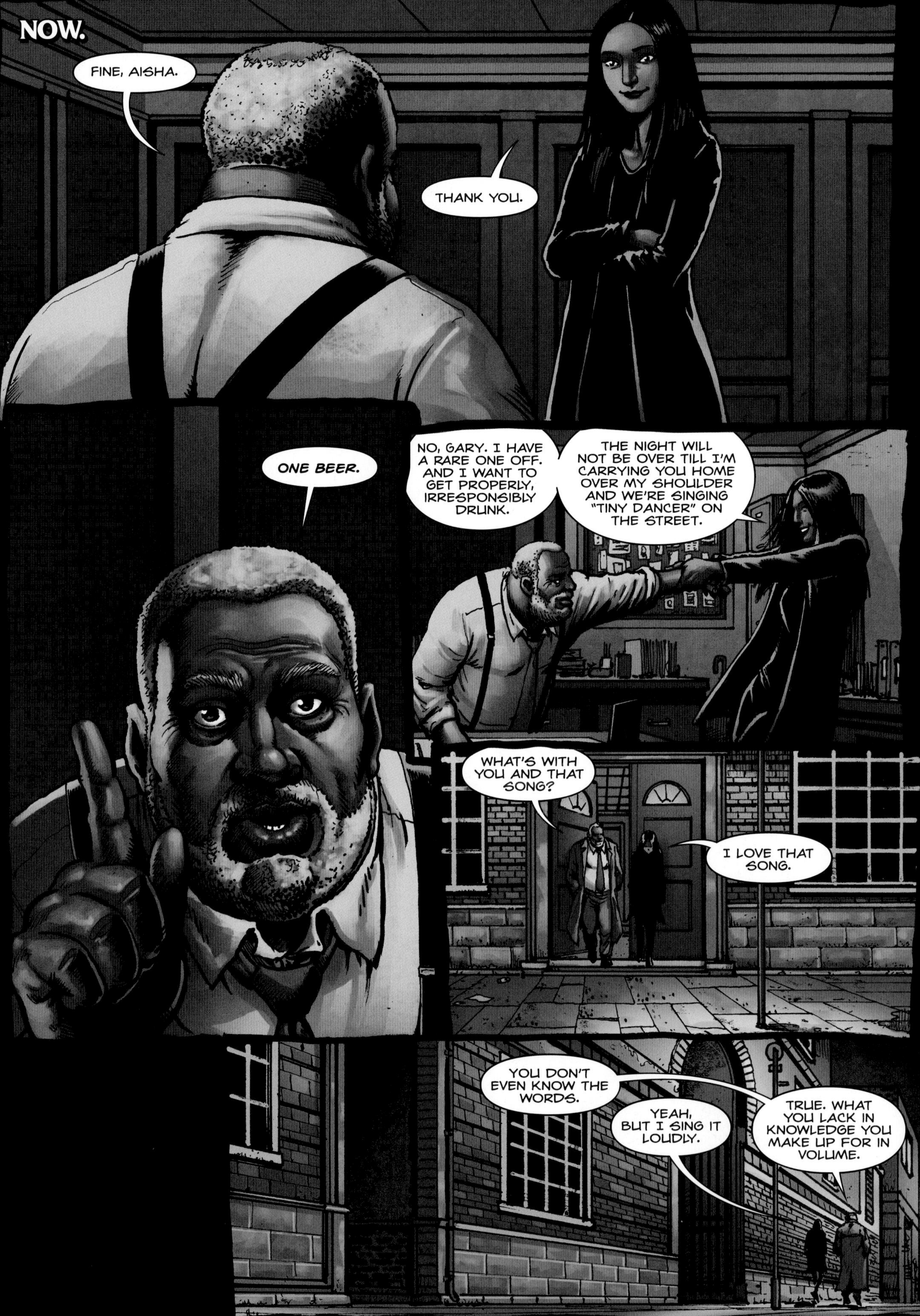
NOW.
FINE, AISHA.
THANK YOU.
ONE BEER.
NO, GARY. I HAVE A RARE ONE OFF. AND I WANT TO GET PROPERLY, IRRESPONSIBLY DRUNK.
THE NIGHT WILL NOT BE OVER TILL I'M CARRYING YOU HOME OVER MY SHOULDER AND WE'RE SINGING "TINY DANCER" ON THE STREET.
WHAT'S WITH YOU AND THAT SONG?
I LOVE THAT SONG.
YOU DON'T EVEN KNOW THE WORDS.
YEAH, BUT I SING IT LOUDLY.
TRUE. WHAT YOU LACK IN KNOWLEDGE YOU MAKE UP FOR IN VOLUME.

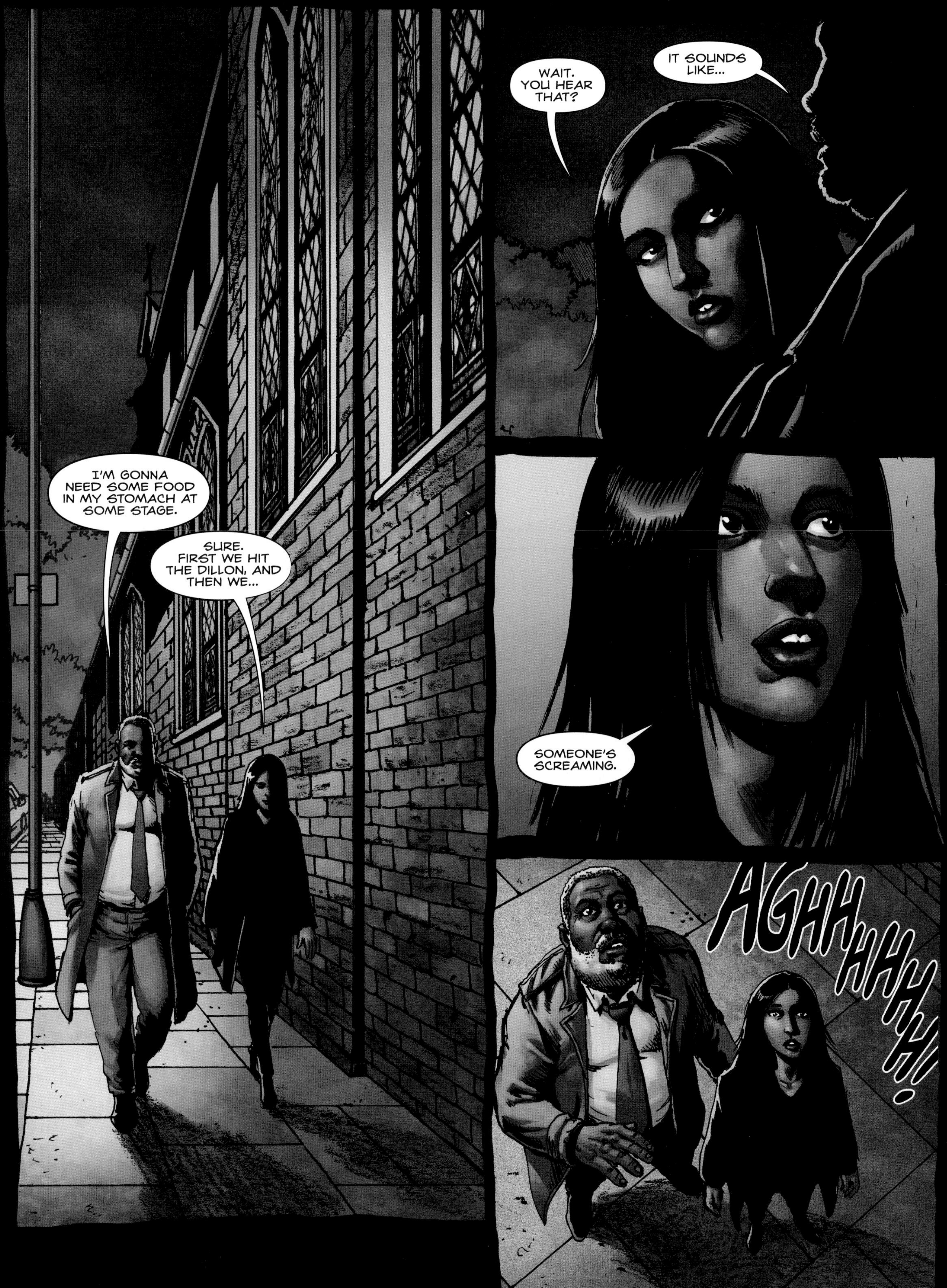
I'M GONNA NEED SOME FOOD IN MY STOMACH AT SOME STAGE.
SURE. FIRST WE HIT THE DILLON, AND THEN WE...
WAIT. YOU HEAR THAT?
IT SOUNDS LIKE...
SOMEONE'S SCREAMING.
AGHHHHHH!!

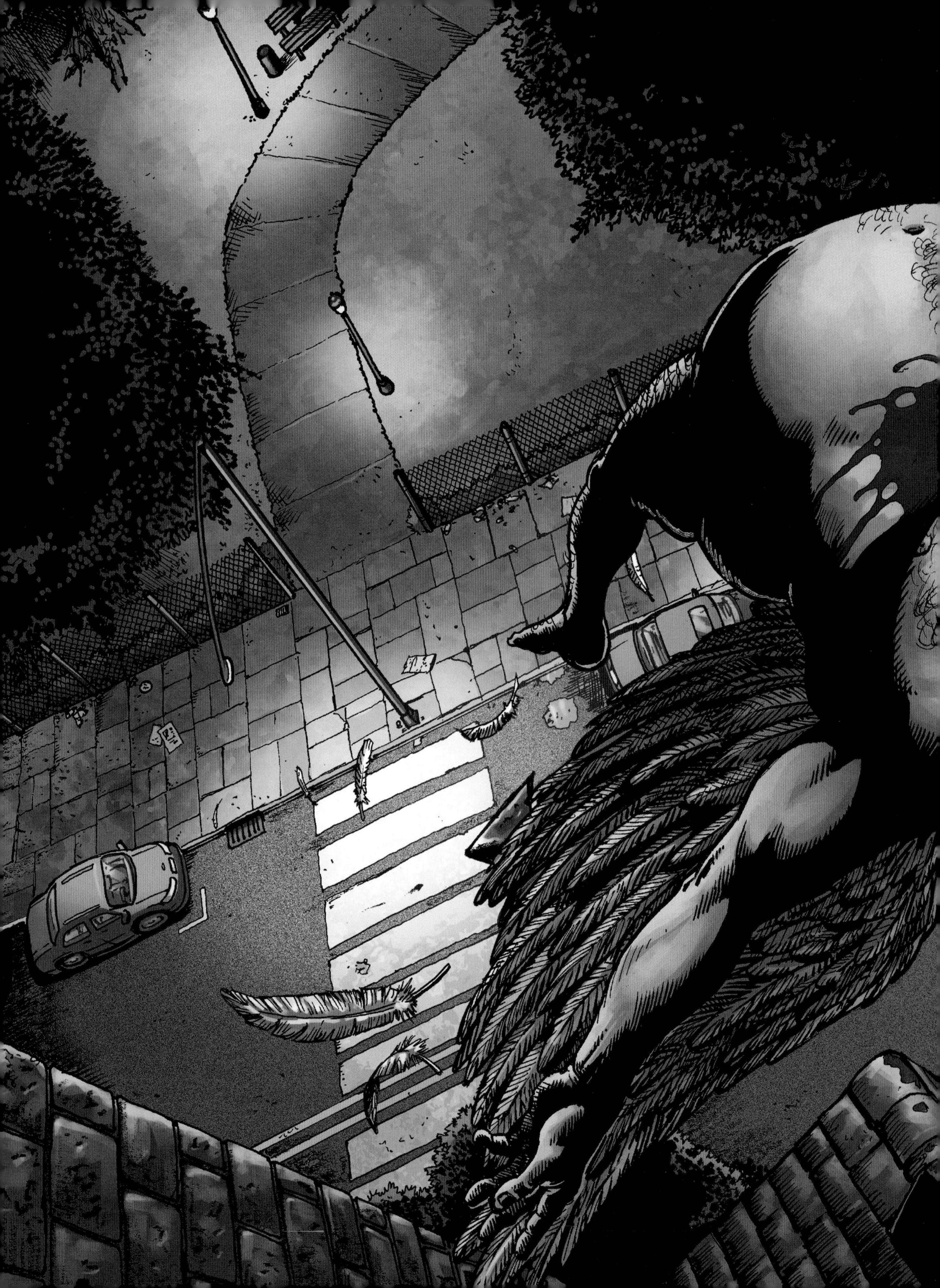

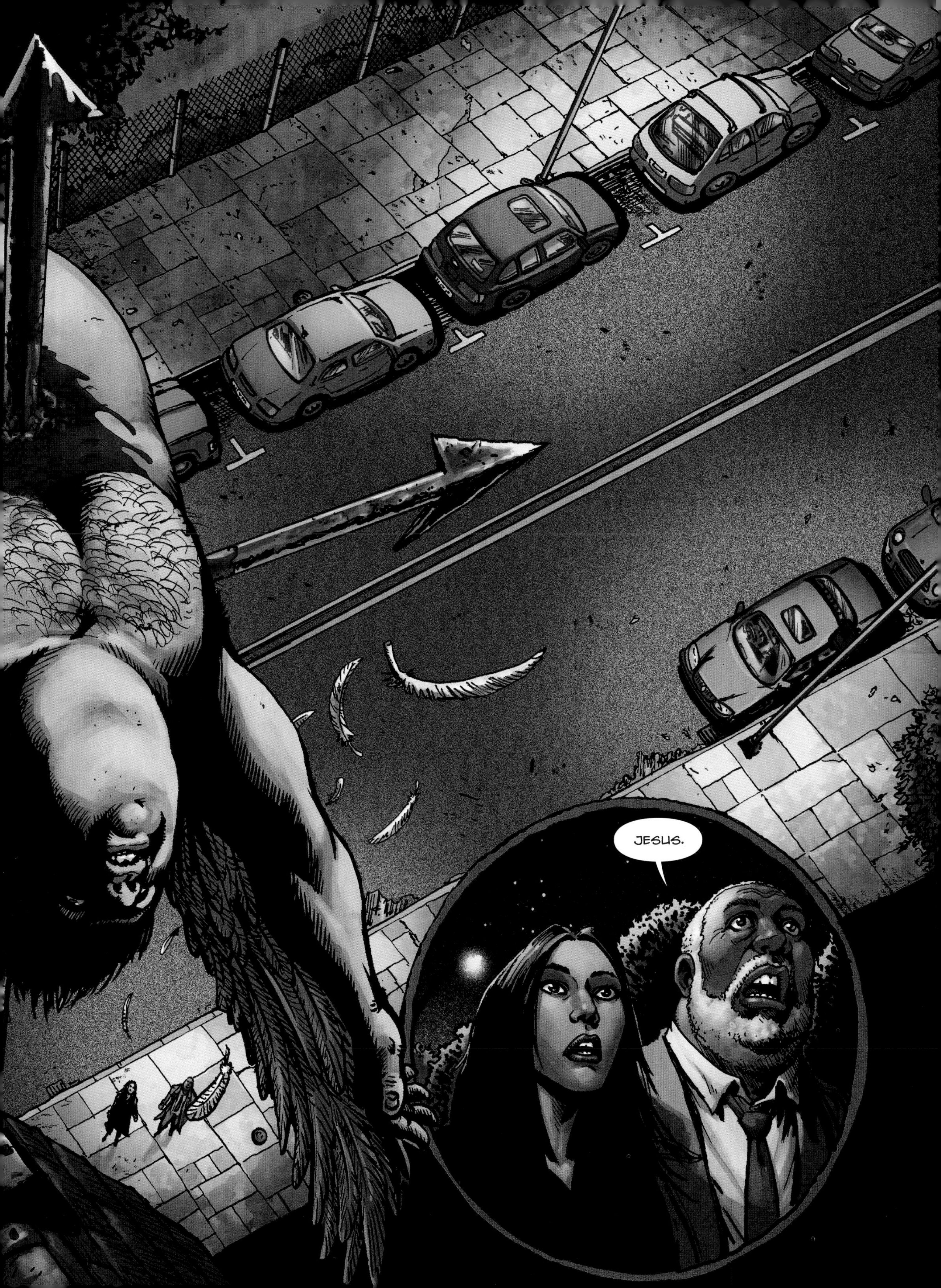
JESUS.

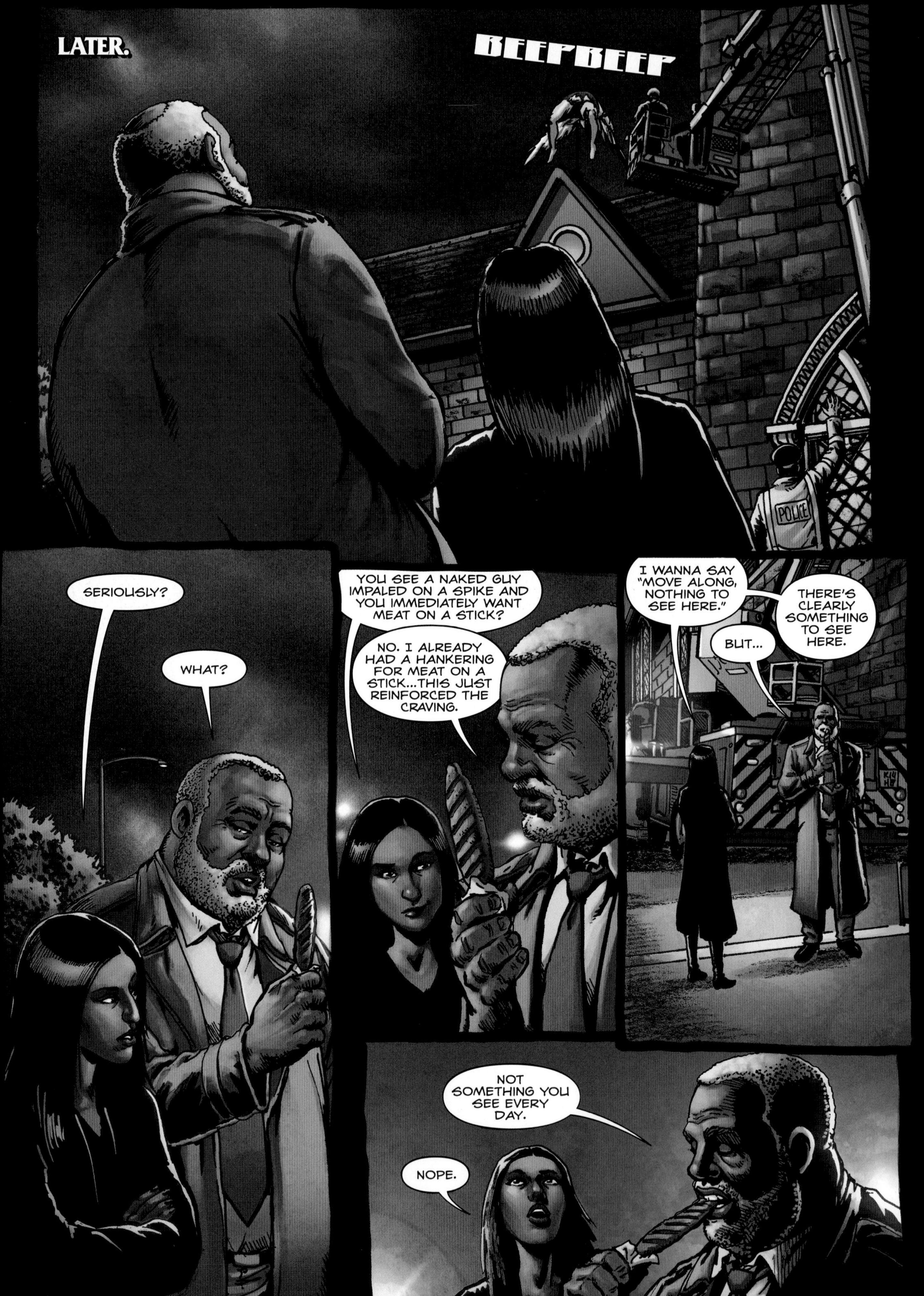
LATER.
BEEPBEEP
POLICE
SERIOUSLY?
WHAT?
YOU SEE A NAKED GUY IMPALED ON A SPIKE AND YOU IMMEDIATELY WANT MEAT ON A STICK?
NO. I ALREADY HAD A HANKERING FOR MEAT ON A STICK...THIS JUST REINFORCED THE CRAVING.
I WANNA SAY "MOVE ALONG, NOTHING TO SEE HERE."
BUT...
THERE'S CLEARLY SOMETHING TO SEE HERE.
NOT SOMETHING YOU SEE EVERY DAY.
NOPE.

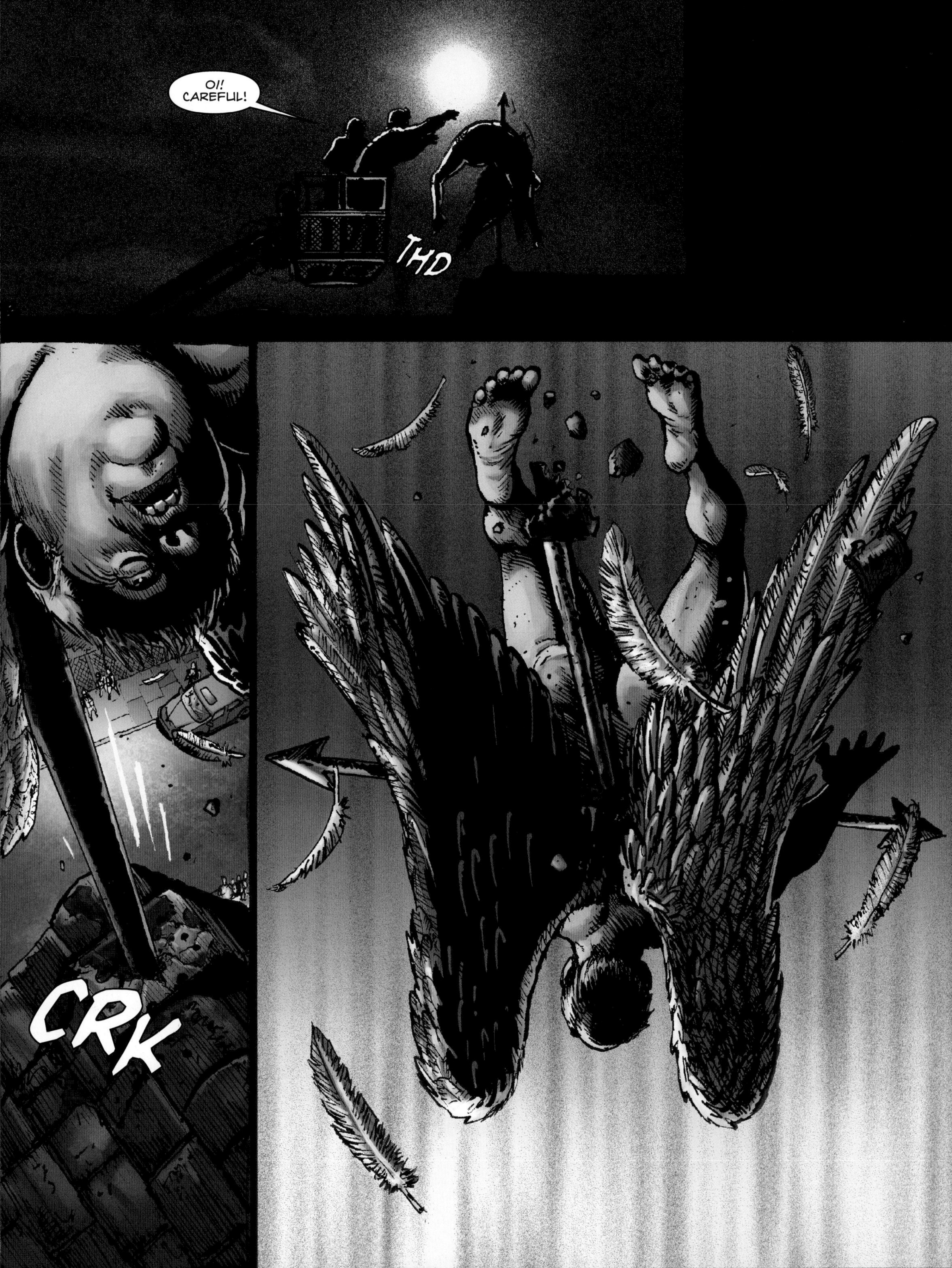
OI! CAREFUL!
THD
CRK

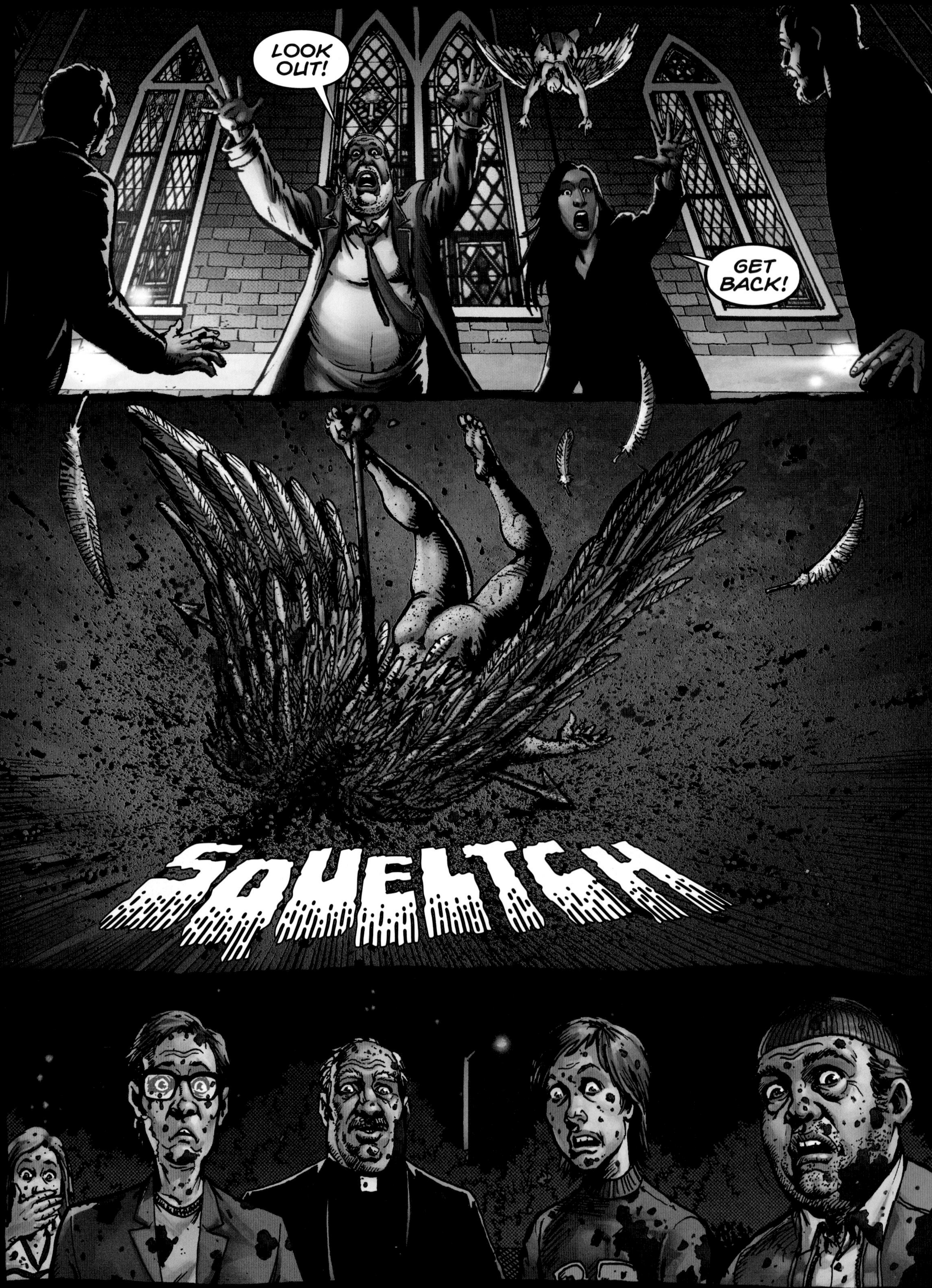
LOOK OUT!
GET BACK!
SQUELTCH

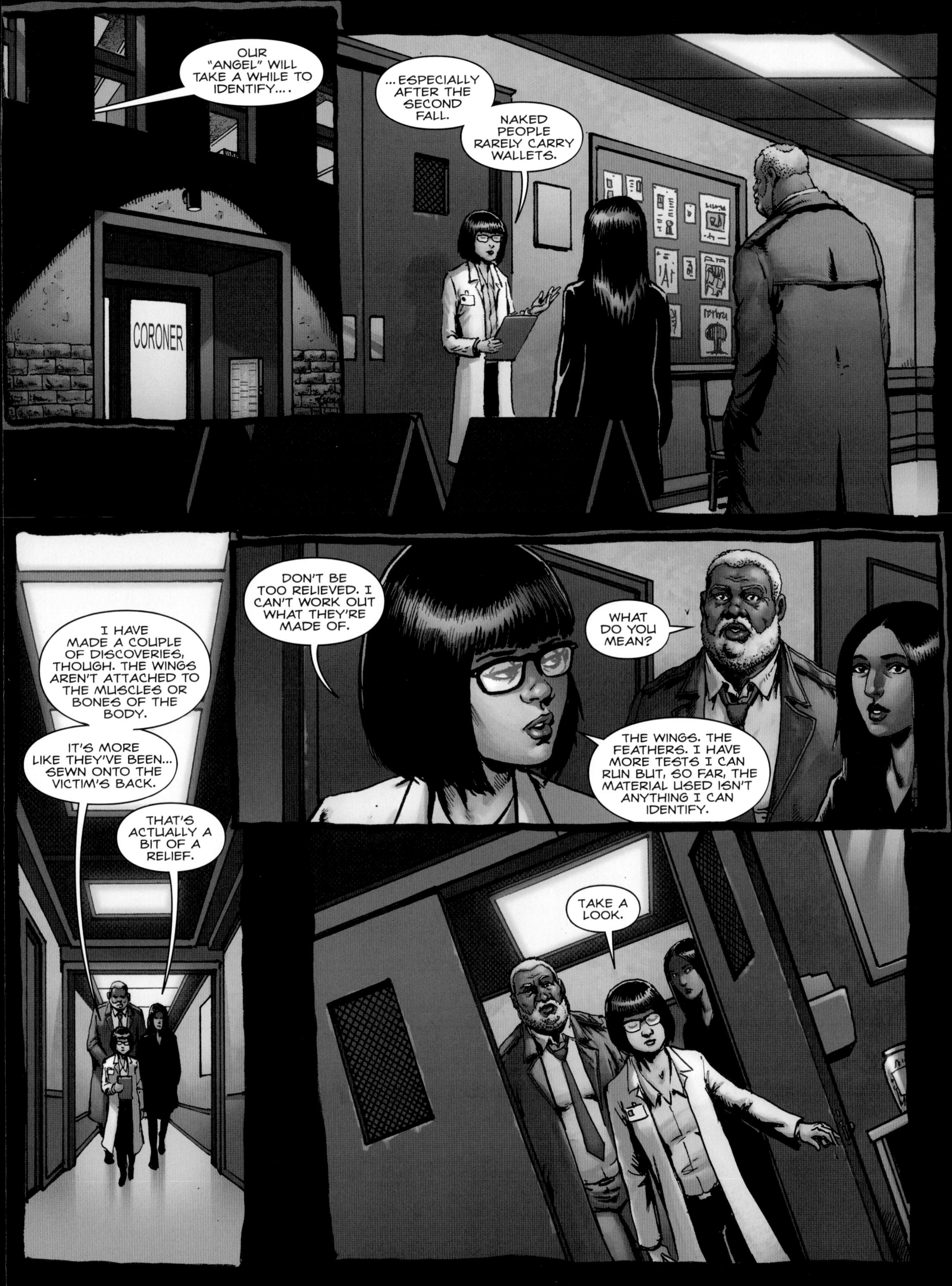
OUR "ANGEL" WILL TAKE A WHILE TO IDENTIFY....
...ESPECIALLY AFTER THE SECOND FALL.
NAKED PEOPLE RARELY CARRY WALLETS.
CORONER
I HAVE MADE A COUPLE OF DISCOVERIES, THOUGH. THE WINGS AREN'T ATTACHED TO THE MUSCLES OR BONES OF THE BODY.
IT'S MORE LIKE THEY'VE BEEN... SEWN ONTO THE VICTIM'S BACK.
THAT'S ACTUALLY A BIT OF A RELIEF.
DON'T BE TOO RELIEVED. I CAN'T WORK OUT WHAT THEY'RE MADE OF.
WHAT DO YOU MEAN?
THE WINGS. THE FEATHERS. I HAVE MORE TESTS I CAN RUN BUT, SO FAR, THE MATERIAL USED ISN'T ANYTHING I CAN IDENTIFY.
TAKE A LOOK.

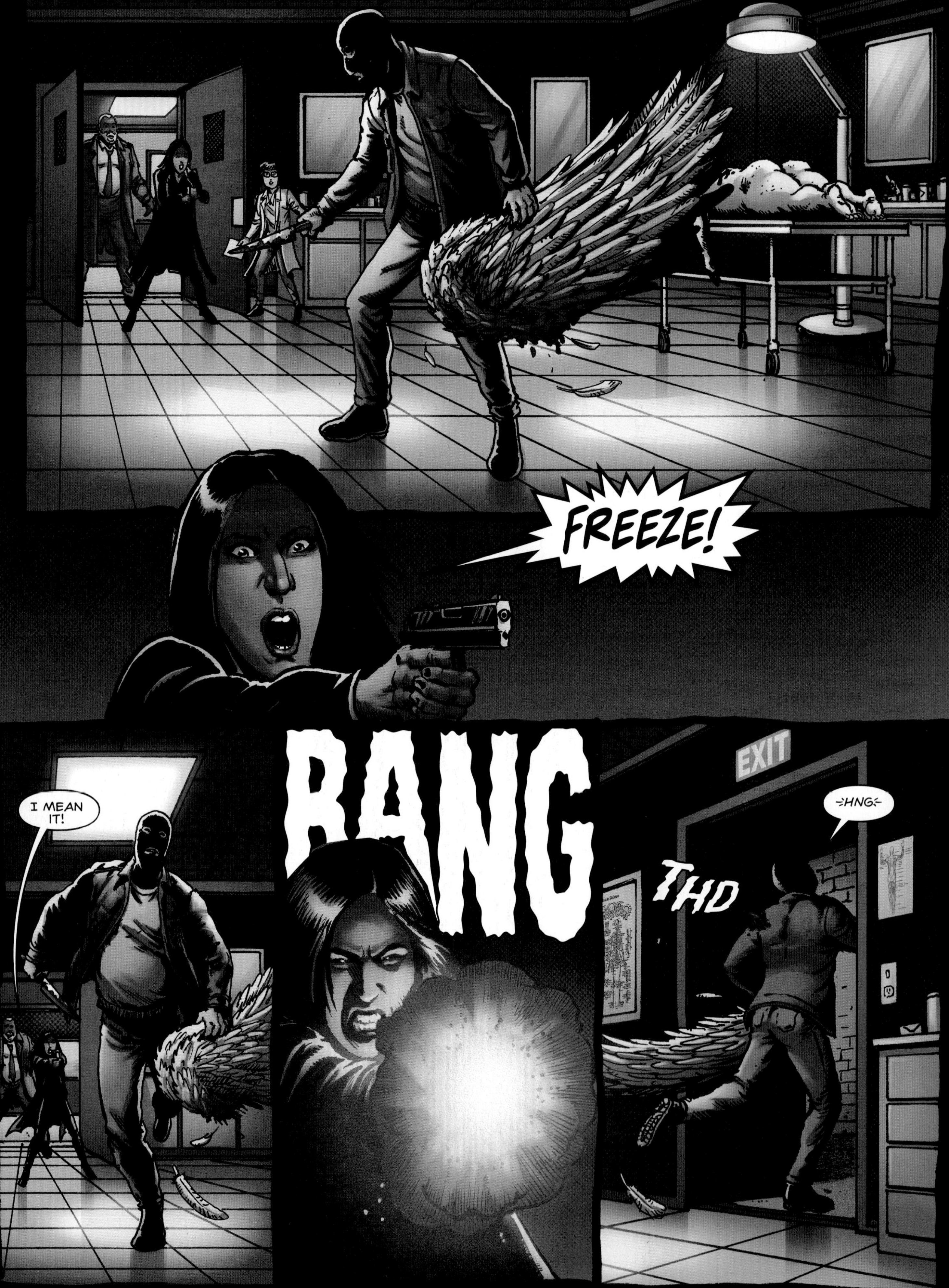
FREEZE!
I MEAN IT!
BANG
EXIT
THD
HNG

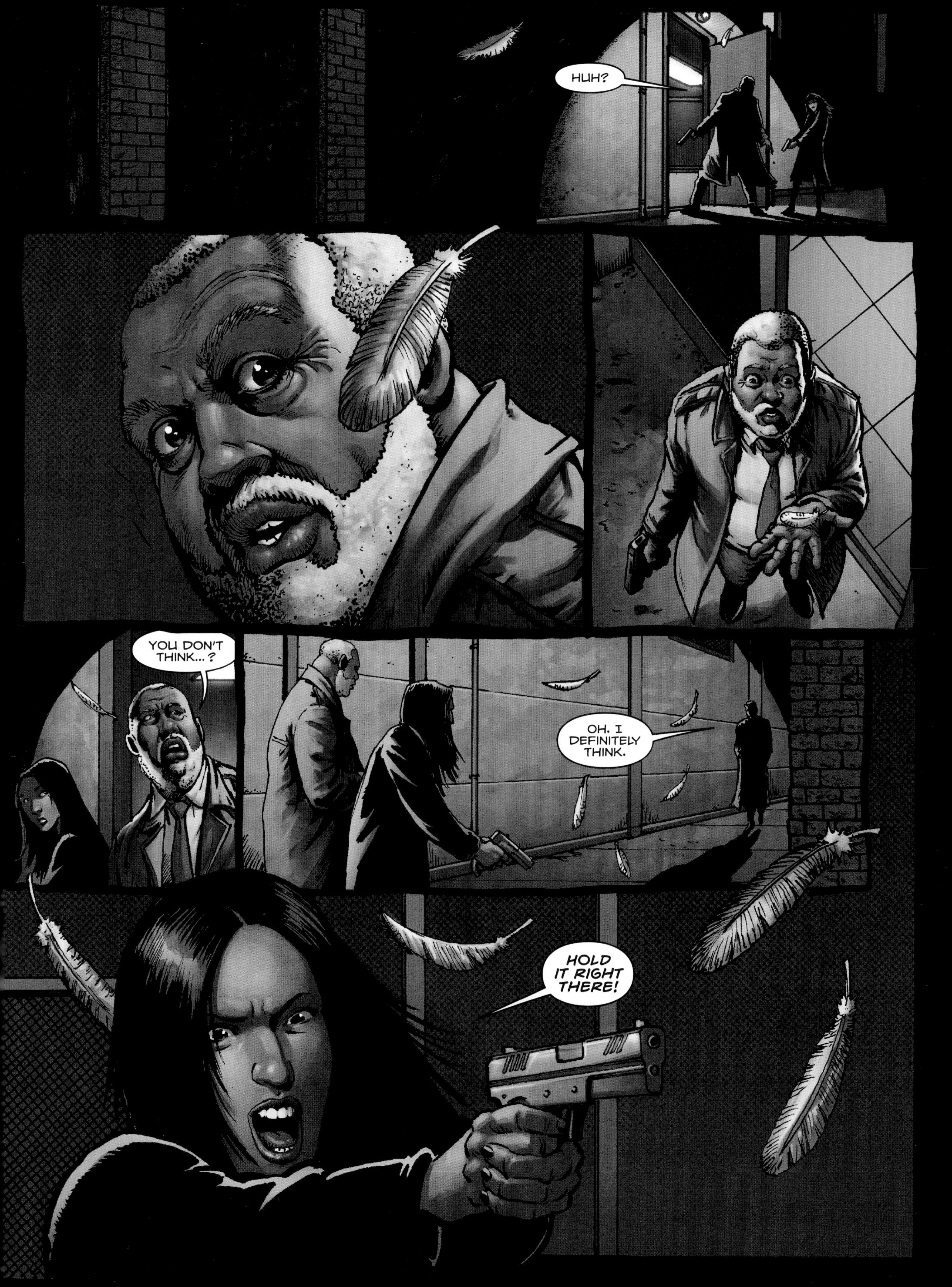
HUH?
YOU DON'T THINK...?
OH. I DEFINITELY THINK.
HOLD IT RIGHT THERE!

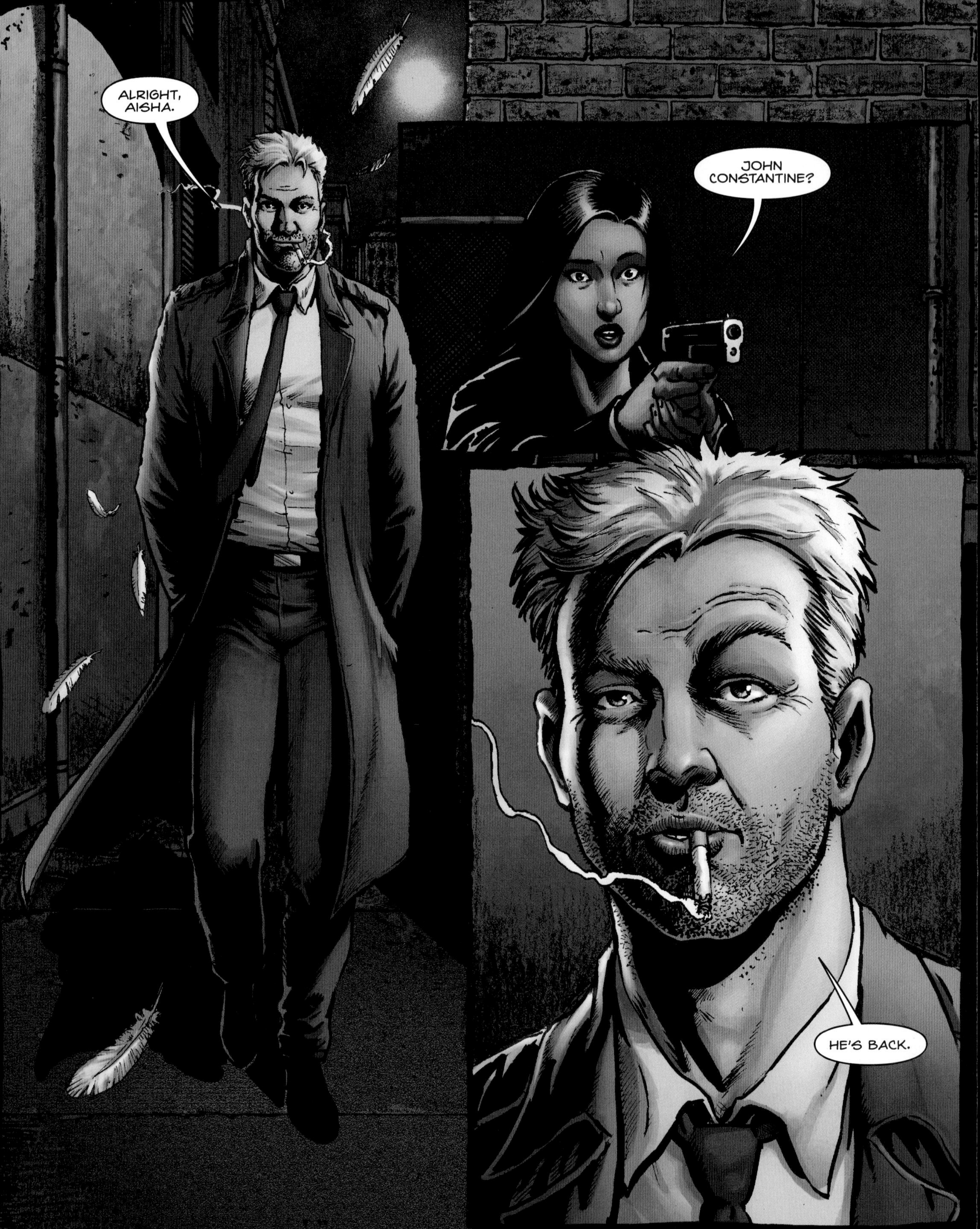
ALRIGHT, AISHA.
JOHN CONSTANTINE?
HE'S BACK.

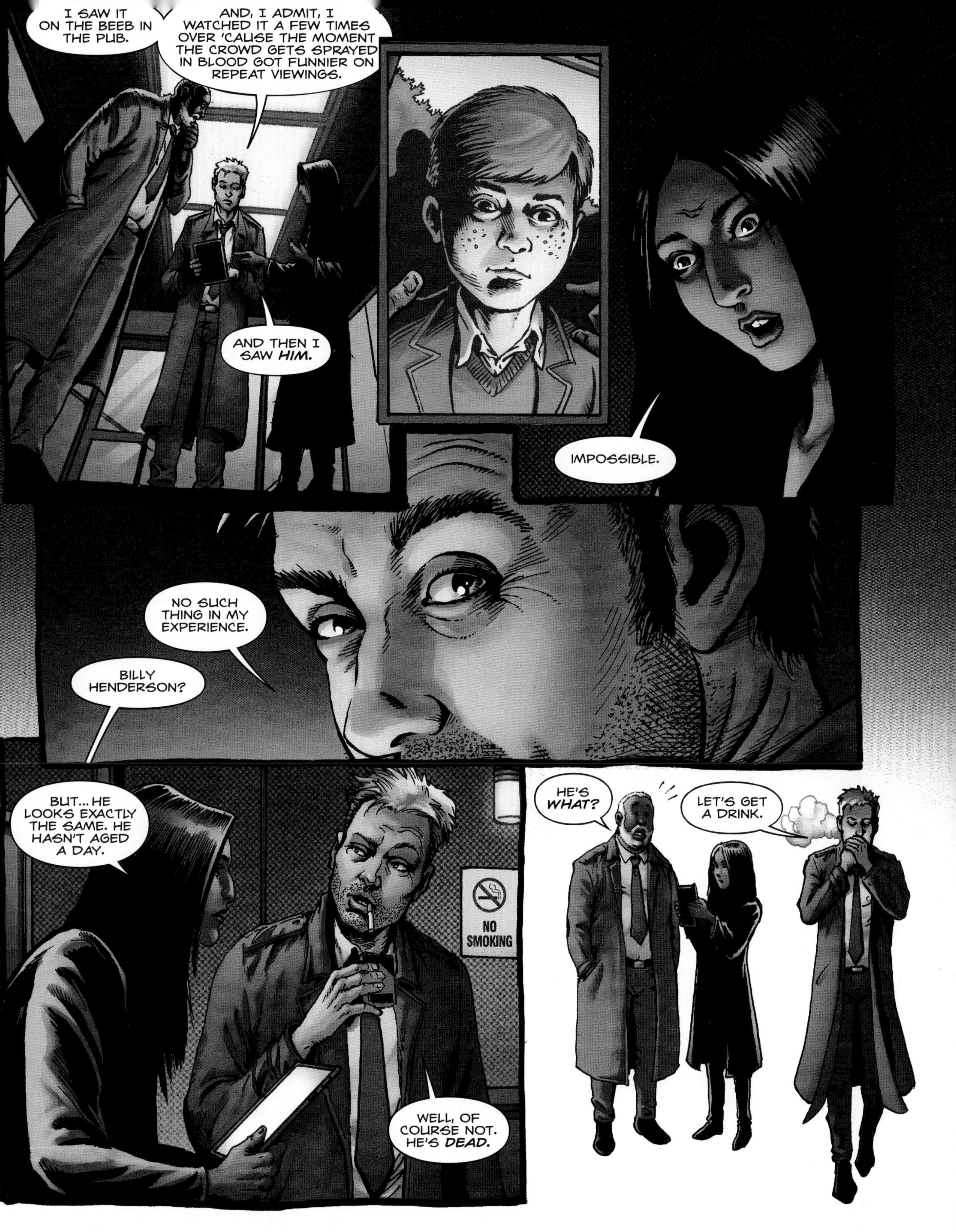
I SAW IT ON THE BEEB IN THE PUB.
AND, I ADMIT, I WATCHED IT A FEW TIMES OVER 'CAUSE THE MOMENT THE CROWD GETS SPRAYED IN BLOOD GOT FUNNIER ON REPEAT VIEWINGS.
AND THEN I SAW *HIM.*
IMPOSSIBLE.
NO SUCH THING IN MY EXPERIENCE.
BILLY HENDERSON?
BUT... HE LOOKS EXACTLY THE SAME. HE HASN'T AGED A DAY.
NO SMOKING
WELL, OF COURSE NOT. HE'S *DEAD.*
HE'S *WHAT?*
LET'S GET A DRINK.

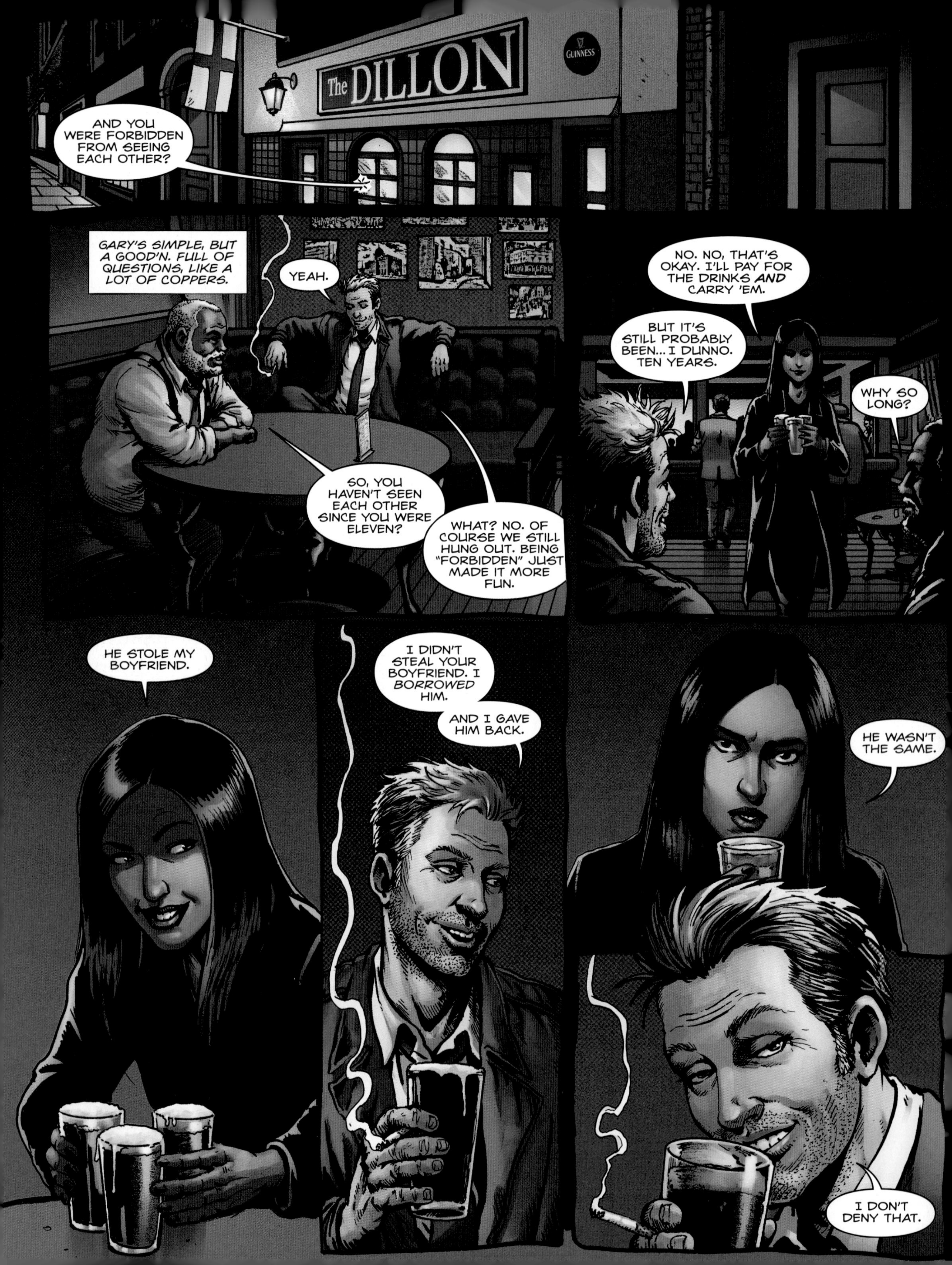
The DILLON
GUINNESS
AND YOU WERE FORBIDDEN FROM SEEING EACH OTHER?
GARY'S SIMPLE, BUT A GOOD'N. FULL OF QUESTIONS, LIKE A LOT OF COPPERS.
YEAH.
SO, YOU HAVEN'T SEEN EACH OTHER SINCE YOU WERE ELEVEN?
WHAT? NO. OF COURSE WE STILL HUNG OUT. BEING "FORBIDDEN" JUST MADE IT MORE FUN.
NO. NO, THAT'S OKAY. I'LL PAY FOR THE DRINKS *AND* CARRY 'EM.
BUT IT'S STILL PROBABLY BEEN... I DUNNO. TEN YEARS.
WHY SO LONG?
HE STOLE MY BOYFRIEND.
I DIDN'T STEAL YOUR BOYFRIEND. I *BORROWED* HIM.
AND I GAVE HIM BACK.
HE WASN'T THE SAME.
I DON'T DENY THAT.

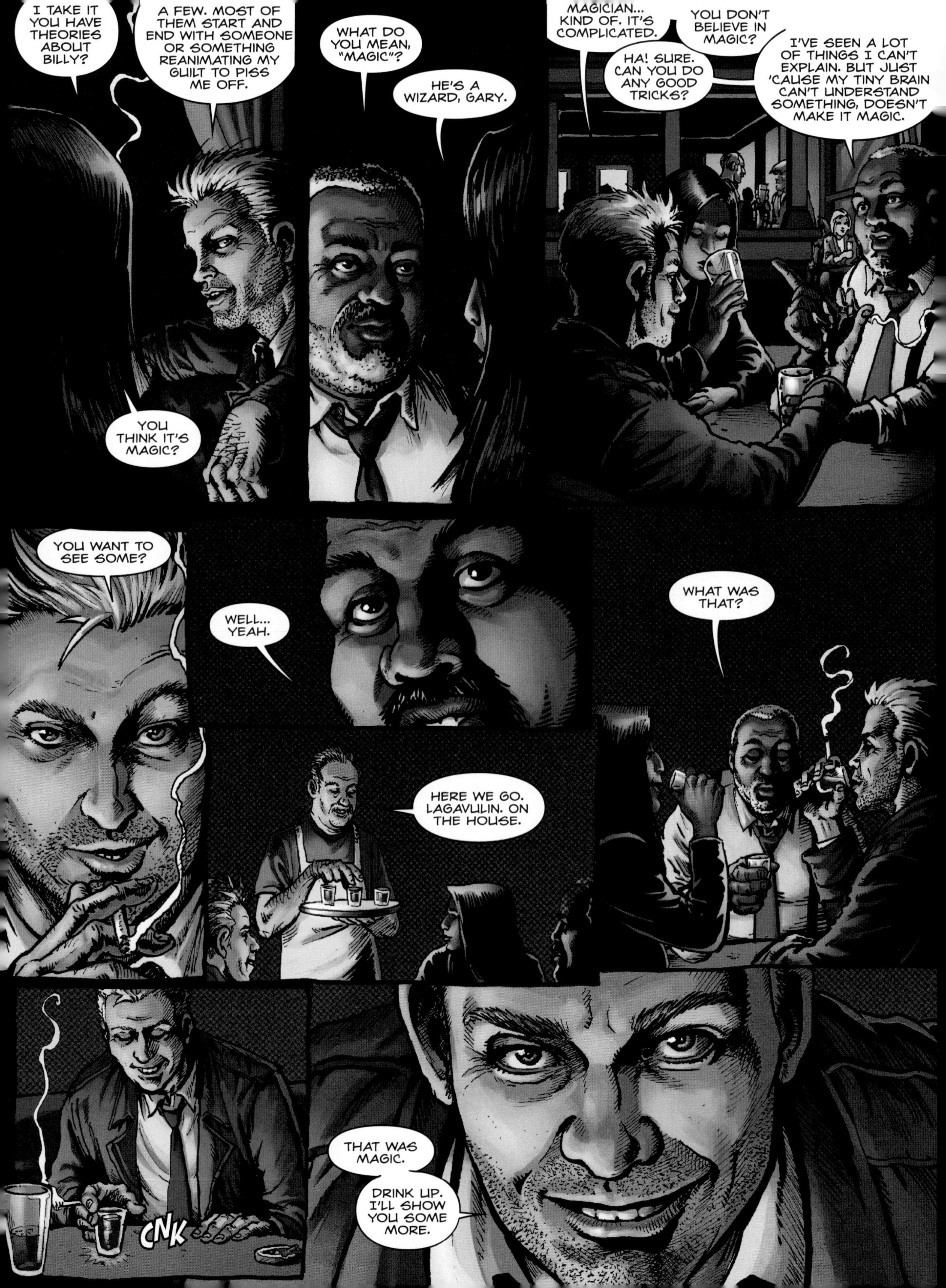
I TAKE IT YOU HAVE THEORIES ABOUT BILLY?
A FEW. MOST OF THEM START AND END WITH SOMEONE OR SOMETHING REANIMATING MY GUILT TO PISS ME OFF.
YOU THINK IT'S MAGIC?
WHAT DO YOU MEAN, "MAGIC"?
HE'S A WIZARD, GARY.
MAGICIAN... KIND OF. IT'S COMPLICATED.
YOU DON'T BELIEVE IN MAGIC?
HA! SURE. CAN YOU DO ANY GOOD TRICKS?
I'VE SEEN A LOT OF THINGS I CAN'T EXPLAIN. BUT JUST 'CAUSE MY TINY BRAIN CAN'T UNDERSTAND SOMETHING, DOESN'T MAKE IT MAGIC.
YOU WANT TO SEE SOME?
WELL... YEAH.
HERE WE GO. LAGAVULIN. ON THE HOUSE.
WHAT WAS THAT?
CNK
THAT WAS MAGIC.
DRINK UP. I'LL SHOW YOU SOME MORE.

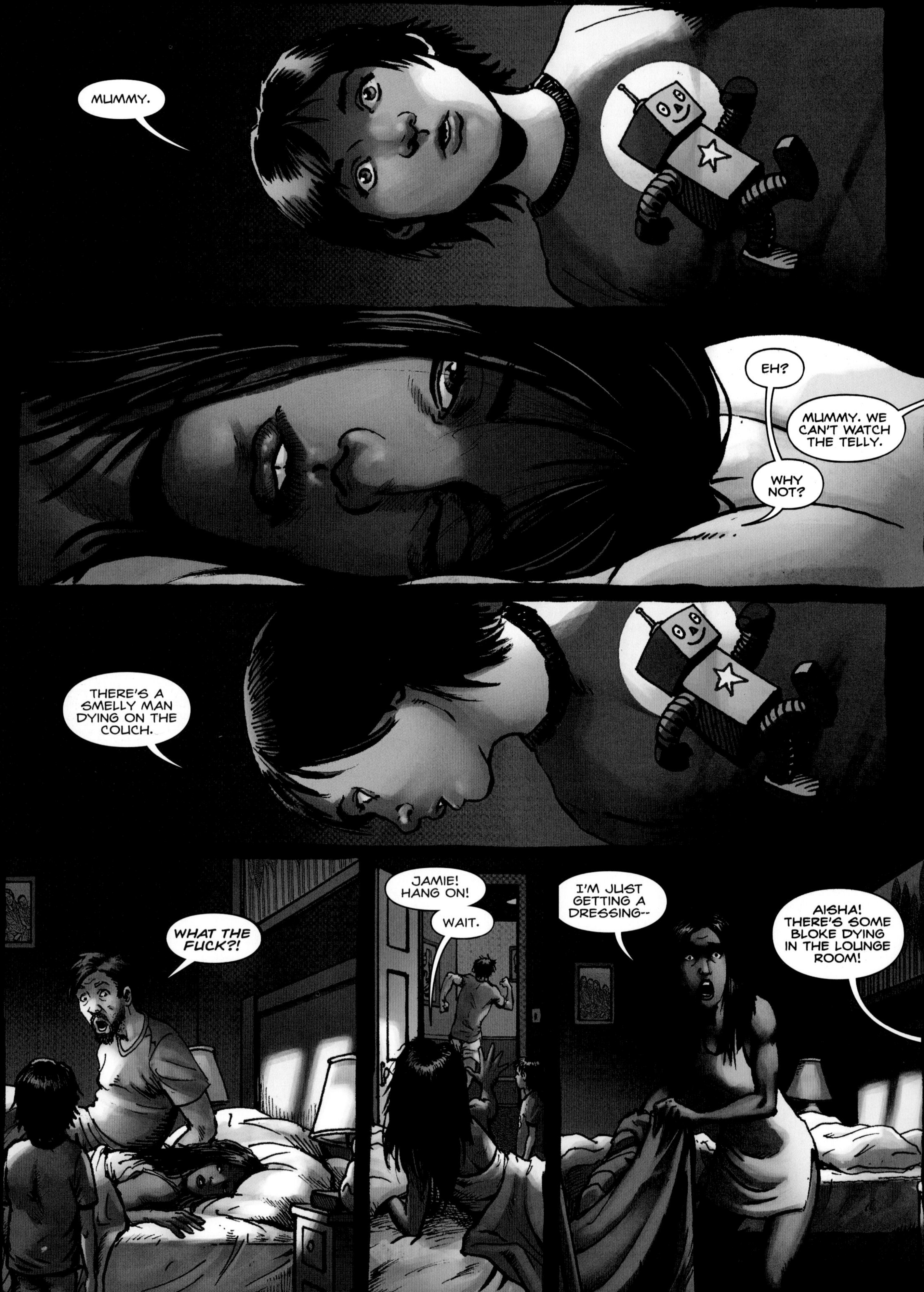
MUMMY.
EH?
MUMMY. WE CAN'T WATCH THE TELLY.
WHY NOT?
THERE'S A SMELLY MAN DYING ON THE COUCH.
WHAT THE FUCK?!
JAMIE! HANG ON!
WAIT.
I'M JUST GETTING A DRESSING--
AISHA! THERE'S SOME BLOKE DYING IN THE LOUNGE ROOM!

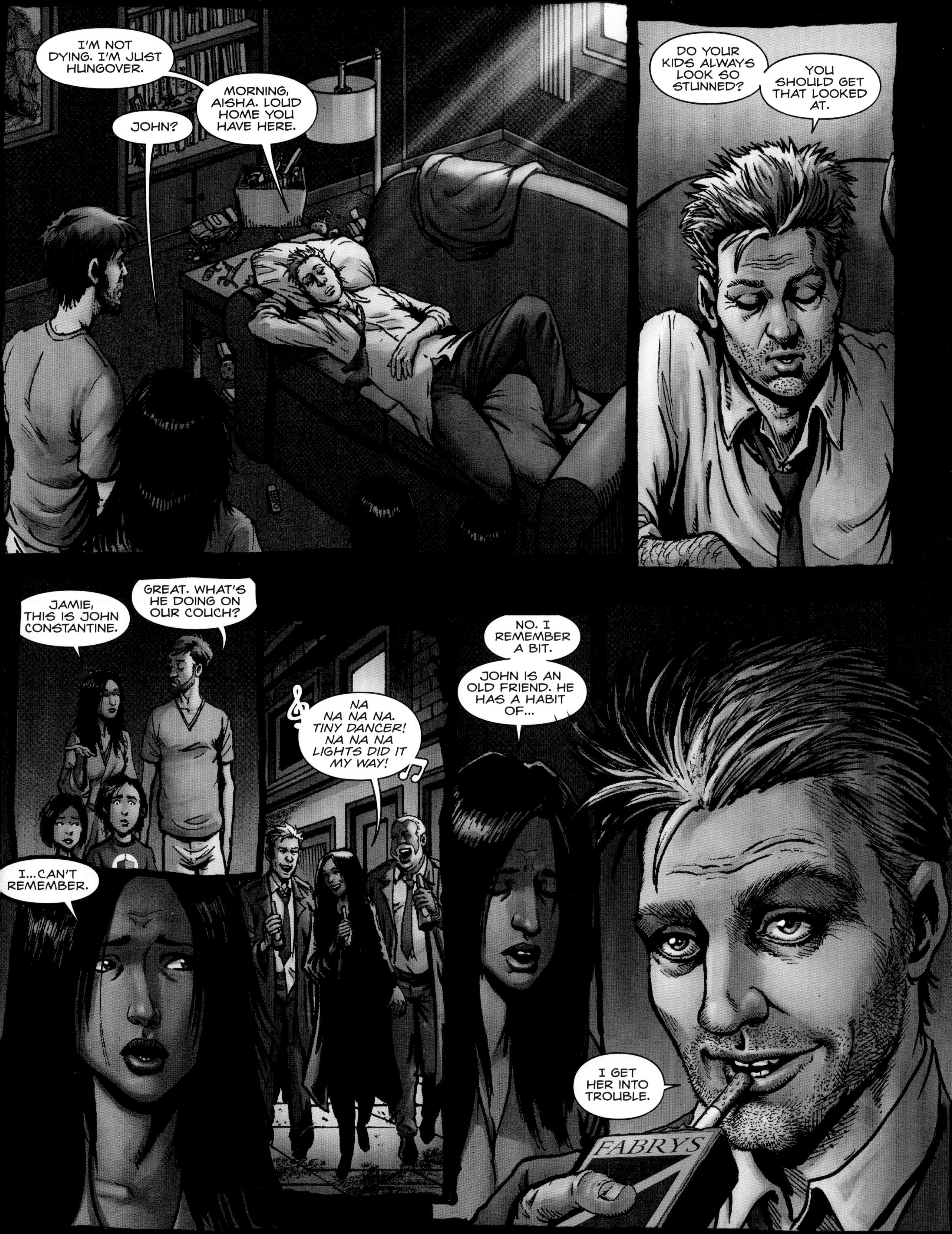

I'M NOT DYING. I'M JUST HUNGOVER.
JOHN?
MORNING, AISHA. LOUD HOME YOU HAVE HERE.
DO YOUR KIDS ALWAYS LOOK SO STUNNED?
YOU SHOULD GET THAT LOOKED AT.
JAMIE, THIS IS JOHN CONSTANTINE.
GREAT. WHAT'S HE DOING ON OUR COUCH?
I...CAN'T REMEMBER.
NA NA NA NA. TINY DANCER! NA NA NA LIGHTS DID IT MY WAY!
NO. I REMEMBER A BIT.
JOHN IS AN OLD FRIEND. HE HAS A HABIT OF...
I GET HER INTO TROUBLE.
FABRYS

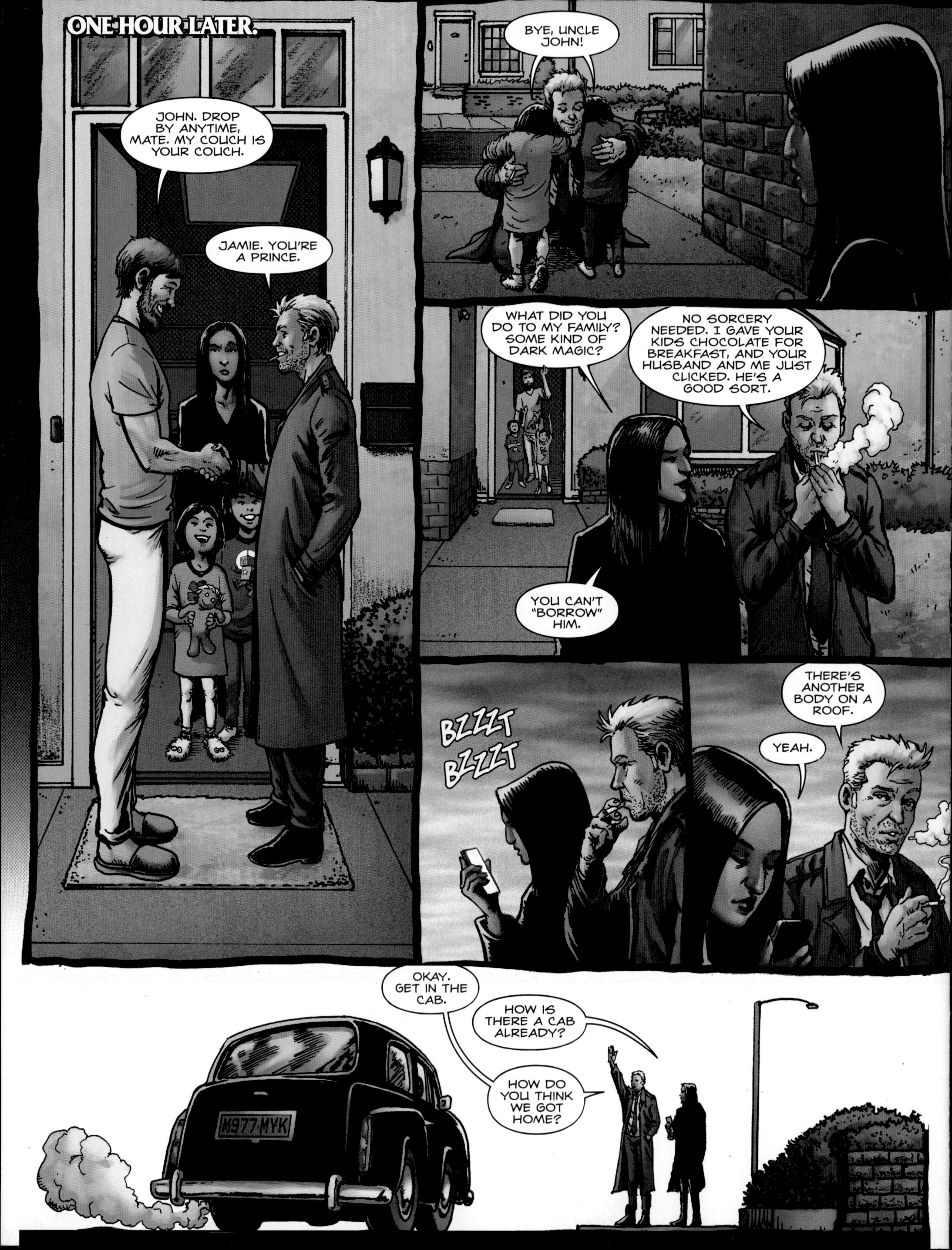
ONE HOUR LATER.
JOHN. DROP BY ANYTIME, MATE. MY COUCH IS YOUR COUCH.
JAMIE. YOU'RE A PRINCE.
BYE, UNCLE JOHN!
WHAT DID YOU DO TO MY FAMILY? SOME KIND OF DARK MAGIC?
NO SORCERY NEEDED. I GAVE YOUR KIDS CHOCOLATE FOR BREAKFAST, AND YOUR HUSBAND AND ME JUST CLICKED. HE'S A GOOD SORT.
YOU CAN'T "BORROW" HIM.
BZZZT BZZZT
THERE'S ANOTHER BODY ON A ROOF.
YEAH.
OKAY. GET IN THE CAB.
HOW IS THERE A CAB ALREADY?
HOW DO YOU THINK WE GOT HOME?
M977 MYK

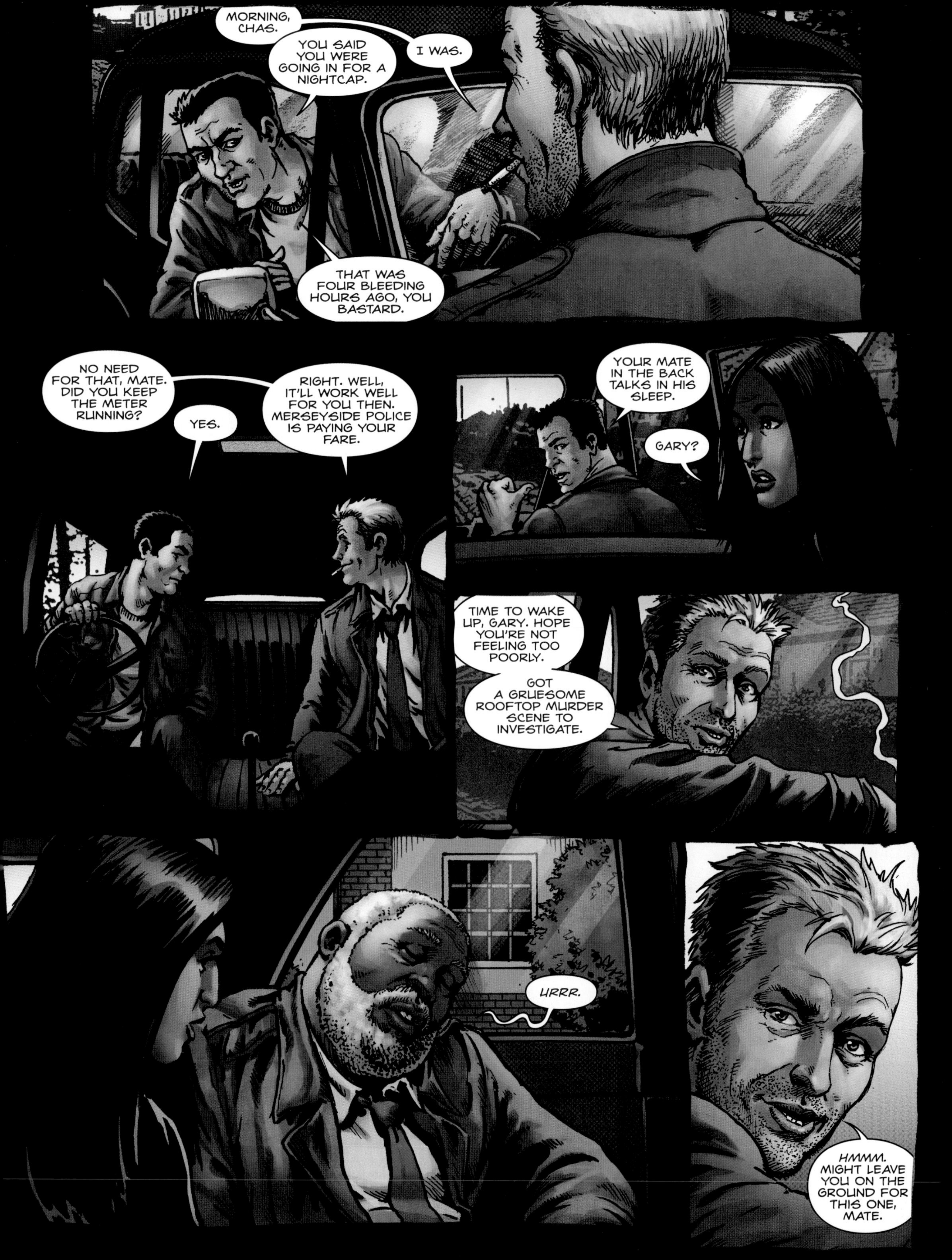
MORNING, CHAS.
YOU SAID YOU WERE GOING IN FOR A NIGHTCAP.
I WAS.
THAT WAS FOUR BLEEDING HOURS AGO, YOU BASTARD.
NO NEED FOR THAT, MATE. DID YOU KEEP THE METER RUNNING?
YES.
RIGHT. WELL, IT'LL WORK WELL FOR YOU THEN. MERSEYSIDE POLICE IS PAYING YOUR FARE.
YOUR MATE IN THE BACK TALKS IN HIS SLEEP.
GARY?
TIME TO WAKE UP, GARY. HOPE YOU'RE NOT FEELING TOO POORLY.
GOT A GRUESOME ROOFTOP MURDER SCENE TO INVESTIGATE.
URRR.
HMMM. MIGHT LEAVE YOU ON THE GROUND FOR THIS ONE, MATE.

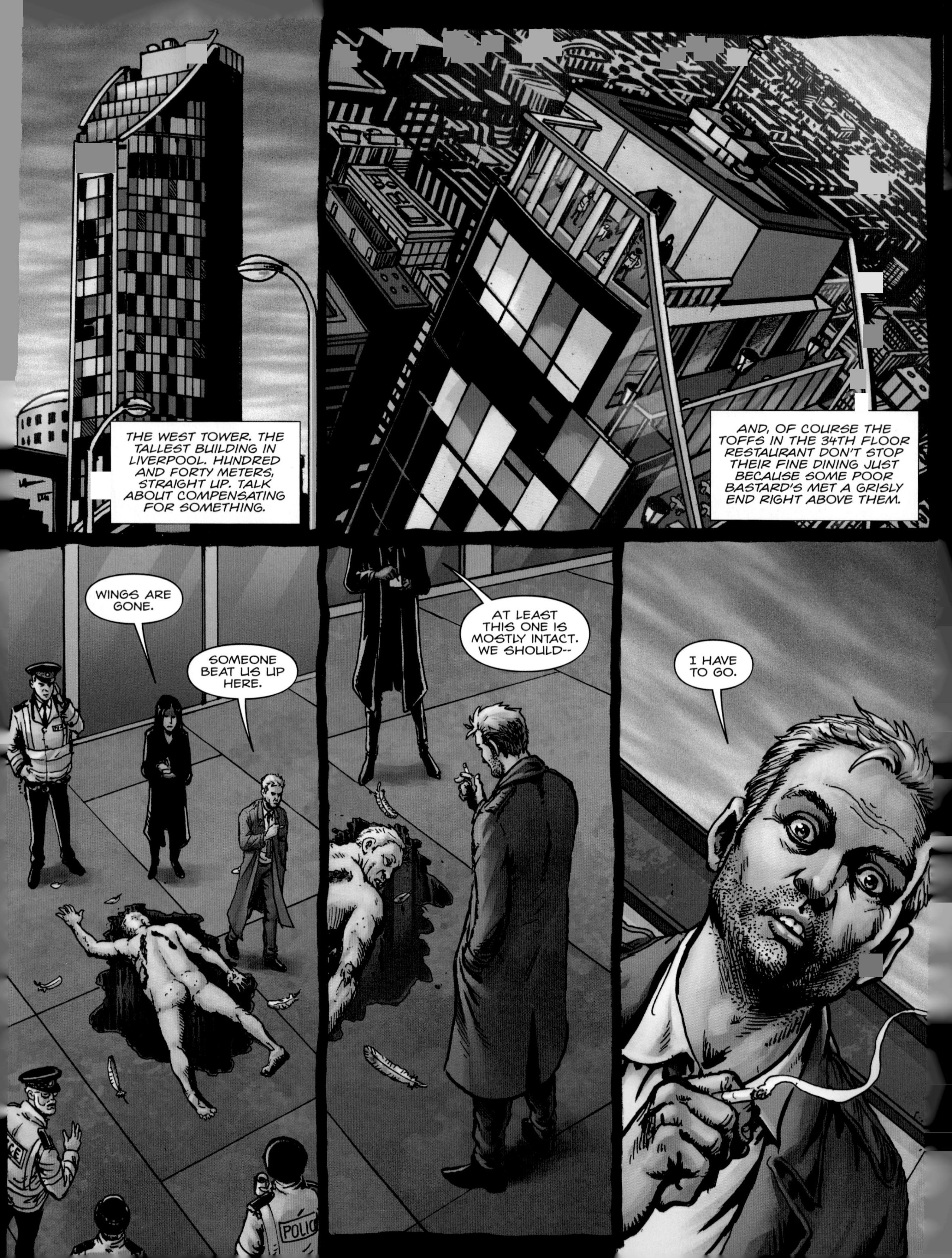
THE WEST TOWER. THE TALLEST BUILDING IN LIVERPOOL. HUNDRED AND FORTY METERS, STRAIGHT UP. TALK ABOUT COMPENSATING FOR SOMETHING.
AND, OF COURSE THE TOFFS IN THE 34TH FLOOR RESTAURANT DON'T STOP THEIR FINE DINING JUST BECAUSE SOME POOR BASTARD'S MET A GRISLY END RIGHT ABOVE THEM.
WINGS ARE GONE.
SOMEONE BEAT US UP HERE.
AT LEAST THIS ONE IS MOSTLY INTACT. WE SHOULD--
I HAVE TO GO.

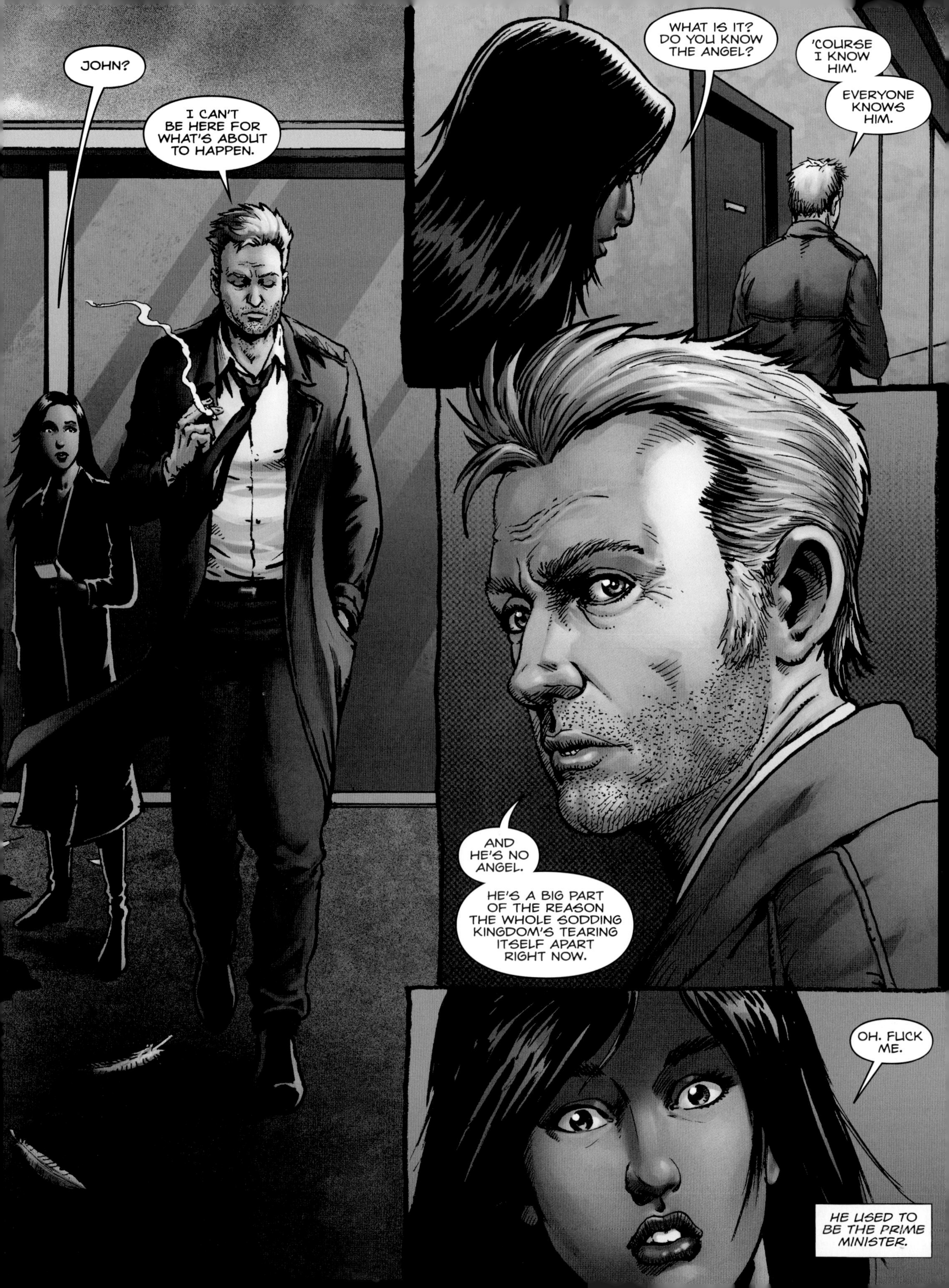
JOHN?
I CAN'T BE HERE FOR WHAT'S ABOUT TO HAPPEN.
WHAT IS IT? DO YOU KNOW THE ANGEL?
'COURSE I KNOW HIM.
EVERYONE KNOWS HIM.
AND HE'S NO ANGEL.
HE'S A BIG PART OF THE REASON THE WHOLE SODDING KINGDOM'S TEARING ITSELF APART RIGHT NOW.
OH. FUCK ME.
HE USED TO BE THE PRIME MINISTER.

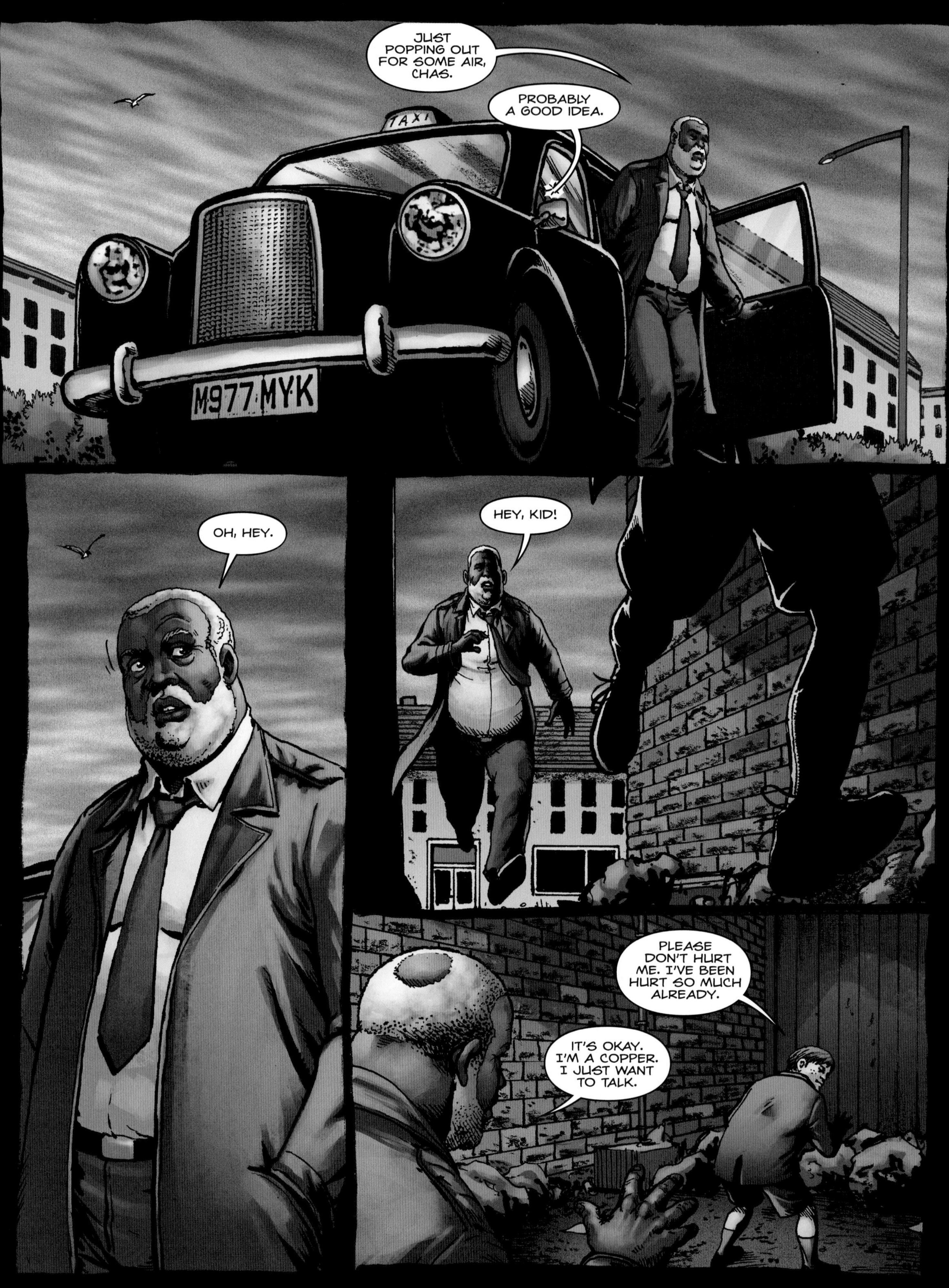
JUST POPPING OUT FOR SOME AIR, CHAS.
PROBABLY A GOOD IDEA.
TAXI
M977 MYK
OH, HEY.
HEY, KID!
PLEASE DON'T HURT ME. I'VE BEEN HURT SO MUCH ALREADY.
IT'S OKAY. I'M A COPPER. I JUST WANT TO TALK.

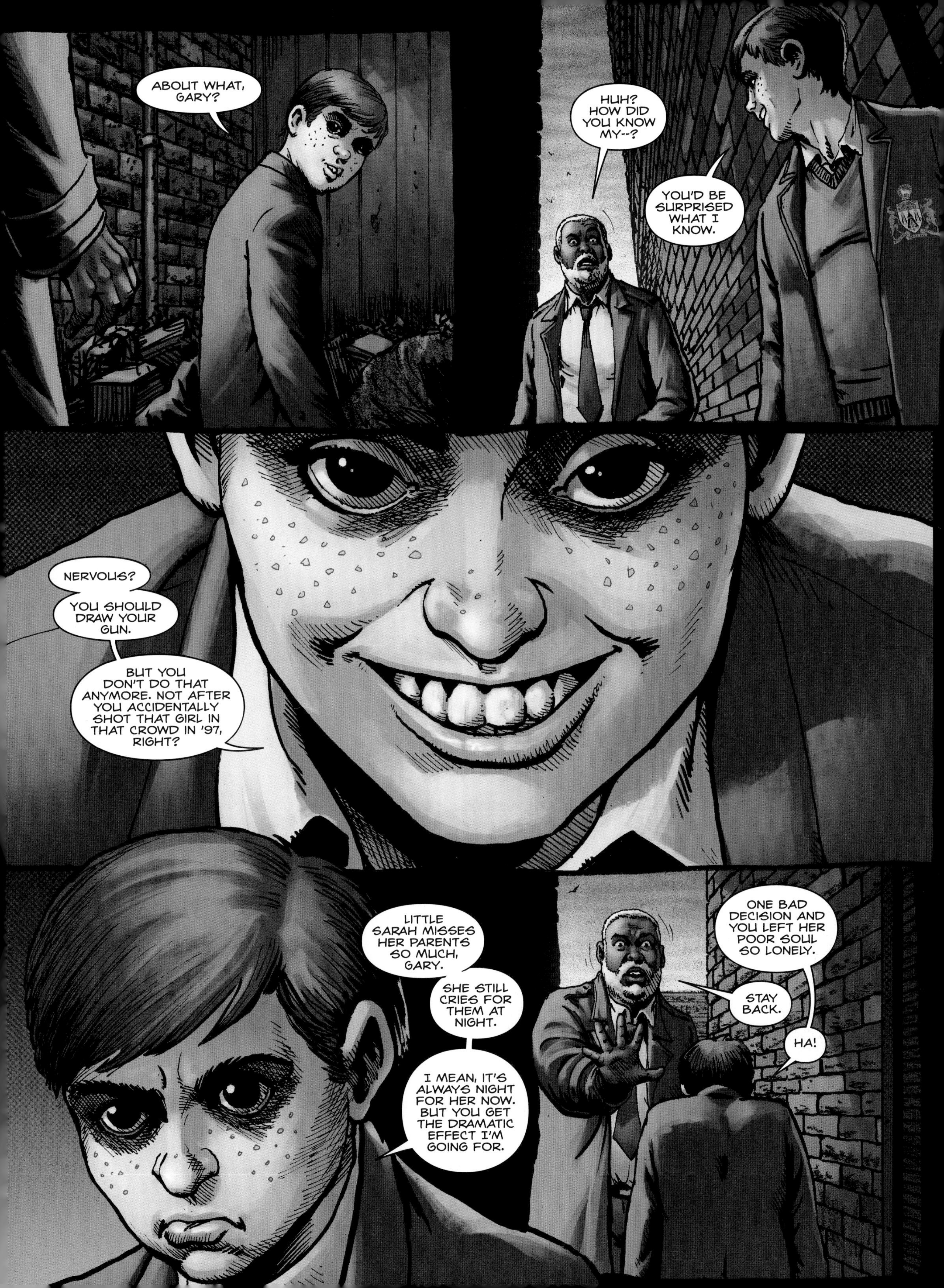
ABOUT WHAT, GARY?
HUH? HOW DID YOU KNOW MY--?
YOU'D BE SURPRISED WHAT I KNOW.
NERVOUS?
YOU SHOULD DRAW YOUR GUN.
BUT YOU DON'T DO THAT ANYMORE. NOT AFTER YOU ACCIDENTALLY SHOT THAT GIRL IN THAT CROWD IN '97, RIGHT?
LITTLE SARAH MISSES HER PARENTS SO MUCH, GARY.
SHE STILL CRIES FOR THEM AT NIGHT.
I MEAN, IT'S ALWAYS NIGHT FOR HER NOW. BUT YOU GET THE DRAMATIC EFFECT I'M GOING FOR.
ONE BAD DECISION AND YOU LEFT HER POOR SOUL SO LONELY.
STAY BACK.
HA!

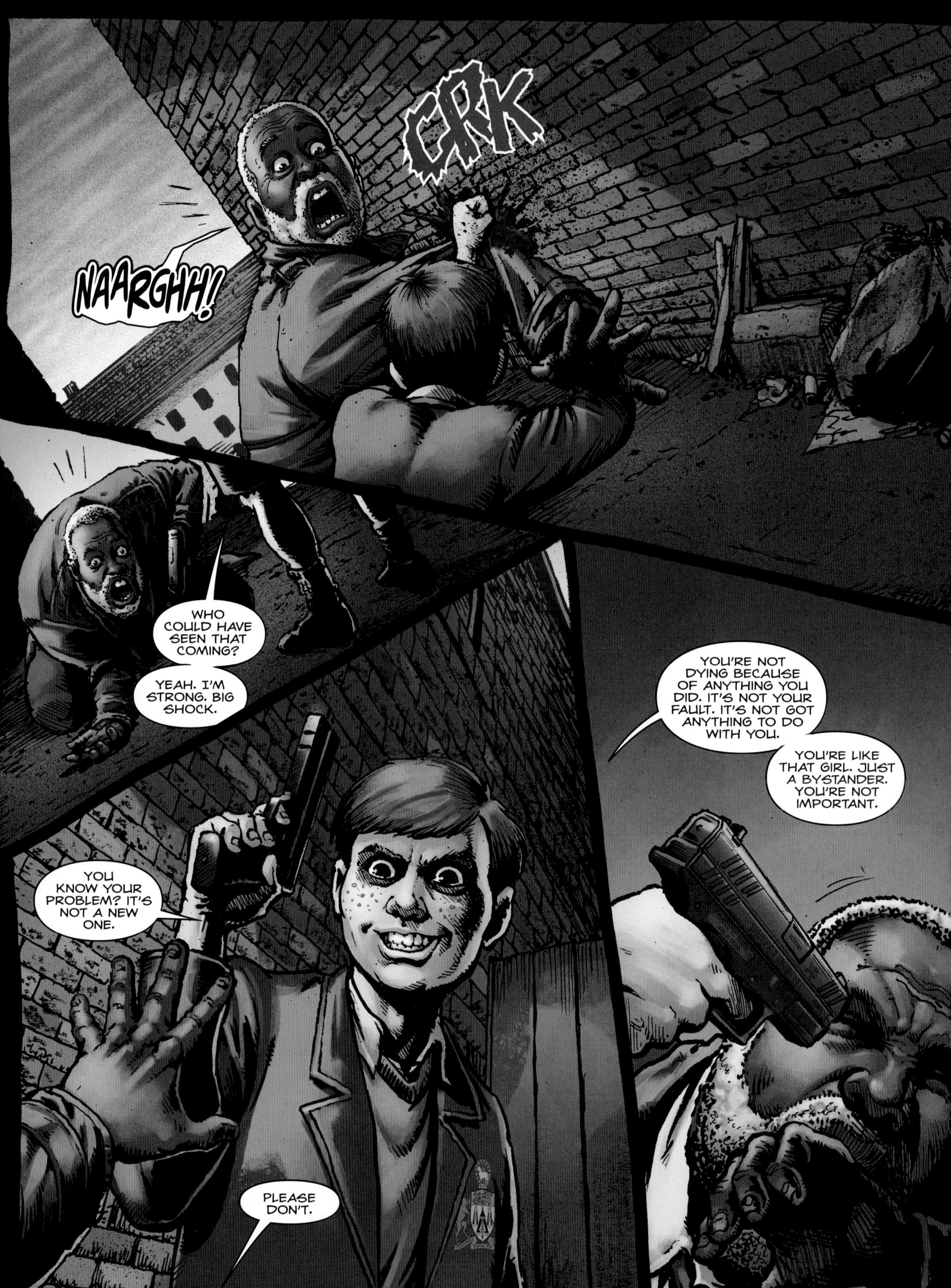
CRK
NAARGHH!
WHO COULD HAVE SEEN THAT COMING?
YEAH. I'M STRONG. BIG SHOCK.
YOU KNOW YOUR PROBLEM? IT'S NOT A NEW ONE.
PLEASE DON'T.
YOU'RE NOT DYING BECAUSE OF ANYTHING YOU DID. IT'S NOT YOUR FAULT. IT'S NOT GOT ANYTHING TO DO WITH YOU.
YOU'RE LIKE THAT GIRL. JUST A BYSTANDER. YOU'RE NOT IMPORTANT.

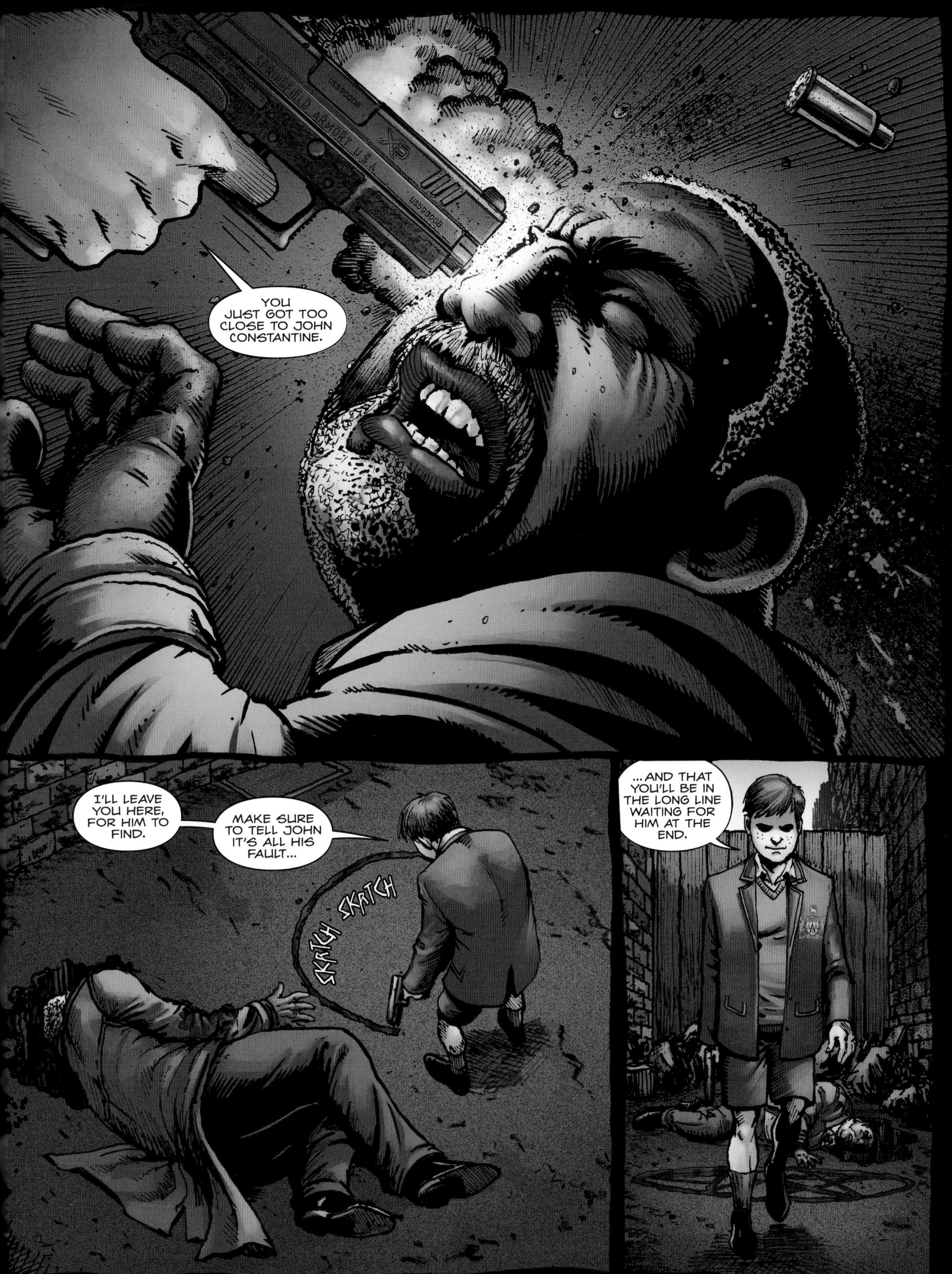

YOU JUST GOT TOO CLOSE TO JOHN CONSTANTINE.
I'LL LEAVE YOU HERE, FOR HIM TO FIND.
MAKE SURE TO TELL JOHN IT'S ALL HIS FAULT...
SKRTCH SKRTCH
...AND THAT YOU'LL BE IN THE LONG LINE WAITING FOR HIM AT THE END.

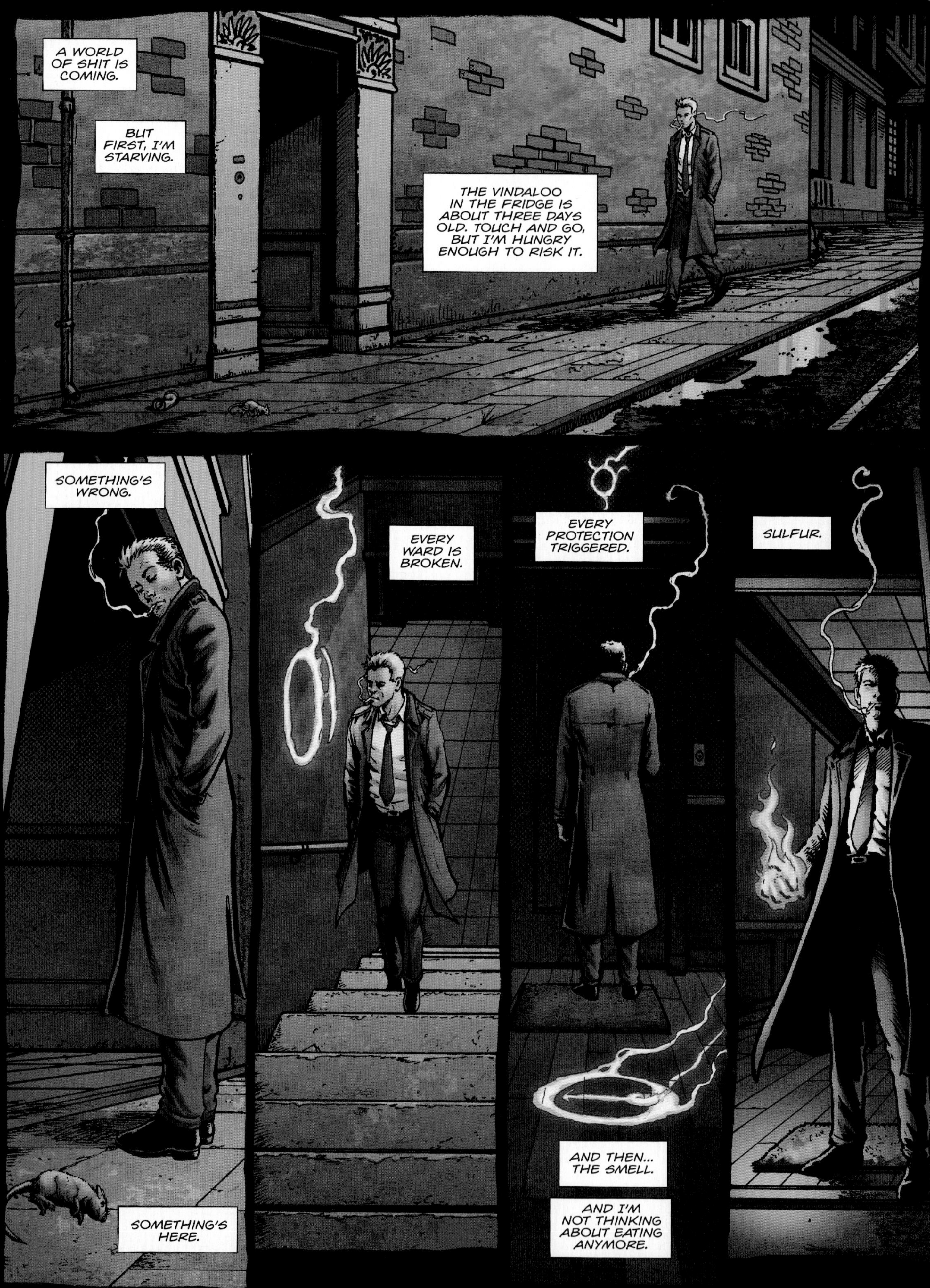
A WORLD OF SHIT IS COMING.
BUT FIRST, I'M STARVING.
THE VINDALOO IN THE FRIDGE IS ABOUT THREE DAYS OLD. TOUCH AND GO, BUT I'M HUNGRY ENOUGH TO RISK IT.
SOMETHING'S WRONG.
SOMETHING'S HERE.
EVERY WARD IS BROKEN.
EVERY PROTECTION TRIGGERED.
AND THEN... THE SMELL.
AND I'M NOT THINKING ABOUT EATING ANYMORE.
SULFUR.

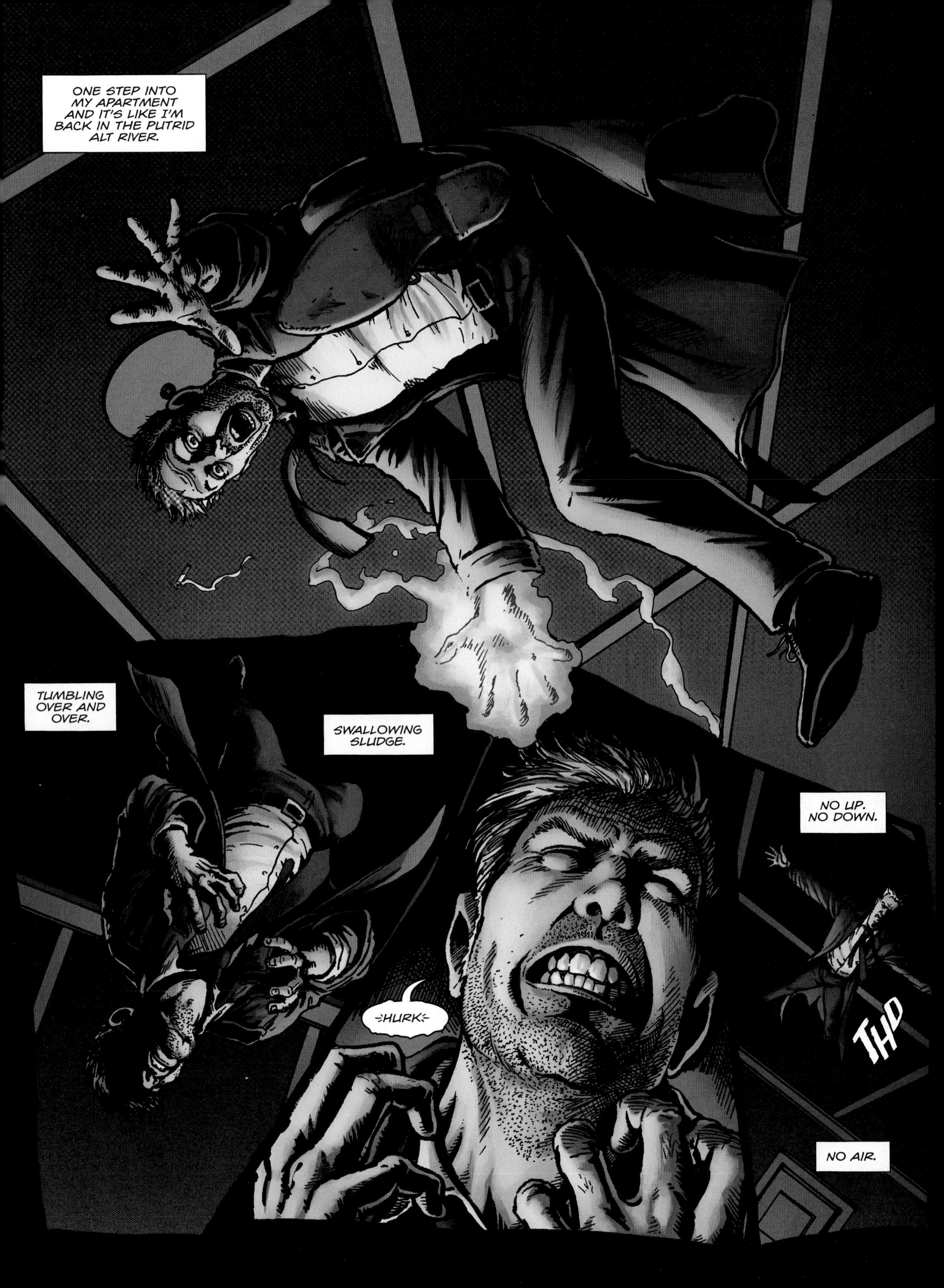
ONE STEP INTO MY APARTMENT AND IT'S LIKE I'M BACK IN THE PUTRID ALT RIVER.
TUMBLING OVER AND OVER.
SWALLOWING SLUDGE.
NO UP. NO DOWN.
HURK
NO AIR.
THP

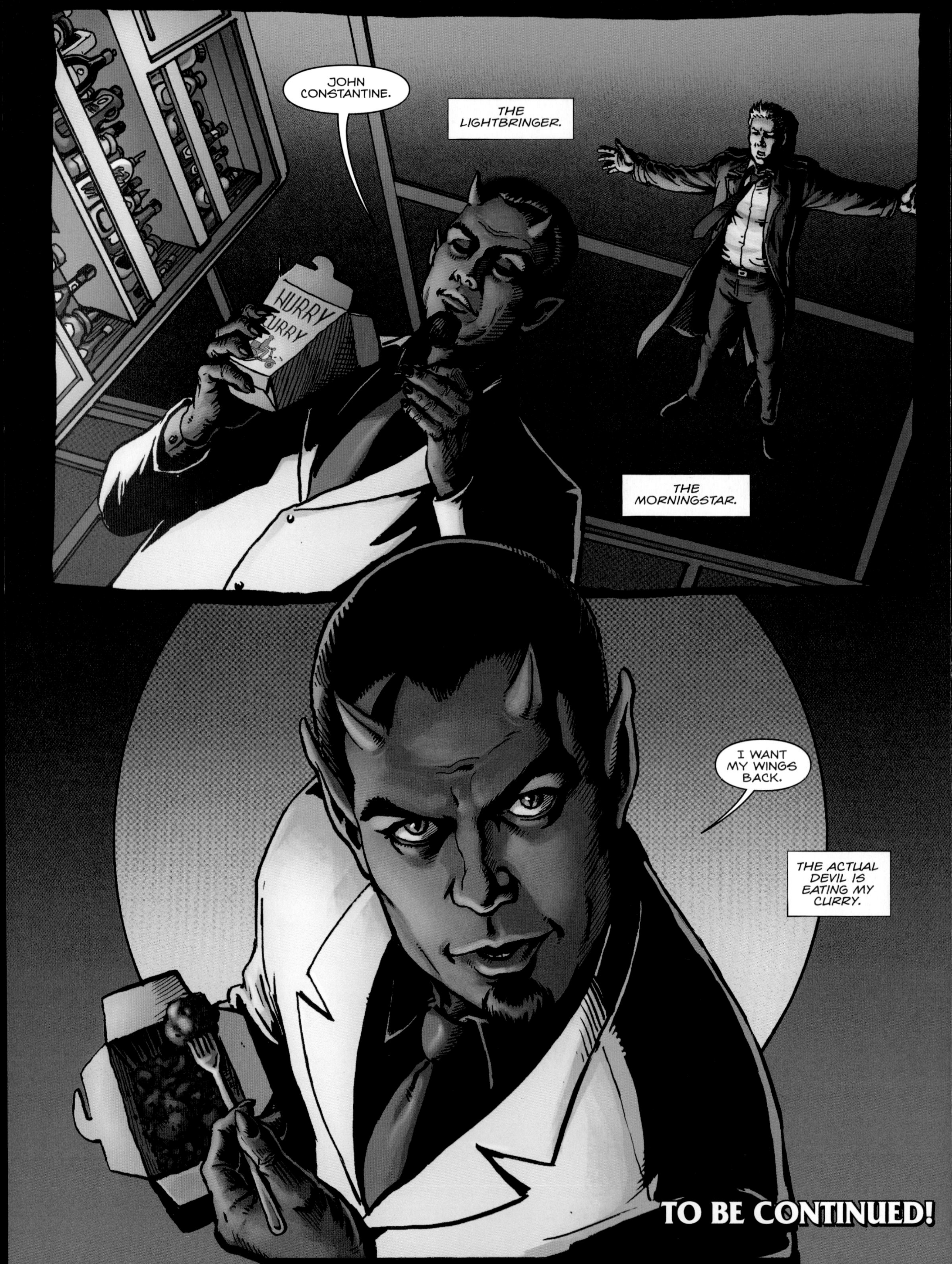
JOHN CONSTANTINE.
THE LIGHTBRINGER.
THE MORNINGSTAR.
I WANT MY WINGS BACK.
THE ACTUAL DEVIL IS EATING MY CURRY.
TO BE CONTINUED!

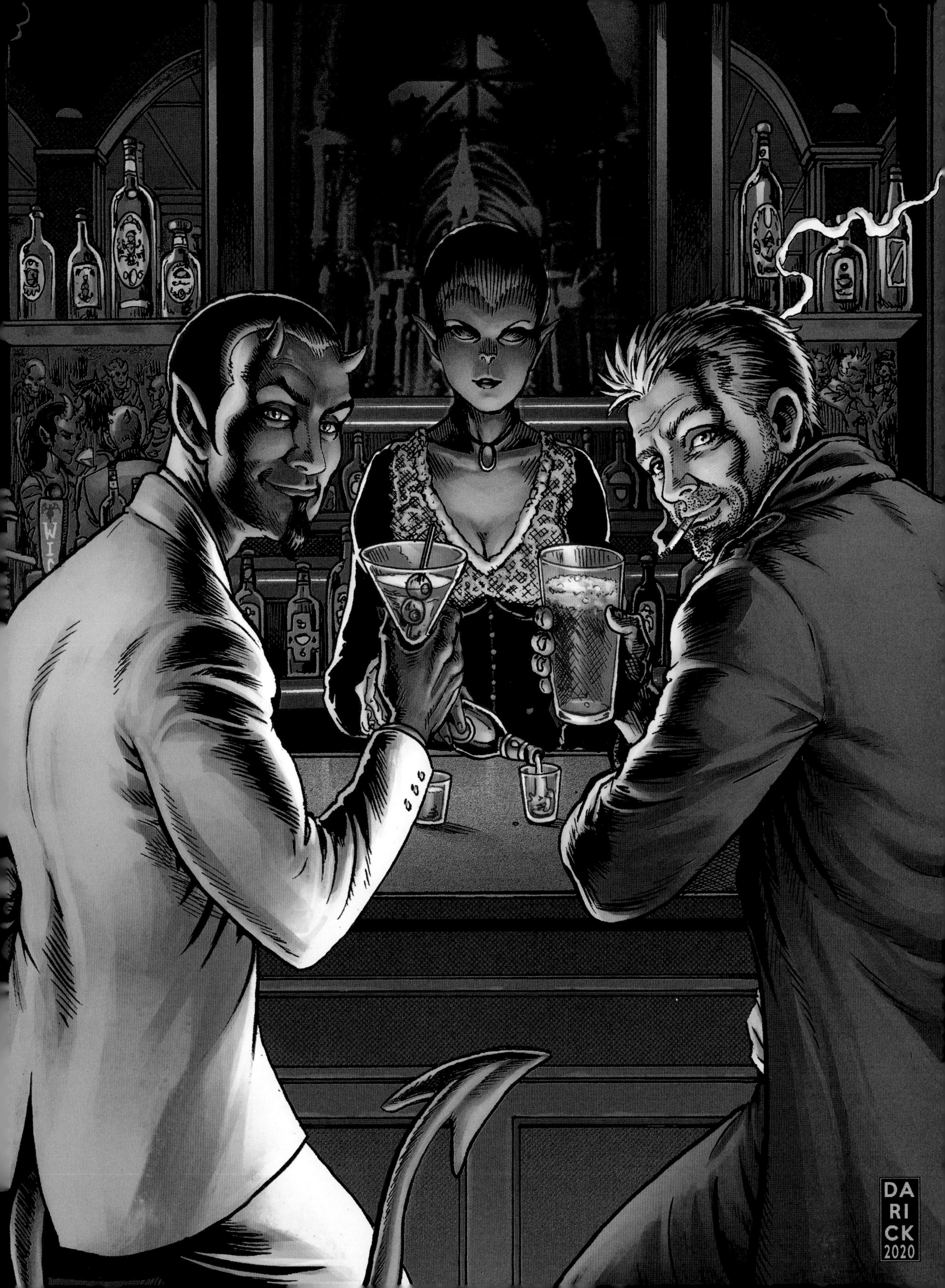
DA
RI
CK
2020

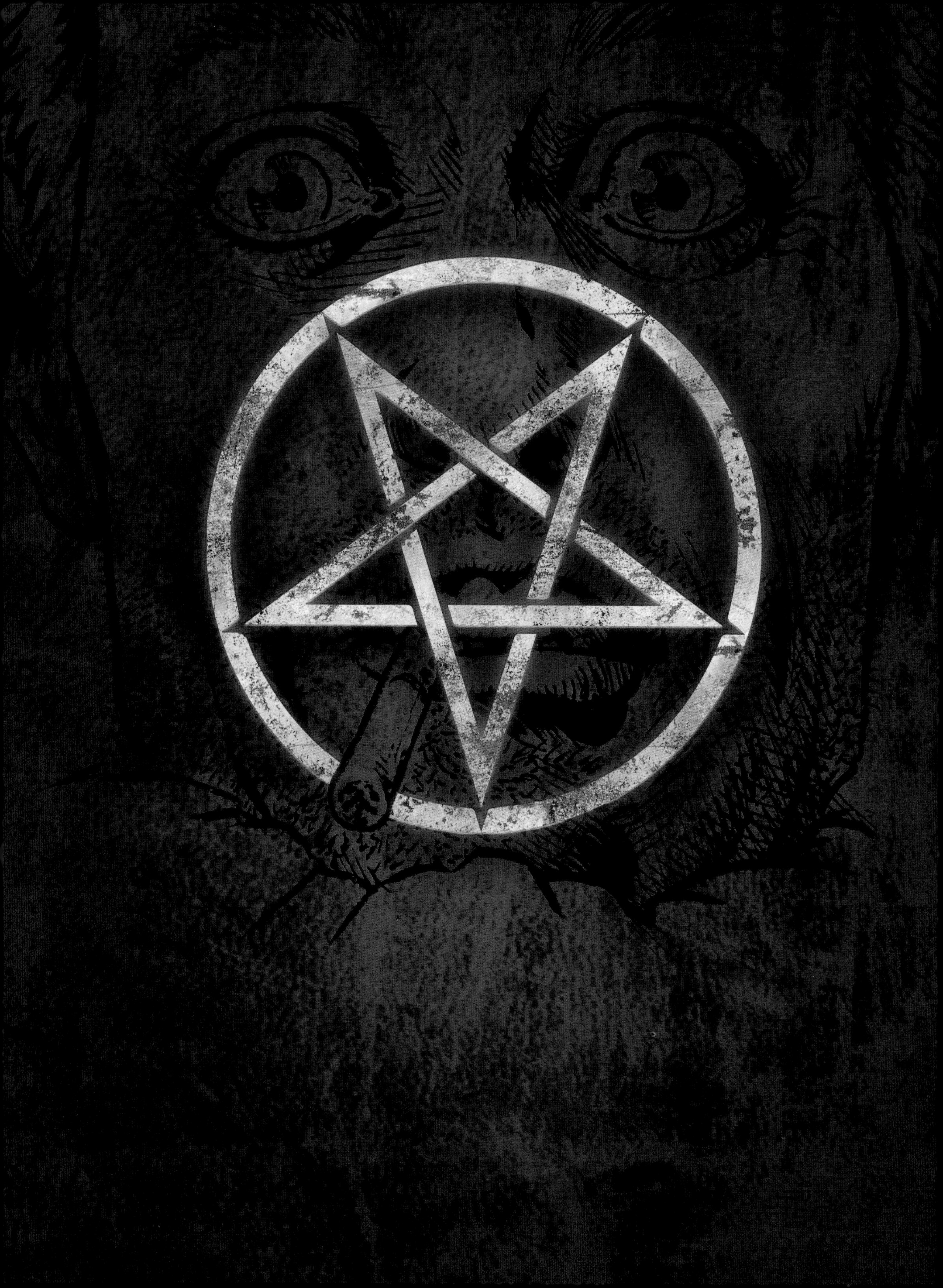

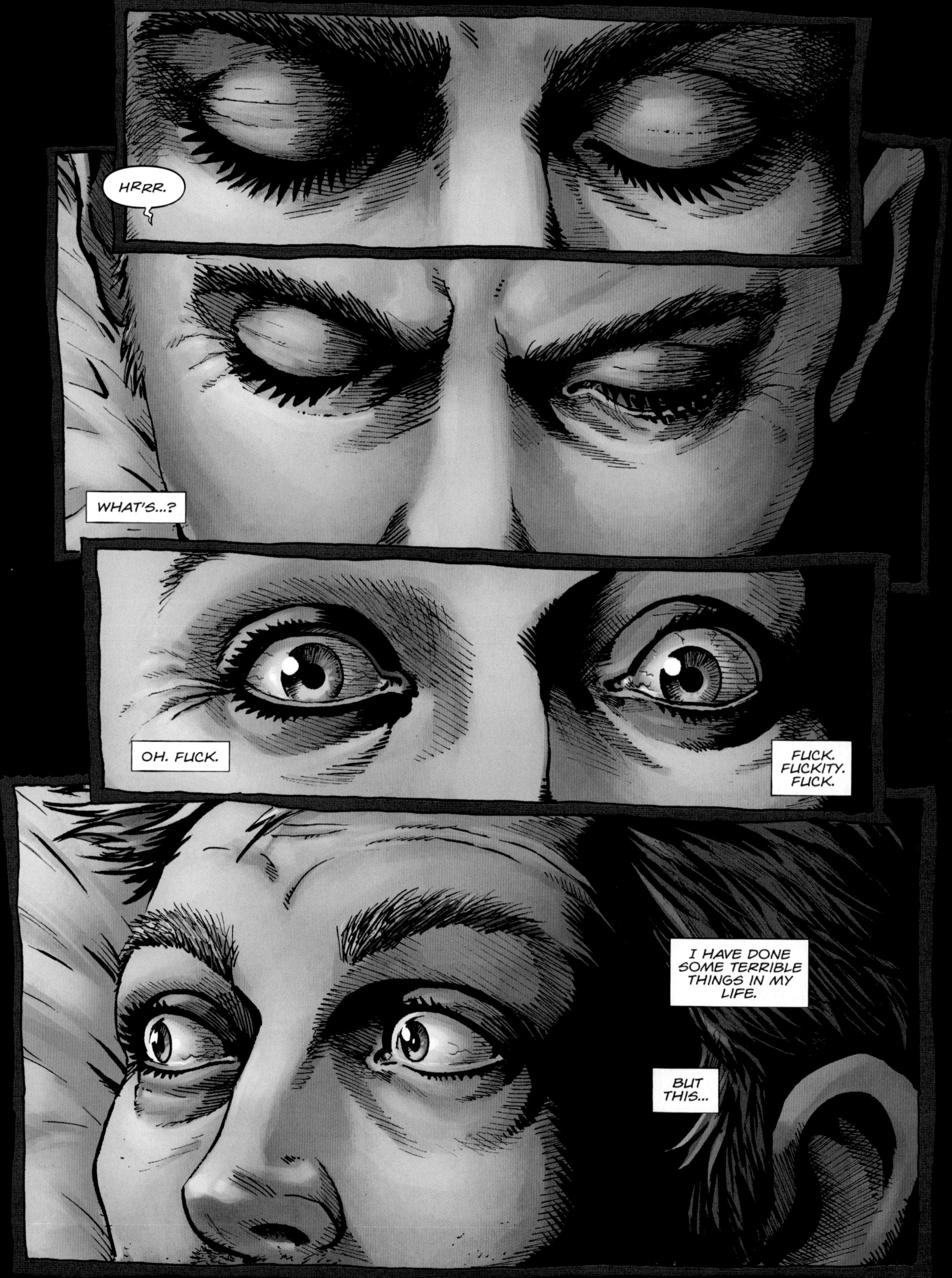
HRRR.
WHAT'S...?
OH. FUCK.
FUCK. FUCKITY. FUCK.
I HAVE DONE SOME TERRIBLE THINGS IN MY LIFE.
BUT THIS...

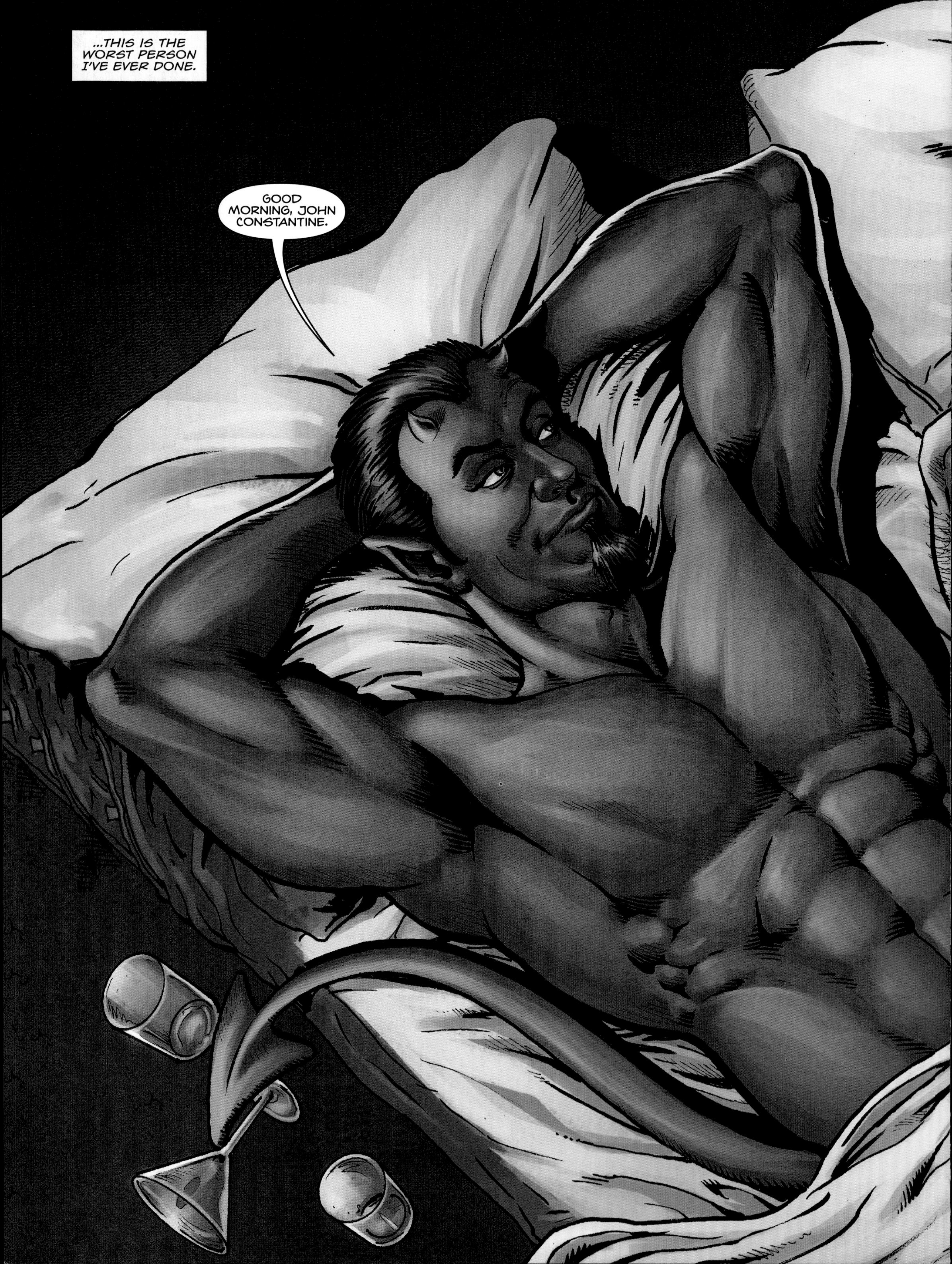
...THIS IS THE WORST PERSON I'VE EVER DONE.
GOOD MORNING, JOHN CONSTANTINE.

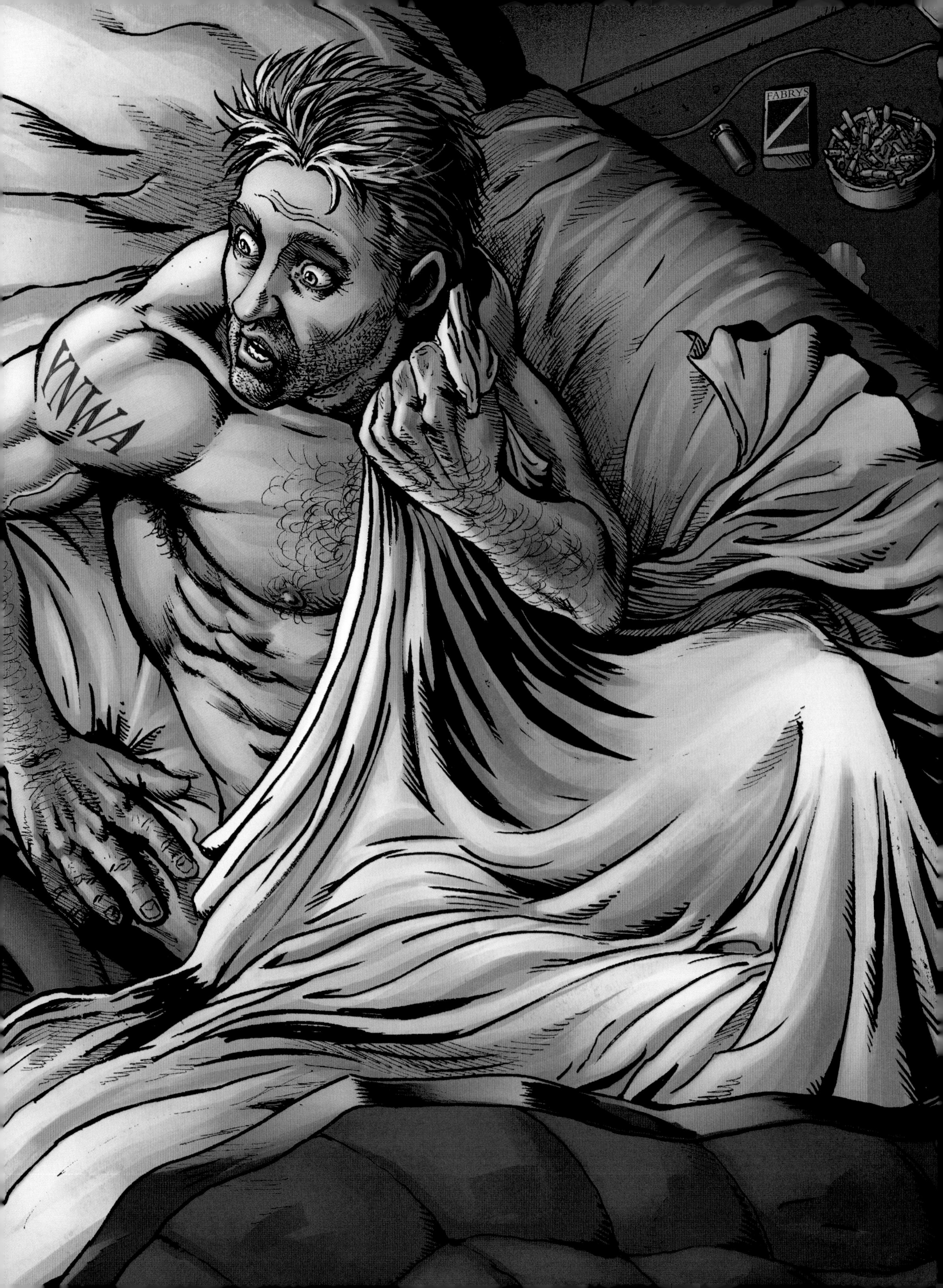
FABRYS
YNWA

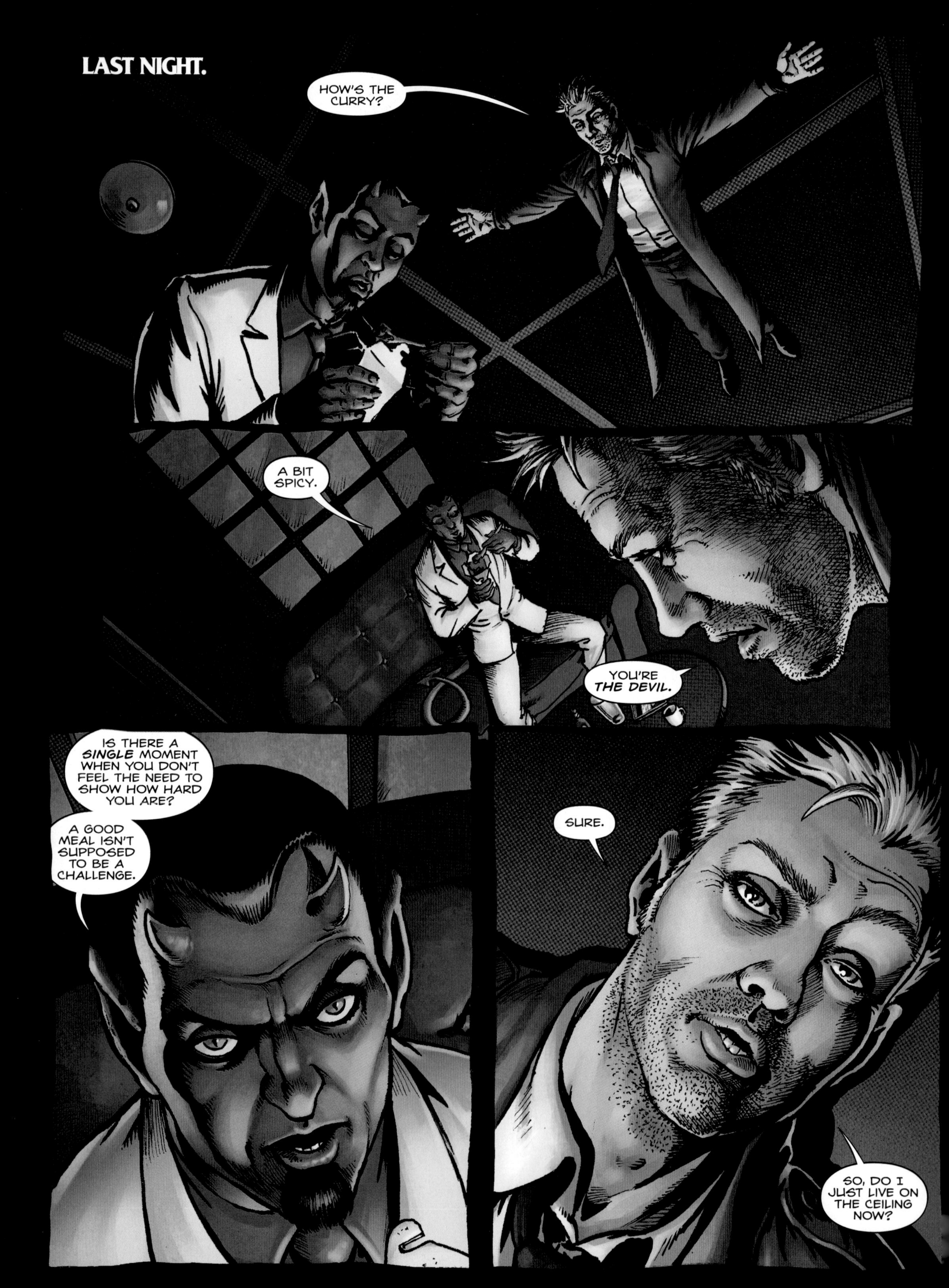
LAST NIGHT.
HOW'S THE CURRY?
A BIT SPICY.
YOU'RE THE DEVIL.
IS THERE A SINGLE MOMENT WHEN YOU DON'T FEEL THE NEED TO SHOW HOW HARD YOU ARE?
A GOOD MEAL ISN'T SUPPOSED TO BE A CHALLENGE.
SURE.
SO, DO I JUST LIVE ON THE CEILING NOW?

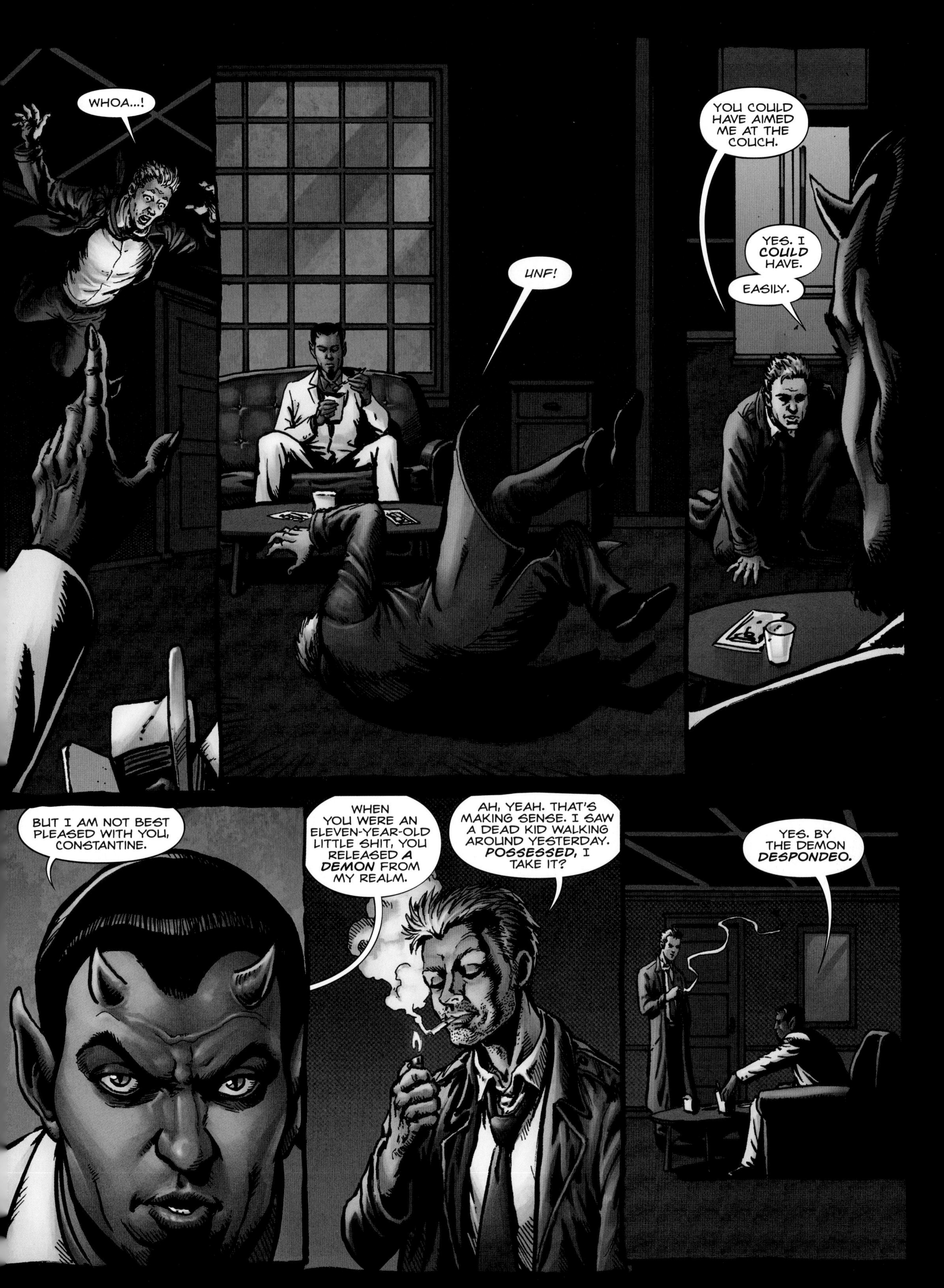
WHOA...!
UNF!
YOU COULD HAVE AIMED ME AT THE COUCH.
YES. I COULD HAVE.
EASILY.
BUT I AM NOT BEST PLEASED WITH YOU, CONSTANTINE.
WHEN YOU WERE AN ELEVEN-YEAR-OLD LITTLE SHIT, YOU RELEASED A DEMON FROM MY REALM.
AH, YEAH. THAT'S MAKING SENSE. I SAW A DEAD KID WALKING AROUND YESTERDAY. POSSESSED, I TAKE IT?
YES. BY THE DEMON DESPONDEO.

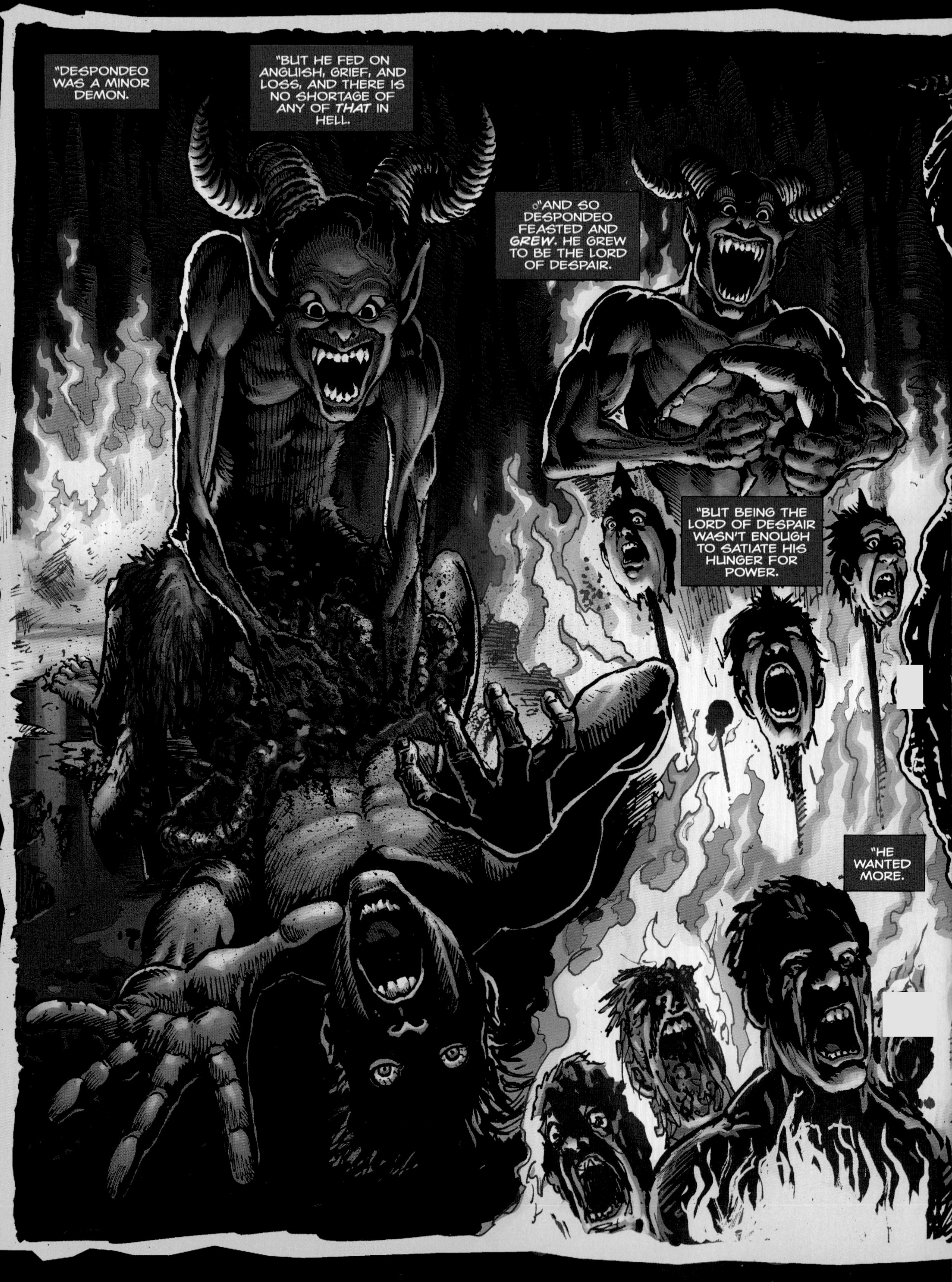
"DESPONDEO WAS A MINOR DEMON.
"BUT HE FED ON ANGUISH, GRIEF, AND LOSS, AND THERE IS NO SHORTAGE OF ANY OF *THAT* IN HELL.
"AND SO DESPONDEO FEASTED AND *GREW*. HE GREW TO BE THE LORD OF DESPAIR.
"BUT BEING THE LORD OF DESPAIR WASN'T ENOUGH TO SATIATE HIS HUNGER FOR POWER.
"HE WANTED MORE.

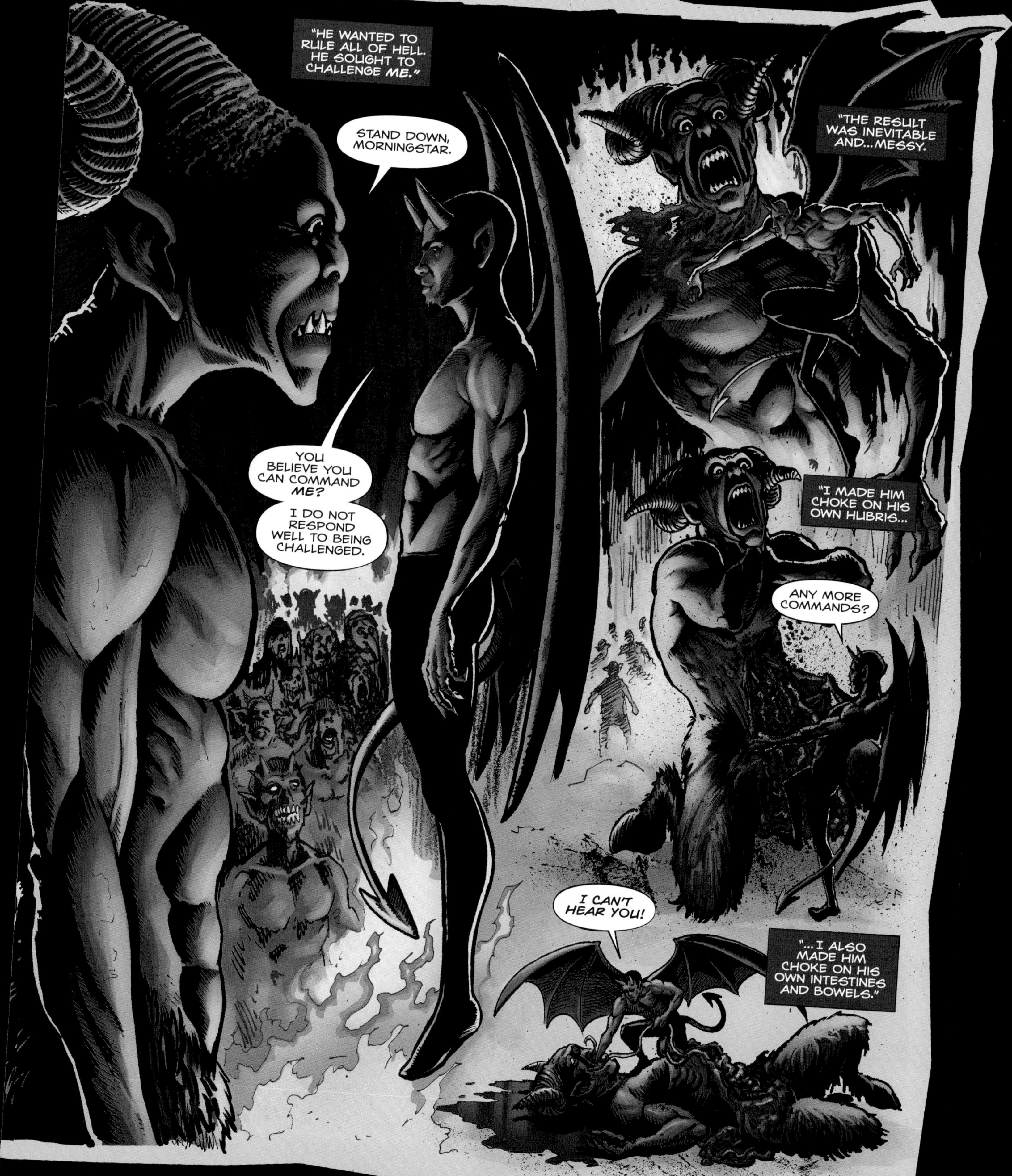
"HE WANTED TO RULE ALL OF HELL. HE SOUGHT TO CHALLENGE *ME*."
STAND DOWN, MORNINGSTAR.
YOU BELIEVE YOU CAN COMMAND *ME*?
I DO NOT RESPOND WELL TO BEING CHALLENGED.
"THE RESULT WAS INEVITABLE AND...MESSY.
"I MADE HIM CHOKE ON HIS OWN HUBRIS...
ANY MORE COMMANDS?
I CAN'T HEAR YOU!
"...I ALSO MADE HIM CHOKE ON HIS OWN INTESTINES AND BOWELS."

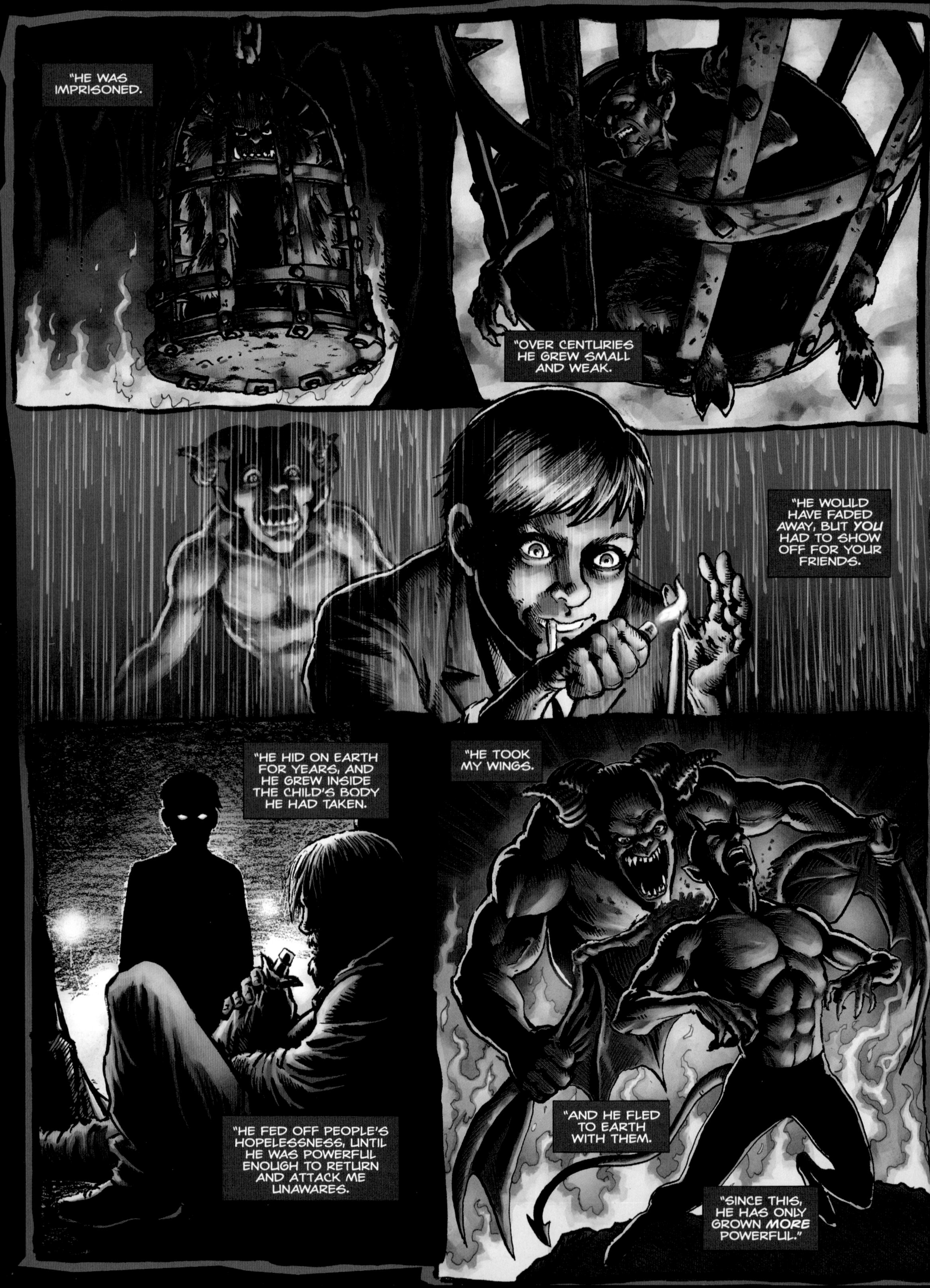
"HE WAS IMPRISONED.
"OVER CENTURIES HE GREW SMALL AND WEAK.
"HE WOULD HAVE FADED AWAY, BUT YOU HAD TO SHOW OFF FOR YOUR FRIENDS.
"HE HID ON EARTH FOR YEARS, AND HE GREW INSIDE THE CHILD'S BODY HE HAD TAKEN.
"HE FED OFF PEOPLE'S HOPELESSNESS, UNTIL HE WAS POWERFUL ENOUGH TO RETURN AND ATTACK ME UNAWARES.
"HE TOOK MY WINGS.
"AND HE FLED TO EARTH WITH THEM.
"SINCE THIS, HE HAS ONLY GROWN MORE POWERFUL."

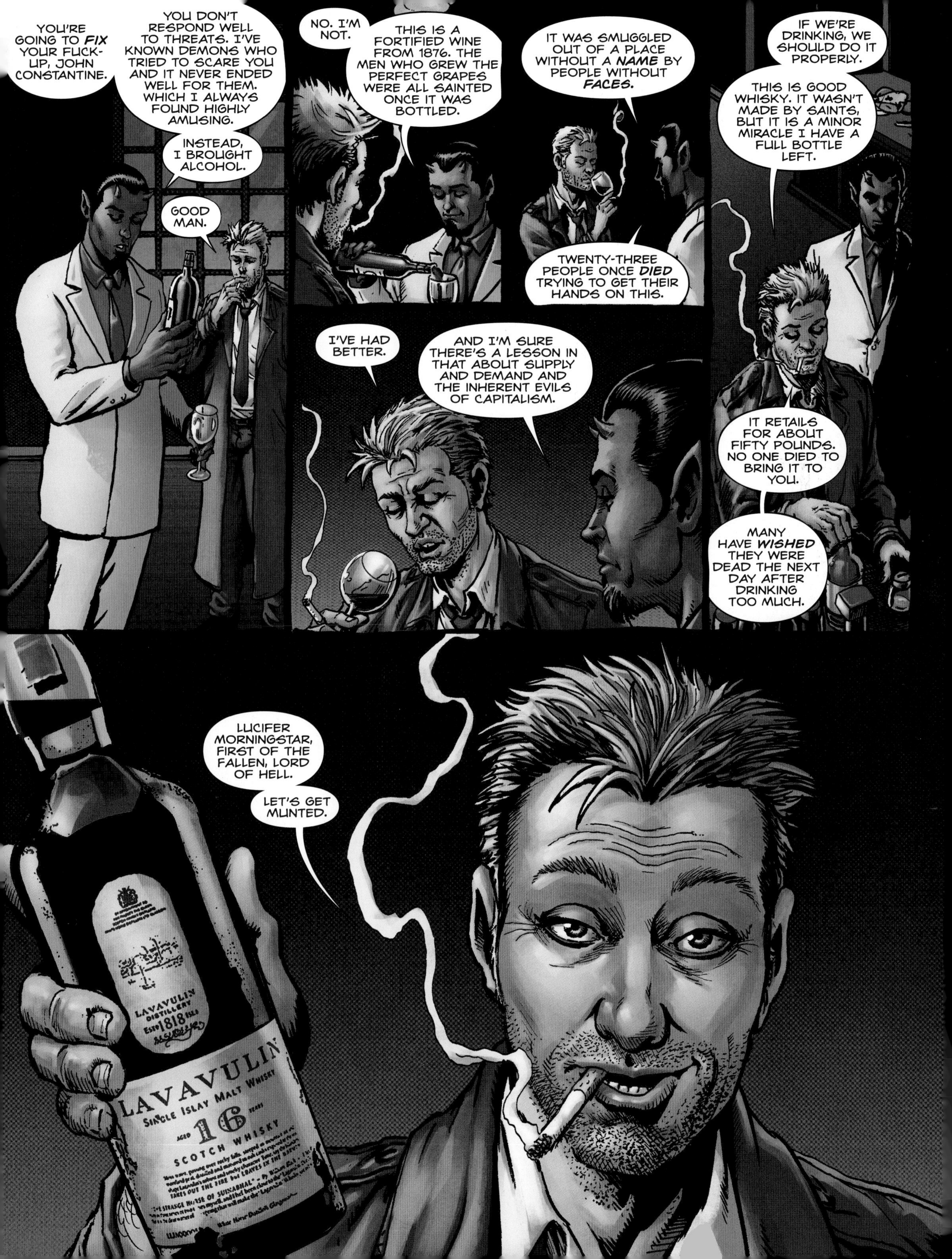

YOU'RE GOING TO FIX YOUR FUCK-UP, JOHN CONSTANTINE.
YOU DON'T RESPOND WELL TO THREATS. I'VE KNOWN DEMONS WHO TRIED TO SCARE YOU AND IT NEVER ENDED WELL FOR THEM. WHICH I ALWAYS FOUND HIGHLY AMUSING.
INSTEAD, I BROUGHT ALCOHOL.
GOOD MAN.
NO. I'M NOT.
THIS IS A FORTIFIED WINE FROM 1876. THE MEN WHO GREW THE PERFECT GRAPES WERE ALL SAINTED ONCE IT WAS BOTTLED.
IT WAS SMUGGLED OUT OF A PLACE WITHOUT A NAME BY PEOPLE WITHOUT FACES.
TWENTY-THREE PEOPLE ONCE DIED TRYING TO GET THEIR HANDS ON THIS.
I'VE HAD BETTER.
AND I'M SURE THERE'S A LESSON IN THAT ABOUT SUPPLY AND DEMAND AND THE INHERENT EVILS OF CAPITALISM.
IF WE'RE DRINKING, WE SHOULD DO IT PROPERLY.
THIS IS GOOD WHISKY. IT WASN'T MADE BY SAINTS, BUT IT IS A MINOR MIRACLE I HAVE A FULL BOTTLE LEFT.
IT RETAILS FOR ABOUT FIFTY POUNDS. NO ONE DIED TO BRING IT TO YOU.
MANY HAVE WISHED THEY WERE DEAD THE NEXT DAY AFTER DRINKING TOO MUCH.
LUCIFER MORNINGSTAR, FIRST OF THE FALLEN, LORD OF HELL.
LET'S GET MUNTED.
LAGAVULIN DISTILLERY ESTD 1818
LAGAVULIN
SINGLE ISLAY MALT WHISKY
AGED 16 YEARS
SCOTCH WHISKY

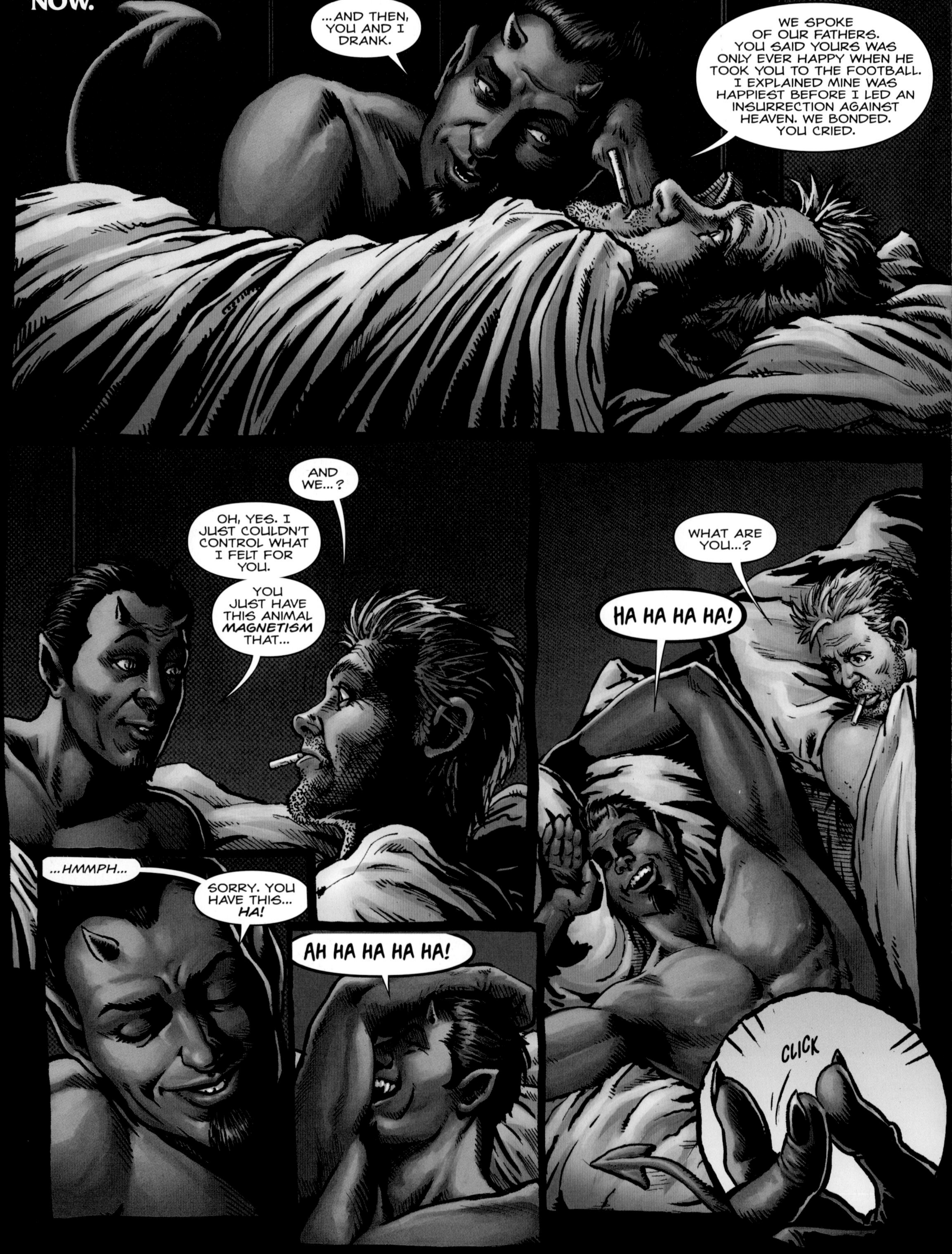
NOW.
...AND THEN, YOU AND I DRANK.
WE SPOKE OF OUR FATHERS. YOU SAID YOURS WAS ONLY EVER HAPPY WHEN HE TOOK YOU TO THE FOOTBALL. I EXPLAINED MINE WAS HAPPIEST BEFORE I LED AN INSURRECTION AGAINST HEAVEN. WE BONDED. YOU CRIED.
AND WE...?
OH, YES. I JUST COULDN'T CONTROL WHAT I FELT FOR YOU.
YOU JUST HAVE THIS ANIMAL *MAGNETISM* THAT...
...HMMPH...
SORRY. YOU HAVE THIS... *HA!*
AH HA HA HA HA!
WHAT ARE YOU...?
HA HA HA HA!
CLICK

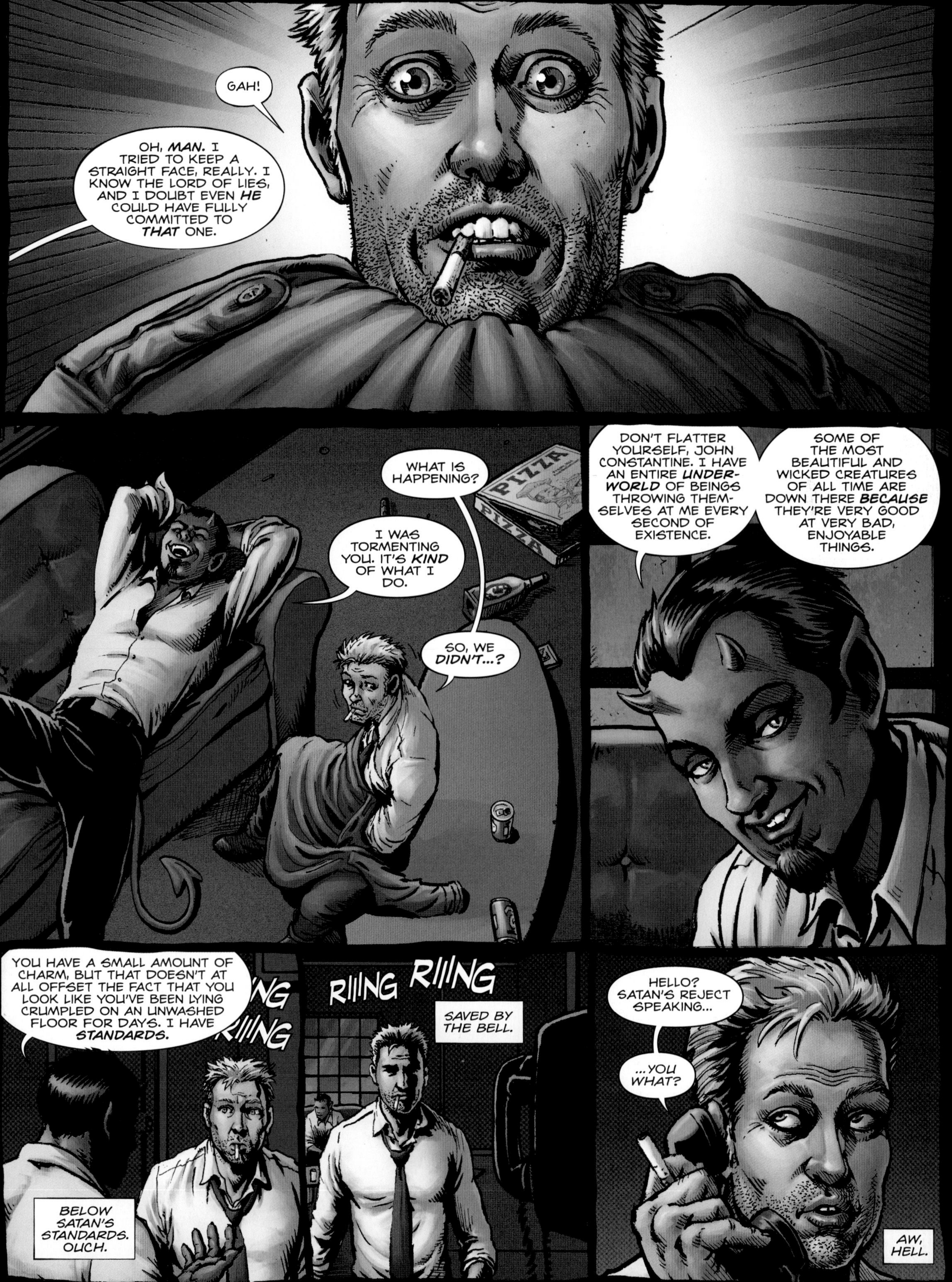
GAH!
OH, MAN. I TRIED TO KEEP A STRAIGHT FACE, REALLY. I KNOW THE LORD OF LIES, AND I DOUBT EVEN HE COULD HAVE FULLY COMMITTED TO THAT ONE.
WHAT IS HAPPENING?
I WAS TORMENTING YOU. IT'S KIND OF WHAT I DO.
SO, WE DIDN'T...?
PIZZA
DON'T FLATTER YOURSELF, JOHN CONSTANTINE. I HAVE AN ENTIRE UNDER-WORLD OF BEINGS THROWING THEM-SELVES AT ME EVERY SECOND OF EXISTENCE.
SOME OF THE MOST BEAUTIFUL AND WICKED CREATURES OF ALL TIME ARE DOWN THERE BECAUSE THEY'RE VERY GOOD AT VERY BAD, ENJOYABLE THINGS.
YOU HAVE A SMALL AMOUNT OF CHARM, BUT THAT DOESN'T AT ALL OFFSET THE FACT THAT YOU LOOK LIKE YOU'VE BEEN LYING CRUMPLED ON AN UNWASHED FLOOR FOR DAYS. I HAVE STANDARDS.
BELOW SATAN'S STANDARDS. OUCH.
RIIING RIIING
SAVED BY THE BELL.
HELLO? SATAN'S REJECT SPEAKING...
...YOU WHAT?
AW, HELL.

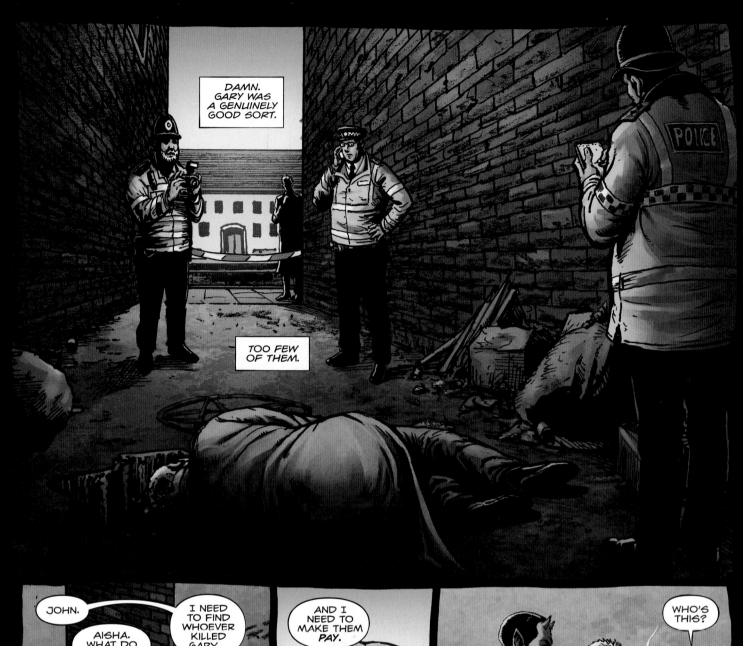

DAMN. GARY WAS A GENUINELY GOOD SORT.

TOO FEW OF THEM.

JOHN.

AISHA. WHAT DO YOU NEED?

I NEED TO FIND WHOEVER KILLED GARY...

AND I NEED TO MAKE THEM PAY.

WHO'S THIS?

WHO'S...?

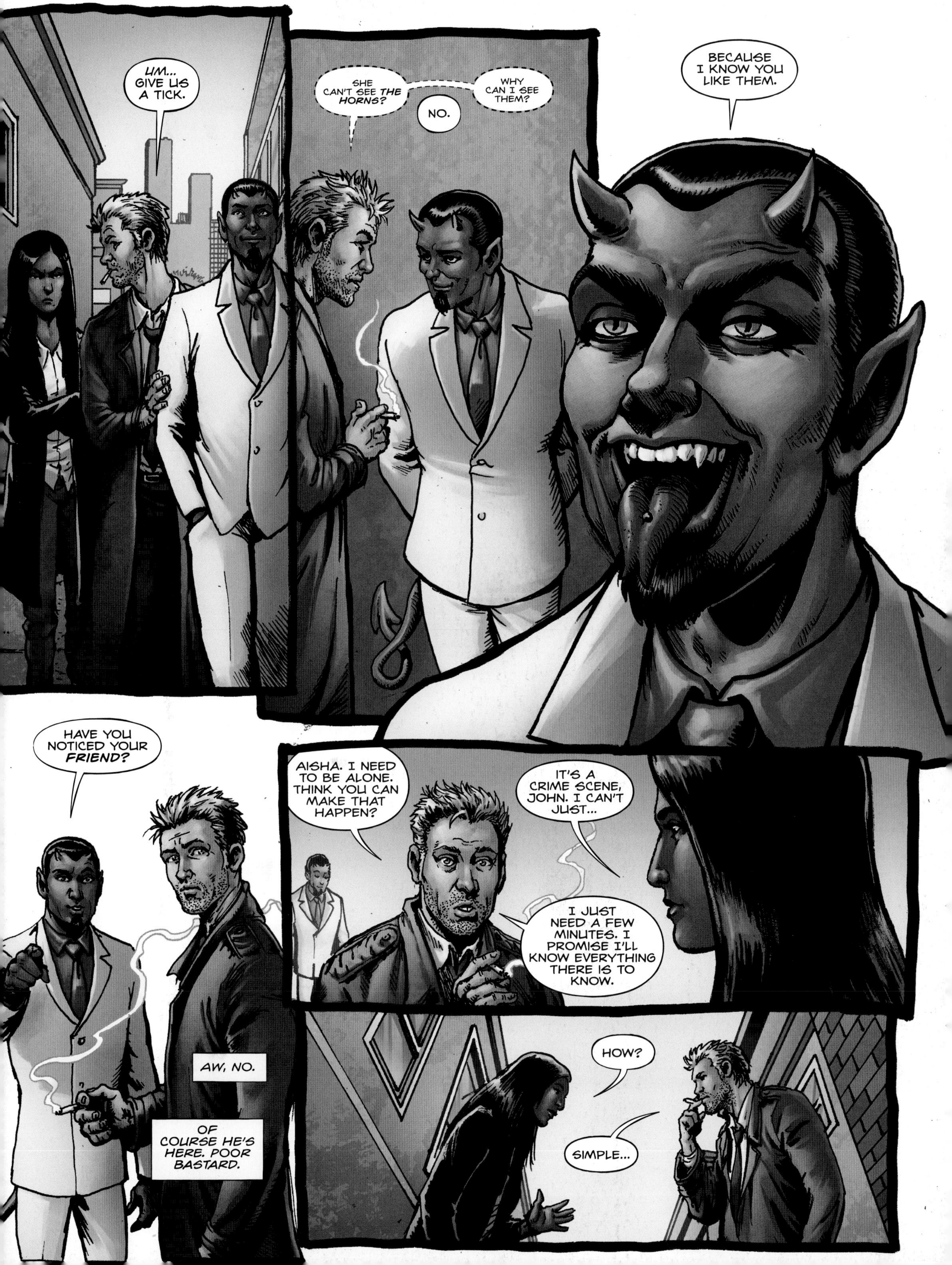
UM... GIVE US A TICK.
SHE CAN'T SEE THE HORNS?
NO.
WHY CAN I SEE THEM?
BECAUSE I KNOW YOU LIKE THEM.
HAVE YOU NOTICED YOUR FRIEND?
AW, NO.
OF COURSE HE'S HERE. POOR BASTARD.
AISHA. I NEED TO BE ALONE. THINK YOU CAN MAKE THAT HAPPEN?
IT'S A CRIME SCENE, JOHN. I CAN'T JUST...
I JUST NEED A FEW MINUTES. I PROMISE I'LL KNOW EVERYTHING THERE IS TO KNOW.
HOW?
SIMPLE...

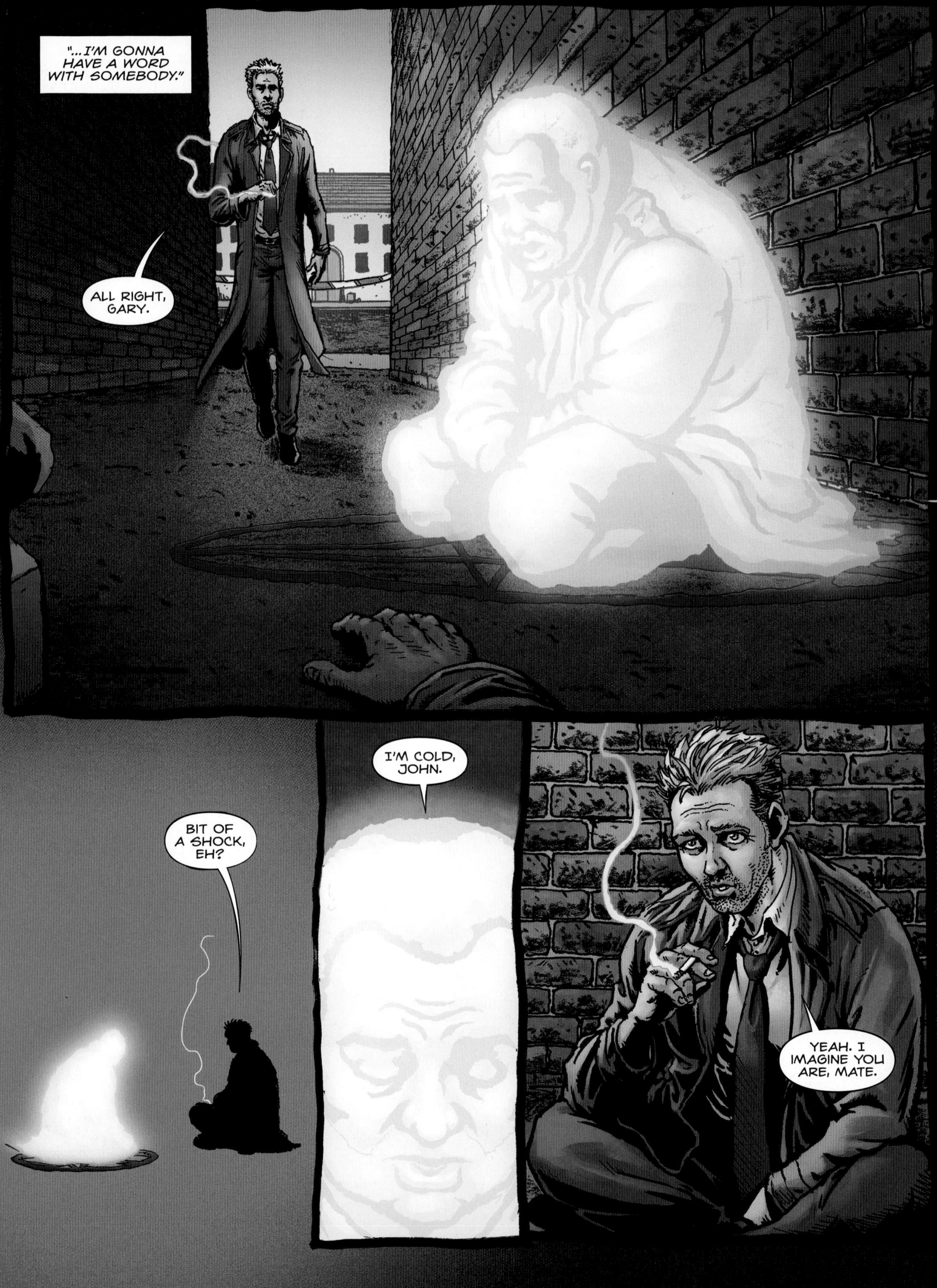
"...I'M GONNA HAVE A WORD WITH SOMEBODY."
ALL RIGHT, GARY.
BIT OF A SHOCK, EH?
I'M COLD, JOHN.
YEAH. I IMAGINE YOU ARE, MATE.

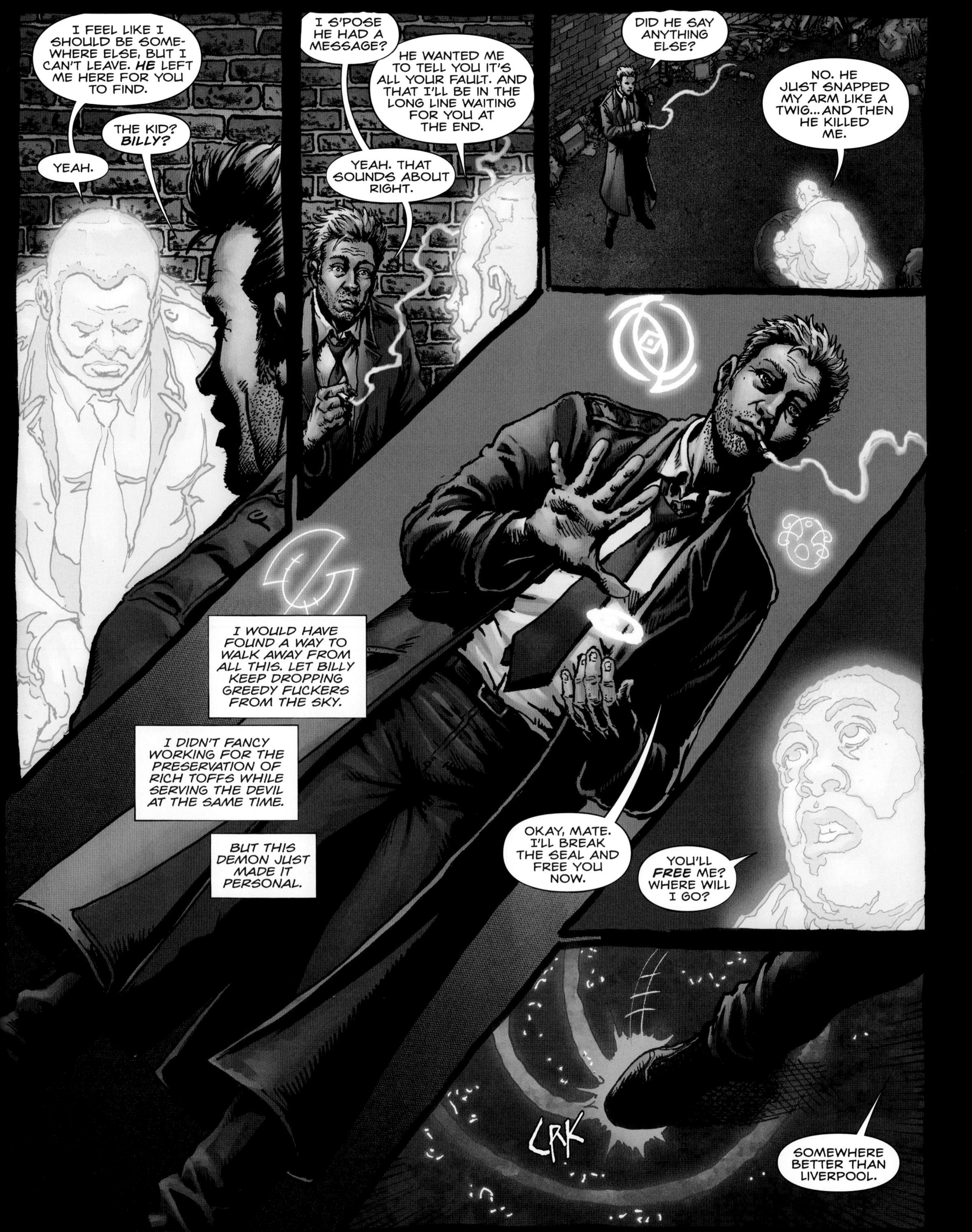
I FEEL LIKE I SHOULD BE SOMEWHERE ELSE, BUT I CAN'T LEAVE. HE LEFT ME HERE FOR YOU TO FIND.
THE KID? BILLY?
YEAH.
I S'POSE HE HAD A MESSAGE?
HE WANTED ME TO TELL YOU IT'S ALL YOUR FAULT. AND THAT I'LL BE IN THE LONG LINE WAITING FOR YOU AT THE END.
YEAH. THAT SOUNDS ABOUT RIGHT.
DID HE SAY ANYTHING ELSE?
NO. HE JUST SNAPPED MY ARM LIKE A TWIG...AND THEN HE KILLED ME.
I WOULD HAVE FOUND A WAY TO WALK AWAY FROM ALL THIS. LET BILLY KEEP DROPPING GREEDY FUCKERS FROM THE SKY.
I DIDN'T FANCY WORKING FOR THE PRESERVATION OF RICH TOFFS WHILE SERVING THE DEVIL AT THE SAME TIME.
BUT THIS DEMON JUST MADE IT PERSONAL.
OKAY, MATE. I'LL BREAK THE SEAL AND FREE YOU NOW.
YOU'LL FREE ME? WHERE WILL I GO?
CRK
SOMEWHERE BETTER THAN LIVERPOOL.

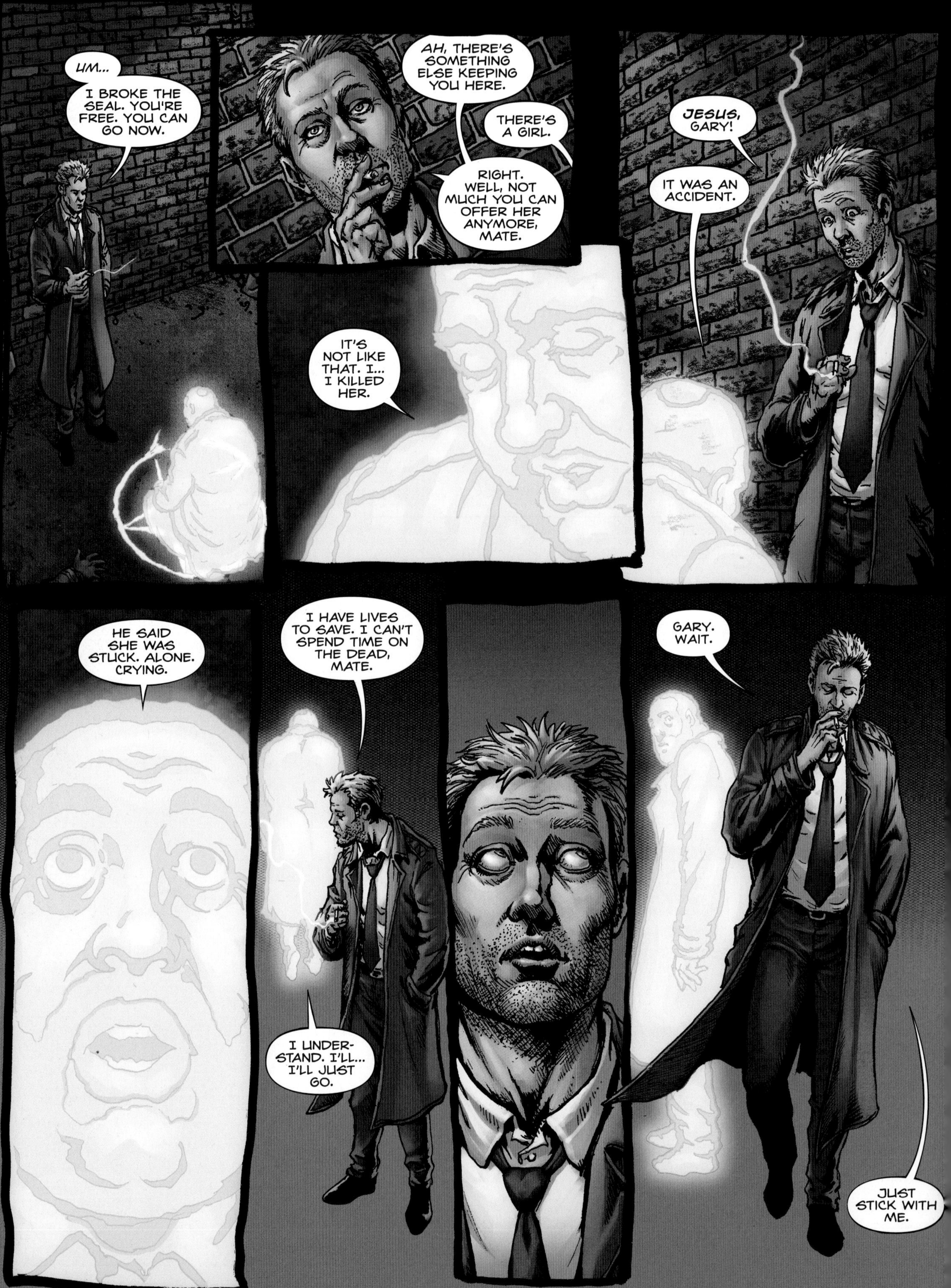
UM...
I BROKE THE SEAL. YOU'RE FREE. YOU CAN GO NOW.
AH, THERE'S SOMETHING ELSE KEEPING YOU HERE.
THERE'S A GIRL.
RIGHT. WELL, NOT MUCH YOU CAN OFFER HER ANYMORE, MATE.
IT'S NOT LIKE THAT. I... I KILLED HER.
JESUS, GARY!
IT WAS AN ACCIDENT.
HE SAID SHE WAS STUCK. ALONE. CRYING.
I HAVE LIVES TO SAVE. I CAN'T SPEND TIME ON THE DEAD, MATE.
I UNDER-STAND. I'LL... I'LL JUST GO.
GARY. WAIT.
JUST STICK WITH ME.

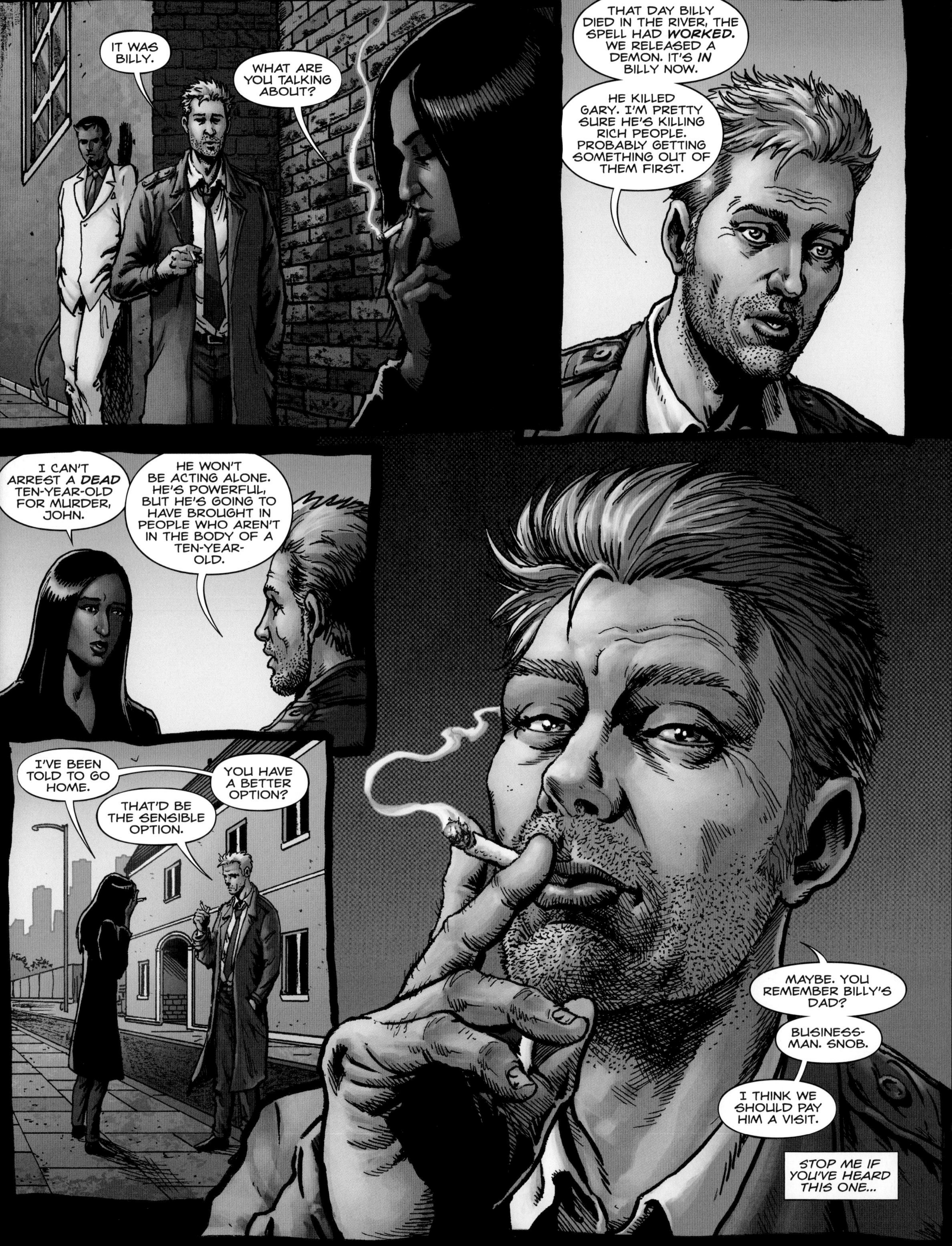
IT WAS BILLY.
WHAT ARE YOU TALKING ABOUT?
THAT DAY BILLY DIED IN THE RIVER, THE SPELL HAD WORKED. WE RELEASED A DEMON. IT'S IN BILLY NOW.
HE KILLED GARY. I'M PRETTY SURE HE'S KILLING RICH PEOPLE. PROBABLY GETTING SOMETHING OUT OF THEM FIRST.
I CAN'T ARREST A DEAD TEN-YEAR-OLD FOR MURDER, JOHN.
HE WON'T BE ACTING ALONE. HE'S POWERFUL, BUT HE'S GOING TO HAVE BROUGHT IN PEOPLE WHO AREN'T IN THE BODY OF A TEN-YEAR-OLD.
I'VE BEEN TOLD TO GO HOME.
THAT'D BE THE SENSIBLE OPTION.
YOU HAVE A BETTER OPTION?
MAYBE. YOU REMEMBER BILLY'S DAD?
BUSINESS-MAN. SNOB.
I THINK WE SHOULD PAY HIM A VISIT.
STOP ME IF YOU'VE HEARD THIS ONE...

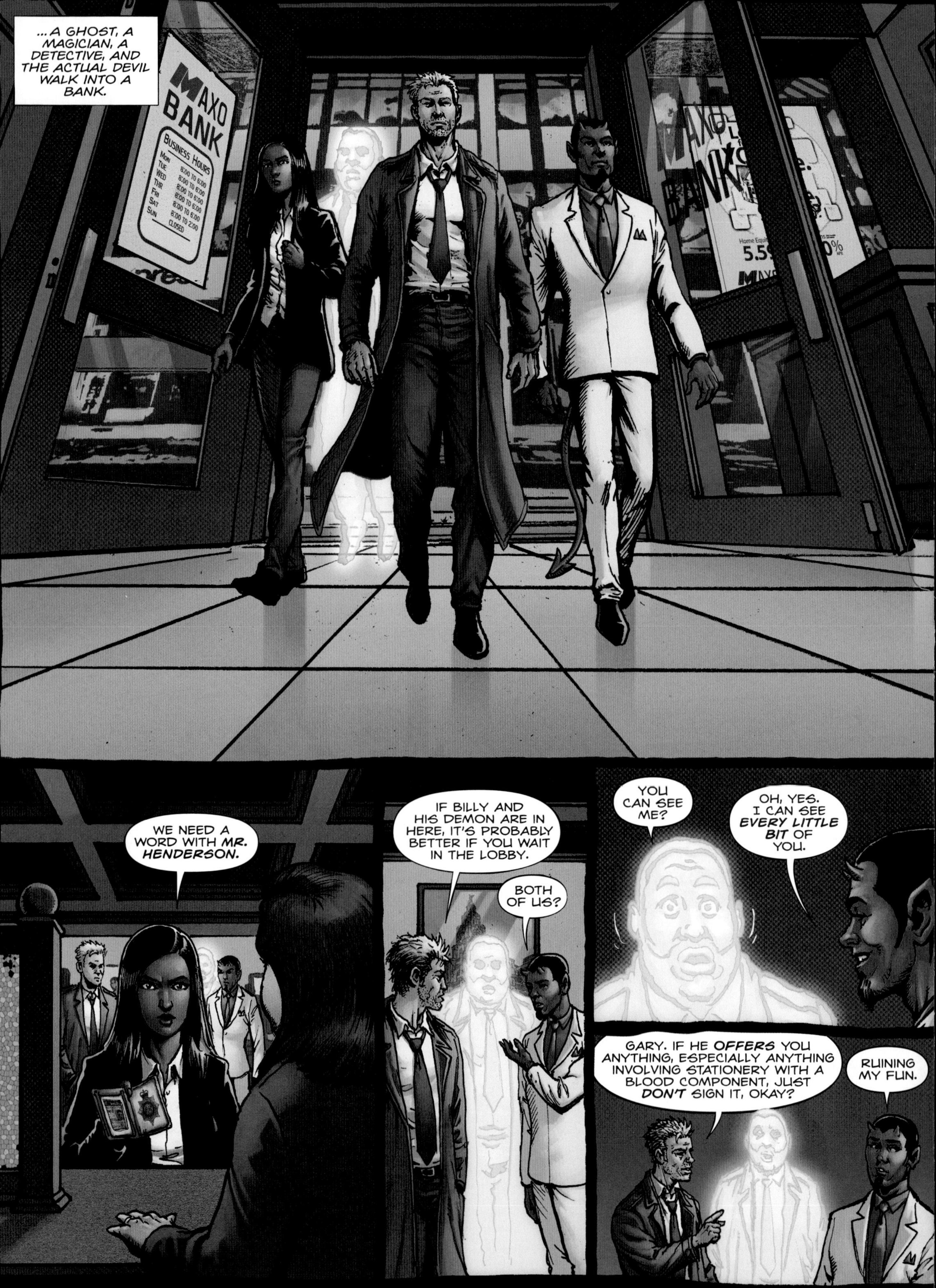
...A GHOST, A MAGICIAN, A DETECTIVE, AND THE ACTUAL DEVIL WALK INTO A BANK.
MAXO BANK
BUSINESS HOURS
MON 8:00 TO 6:00
TUE 8:00 TO 6:00
WED 8:00 TO 6:00
THR 8:00 TO 6:00
FRI 8:00 TO 6:00
SAT 8:00 TO 2:00
SUN CLOSED
WE NEED A WORD WITH MR. HENDERSON.
IF BILLY AND HIS DEMON ARE IN HERE, IT'S PROBABLY BETTER IF YOU WAIT IN THE LOBBY.
BOTH OF US?
YOU CAN SEE ME?
OH, YES. I CAN SEE EVERY LITTLE BIT OF YOU.
GARY. IF HE OFFERS YOU ANYTHING, ESPECIALLY ANYTHING INVOLVING STATIONERY WITH A BLOOD COMPONENT, JUST DON'T SIGN IT, OKAY?
RUINING MY FUN.

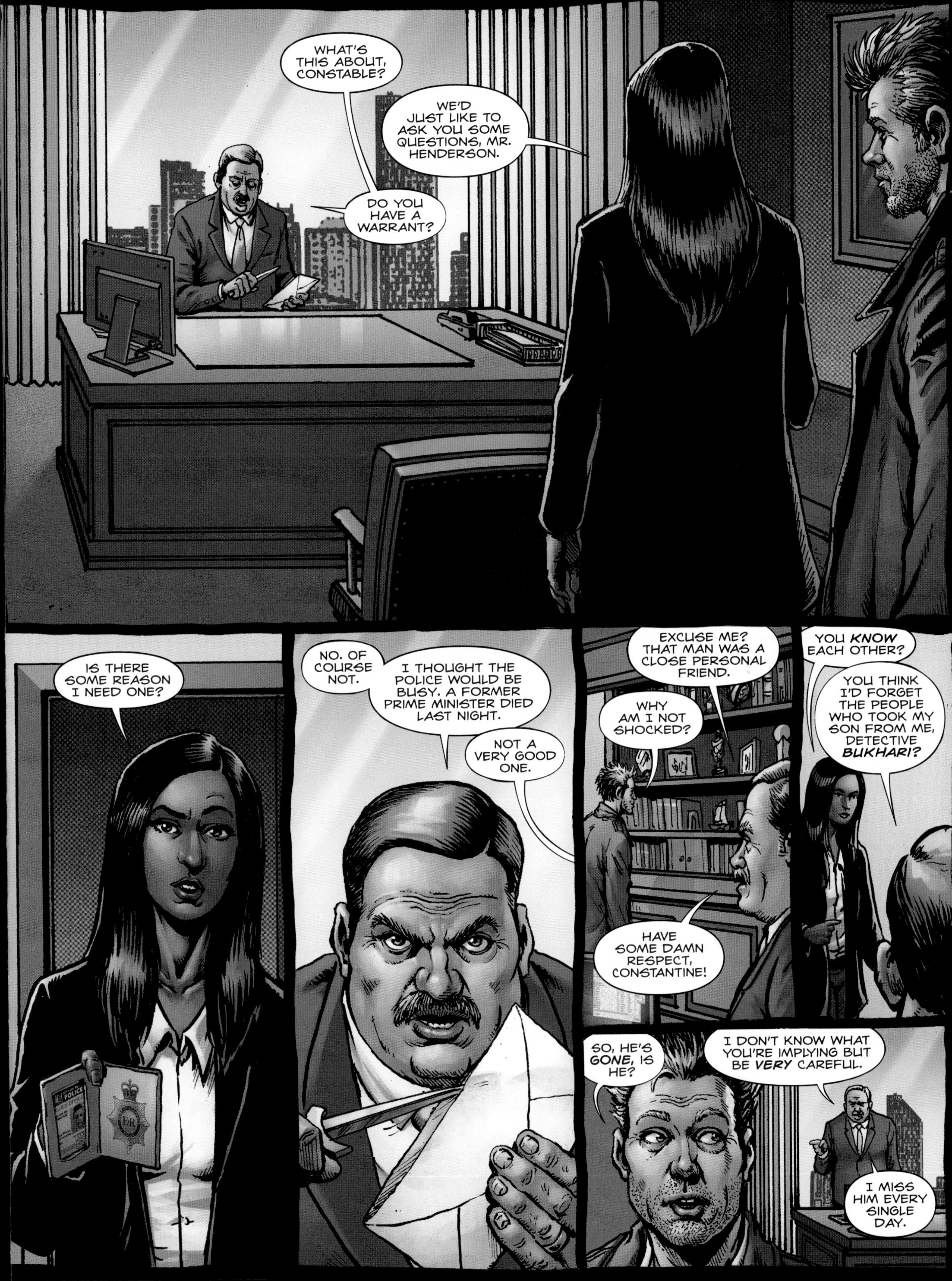
WHAT'S THIS ABOUT, CONSTABLE?
WE'D JUST LIKE TO ASK YOU SOME QUESTIONS, MR. HENDERSON.
DO YOU HAVE A WARRANT?
IS THERE SOME REASON I NEED ONE?
NO. OF COURSE NOT.
I THOUGHT THE POLICE WOULD BE BUSY. A FORMER PRIME MINISTER DIED LAST NIGHT.
NOT A VERY GOOD ONE.
EXCUSE ME? THAT MAN WAS A CLOSE PERSONAL FRIEND.
WHY AM I NOT SHOCKED?
HAVE SOME DAMN RESPECT, CONSTANTINE!
YOU *KNOW* EACH OTHER?
YOU THINK I'D FORGET THE PEOPLE WHO TOOK MY SON FROM ME, DETECTIVE *BUKHARI?*
SO, HE'S *GONE,* IS HE?
I DON'T KNOW WHAT YOU'RE IMPLYING BUT BE *VERY* CAREFUL.
I MISS HIM EVERY SINGLE DAY.

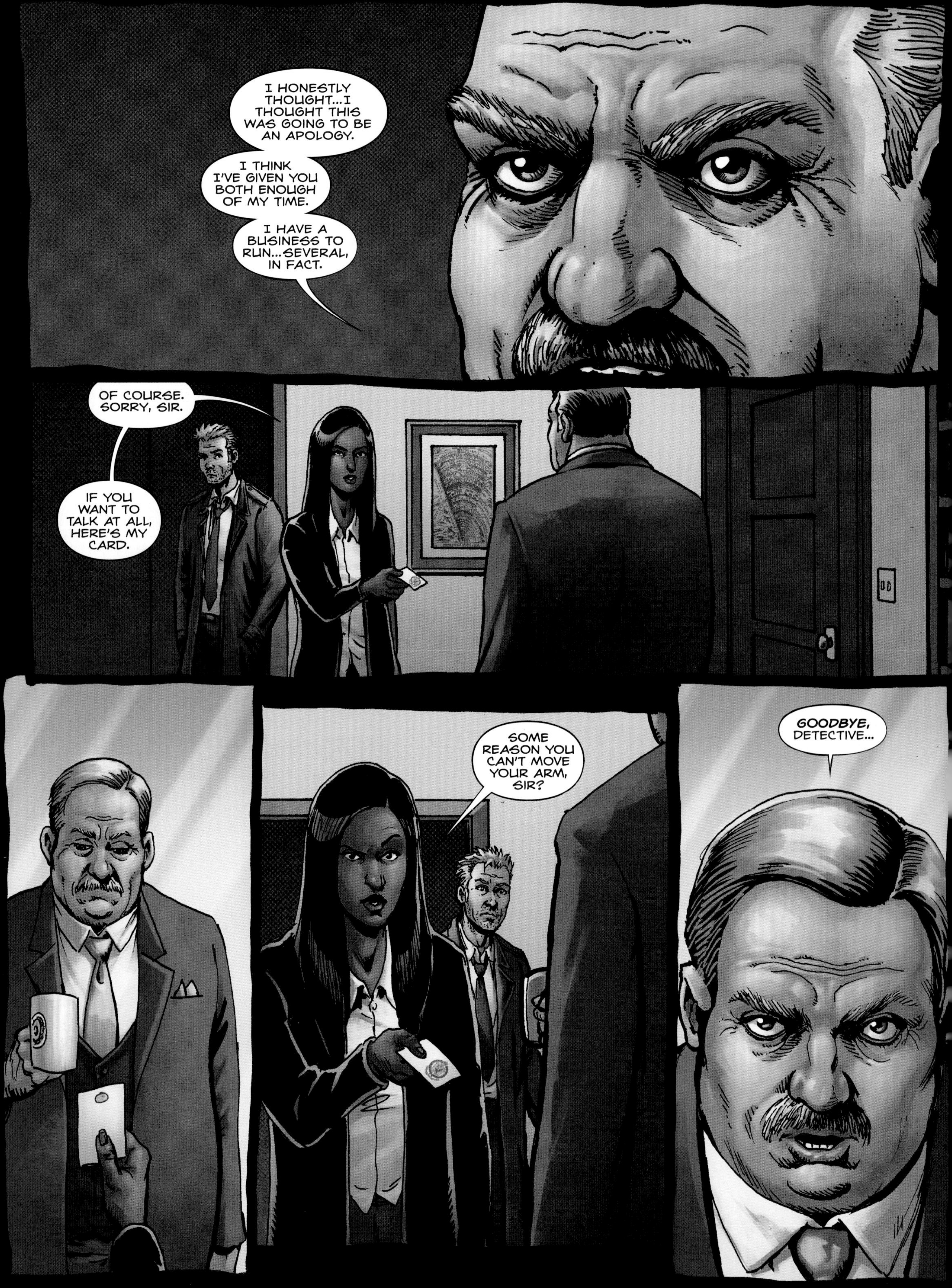
I HONESTLY THOUGHT...I THOUGHT THIS WAS GOING TO BE AN APOLOGY.
I THINK I'VE GIVEN YOU BOTH ENOUGH OF MY TIME.
I HAVE A BUSINESS TO RUN...SEVERAL, IN FACT.
OF COURSE. SORRY, SIR.
IF YOU WANT TO TALK AT ALL, HERE'S MY CARD.
SOME REASON YOU CAN'T MOVE YOUR ARM, SIR?
GOODBYE, DETECTIVE...

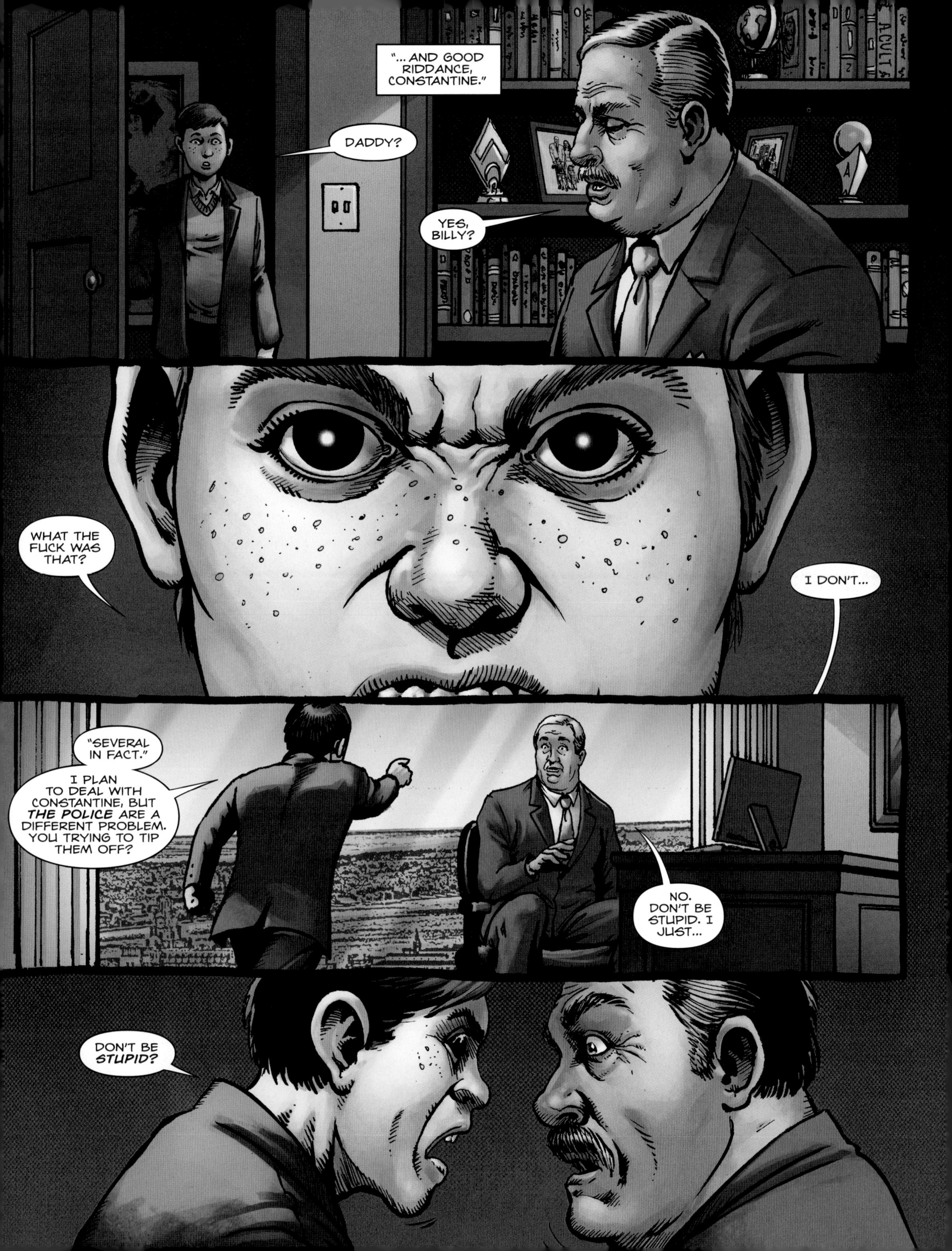
"...AND GOOD RIDDANCE, CONSTANTINE."
DADDY?
YES, BILLY?
WHAT THE FUCK WAS THAT?
I DON'T...
"SEVERAL IN FACT."
I PLAN TO DEAL WITH CONSTANTINE, BUT *THE POLICE* ARE A DIFFERENT PROBLEM. YOU TRYING TO TIP THEM OFF?
NO. DON'T BE STUPID. I JUST...
DON'T BE *STUPID*?

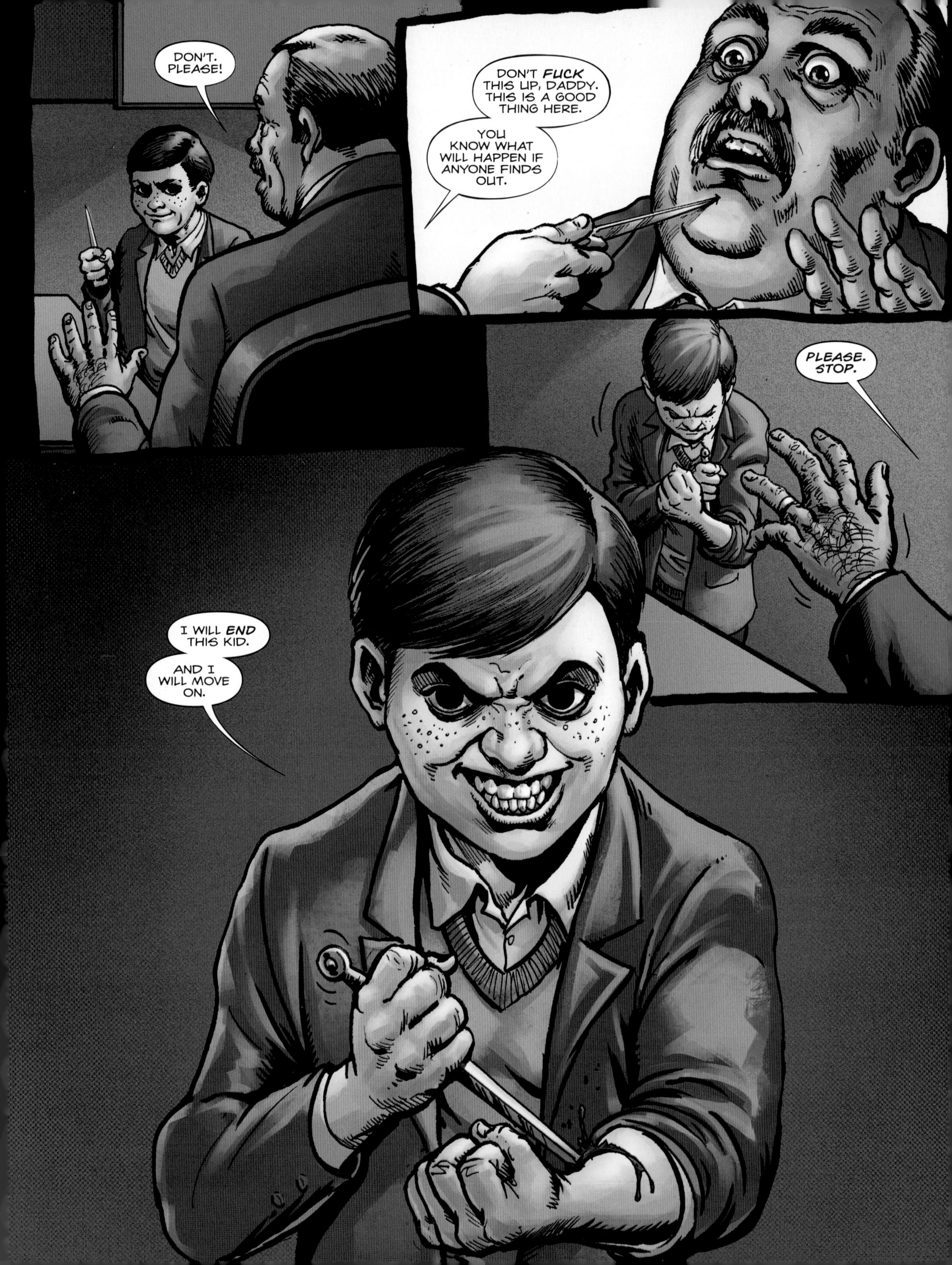
DON'T. PLEASE!
DON'T FUCK THIS UP, DADDY. THIS IS A GOOD THING HERE.
YOU KNOW WHAT WILL HAPPEN IF ANYONE FINDS OUT.
PLEASE. STOP.
I WILL END THIS KID.
AND I WILL MOVE ON.

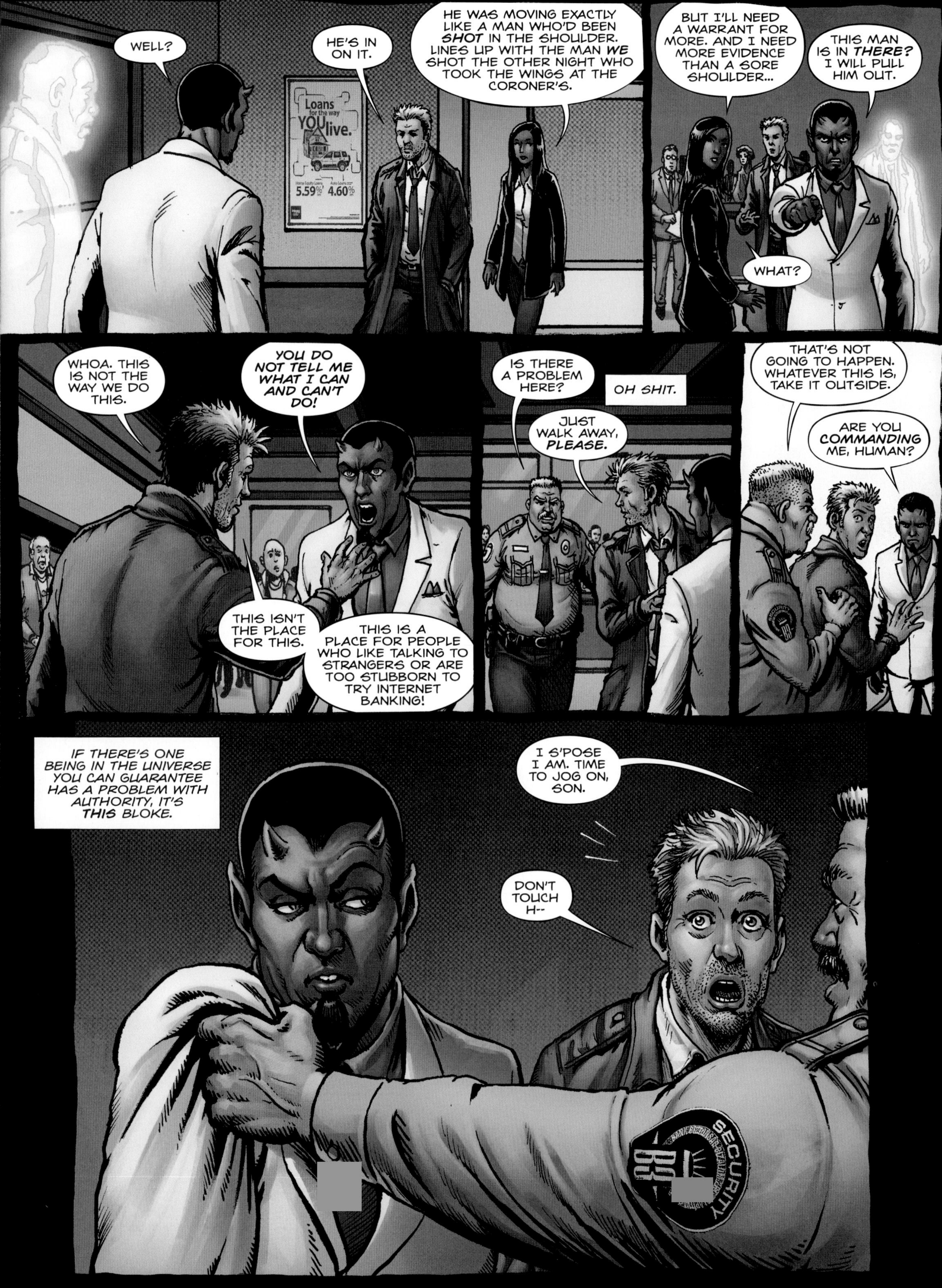

WELL?
HE'S IN ON IT.
HE WAS MOVING EXACTLY LIKE A MAN WHO'D BEEN SHOT IN THE SHOULDER. LINES UP WITH THE MAN WE SHOT THE OTHER NIGHT WHO TOOK THE WINGS AT THE CORONER'S.
Loans for the way YOU live.
5.59%
4.60%
BUT I'LL NEED A WARRANT FOR MORE. AND I NEED MORE EVIDENCE THAN A SORE SHOULDER...
THIS MAN IS IN THERE? I WILL PULL HIM OUT.
WHAT?
WHOA. THIS IS NOT THE WAY WE DO THIS.
YOU DO NOT TELL ME WHAT I CAN AND CAN'T DO!
THIS ISN'T THE PLACE FOR THIS.
THIS IS A PLACE FOR PEOPLE WHO LIKE TALKING TO STRANGERS OR ARE TOO STUBBORN TO TRY INTERNET BANKING!
IS THERE A PROBLEM HERE?
OH SHIT.
JUST WALK AWAY, PLEASE.
THAT'S NOT GOING TO HAPPEN. WHATEVER THIS IS, TAKE IT OUTSIDE.
ARE YOU COMMANDING ME, HUMAN?
IF THERE'S ONE BEING IN THE UNIVERSE YOU CAN GUARANTEE HAS A PROBLEM WITH AUTHORITY, IT'S THIS BLOKE.
I S'POSE I AM. TIME TO JOG ON, SON.
DON'T TOUCH H--
SECURITY

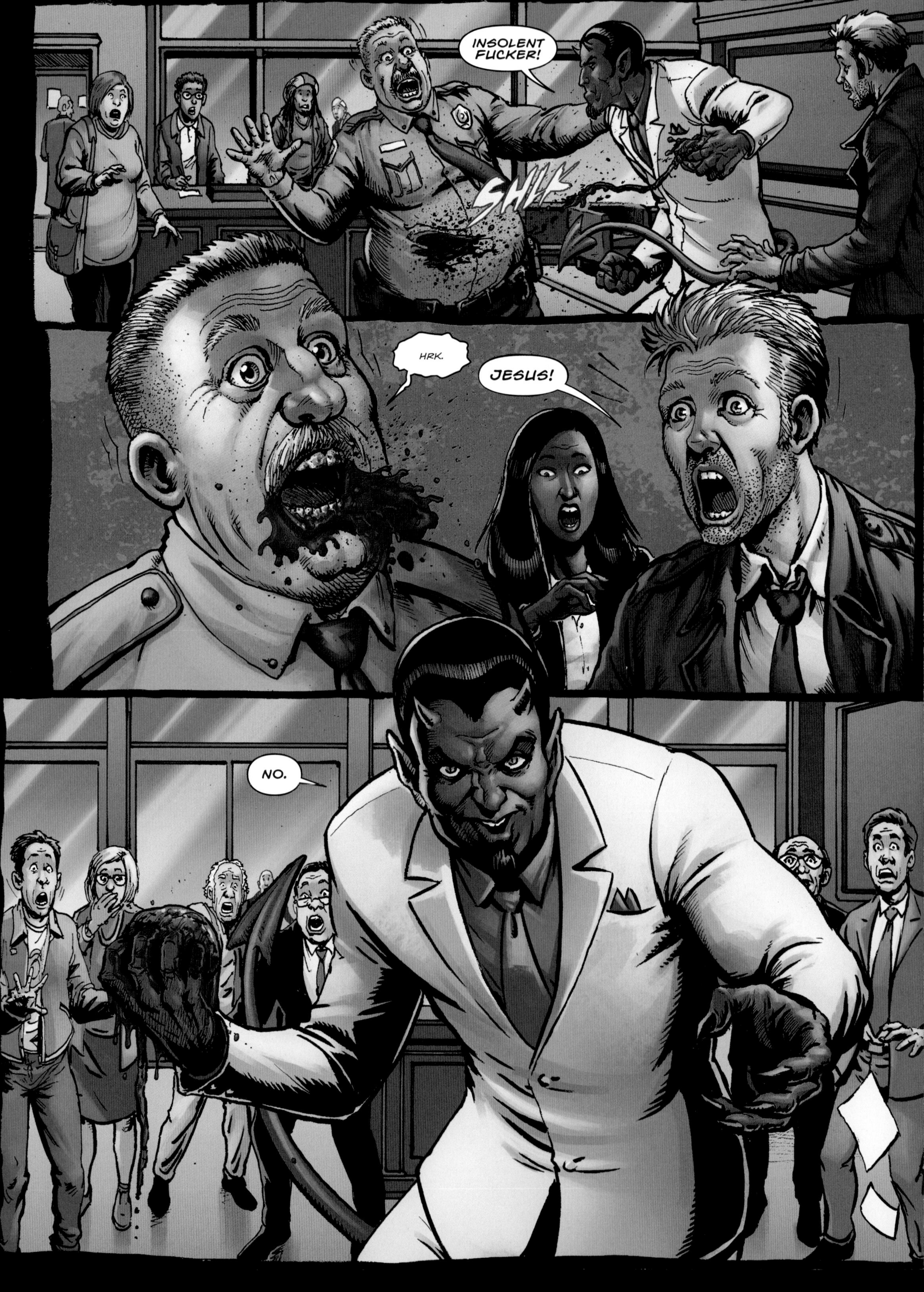

INSOLENT FUCKER!
SHLK
HRK.
JESUS!
NO.

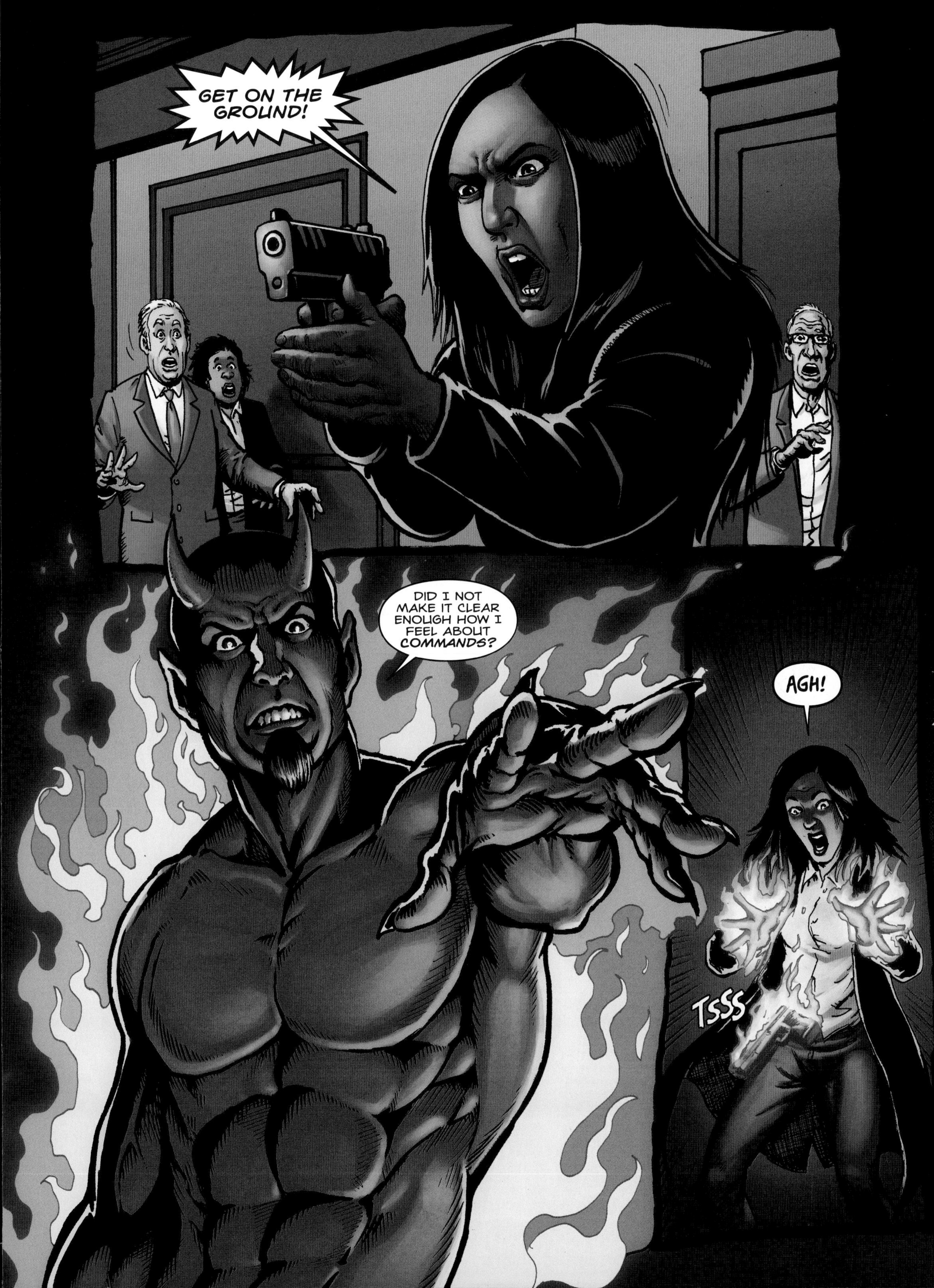
GET ON THE GROUND!
DID I NOT MAKE IT CLEAR ENOUGH HOW I FEEL ABOUT COMMANDS?
AGH!
TSSS

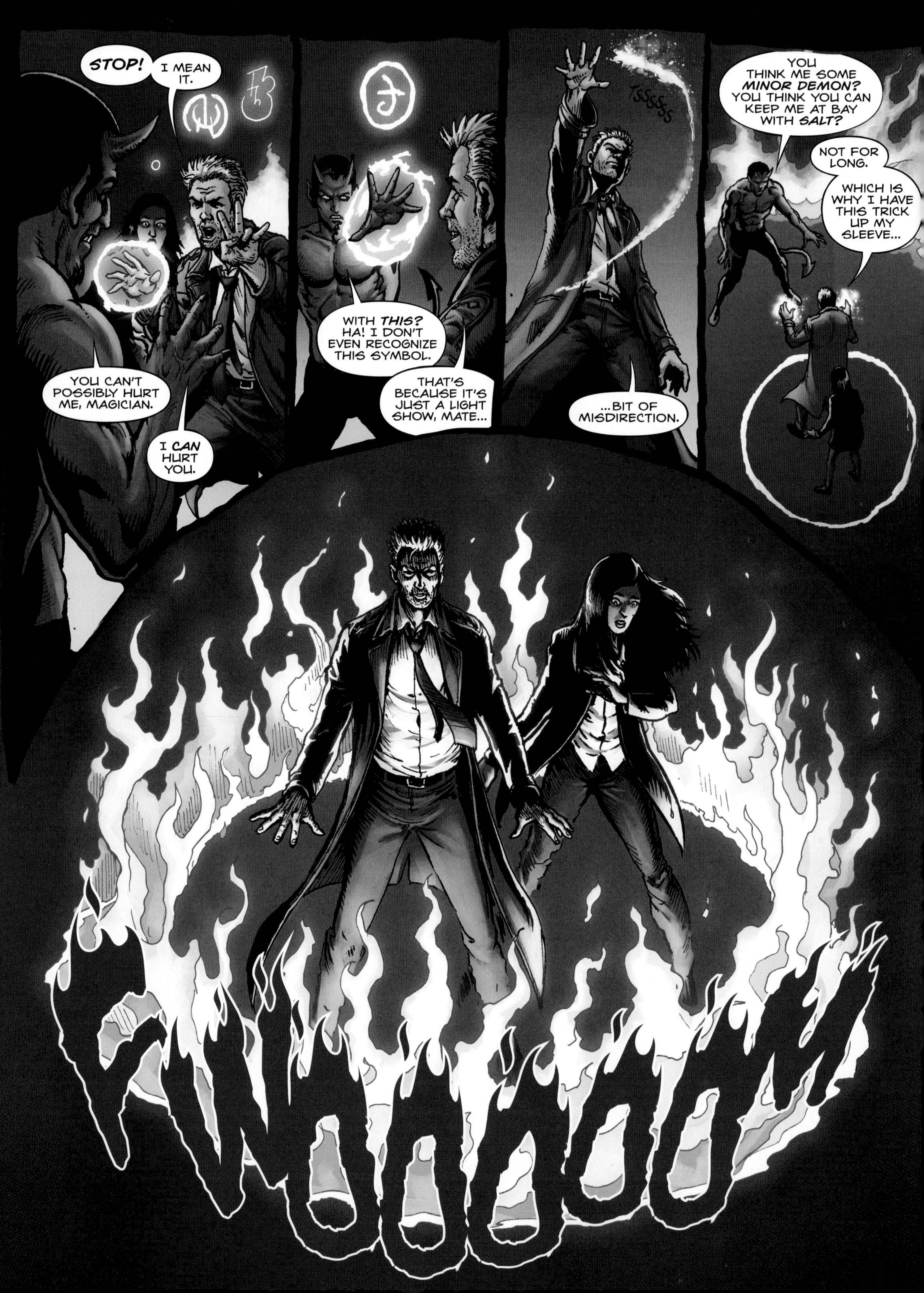
STOP!
I MEAN IT.
YOU CAN'T POSSIBLY HURT ME, MAGICIAN.
I CAN HURT YOU.
WITH THIS? HA! I DON'T EVEN RECOGNIZE THIS SYMBOL.
THAT'S BECAUSE IT'S JUST A LIGHT SHOW, MATE...
TSSSSSS
...BIT OF MISDIRECTION.
YOU THINK ME SOME MINOR DEMON? YOU THINK YOU CAN KEEP ME AT BAY WITH SALT?
NOT FOR LONG.
WHICH IS WHY I HAVE THIS TRICK UP MY SLEEVE...

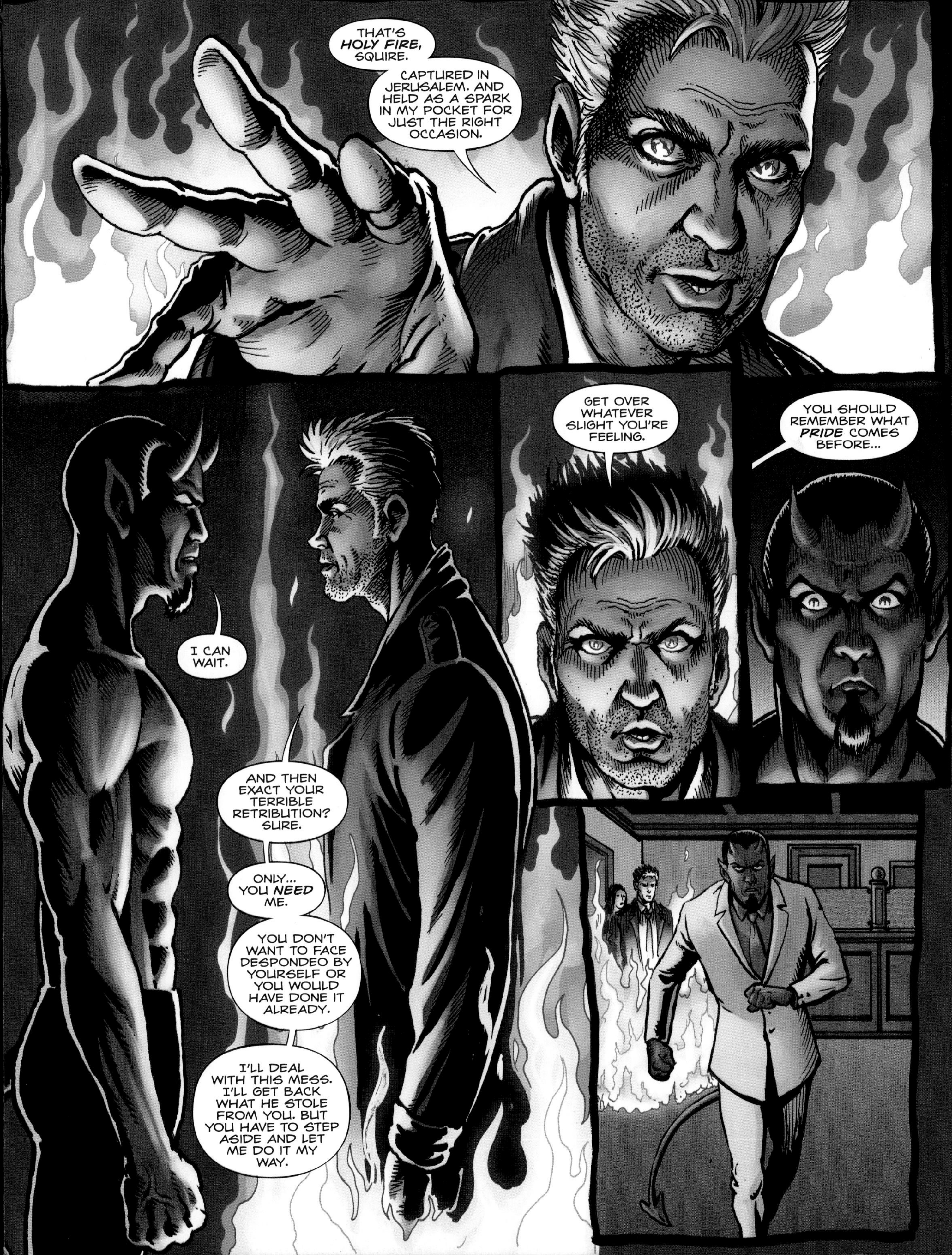
THAT'S *HOLY FIRE,* SQUIRE.
CAPTURED IN JERUSALEM. AND HELD AS A SPARK IN MY POCKET FOR JUST THE RIGHT OCCASION.
I CAN WAIT.
AND THEN EXACT YOUR TERRIBLE RETRIBUTION? SURE.
ONLY... YOU *NEED* ME.
YOU DON'T WANT TO FACE DESPONDEO BY YOURSELF OR YOU WOULD HAVE DONE IT ALREADY.
I'LL DEAL WITH THIS MESS. I'LL GET BACK WHAT HE STOLE FROM YOU. BUT YOU HAVE TO STEP ASIDE AND LET ME DO IT MY WAY.
GET OVER WHATEVER SLIGHT YOU'RE FEELING.
YOU SHOULD REMEMBER WHAT *PRIDE* COMES BEFORE...

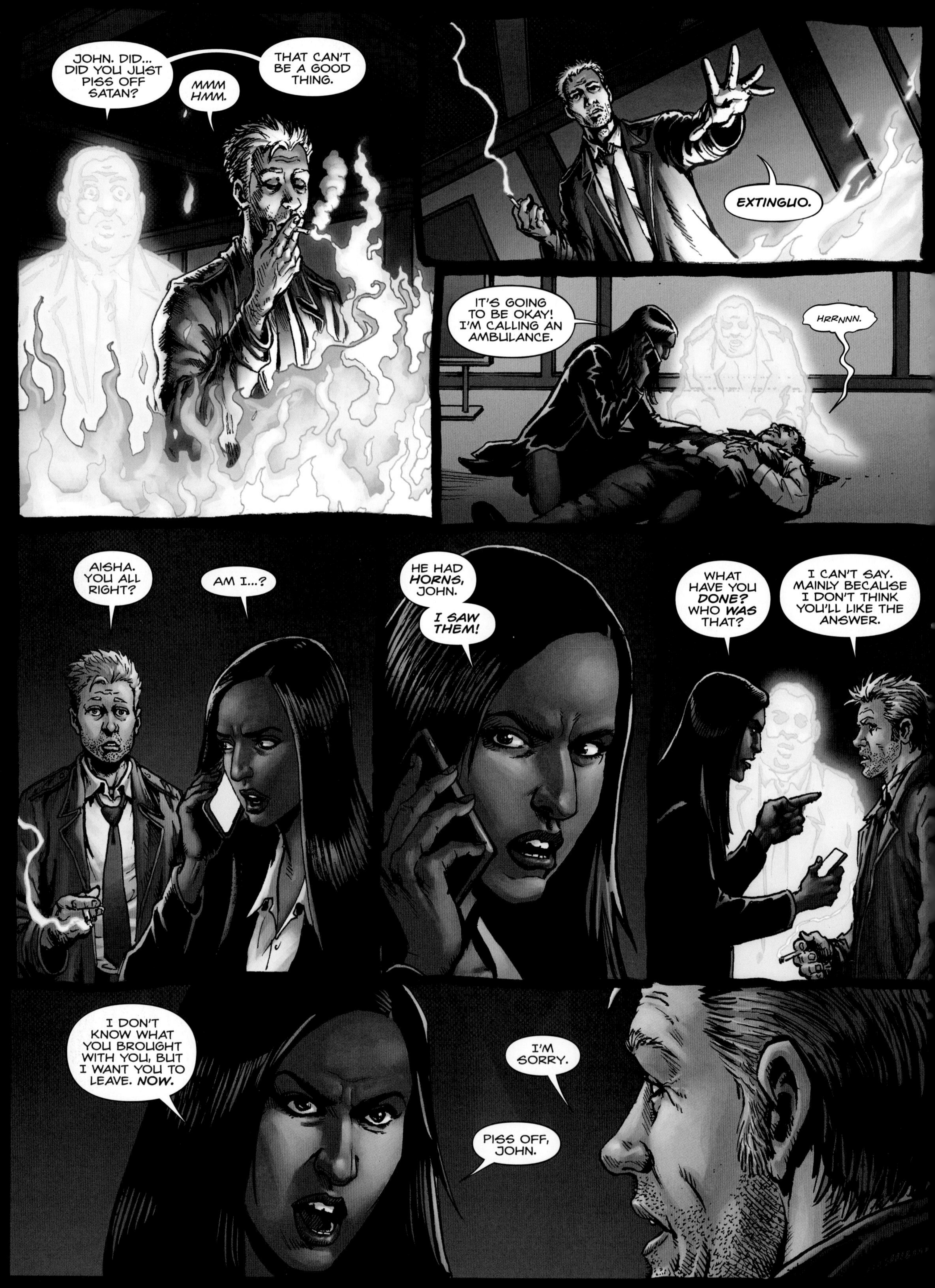
JOHN. DID... DID YOU JUST PISS OFF SATAN?
MMM HMM.
THAT CAN'T BE A GOOD THING.
EXTINGUO.
IT'S GOING TO BE OKAY! I'M CALLING AN AMBULANCE.
HRRNNN.
AISHA. YOU ALL RIGHT?
AM I...?
HE HAD HORNS, JOHN.
I SAW THEM!
WHAT HAVE YOU DONE? WHO WAS THAT?
I CAN'T SAY. MAINLY BECAUSE I DON'T THINK YOU'LL LIKE THE ANSWER.
I DON'T KNOW WHAT YOU BROUGHT WITH YOU, BUT I WANT YOU TO LEAVE. NOW.
I'M SORRY.
PISS OFF, JOHN.

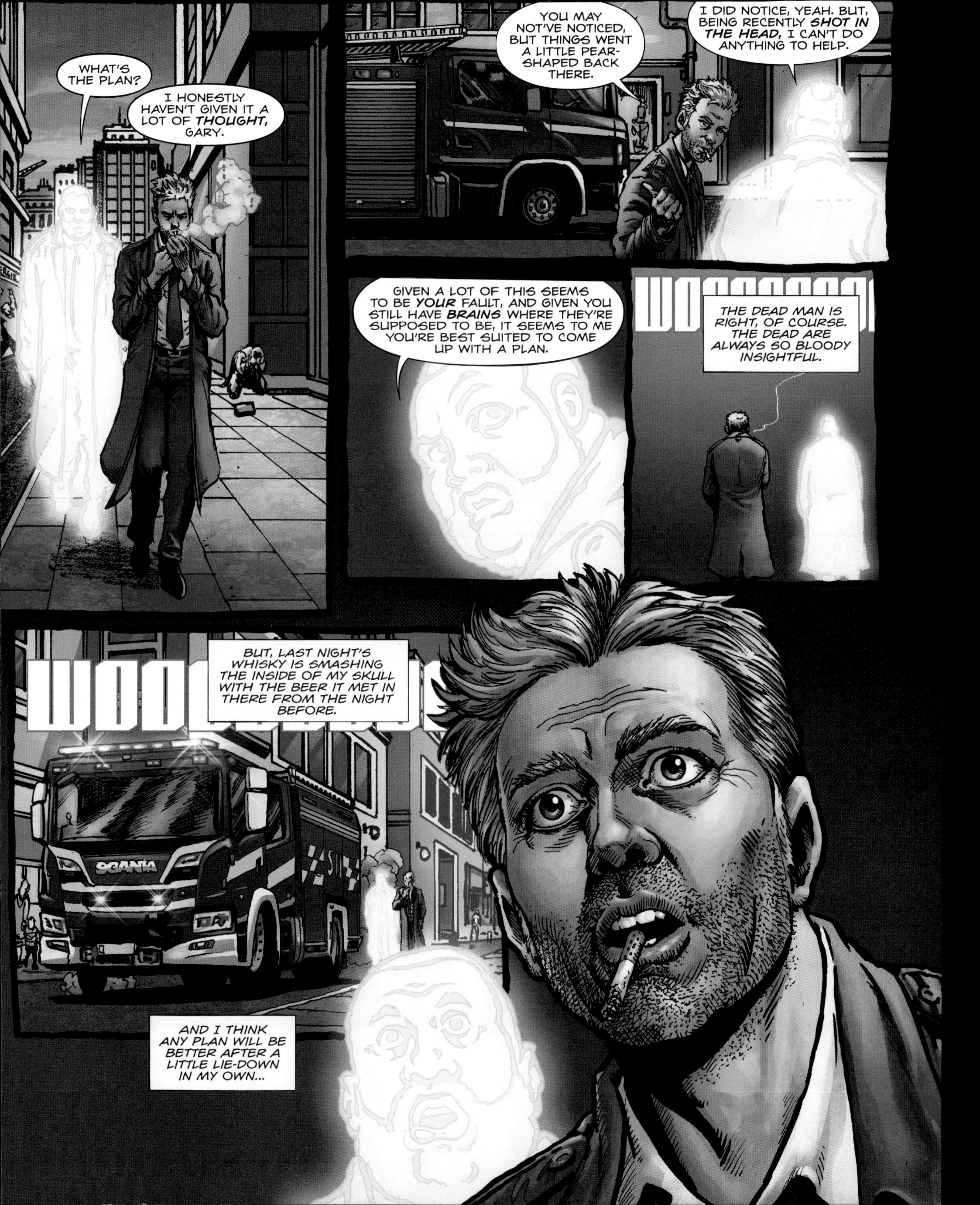
WHAT'S THE PLAN?
I HONESTLY HAVEN'T GIVEN IT A LOT OF THOUGHT, GARY.
YOU MAY NOT'VE NOTICED, BUT THINGS WENT A LITTLE PEAR-SHAPED BACK THERE.
I DID NOTICE, YEAH. BUT, BEING RECENTLY SHOT IN THE HEAD, I CAN'T DO ANYTHING TO HELP.
GIVEN A LOT OF THIS SEEMS TO BE YOUR FAULT, AND GIVEN YOU STILL HAVE BRAINS WHERE THEY'RE SUPPOSED TO BE, IT SEEMS TO ME YOU'RE BEST SUITED TO COME UP WITH A PLAN.
THE DEAD MAN IS RIGHT, OF COURSE. THE DEAD ARE ALWAYS SO BLOODY INSIGHTFUL.
BUT, LAST NIGHT'S WHISKY IS SMASHING THE INSIDE OF MY SKULL WITH THE BEER IT MET IN THERE FROM THE NIGHT BEFORE.
SCANIA
AND I THINK ANY PLAN WILL BE BETTER AFTER A LITTLE LIE-DOWN IN MY OWN...

OH, FUCK ME IN THE EAR WITH A RABID SQUIRREL.
IS THAT YOUR FLAT?
YEAH.
LOOKS LIKE THE DEVIL SET FIRE TO YOUR PLACE.
THAT'S SOME FINE DETECTIVE WORK, GHOST GARY.
WELL, YOU ANGERED THE LORD OF HELL AND NOW YOUR PLACE IS ON FIRE.
THOSE DOTS COME PRECONNECTED.
STAY HERE.
IF YOU GET BORED, DO ME A FAVOR AND HAUNT THE GUY DOWN-STAIRS. HE'S AN ARSEHOLE.
WHERE ARE YOU GOING?
I HAVE TO CONVINCE A JUDGE TO BREAK THE LAW.
AND THAT WOULD HAVE BEEN A LOT EASIER WITH THE DEVIL BESIDE ME.

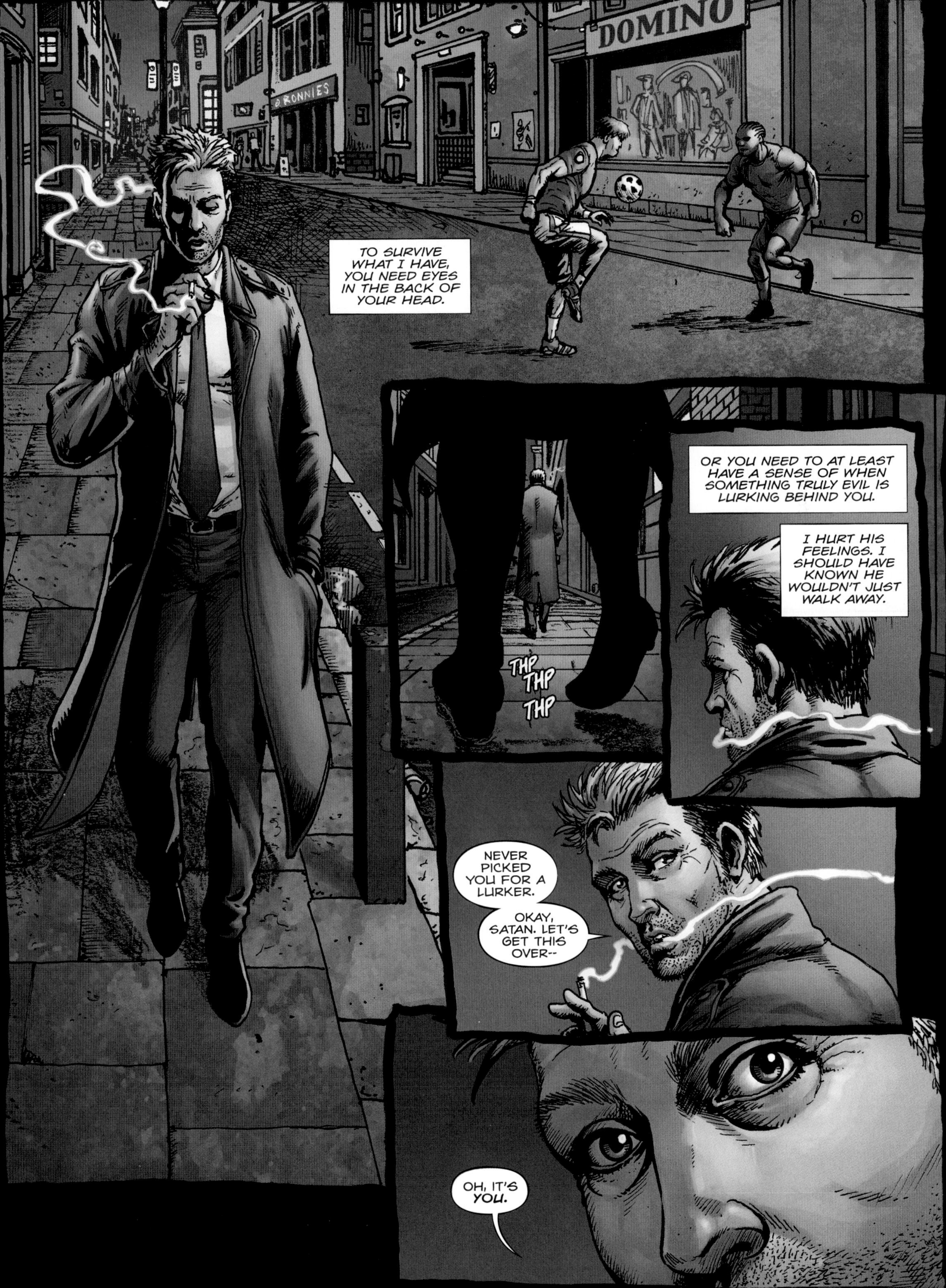
DOMINO
RONNIES
TO SURVIVE WHAT I HAVE, YOU NEED EYES IN THE BACK OF YOUR HEAD.
OR YOU NEED TO AT LEAST HAVE A SENSE OF WHEN SOMETHING TRULY EVIL IS LURKING BEHIND YOU.
THP THP THP
I HURT HIS FEELINGS. I SHOULD HAVE KNOWN HE WOULDN'T JUST WALK AWAY.
NEVER PICKED YOU FOR A LURKER.
OKAY, SATAN. LET'S GET THIS OVER--
OH, IT'S YOU.

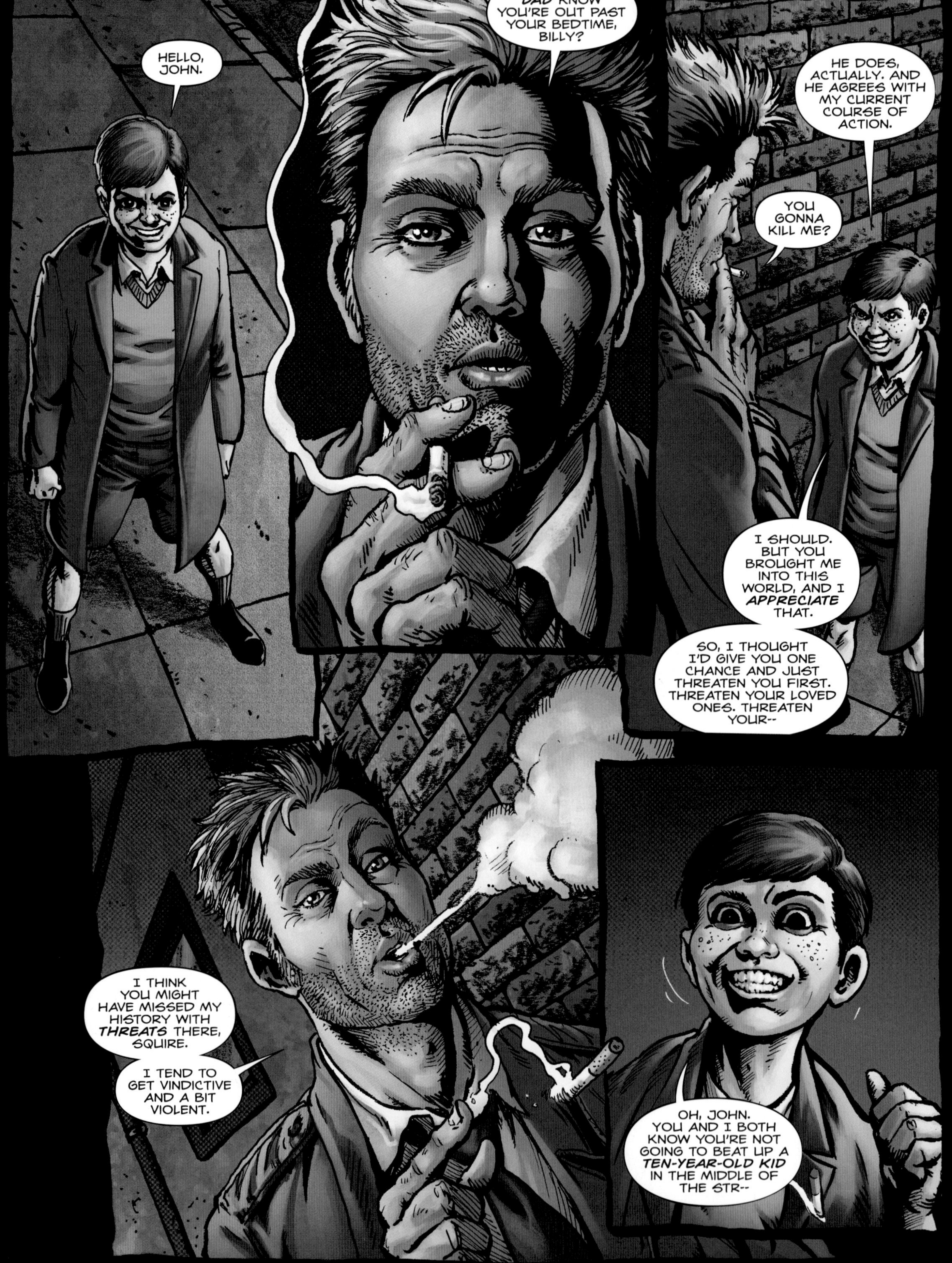
HELLO, JOHN.
DAD KNOW YOU'RE OUT PAST YOUR BEDTIME, BILLY?
HE DOES, ACTUALLY. AND HE AGREES WITH MY CURRENT COURSE OF ACTION.
YOU GONNA KILL ME?
I SHOULD. BUT YOU BROUGHT ME INTO THIS WORLD, AND I *APPRECIATE* THAT.
SO, I THOUGHT I'D GIVE YOU ONE CHANCE AND JUST THREATEN YOU FIRST. THREATEN YOUR LOVED ONES. THREATEN YOUR--
I THINK YOU MIGHT HAVE MISSED MY HISTORY WITH *THREATS* THERE, SQUIRE.
I TEND TO GET VINDICTIVE AND A BIT VIOLENT.
OH, JOHN. YOU AND I BOTH KNOW YOU'RE NOT GOING TO BEAT UP A *TEN-YEAR-OLD KID* IN THE MIDDLE OF THE STR--

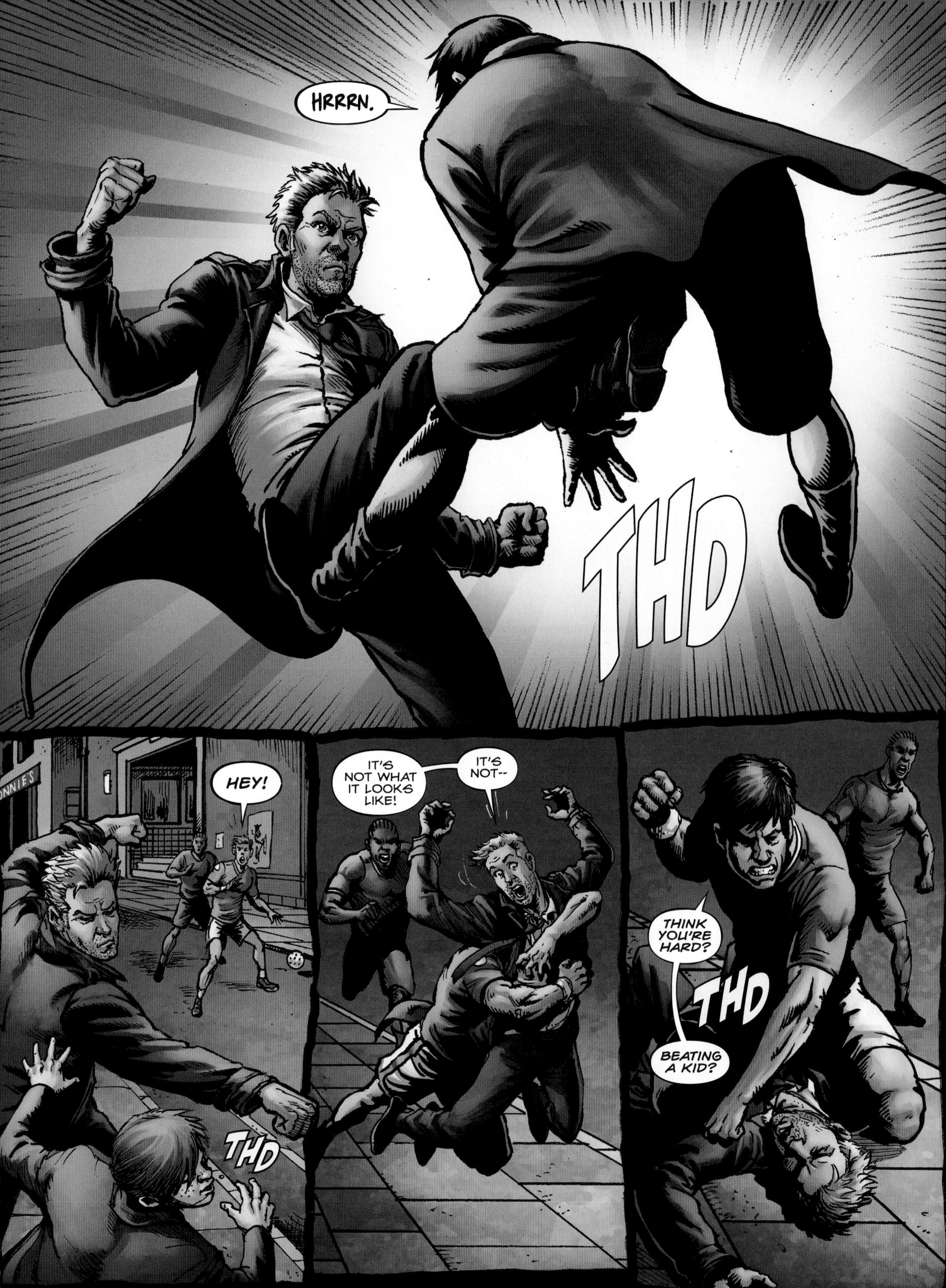
HRRRN.
THD
HEY!
THD
IT'S NOT WHAT IT LOOKS LIKE!
IT'S NOT--
THINK YOU'RE HARD?
THD
BEATING A KID?

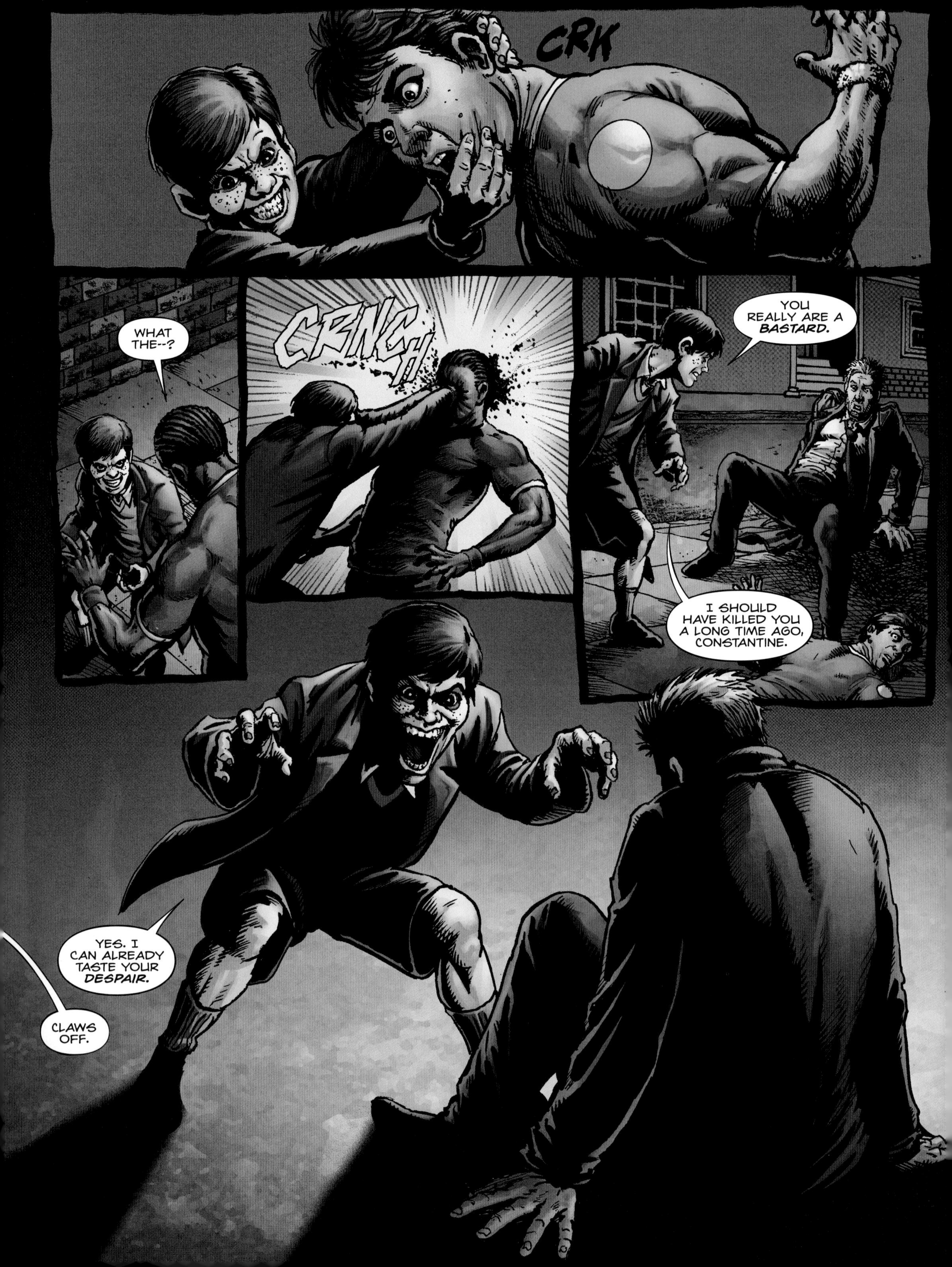
CRK
WHAT THE--?
CRNCH
YOU REALLY ARE A BASTARD.
I SHOULD HAVE KILLED YOU A LONG TIME AGO, CONSTANTINE.
YES. I CAN ALREADY TASTE YOUR DESPAIR.
CLAWS OFF.

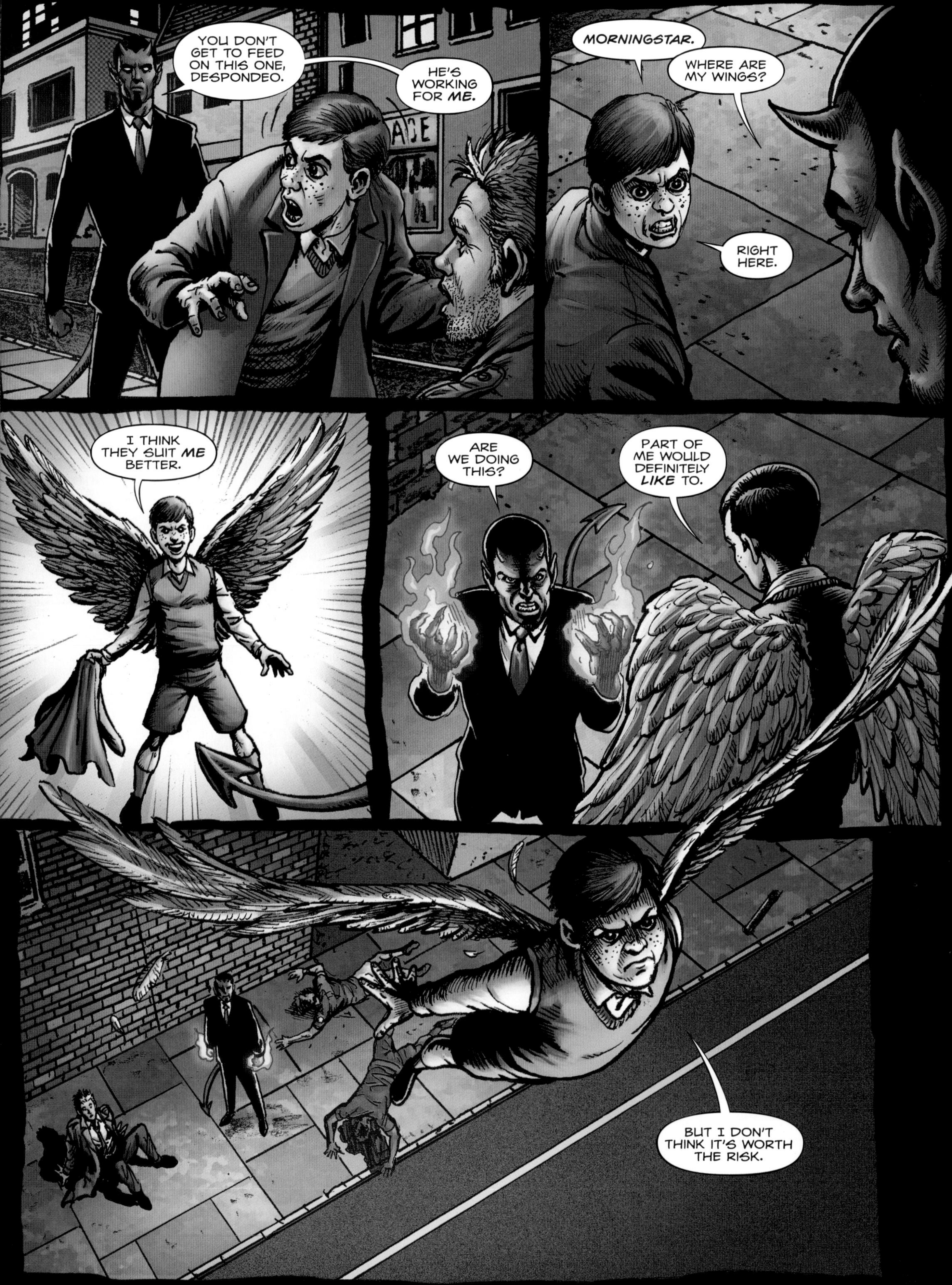

YOU DON'T GET TO FEED ON THIS ONE, DESPONDEO.
HE'S WORKING FOR **ME.**
MORNINGSTAR.
WHERE ARE MY WINGS?
RIGHT HERE.
I THINK THEY SUIT **ME** BETTER.
ARE WE DOING THIS?
PART OF ME WOULD DEFINITELY **LIKE** TO.
BUT I DON'T THINK IT'S WORTH THE RISK.

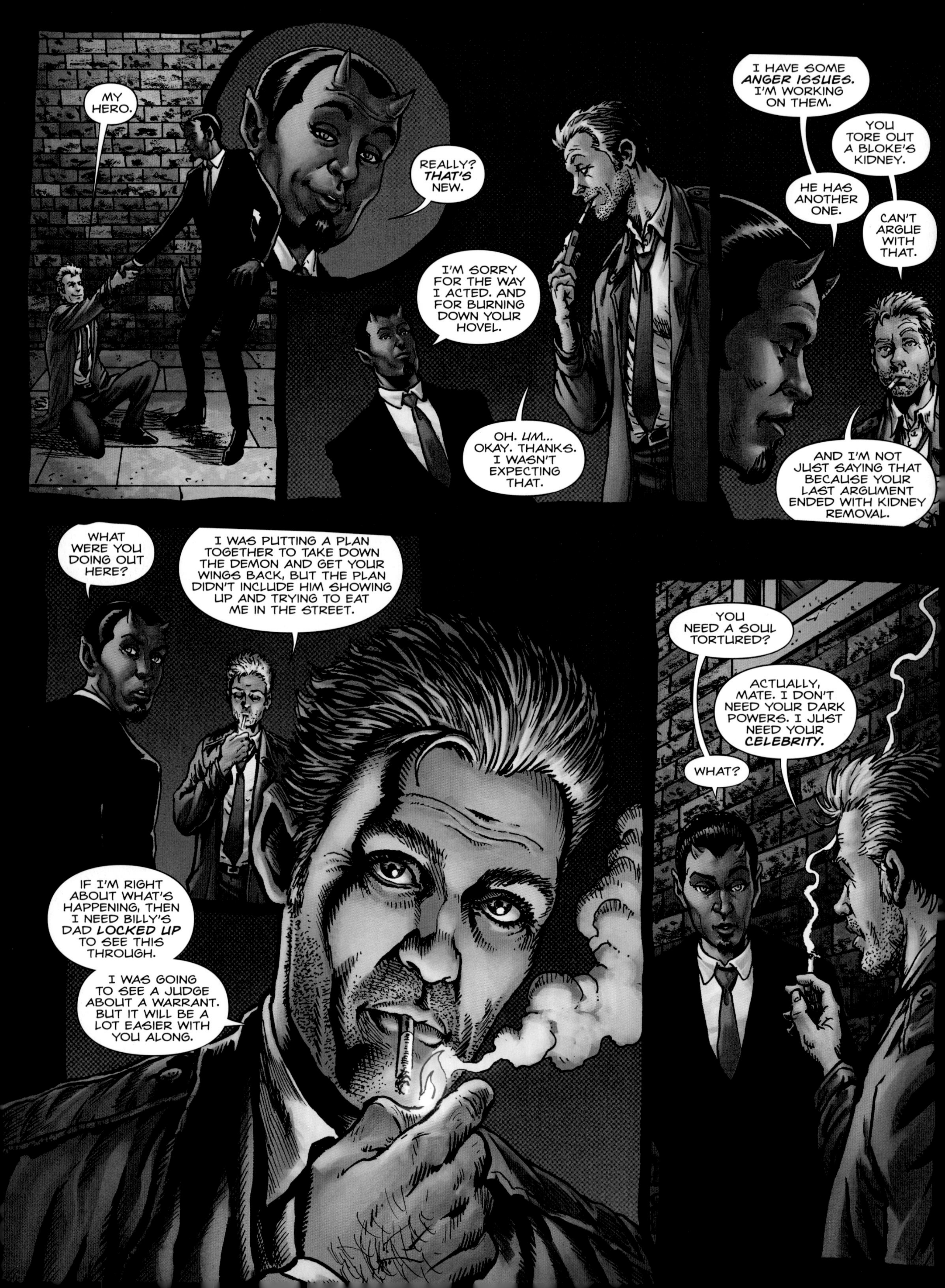
MY HERO.
REALLY? THAT'S NEW.
I'M SORRY FOR THE WAY I ACTED. AND FOR BURNING DOWN YOUR HOVEL.
OH. UM... OKAY. THANKS. I WASN'T EXPECTING THAT.
I HAVE SOME ANGER ISSUES. I'M WORKING ON THEM.
YOU TORE OUT A BLOKE'S KIDNEY.
HE HAS ANOTHER ONE.
CAN'T ARGUE WITH THAT.
AND I'M NOT JUST SAYING THAT BECAUSE YOUR LAST ARGUMENT ENDED WITH KIDNEY REMOVAL.
WHAT WERE YOU DOING OUT HERE?
I WAS PUTTING A PLAN TOGETHER TO TAKE DOWN THE DEMON AND GET YOUR WINGS BACK, BUT THE PLAN DIDN'T INCLUDE HIM SHOWING UP AND TRYING TO EAT ME IN THE STREET.
IF I'M RIGHT ABOUT WHAT'S HAPPENING, THEN I NEED BILLY'S DAD LOCKED UP TO SEE THIS THROUGH.
I WAS GOING TO SEE A JUDGE ABOUT A WARRANT. BUT IT WILL BE A LOT EASIER WITH YOU ALONG.
YOU NEED A SOUL TORTURED?
ACTUALLY, MATE. I DON'T NEED YOUR DARK POWERS. I JUST NEED YOUR CELEBRITY.
WHAT?

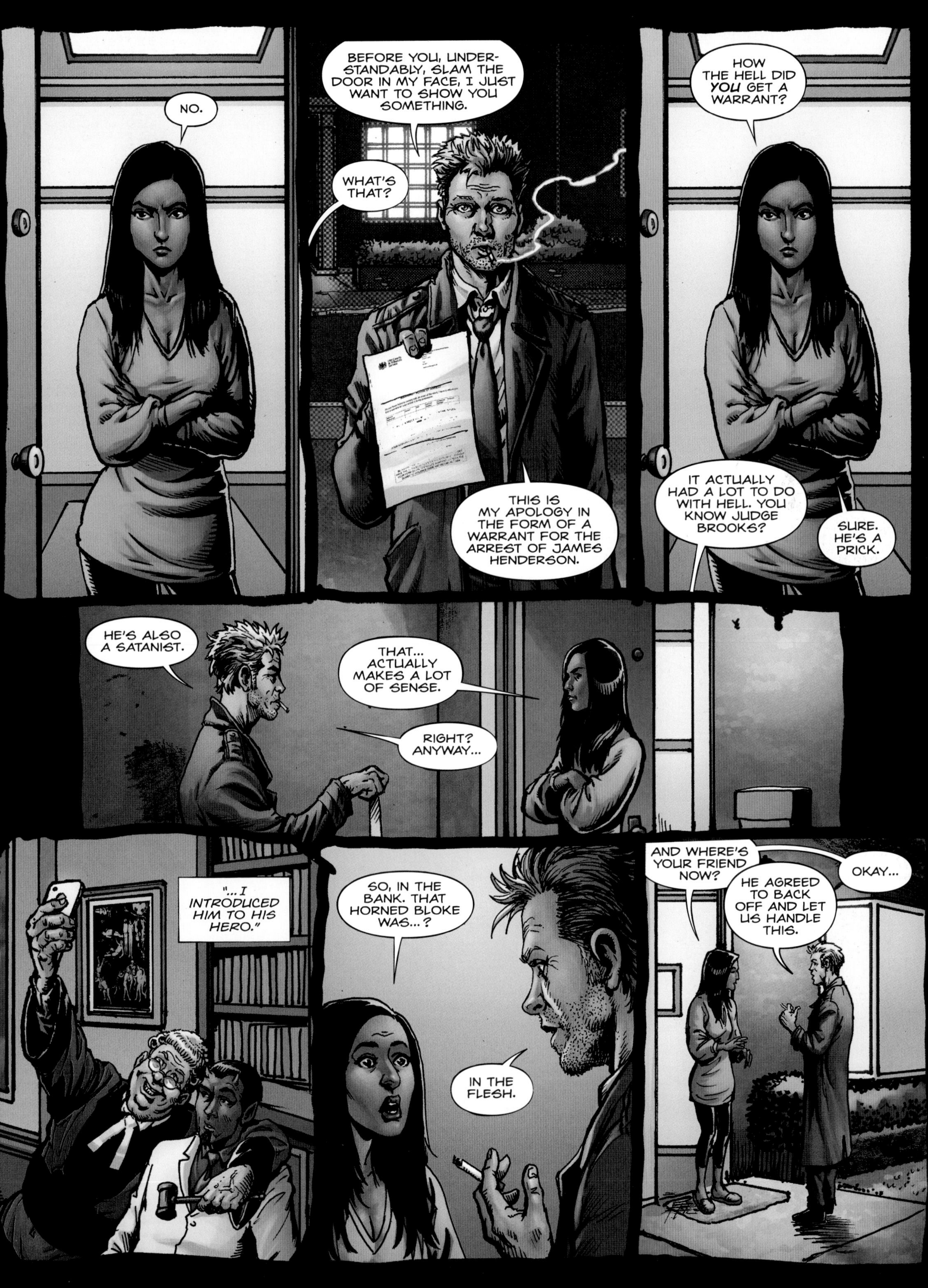
NO.
BEFORE YOU, UNDER-STANDABLY, SLAM THE DOOR IN MY FACE, I JUST WANT TO SHOW YOU SOMETHING.
WHAT'S THAT?
THIS IS MY APOLOGY IN THE FORM OF A WARRANT FOR THE ARREST OF JAMES HENDERSON.
HOW THE HELL DID *YOU* GET A WARRANT?
IT ACTUALLY HAD A LOT TO DO WITH HELL. YOU KNOW JUDGE BROOKS?
SURE. HE'S A PRICK.
HE'S ALSO A SATANIST.
THAT... ACTUALLY MAKES A LOT OF SENSE.
RIGHT? ANYWAY...
"...I INTRODUCED HIM TO HIS HERO."
SO, IN THE BANK. THAT HORNED BLOKE WAS...?
IN THE FLESH.
AND WHERE'S YOUR FRIEND NOW?
OKAY...
HE AGREED TO BACK OFF AND LET US HANDLE THIS.

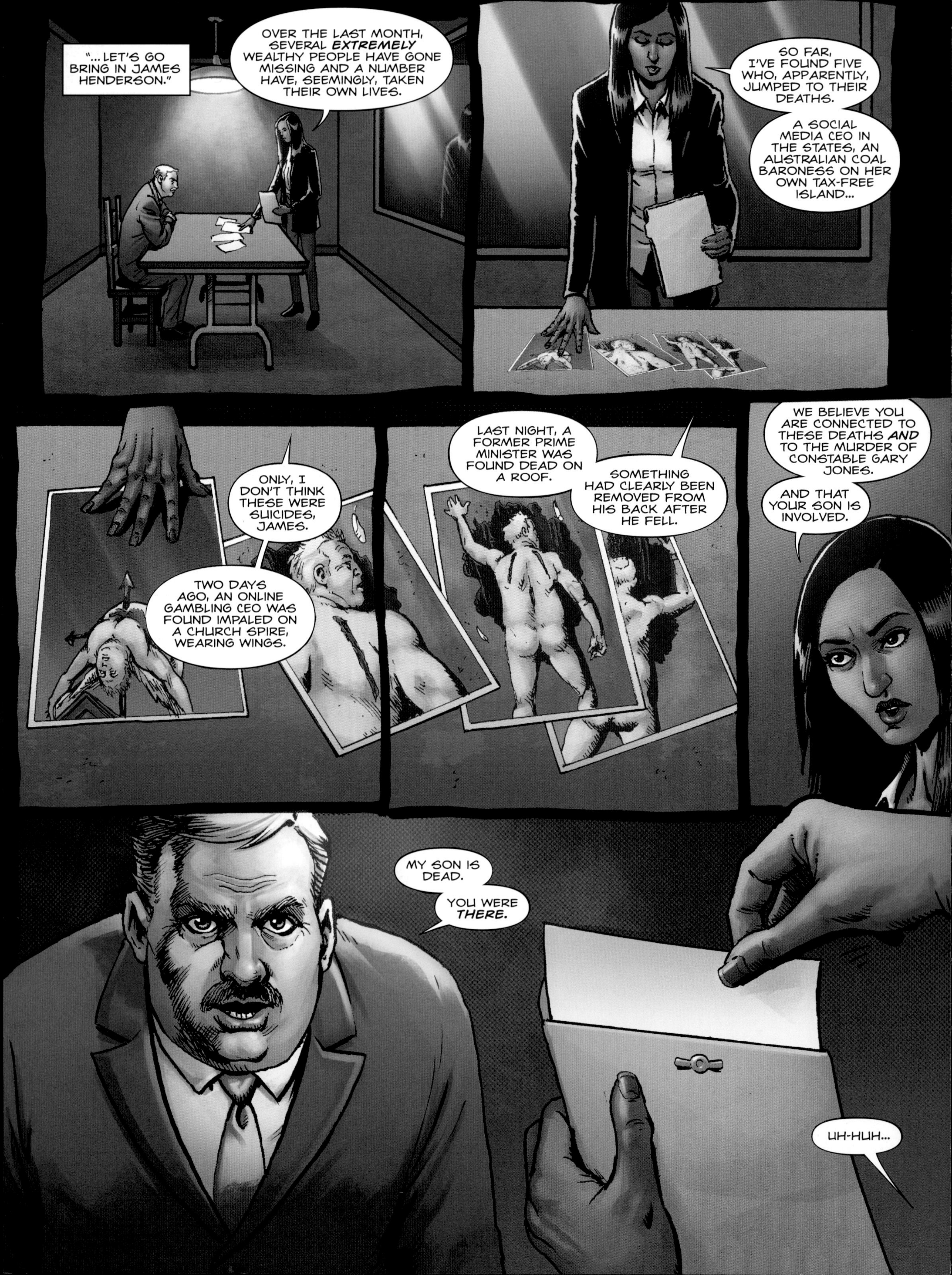
"...LET'S GO BRING IN JAMES HENDERSON."
OVER THE LAST MONTH, SEVERAL EXTREMELY WEALTHY PEOPLE HAVE GONE MISSING AND A NUMBER HAVE, SEEMINGLY, TAKEN THEIR OWN LIVES.
SO FAR, I'VE FOUND FIVE WHO, APPARENTLY, JUMPED TO THEIR DEATHS.
A SOCIAL MEDIA CEO IN THE STATES, AN AUSTRALIAN COAL BARONESS ON HER OWN TAX-FREE ISLAND...
ONLY, I DON'T THINK THESE WERE SUICIDES, JAMES.
TWO DAYS AGO, AN ONLINE GAMBLING CEO WAS FOUND IMPALED ON A CHURCH SPIRE, WEARING WINGS.
LAST NIGHT, A FORMER PRIME MINISTER WAS FOUND DEAD ON A ROOF.
SOMETHING HAD CLEARLY BEEN REMOVED FROM HIS BACK AFTER HE FELL.
WE BELIEVE YOU ARE CONNECTED TO THESE DEATHS AND TO THE MURDER OF CONSTABLE GARY JONES.
AND THAT YOUR SON IS INVOLVED.
MY SON IS DEAD.
YOU WERE THERE.
UH-HUH...

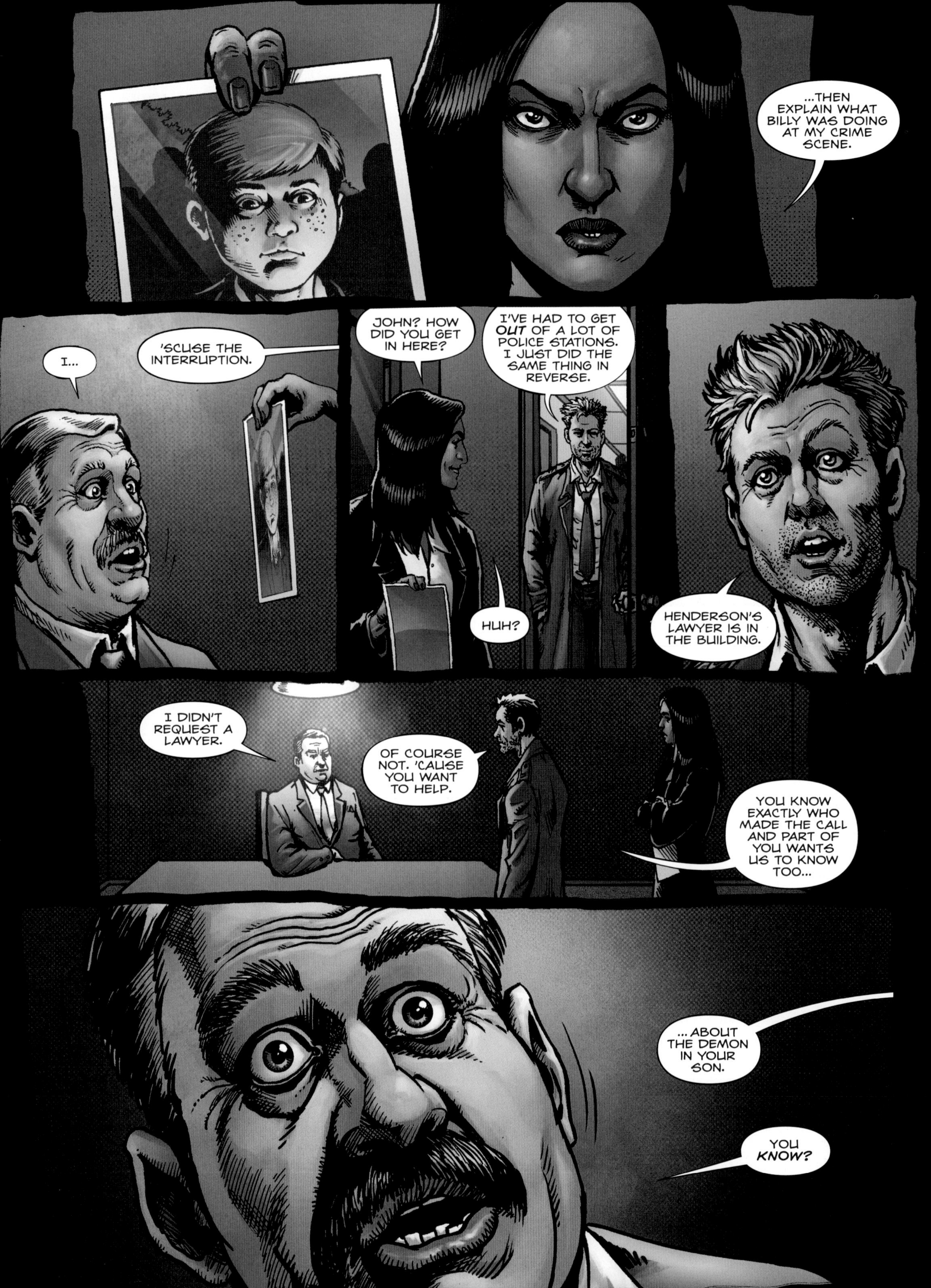

...THEN EXPLAIN WHAT BILLY WAS DOING AT MY CRIME SCENE.
I...
'SCUSE THE INTERRUPTION.
JOHN? HOW DID YOU GET IN HERE?
I'VE HAD TO GET *OUT* OF A LOT OF POLICE STATIONS. I JUST DID THE SAME THING IN REVERSE.
HUH?
HENDERSON'S LAWYER IS IN THE BUILDING.
I DIDN'T REQUEST A LAWYER.
OF COURSE NOT. 'CAUSE YOU WANT TO HELP.
YOU KNOW EXACTLY WHO MADE THE CALL AND PART OF YOU WANTS US TO KNOW TOO...
...ABOUT THE DEMON IN YOUR SON.
YOU *KNOW?*

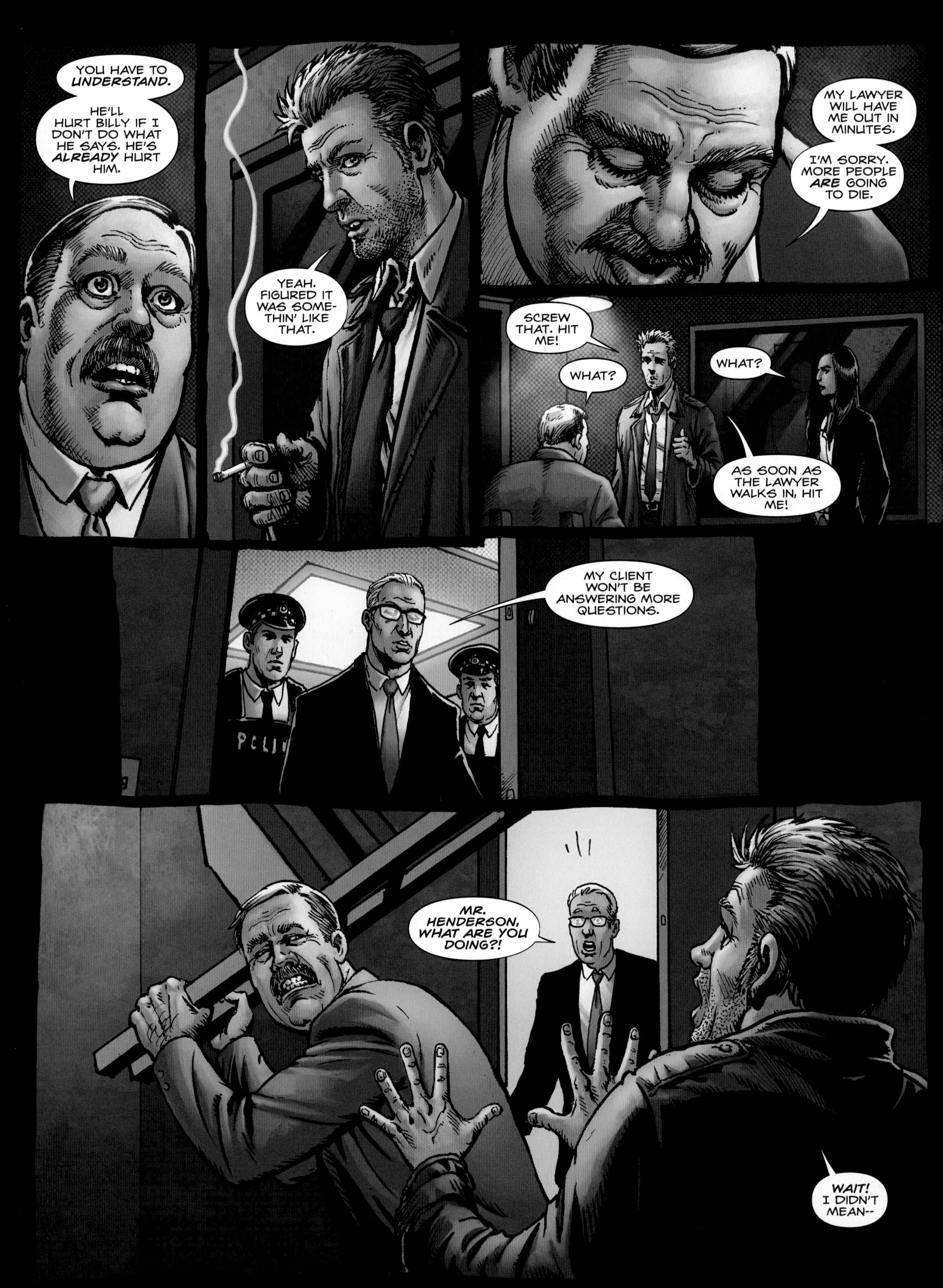

YOU HAVE TO UNDERSTAND.
HE'LL HURT BILLY IF I DON'T DO WHAT HE SAYS. HE'S ALREADY HURT HIM.
YEAH. FIGURED IT WAS SOME-THIN' LIKE THAT.
MY LAWYER WILL HAVE ME OUT IN MINUTES.
I'M SORRY. MORE PEOPLE ARE GOING TO DIE.
SCREW THAT. HIT ME!
WHAT?
WHAT?
AS SOON AS THE LAWYER WALKS IN, HIT ME!
MY CLIENT WON'T BE ANSWERING MORE QUESTIONS.
POLI
MR. HENDERSON, WHAT ARE YOU DOING?!
WAIT! I DIDN'T MEAN--

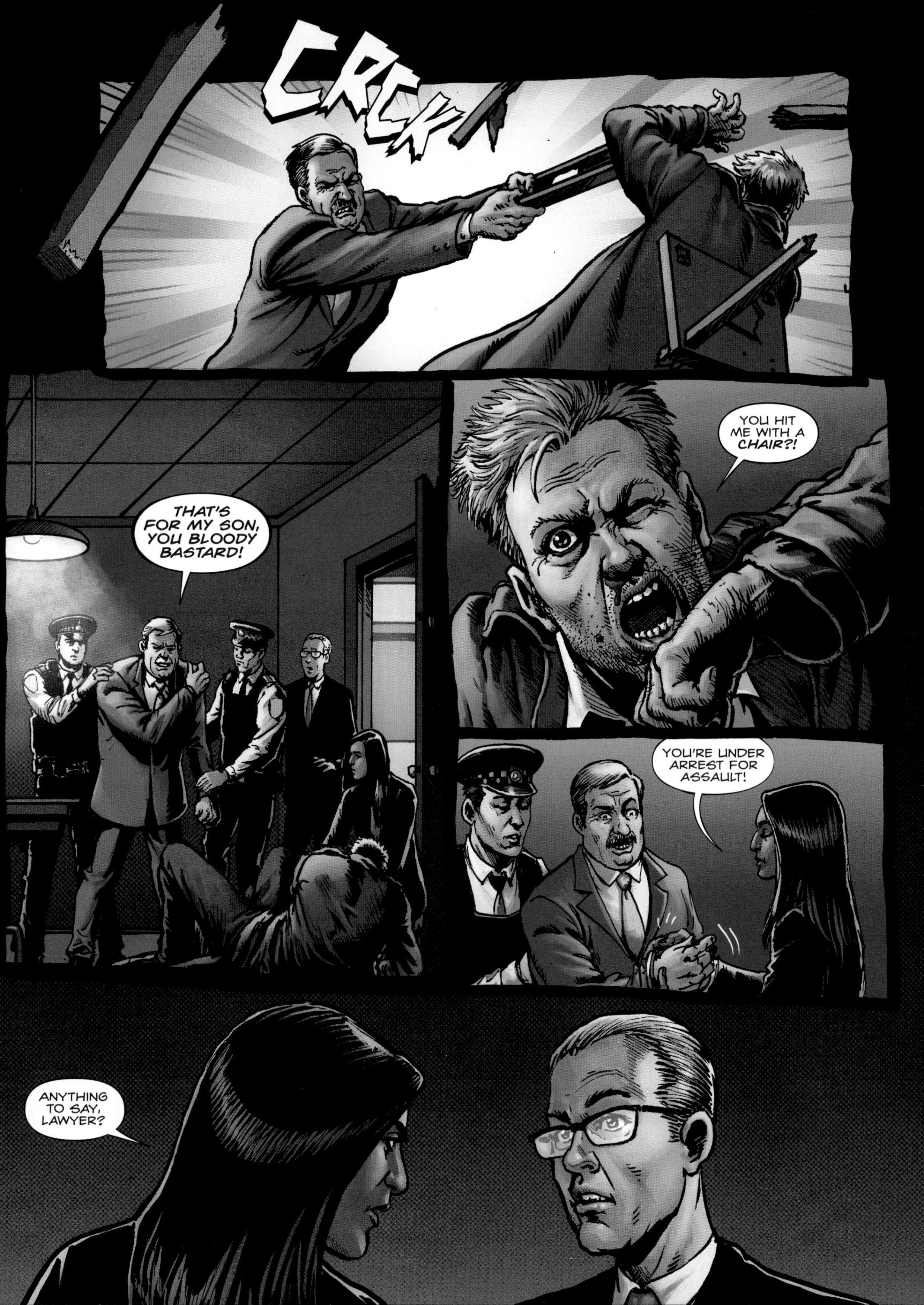
CRCK
THAT'S FOR MY SON, YOU BLOODY BASTARD!
YOU HIT ME WITH A CHAIR?!
YOU'RE UNDER ARREST FOR ASSAULT!
ANYTHING TO SAY, LAWYER?

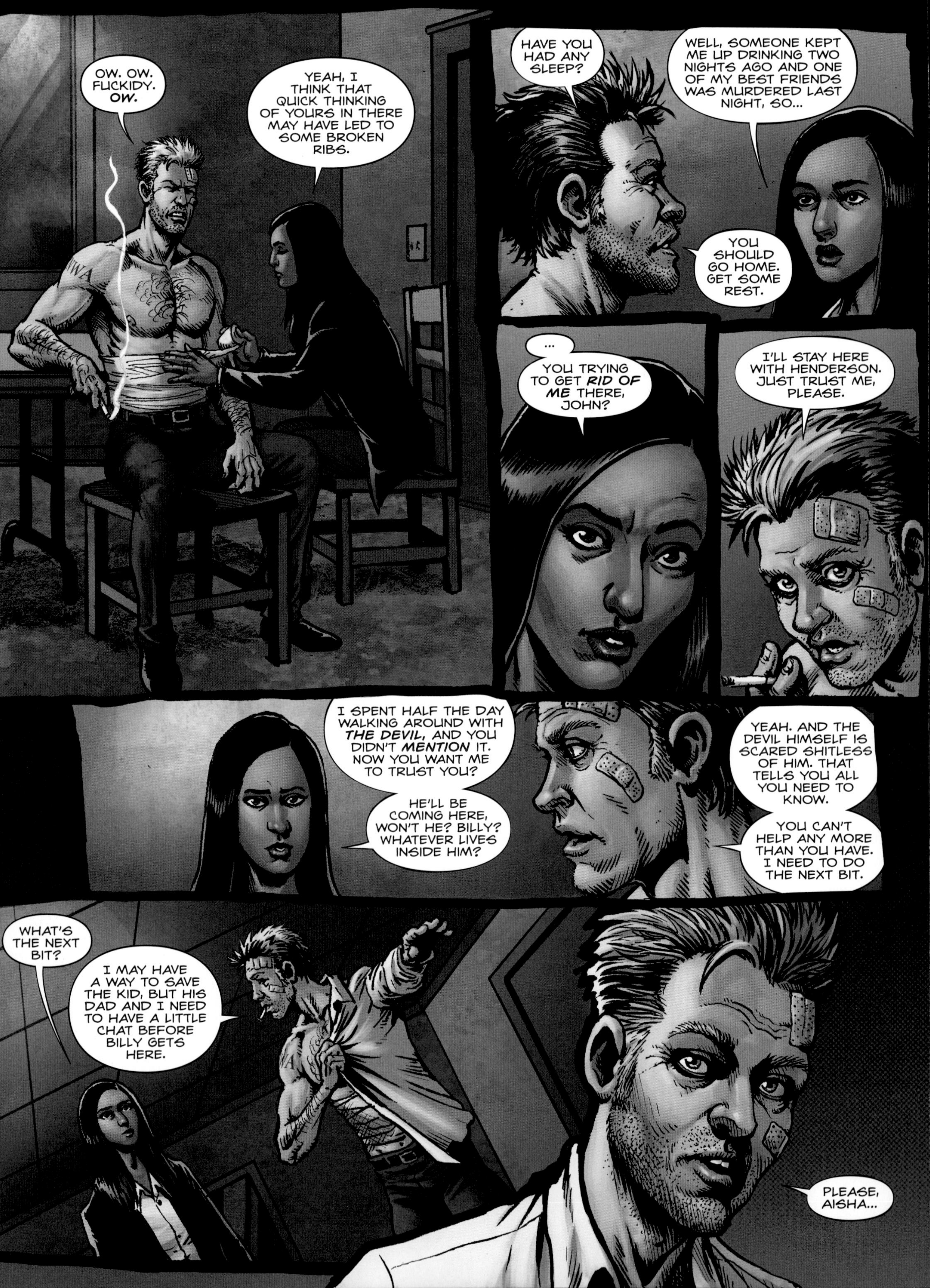
OW. OW. FUCKIDY. **OW.**
YEAH, I THINK THAT QUICK THINKING OF YOURS IN THERE MAY HAVE LED TO SOME BROKEN RIBS.
HAVE YOU HAD ANY SLEEP?
WELL, SOMEONE KEPT ME UP DRINKING TWO NIGHTS AGO AND ONE OF MY BEST FRIENDS WAS MURDERED LAST NIGHT, SO...
YOU SHOULD GO HOME. GET SOME REST.
...
YOU TRYING TO GET ***RID OF ME*** THERE, JOHN?
I'LL STAY HERE WITH HENDERSON. JUST TRUST ME, PLEASE.
I SPENT HALF THE DAY WALKING AROUND WITH ***THE DEVIL***, AND YOU DIDN'T ***MENTION*** IT. NOW YOU WANT ME TO TRUST YOU?
HE'LL BE COMING HERE, WON'T HE? BILLY? WHATEVER LIVES INSIDE HIM?
YEAH. AND THE DEVIL HIMSELF IS SCARED SHITLESS OF HIM. THAT TELLS YOU ALL YOU NEED TO KNOW.
YOU CAN'T HELP ANY MORE THAN YOU HAVE. I NEED TO DO THE NEXT BIT.
WHAT'S THE NEXT BIT?
I MAY HAVE A WAY TO SAVE THE KID, BUT HIS DAD AND I NEED TO HAVE A LITTLE CHAT BEFORE BILLY GETS HERE.
PLEASE, AISHA...

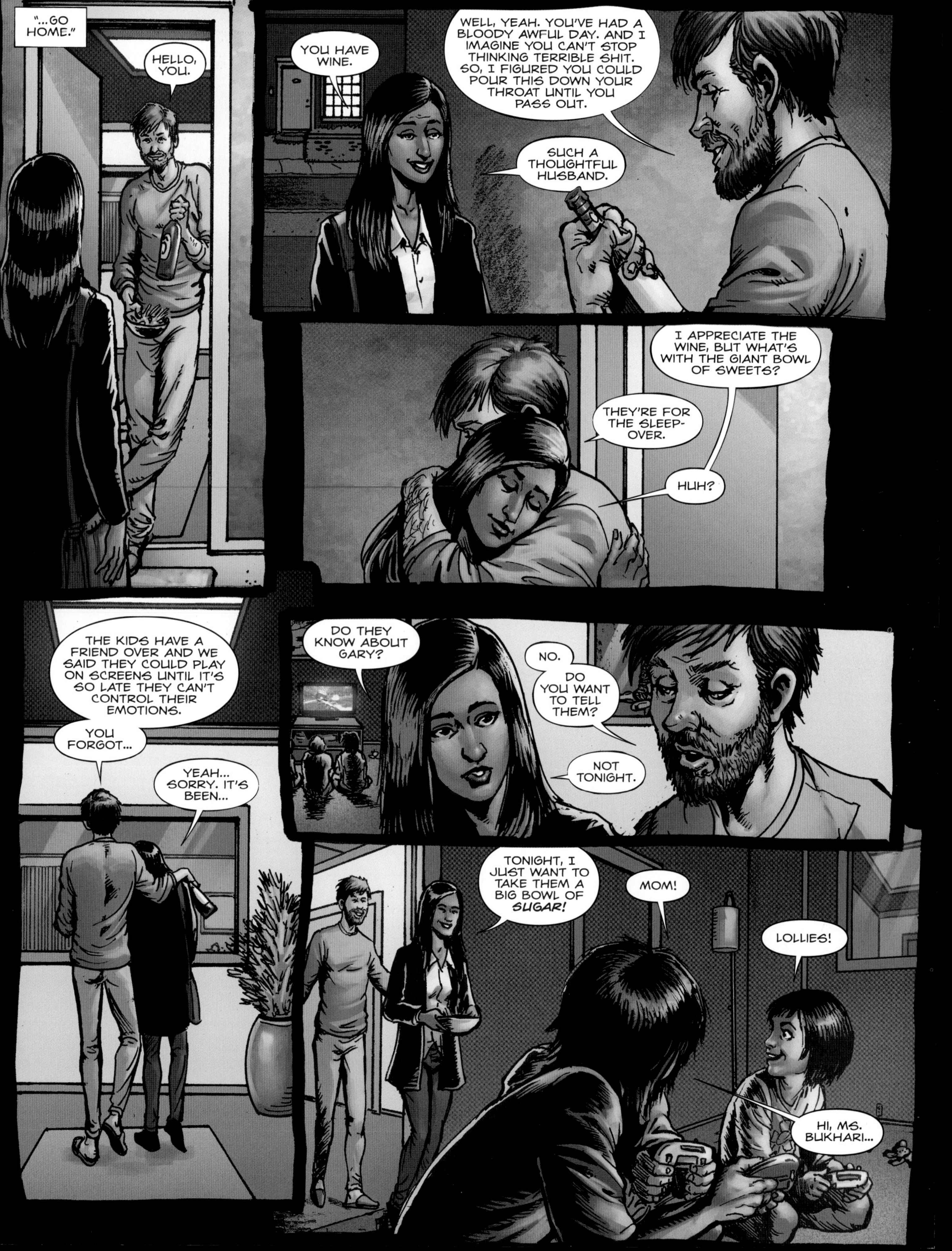
"...GO HOME."
HELLO, YOU.
YOU HAVE WINE.
WELL, YEAH. YOU'VE HAD A BLOODY AWFUL DAY. AND I IMAGINE YOU CAN'T STOP THINKING TERRIBLE SHIT. SO, I FIGURED YOU COULD POUR THIS DOWN YOUR THROAT UNTIL YOU PASS OUT.
SUCH A THOUGHTFUL HUSBAND.
I APPRECIATE THE WINE, BUT WHAT'S WITH THE GIANT BOWL OF SWEETS?
THEY'RE FOR THE SLEEP-OVER.
HUH?
THE KIDS HAVE A FRIEND OVER AND WE SAID THEY COULD PLAY ON SCREENS UNTIL IT'S SO LATE THEY CAN'T CONTROL THEIR EMOTIONS.
YOU FORGOT...
YEAH... SORRY. IT'S BEEN...
DO THEY KNOW ABOUT GARY?
NO.
DO YOU WANT TO TELL THEM?
NOT TONIGHT.
TONIGHT, I JUST WANT TO TAKE THEM A BIG BOWL OF *SUGAR!*
MOM!
LOLLIES!
HI, MS. BUKHARI...

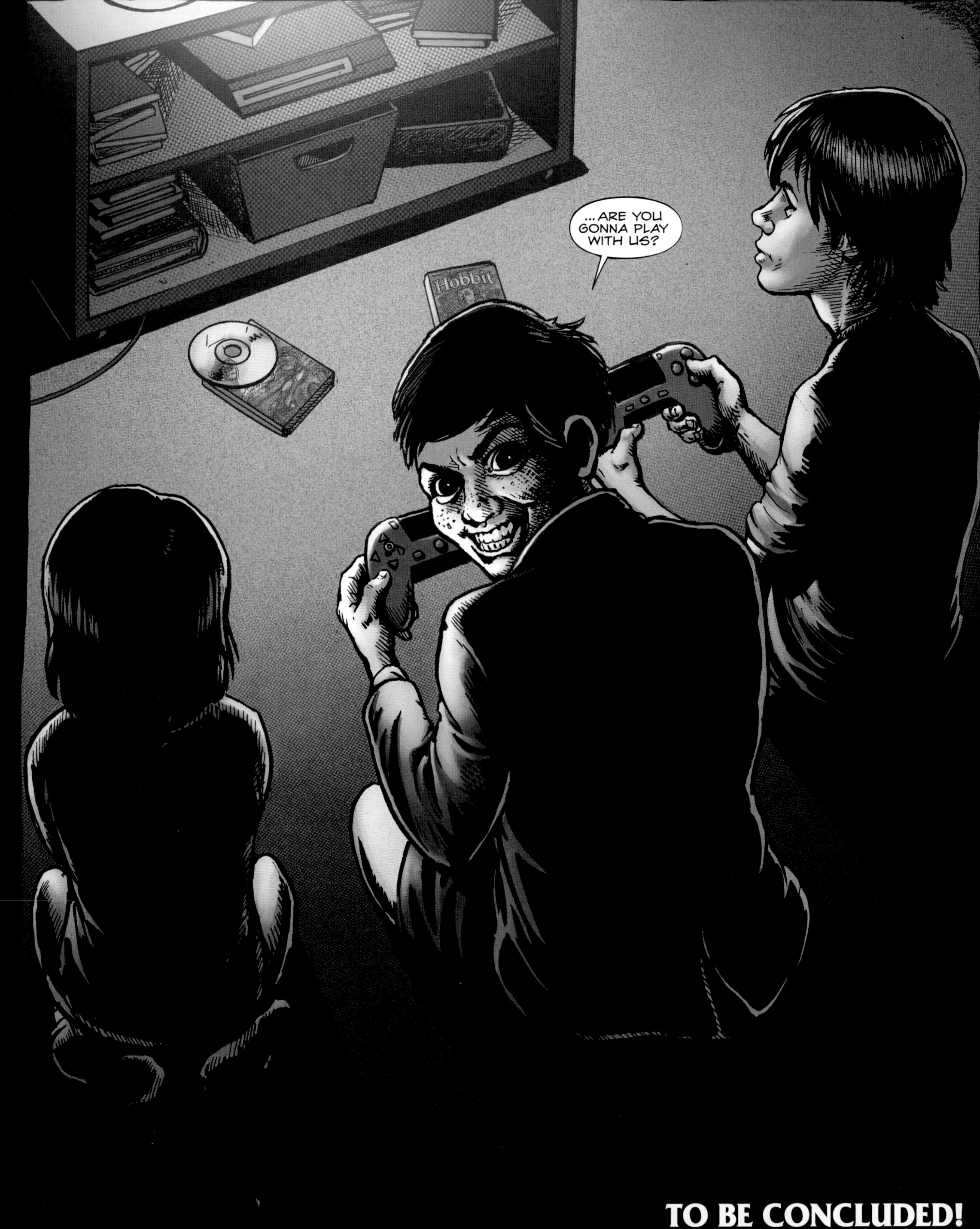
Hobbit
...ARE YOU GONNA PLAY WITH US?
TO BE CONCLUDED!

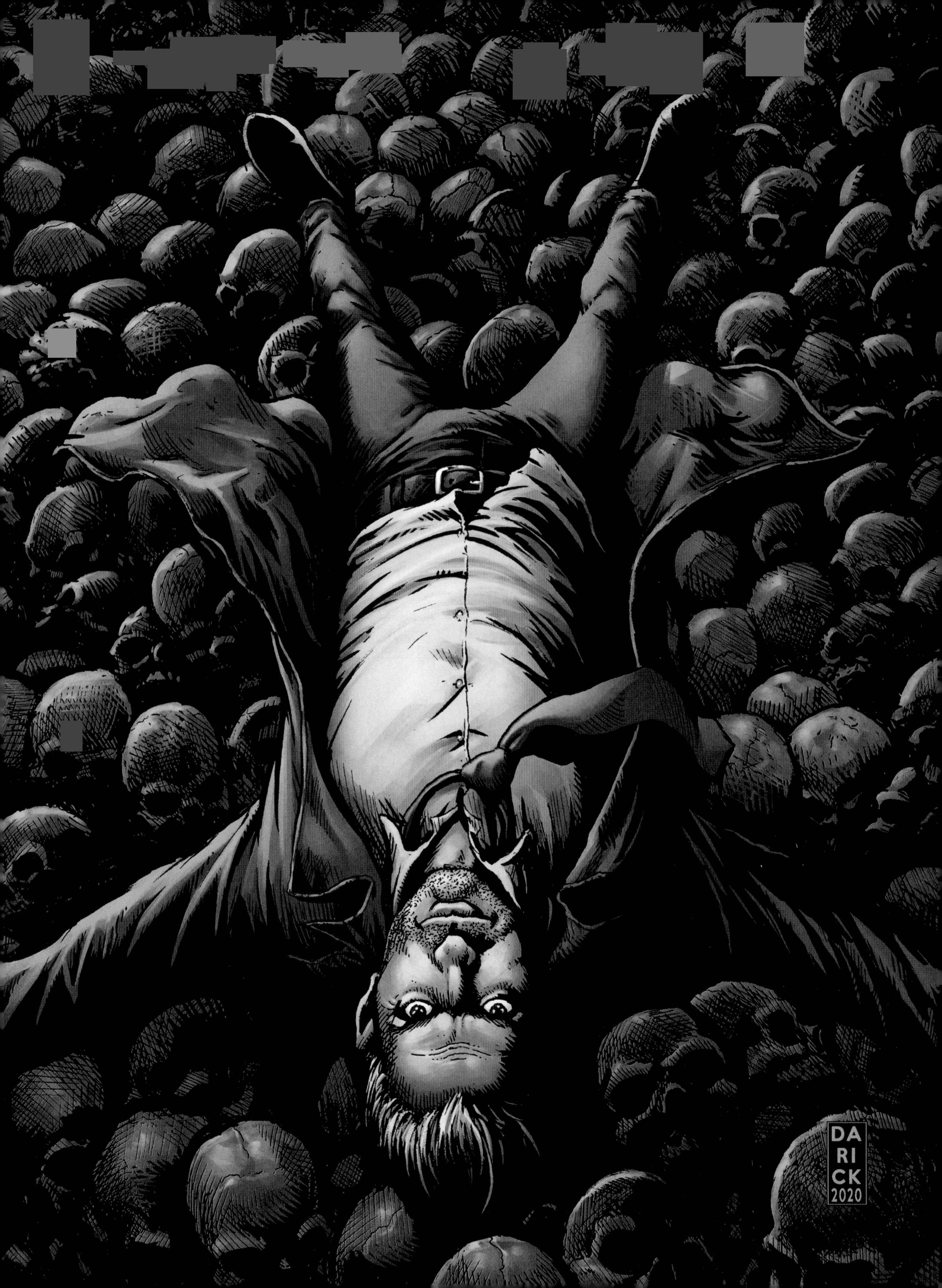
DA
RI
CK
2020

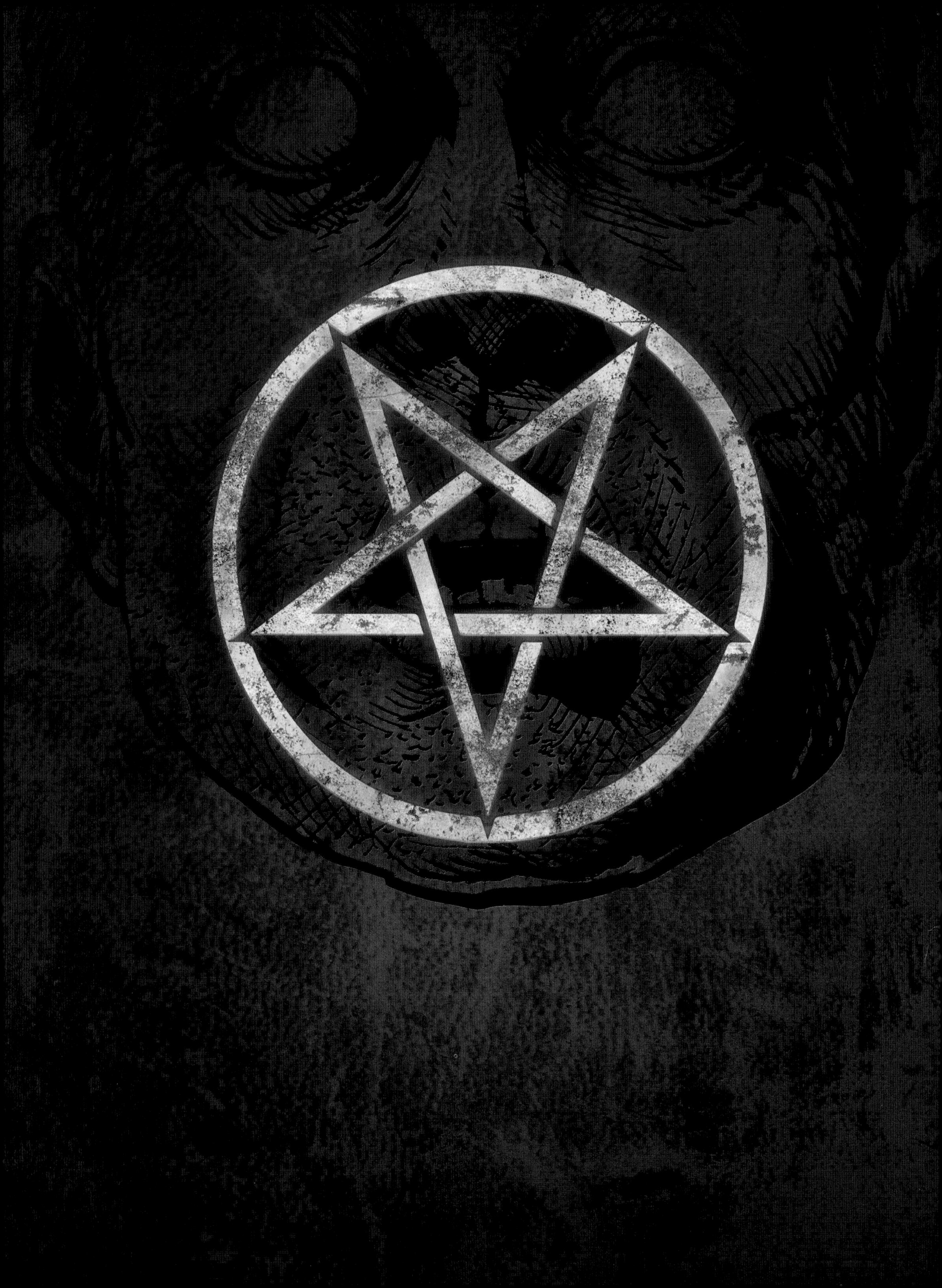

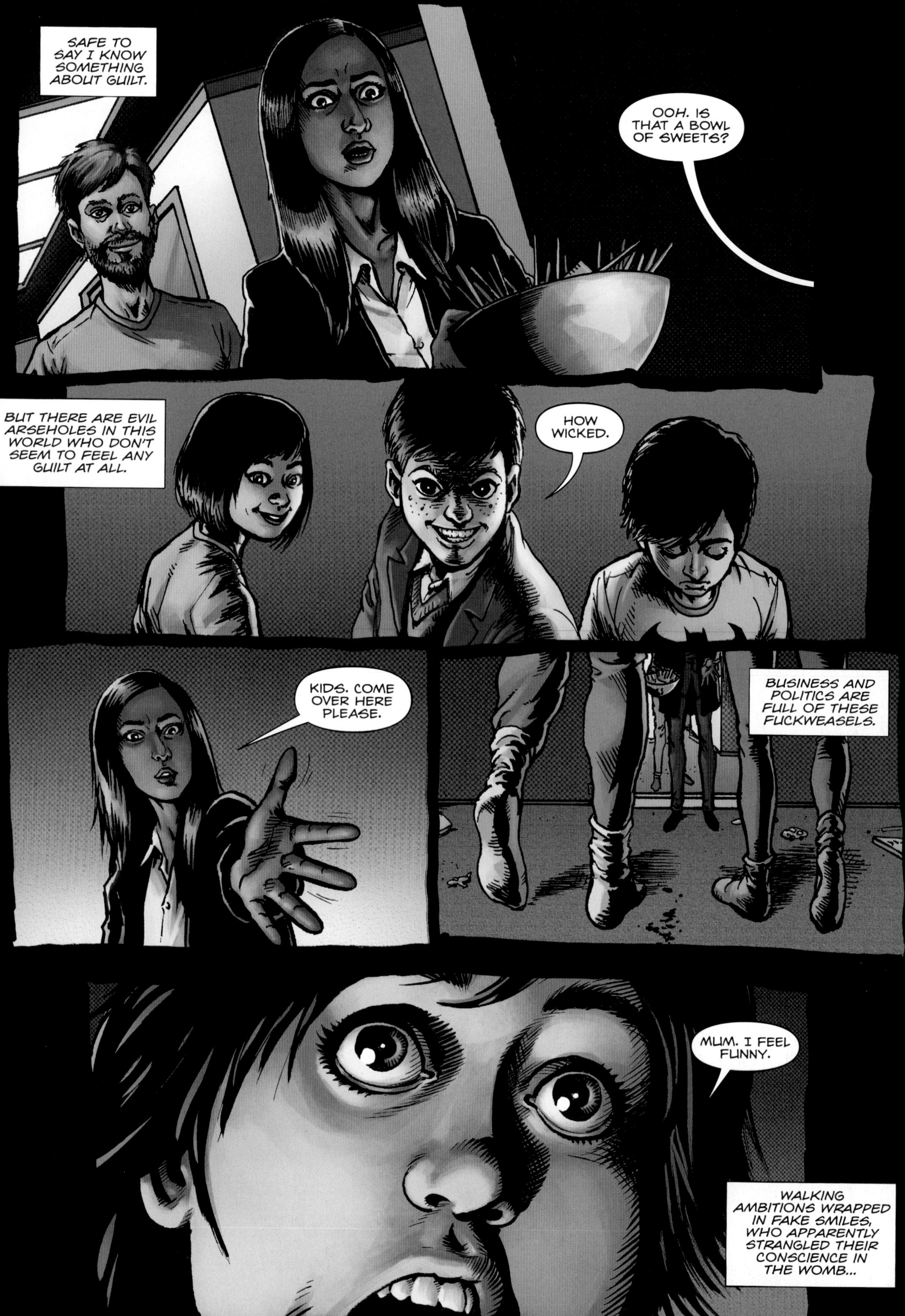

SAFE TO SAY I KNOW SOMETHING ABOUT GUILT.
OOH. IS THAT A BOWL OF SWEETS?
BUT THERE ARE EVIL ARSEHOLES IN THIS WORLD WHO DON'T SEEM TO FEEL ANY GUILT AT ALL.
HOW WICKED.
KIDS. COME OVER HERE PLEASE.
BUSINESS AND POLITICS ARE FULL OF THESE FUCKWEASELS.
MUM. I FEEL FUNNY.
WALKING AMBITIONS WRAPPED IN FAKE SMILES, WHO APPARENTLY STRANGLED THEIR CONSCIENCE IN THE WOMB...

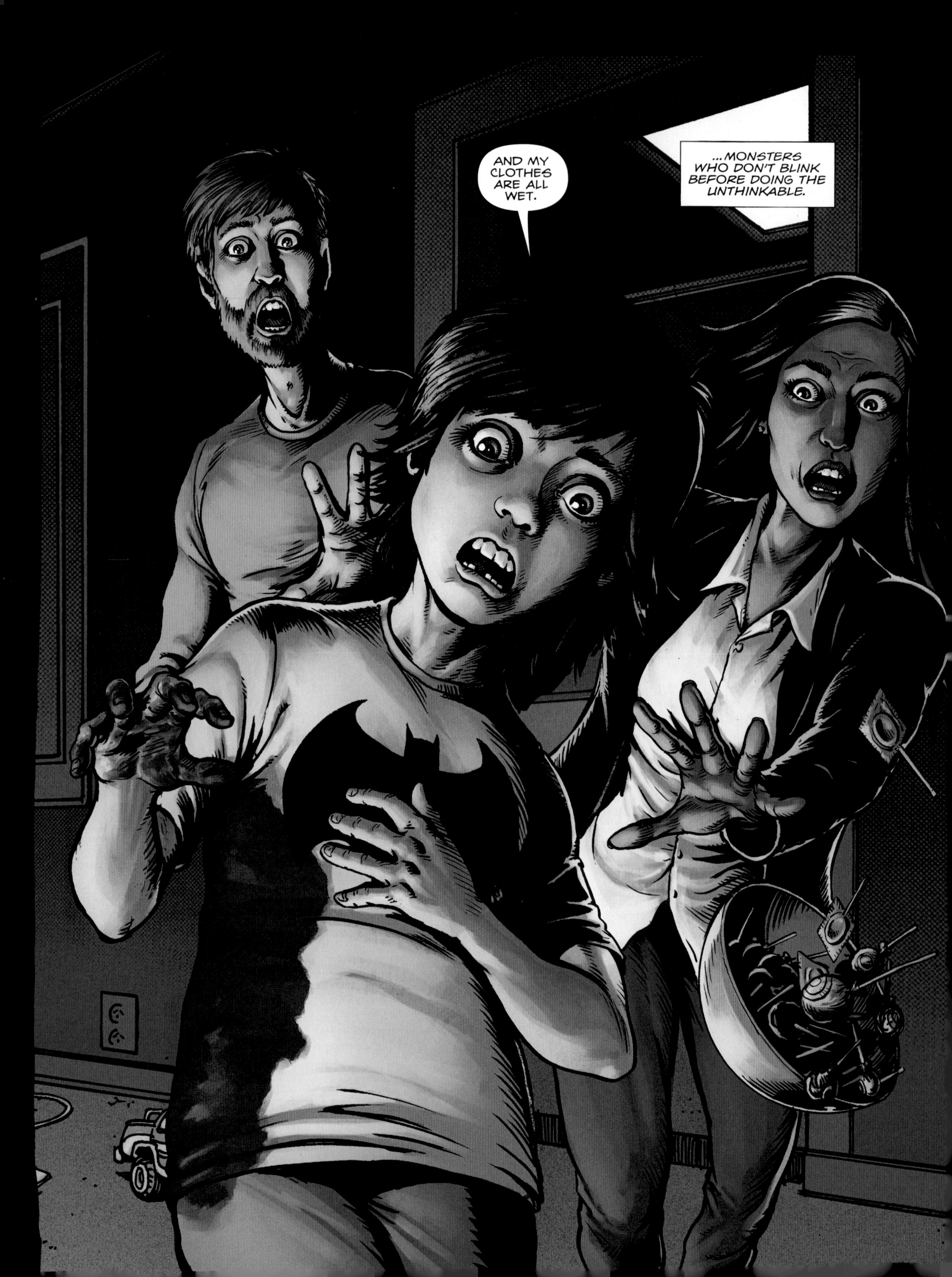
AND MY CLOTHES ARE ALL WET.
...MONSTERS WHO DON'T BLINK BEFORE DOING THE UNTHINKABLE.

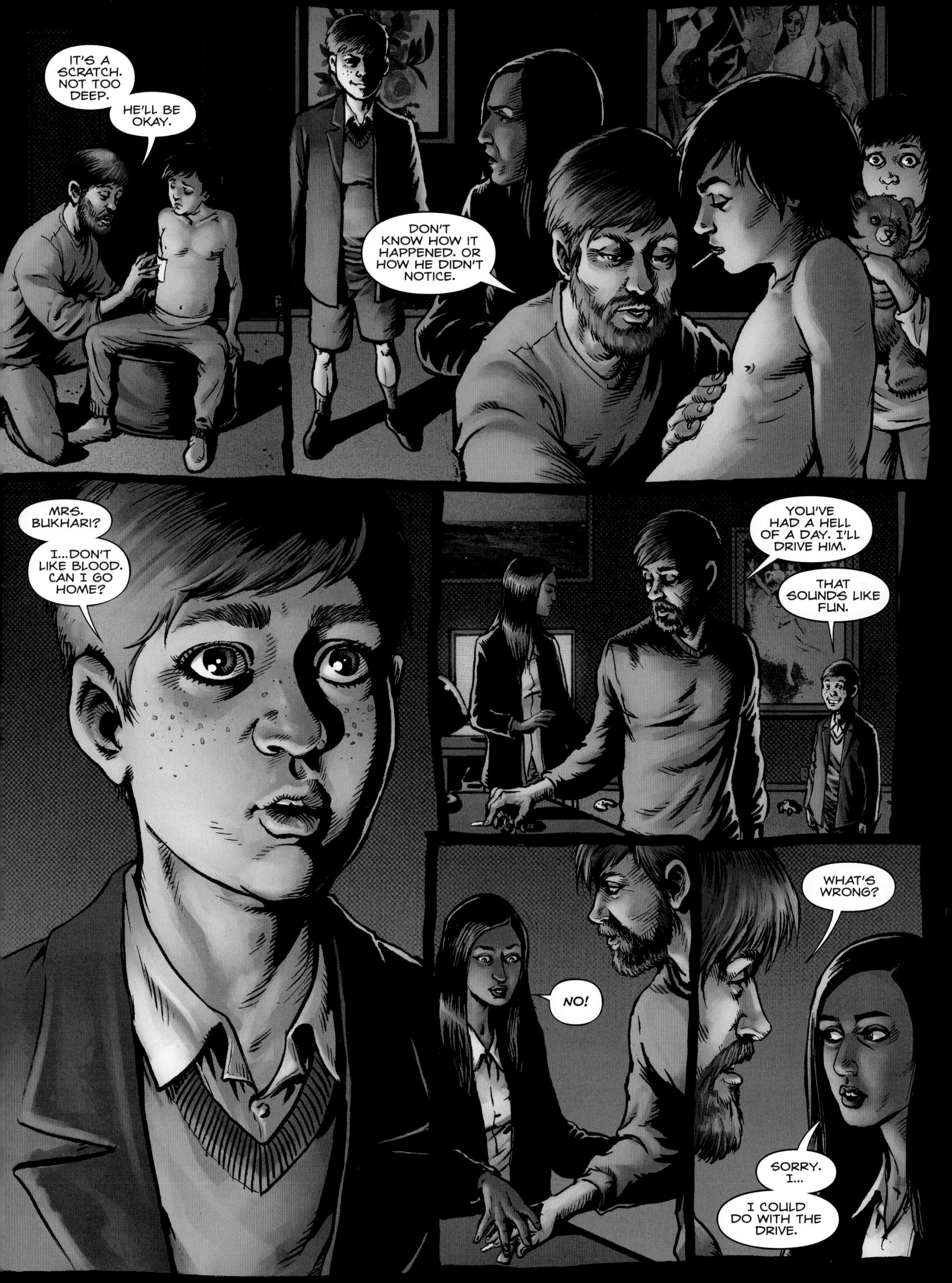
IT'S A SCRATCH. NOT TOO DEEP.
HE'LL BE OKAY.
DON'T KNOW HOW IT HAPPENED. OR HOW HE DIDN'T NOTICE.
MRS. BUKHARI?
I...DON'T LIKE BLOOD. CAN I GO HOME?
YOU'VE HAD A HELL OF A DAY. I'LL DRIVE HIM.
THAT SOUNDS LIKE FUN.
NO!
WHAT'S WRONG?
SORRY. I...
I COULD DO WITH THE DRIVE.

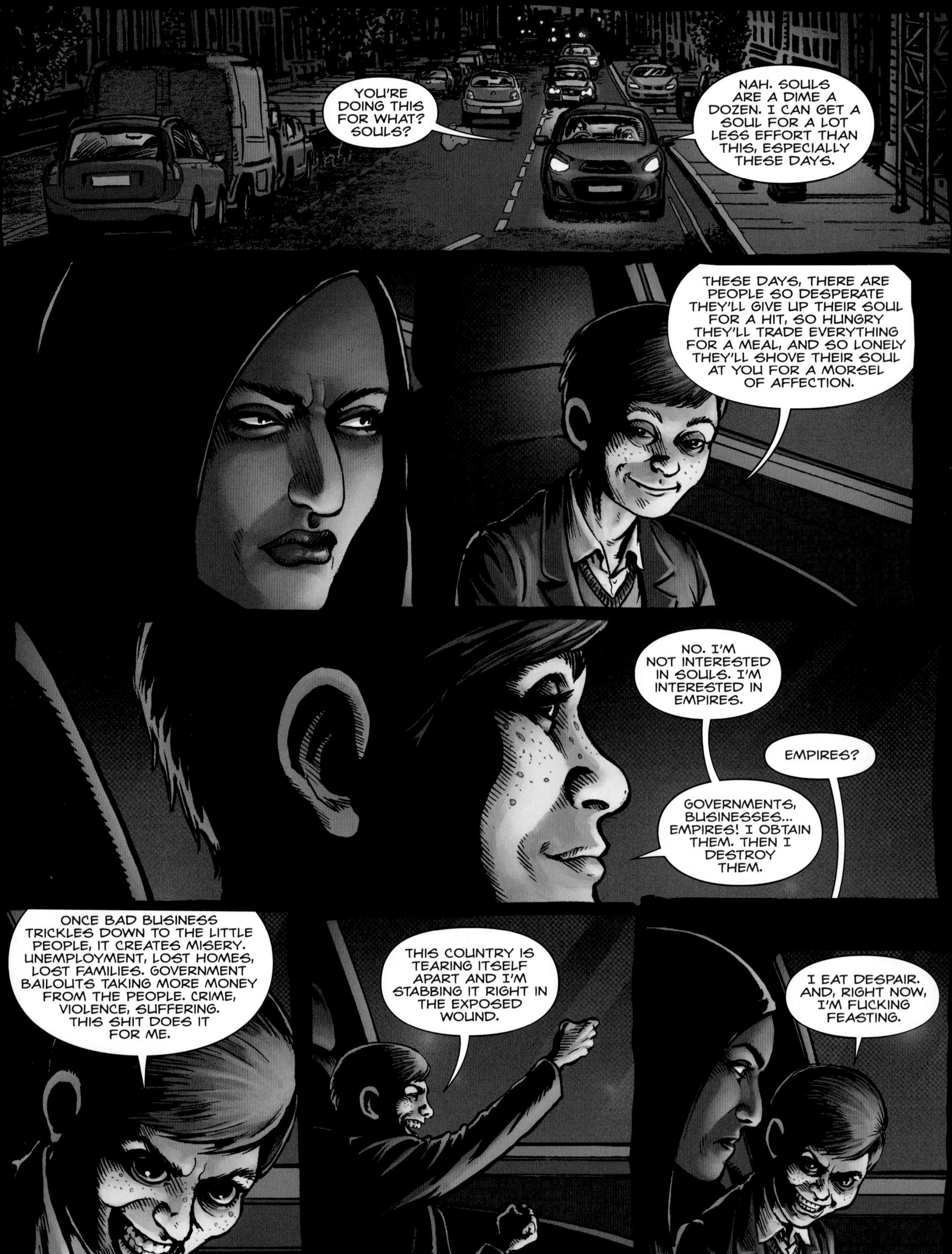
YOU'RE DOING THIS FOR WHAT? SOULS?
NAH. SOULS ARE A DIME A DOZEN. I CAN GET A SOUL FOR A LOT LESS EFFORT THAN THIS, ESPECIALLY THESE DAYS.
THESE DAYS, THERE ARE PEOPLE SO DESPERATE THEY'LL GIVE UP THEIR SOUL FOR A HIT, SO HUNGRY THEY'LL TRADE EVERYTHING FOR A MEAL, AND SO LONELY THEY'LL SHOVE THEIR SOUL AT YOU FOR A MORSEL OF AFFECTION.
NO. I'M NOT INTERESTED IN SOULS. I'M INTERESTED IN EMPIRES.
EMPIRES?
GOVERNMENTS, BUSINESSES... EMPIRES! I OBTAIN THEM. THEN I DESTROY THEM.
ONCE BAD BUSINESS TRICKLES DOWN TO THE LITTLE PEOPLE, IT CREATES MISERY. UNEMPLOYMENT, LOST HOMES, LOST FAMILIES. GOVERNMENT BAILOUTS TAKING MORE MONEY FROM THE PEOPLE. CRIME, VIOLENCE, SUFFERING. THIS SHIT DOES IT FOR ME.
THIS COUNTRY IS TEARING ITSELF APART AND I'M STABBING IT RIGHT IN THE EXPOSED WOUND.
I EAT DESPAIR. AND, RIGHT NOW, I'M FUCKING FEASTING.

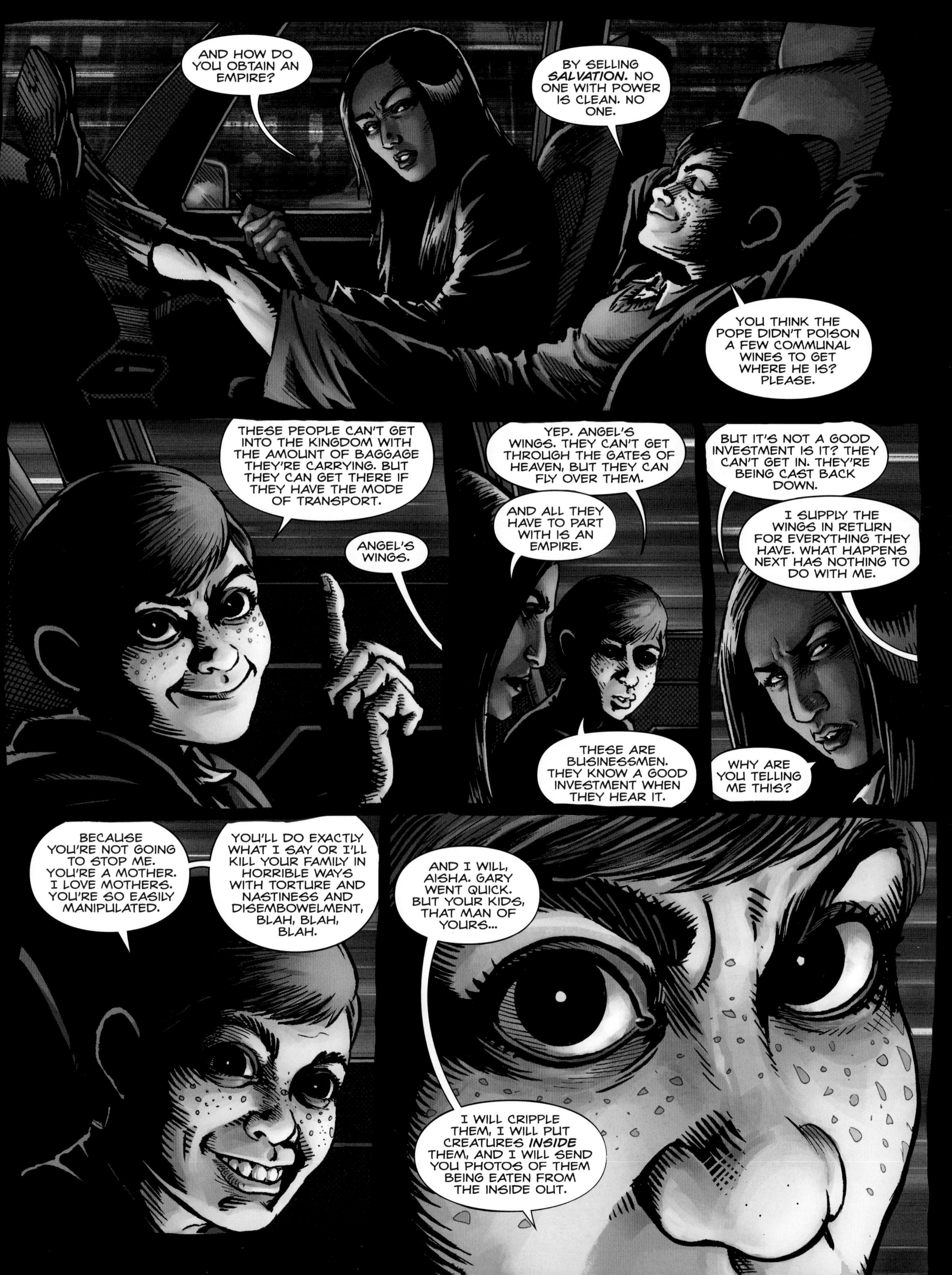
AND HOW DO YOU OBTAIN AN EMPIRE?
BY SELLING *SALVATION.* NO ONE WITH POWER IS CLEAN. NO ONE.
YOU THINK THE POPE DIDN'T POISON A FEW COMMUNAL WINES TO GET WHERE HE IS? PLEASE.
THESE PEOPLE CAN'T GET INTO THE KINGDOM WITH THE AMOUNT OF BAGGAGE THEY'RE CARRYING. BUT THEY CAN GET THERE IF THEY HAVE THE MODE OF TRANSPORT.
ANGEL'S WINGS.
YEP. ANGEL'S WINGS. THEY CAN'T GET THROUGH THE GATES OF HEAVEN, BUT THEY CAN FLY OVER THEM.
AND ALL THEY HAVE TO PART WITH IS AN EMPIRE.
THESE ARE BUSINESSMEN. THEY KNOW A GOOD INVESTMENT WHEN THEY HEAR IT.
BUT IT'S NOT A GOOD INVESTMENT IS IT? THEY CAN'T GET IN. THEY'RE BEING CAST BACK DOWN.
I SUPPLY THE WINGS IN RETURN FOR EVERYTHING THEY HAVE. WHAT HAPPENS NEXT HAS NOTHING TO DO WITH ME.
WHY ARE YOU TELLING ME THIS?
BECAUSE YOU'RE NOT GOING TO STOP ME. YOU'RE A MOTHER. I LOVE MOTHERS. YOU'RE SO EASILY MANIPULATED.
YOU'LL DO EXACTLY WHAT I SAY OR I'LL KILL YOUR FAMILY IN HORRIBLE WAYS WITH TORTURE AND NASTINESS AND DISEMBOWELMENT, BLAH, BLAH, BLAH.
AND I WILL, AISHA. GARY WENT QUICK. BUT YOUR KIDS, THAT MAN OF YOURS...
I WILL CRIPPLE THEM, I WILL PUT CREATURES *INSIDE* THEM, AND I WILL SEND YOU PHOTOS OF THEM BEING EATEN FROM THE INSIDE OUT.

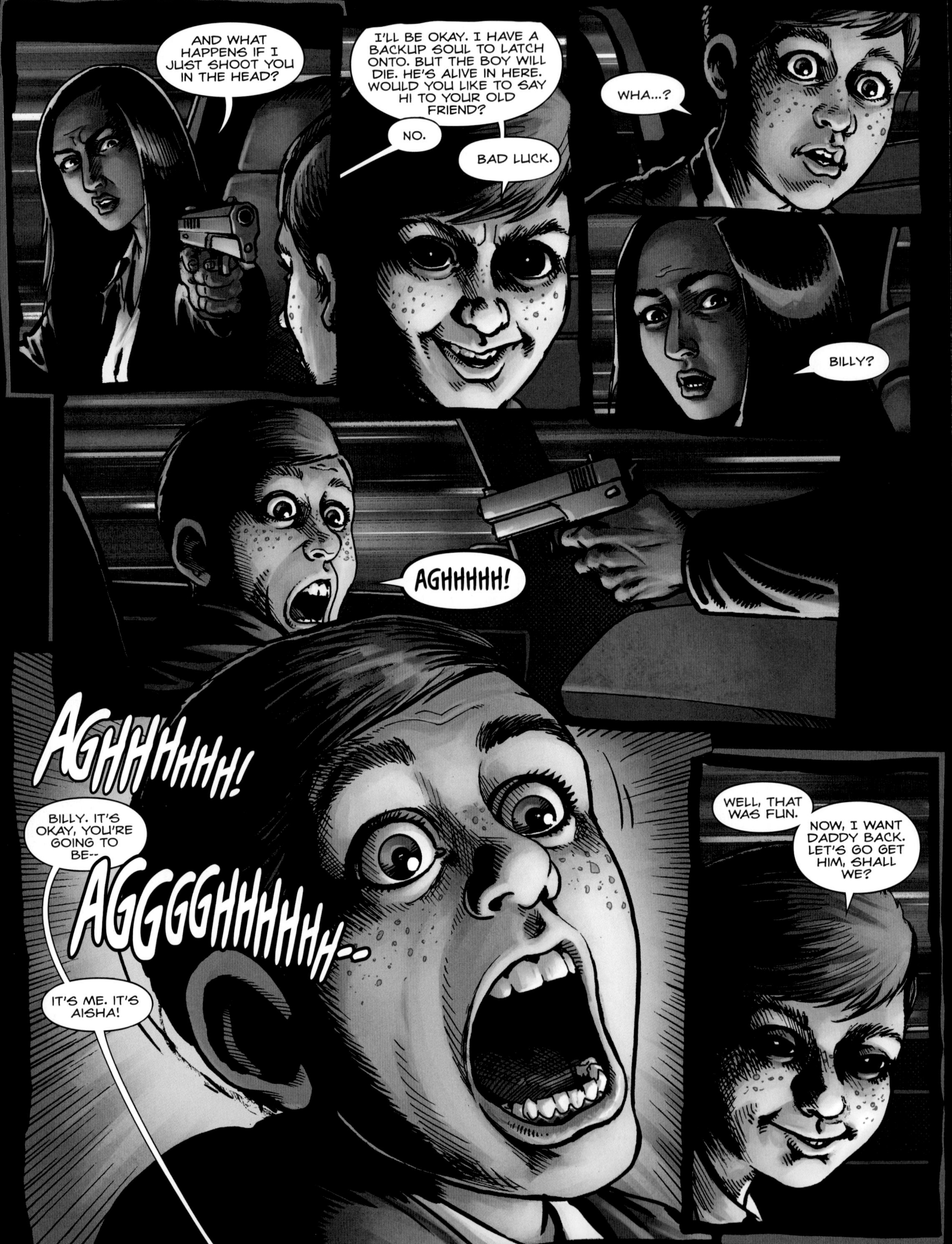
AND WHAT HAPPENS IF I JUST SHOOT YOU IN THE HEAD?
I'LL BE OKAY. I HAVE A BACKUP SOUL TO LATCH ONTO. BUT THE BOY WILL DIE. HE'S ALIVE IN HERE. WOULD YOU LIKE TO SAY HI TO YOUR OLD FRIEND?
NO.
BAD LUCK.
WHA...?
BILLY?
AGHHHHH!
AGHHHHHH!
BILLY. IT'S OKAY, YOU'RE GOING TO BE--
AGGGGHHHHHH--
IT'S ME. IT'S AISHA!
WELL, THAT WAS FUN.
NOW, I WANT DADDY BACK. LET'S GO GET HIM, SHALL WE?

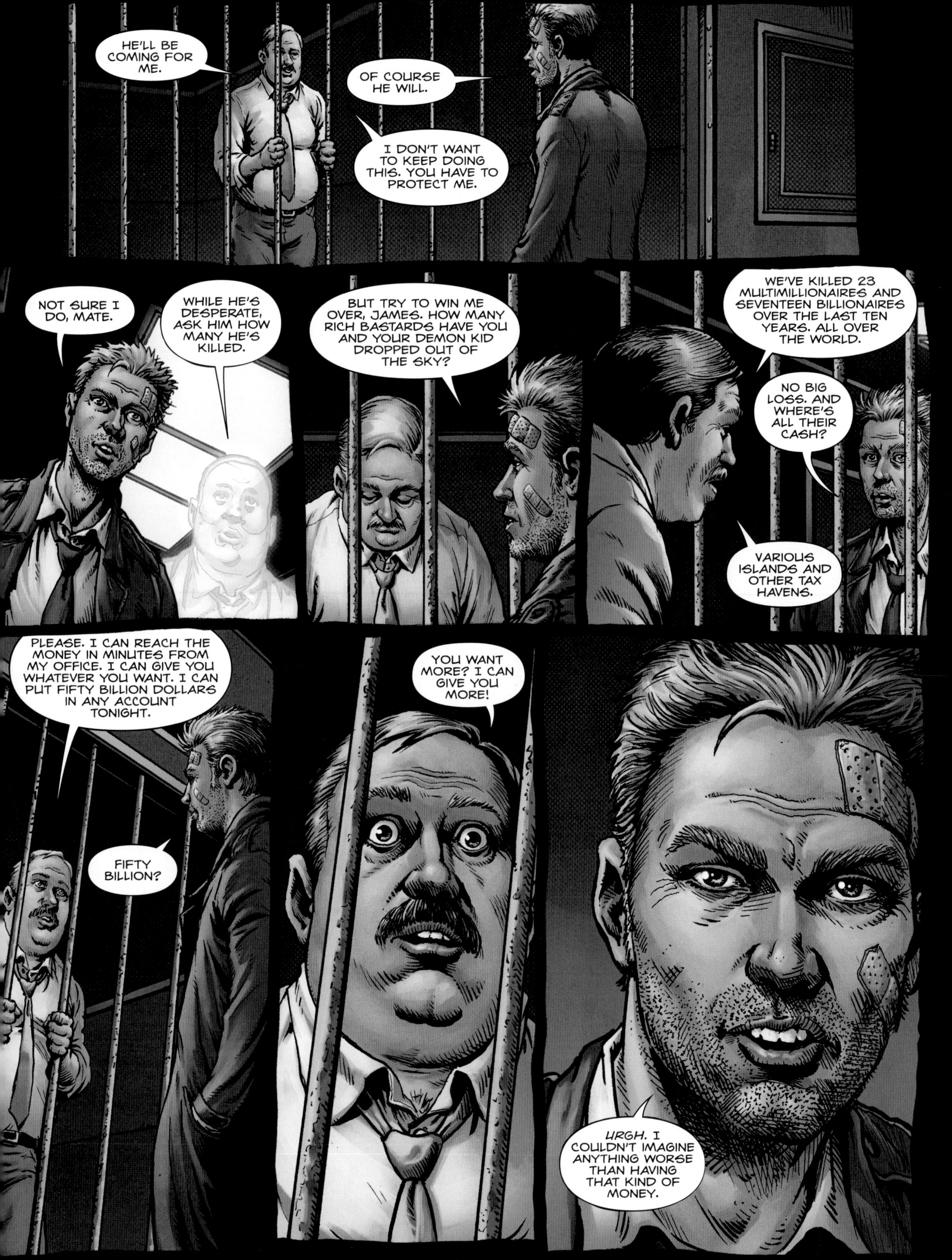
HE'LL BE COMING FOR ME.
OF COURSE HE WILL.
I DON'T WANT TO KEEP DOING THIS. YOU HAVE TO PROTECT ME.
NOT SURE I DO, MATE.
WHILE HE'S DESPERATE, ASK HIM HOW MANY HE'S KILLED.
BUT TRY TO WIN ME OVER, JAMES. HOW MANY RICH BASTARDS HAVE YOU AND YOUR DEMON KID DROPPED OUT OF THE SKY?
WE'VE KILLED 23 MULTIMILLIONAIRES AND SEVENTEEN BILLIONAIRES OVER THE LAST TEN YEARS. ALL OVER THE WORLD.
NO BIG LOSS. AND WHERE'S ALL THEIR CASH?
VARIOUS ISLANDS AND OTHER TAX HAVENS.
PLEASE. I CAN REACH THE MONEY IN MINUTES FROM MY OFFICE. I CAN GIVE YOU WHATEVER YOU WANT. I CAN PUT FIFTY BILLION DOLLARS IN ANY ACCOUNT TONIGHT.
FIFTY BILLION?
YOU WANT MORE? I CAN GIVE YOU MORE!
URGH. I COULDN'T IMAGINE ANYTHING WORSE THAN HAVING THAT KIND OF MONEY.

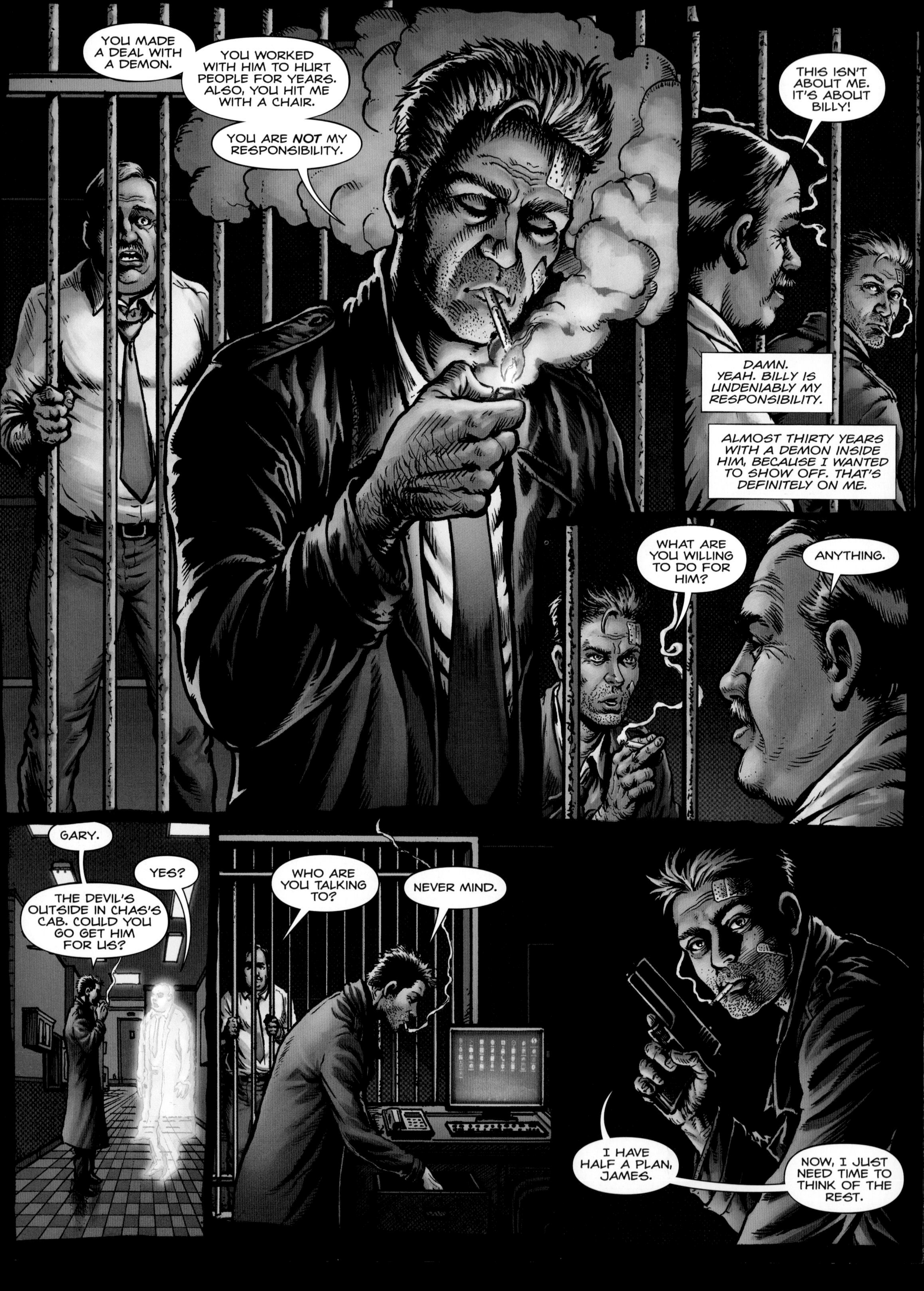
YOU MADE A DEAL WITH A DEMON.
YOU WORKED WITH HIM TO HURT PEOPLE FOR YEARS. ALSO, YOU HIT ME WITH A CHAIR.
YOU ARE *NOT* MY RESPONSIBILITY.
THIS ISN'T ABOUT ME. IT'S ABOUT BILLY!
DAMN. YEAH. BILLY IS UNDENIABLY MY RESPONSIBILITY.
ALMOST THIRTY YEARS WITH A DEMON INSIDE HIM, BECAUSE I WANTED TO SHOW OFF. THAT'S DEFINITELY ON ME.
WHAT ARE YOU WILLING TO DO FOR HIM?
ANYTHING.
GARY.
YES?
THE DEVIL'S OUTSIDE IN CHAS'S CAB. COULD YOU GO GET HIM FOR US?
WHO ARE YOU TALKING TO?
NEVER MIND.
I HAVE HALF A PLAN, JAMES.
NOW, I JUST NEED TIME TO THINK OF THE REST.

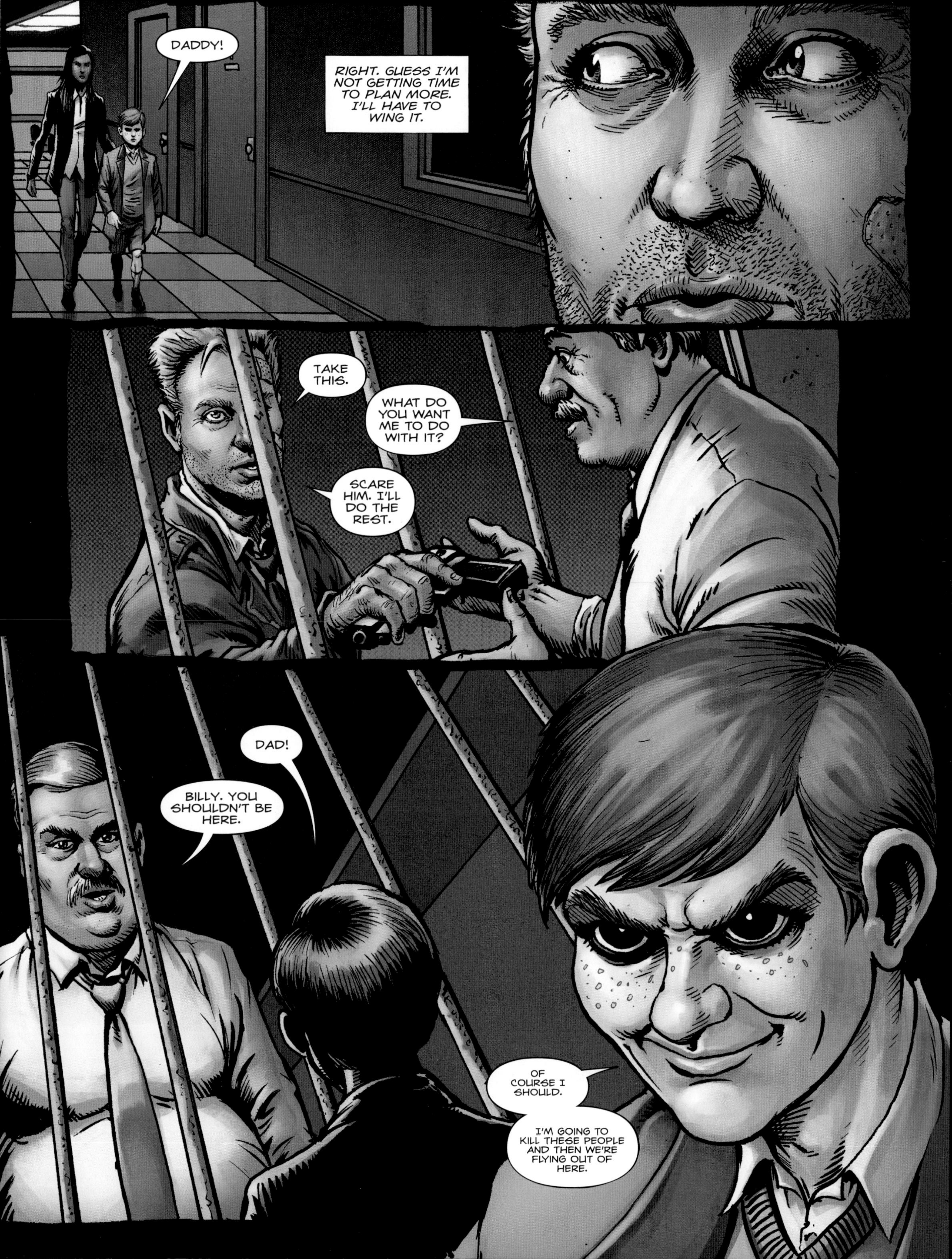
DADDY!
RIGHT. GUESS I'M NOT GETTING TIME TO PLAN MORE. I'LL HAVE TO WING IT.
TAKE THIS.
WHAT DO YOU WANT ME TO DO WITH IT?
SCARE HIM. I'LL DO THE REST.
DAD!
BILLY. YOU SHOULDN'T BE HERE.
OF COURSE I SHOULD.
I'M GOING TO KILL THESE PEOPLE AND THEN WE'RE FLYING OUT OF HERE.

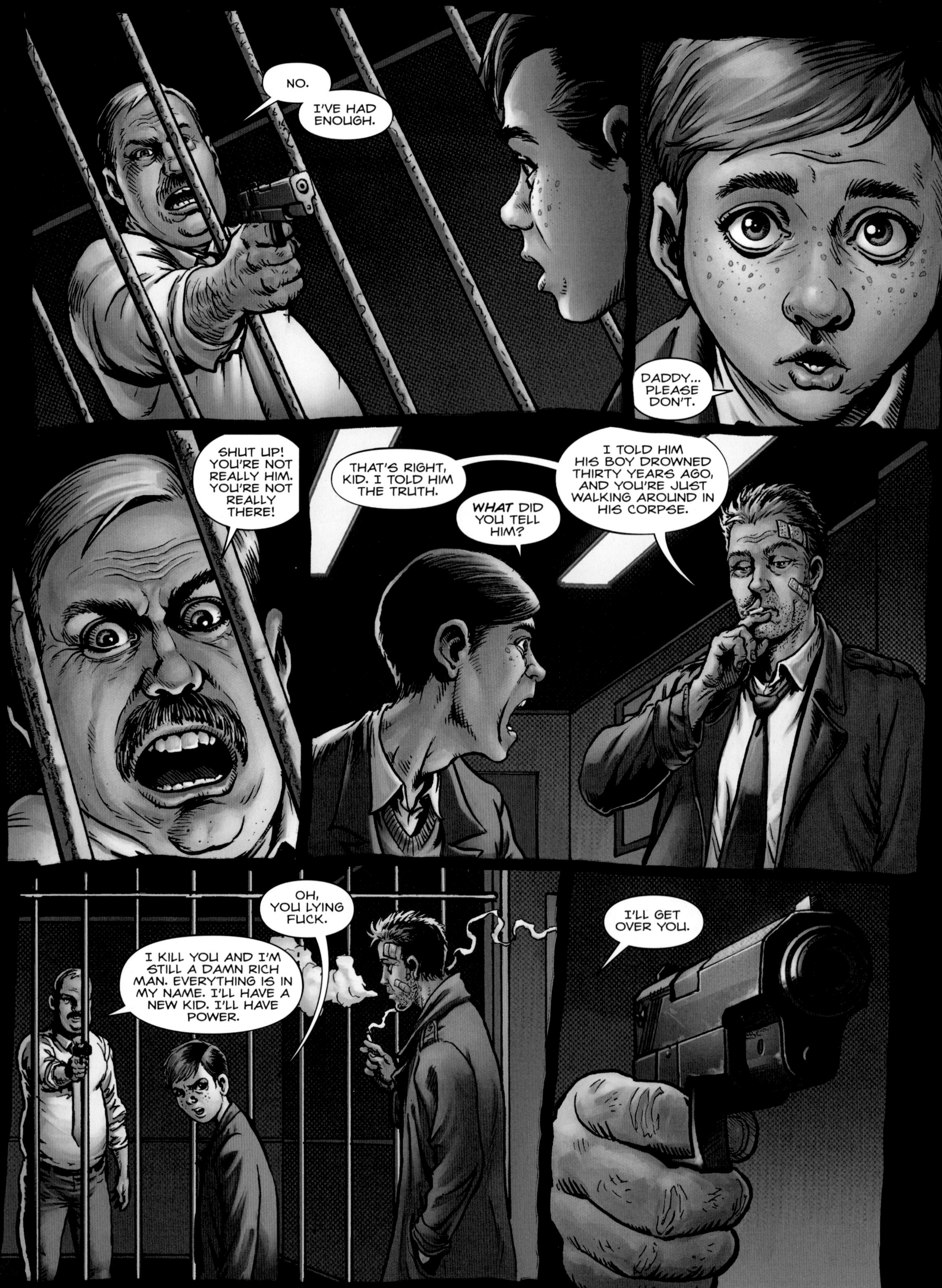
NO.
I'VE HAD ENOUGH.
DADDY... PLEASE DON'T.
SHUT UP! YOU'RE NOT REALLY HIM. YOU'RE NOT REALLY THERE!
WHAT DID YOU TELL HIM?
THAT'S RIGHT, KID. I TOLD HIM THE TRUTH.
I TOLD HIM HIS BOY DROWNED THIRTY YEARS AGO, AND YOU'RE JUST WALKING AROUND IN HIS CORPSE.
OH, YOU LYING FUCK.
I KILL YOU AND I'M STILL A DAMN RICH MAN. EVERYTHING IS IN MY NAME. I'LL HAVE A NEW KID. I'LL HAVE POWER.
I'LL GET OVER YOU.

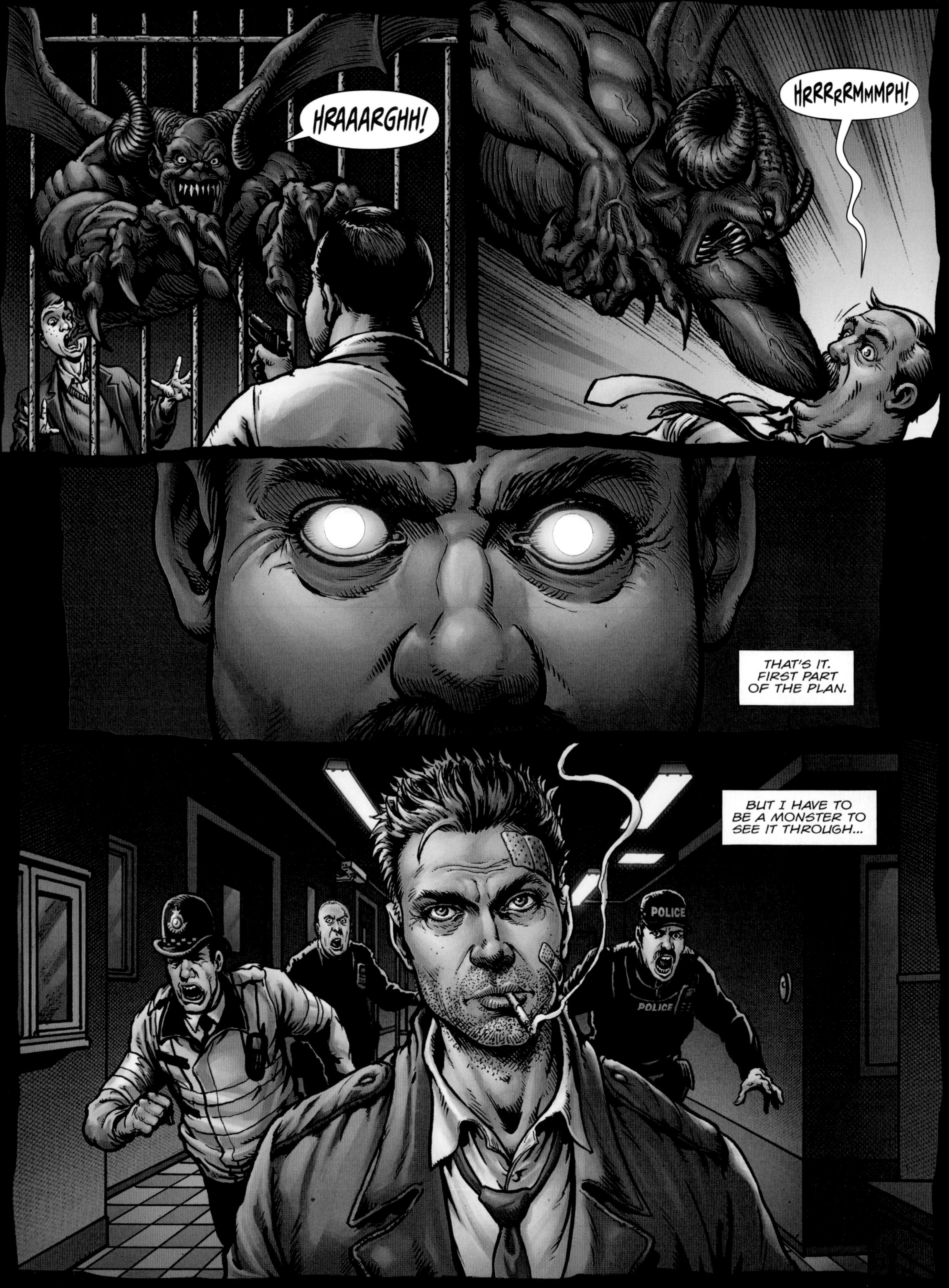
HRAAARGHH!
HRRRRRMMMPH!
THAT'S IT. FIRST PART OF THE PLAN.
BUT I HAVE TO BE A MONSTER TO SEE IT THROUGH...
POLICE
POLICE

...I HAVE TO DO THE UNTHINKABLE.
HE'S GONNA SHOOT THE KID!
TAKE THE GUN OFF THE BOY OR WE WILL DROP YOU!
BANG
BANG
POLICE
BANG
BANG
BANG
BANG
BULLETS AREN'T GOING TO KILL A DEMON...

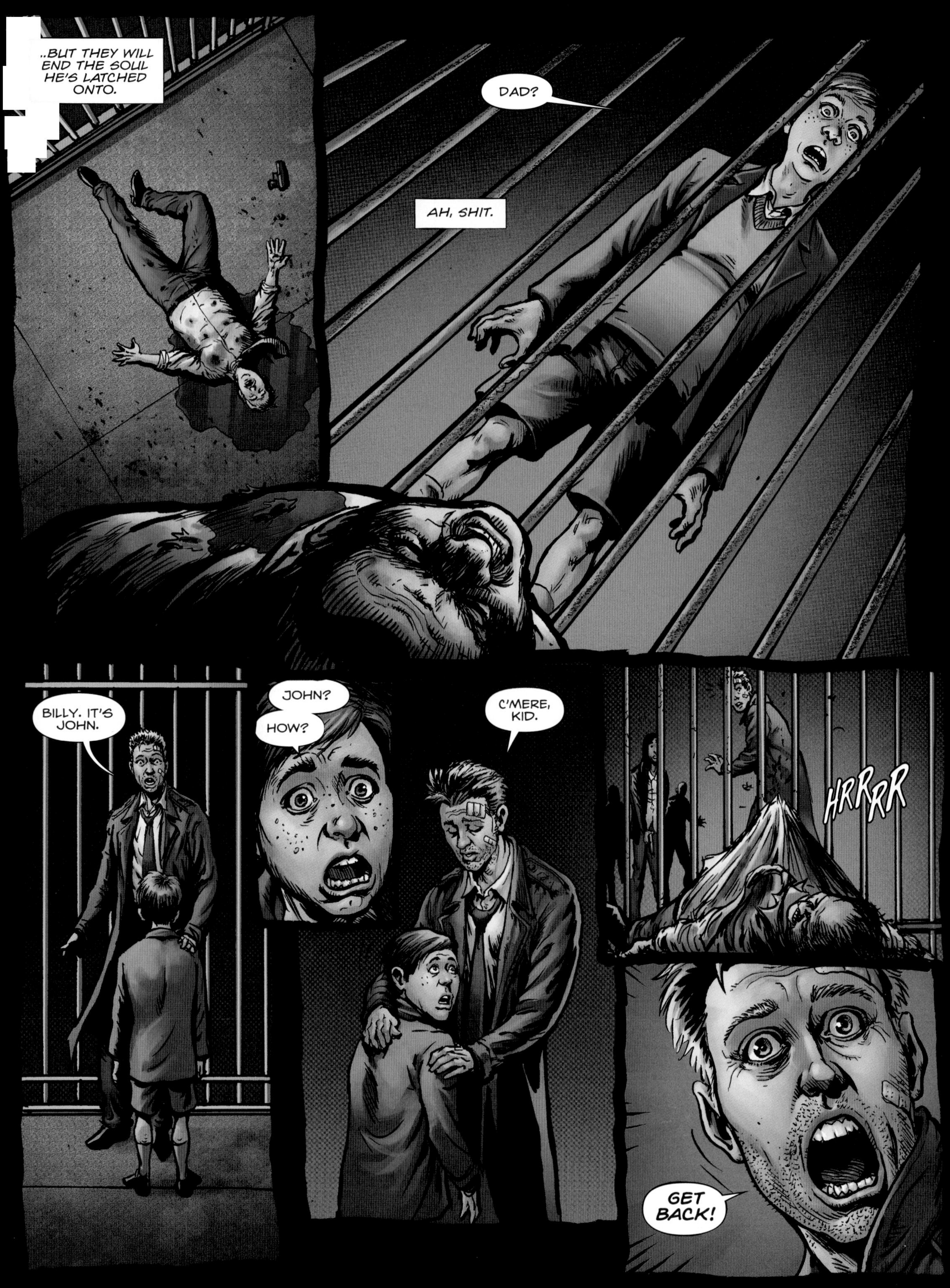
..BUT THEY WILL END THE SOUL HE'S LATCHED ONTO.
DAD?
AH, SHIT.
BILLY. IT'S JOHN.
JOHN?
HOW?
C'MERE, KID.
HRRRR
GET BACK!

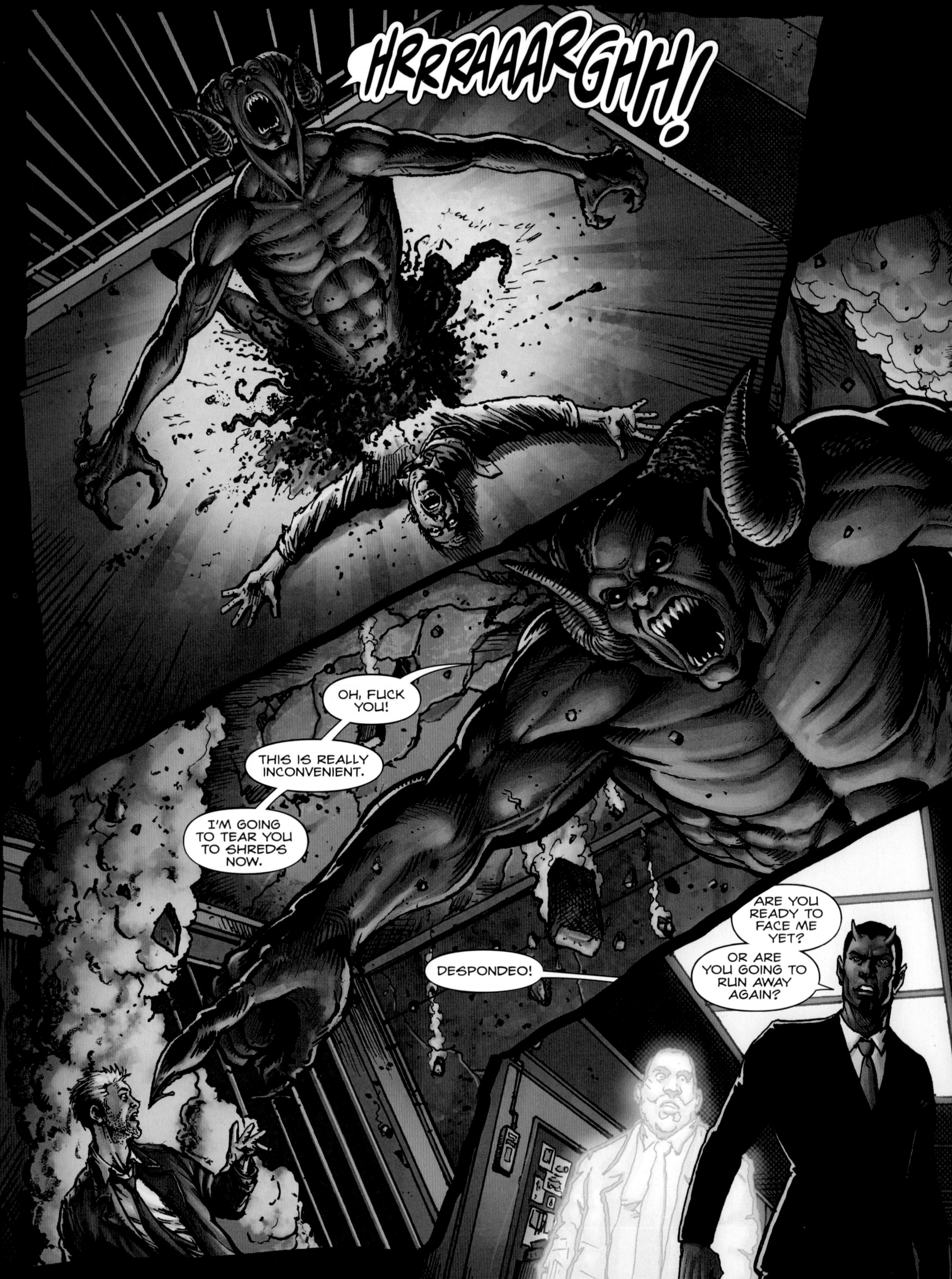
HRRRAAARGHH!
OH, FUCK YOU!
THIS IS REALLY INCONVENIENT.
I'M GOING TO TEAR YOU TO SHREDS NOW.
ARE YOU READY TO FACE ME YET?
OR ARE YOU GOING TO RUN AWAY AGAIN?
DESPONDEO!

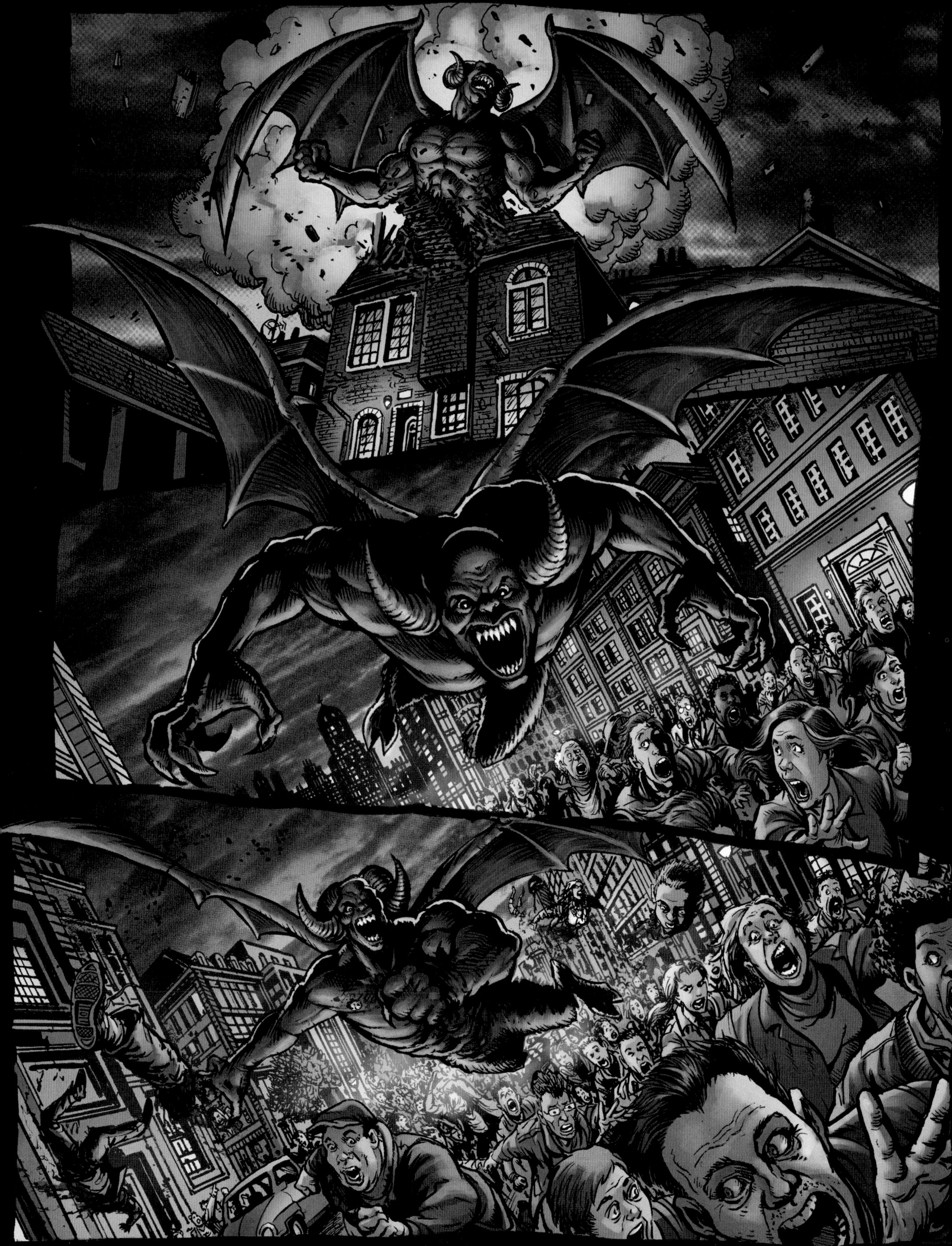

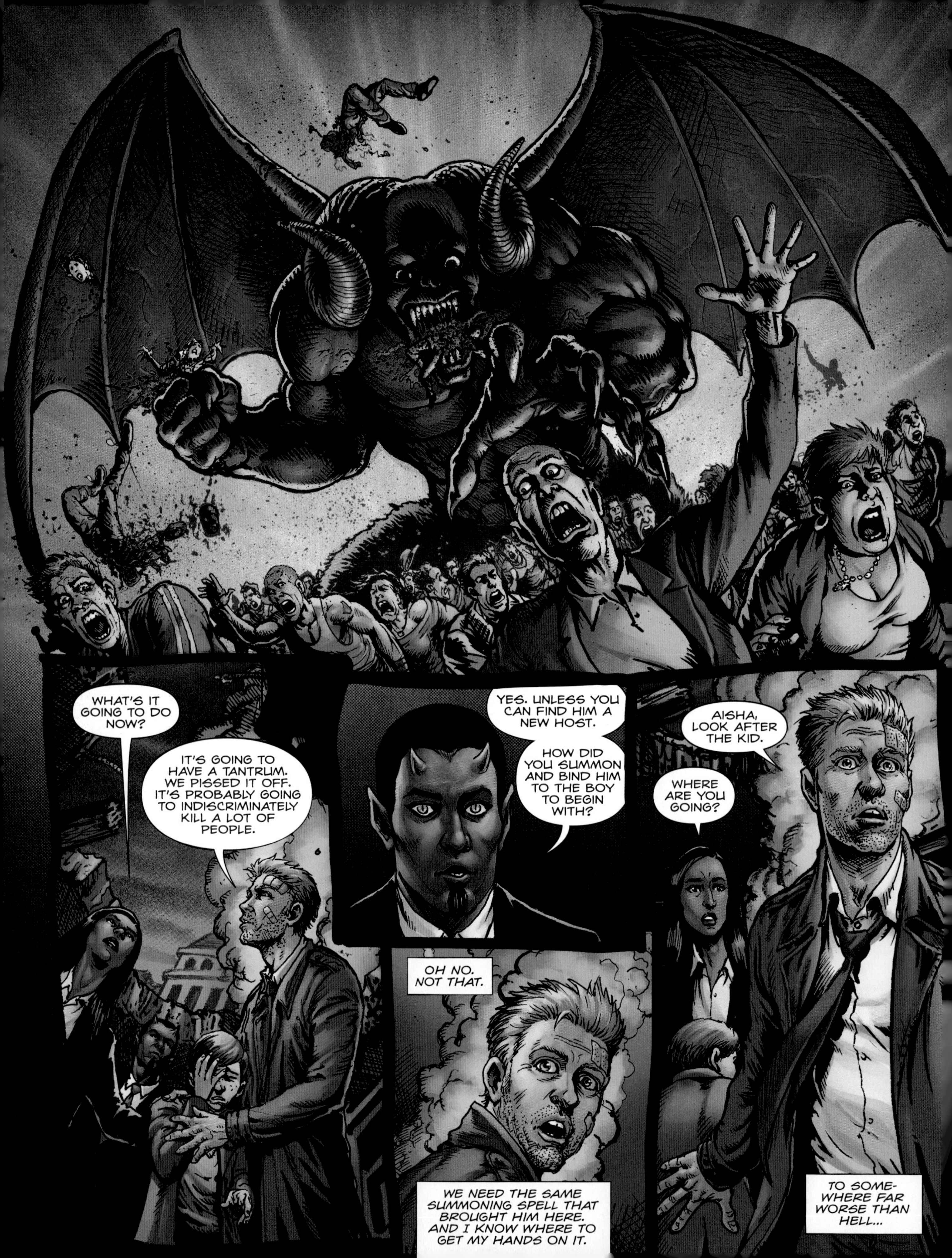
WHAT'S IT GOING TO DO NOW?
IT'S GOING TO HAVE A TANTRUM. WE PISSED IT OFF. IT'S PROBABLY GOING TO INDISCRIMINATELY KILL A LOT OF PEOPLE.
YES. UNLESS YOU CAN FIND HIM A NEW HOST.
HOW DID YOU SUMMON AND BIND HIM TO THE BOY TO BEGIN WITH?
OH NO. NOT THAT.
WE NEED THE SAME SUMMONING SPELL THAT BROUGHT HIM HERE. AND I KNOW WHERE TO GET MY HANDS ON IT.
AISHA, LOOK AFTER THE KID.
WHERE ARE YOU GOING?
TO SOME-WHERE FAR WORSE THAN HELL...

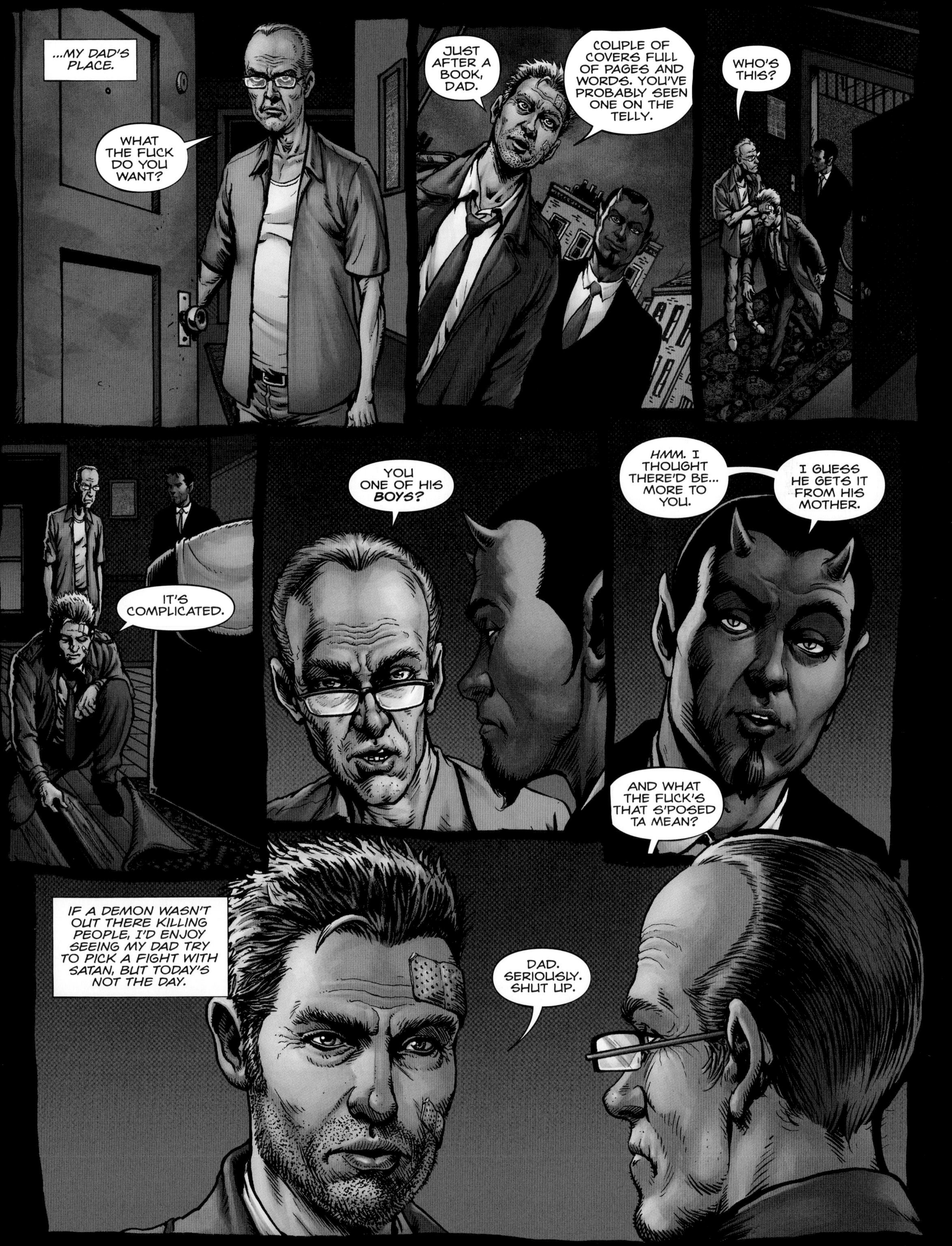
...MY DAD'S PLACE.
WHAT THE FUCK DO YOU WANT?
JUST AFTER A BOOK, DAD.
COUPLE OF COVERS FULL OF PAGES AND WORDS. YOU'VE PROBABLY SEEN ONE ON THE TELLY.
WHO'S THIS?
IT'S COMPLICATED.
YOU ONE OF HIS *BOYS?*
HMM. I THOUGHT THERE'D BE... MORE TO YOU.
I GUESS HE GETS IT FROM HIS MOTHER.
AND WHAT THE FUCK'S THAT S'POSED TA MEAN?
IF A DEMON WASN'T OUT THERE KILLING PEOPLE, I'D ENJOY SEEING MY DAD TRY TO PICK A FIGHT WITH SATAN, BUT TODAY'S NOT THE DAY.
DAD. SERIOUSLY. SHUT UP.

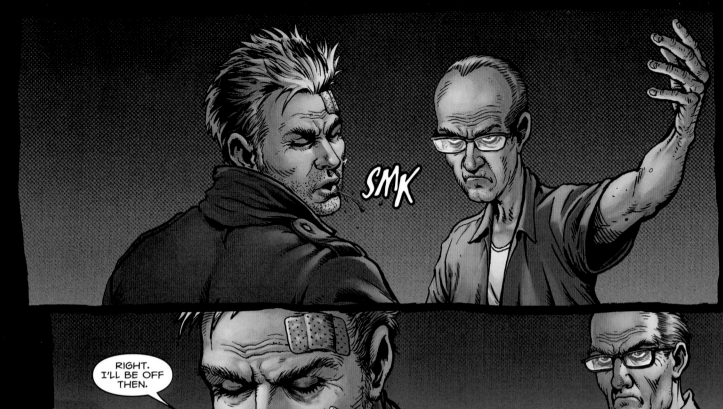

SMK

RIGHT. I'LL BE OFF THEN.

ALWAYS GOOD TO CATCH UP, DAD.

HE DISAPPROVES OF ME TEARING OUT KIDNEYS.

SO, LET'S JUST TALK, SHALL WE, THOMAS?

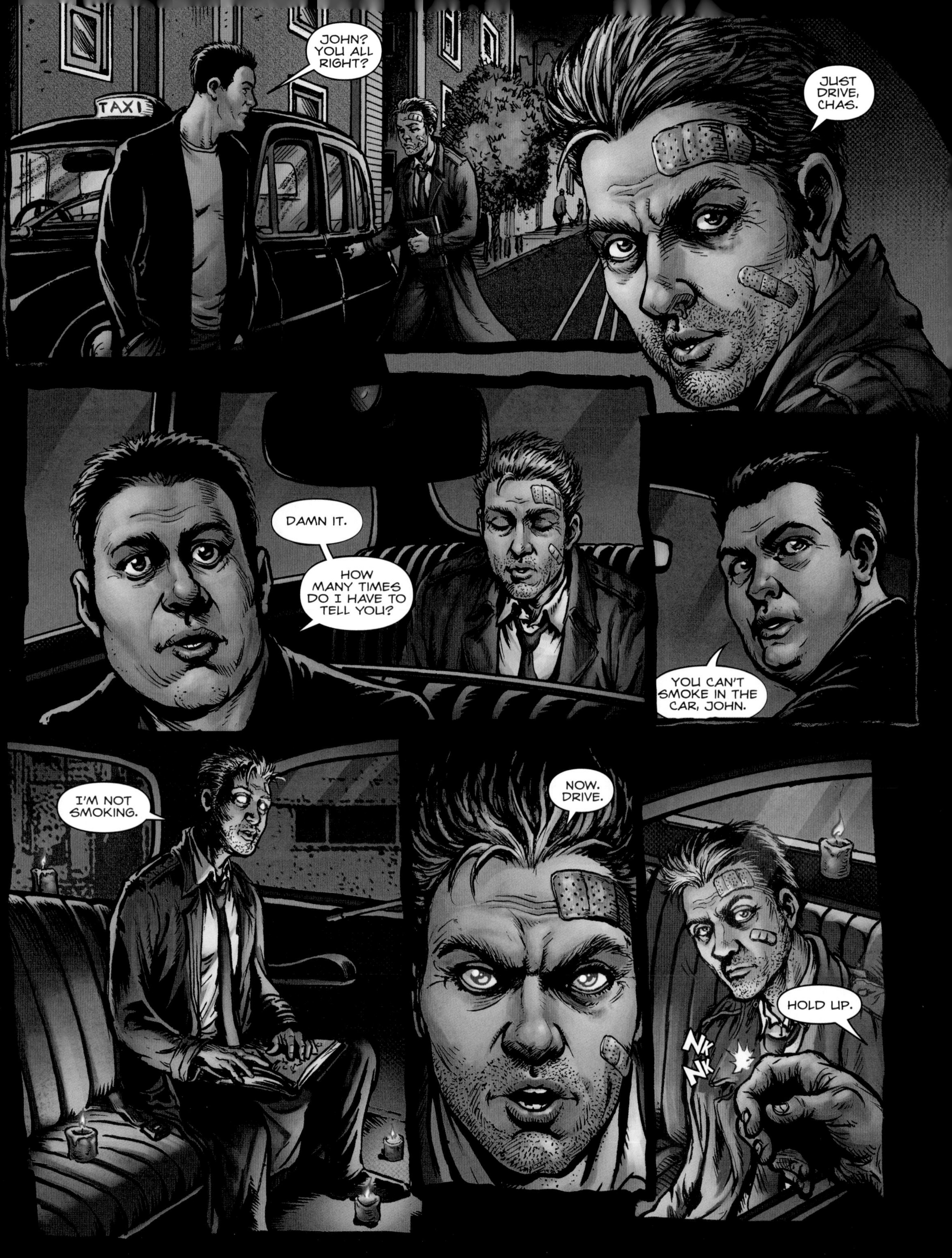
JOHN? YOU ALL RIGHT?
JUST DRIVE, CHAS.
DAMN IT.
HOW MANY TIMES DO I HAVE TO TELL YOU?
YOU CAN'T SMOKE IN THE CAR, JOHN.
I'M NOT SMOKING.
NOW. DRIVE.
HOLD UP.
NK NK

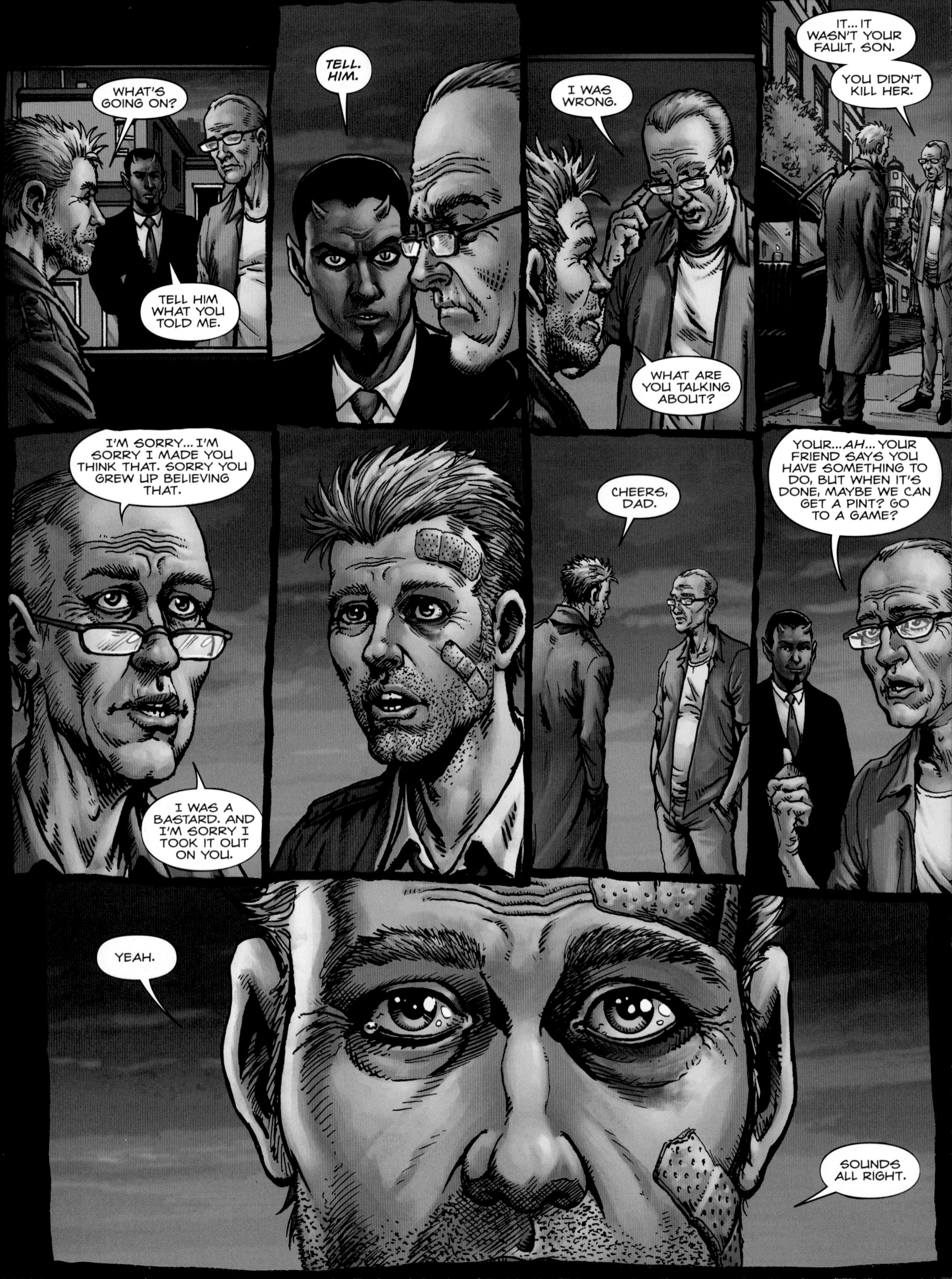
WHAT'S GOING ON?
TELL HIM WHAT YOU TOLD ME.
TELL. HIM.
I WAS WRONG.
WHAT ARE YOU TALKING ABOUT?
IT... IT WASN'T YOUR FAULT, SON.
YOU DIDN'T KILL HER.
I'M SORRY... I'M SORRY I MADE YOU THINK THAT. SORRY YOU GREW UP BELIEVING THAT.
I WAS A BASTARD. AND I'M SORRY I TOOK IT OUT ON YOU.
CHEERS, DAD.
YOUR... AH... YOUR FRIEND SAYS YOU HAVE SOMETHING TO DO, BUT WHEN IT'S DONE, MAYBE WE CAN GET A PINT? GO TO A GAME?
YEAH.
SOUNDS ALL RIGHT.

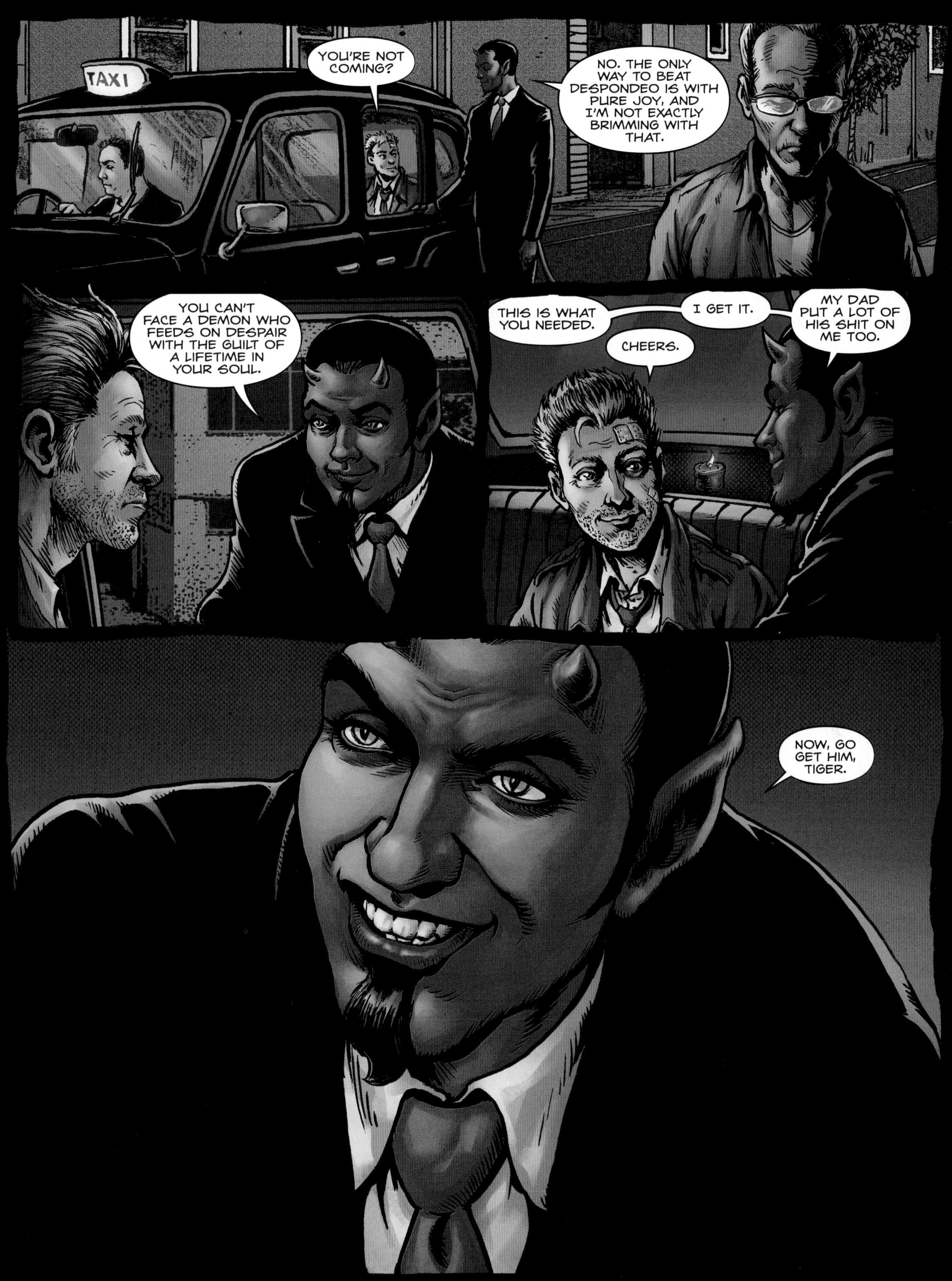
TAXI
YOU'RE NOT COMING?
NO. THE ONLY WAY TO BEAT DESPONDEO IS WITH PURE JOY, AND I'M NOT EXACTLY BRIMMING WITH THAT.
YOU CAN'T FACE A DEMON WHO FEEDS ON DESPAIR WITH THE GUILT OF A LIFETIME IN YOUR SOUL.
THIS IS WHAT YOU NEEDED.
I GET IT.
MY DAD PUT A LOT OF HIS SHIT ON ME TOO.
CHEERS.
NOW, GO GET HIM, TIGER.

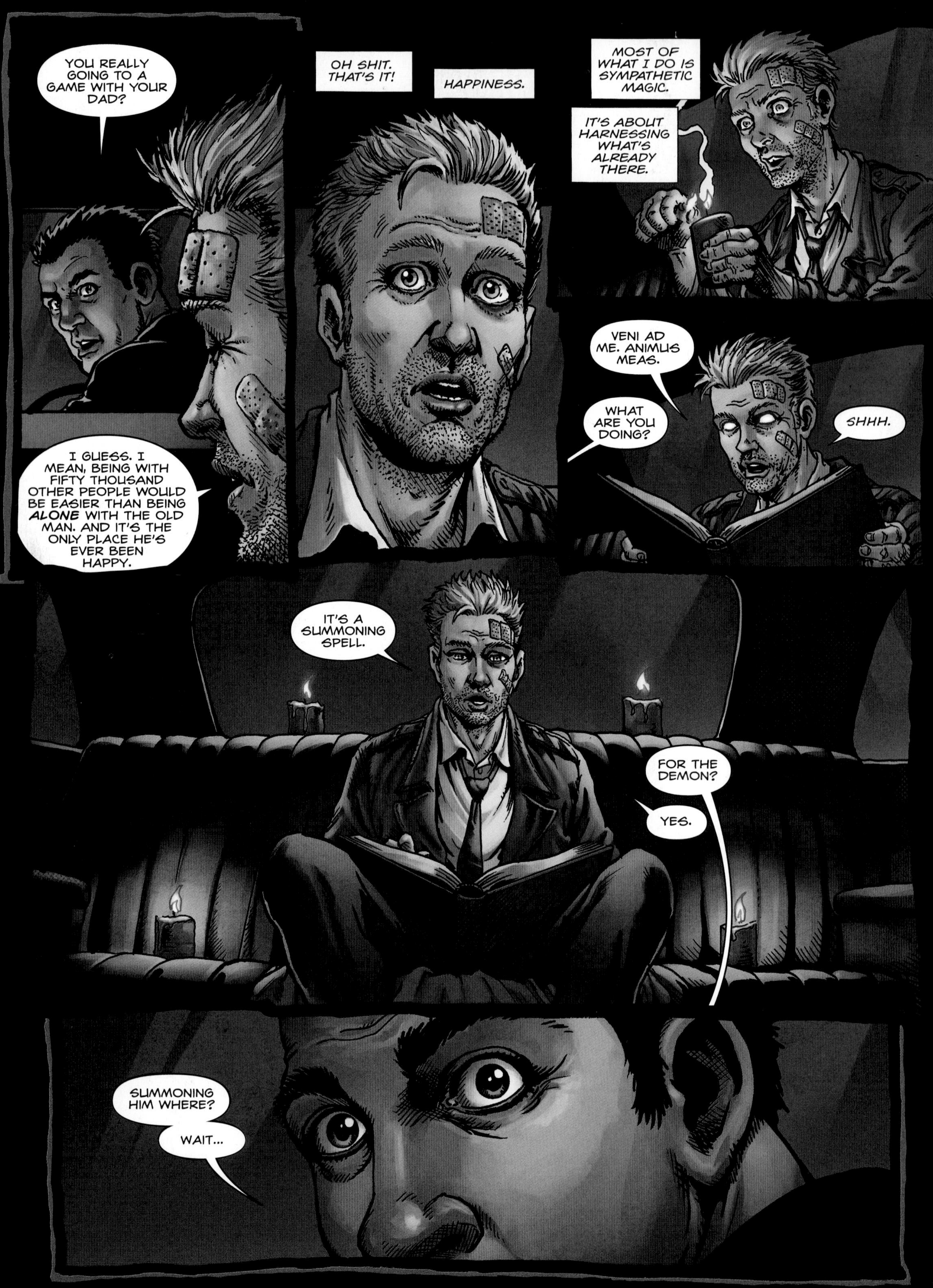
YOU REALLY GOING TO A GAME WITH YOUR DAD?
I GUESS. I MEAN, BEING WITH FIFTY THOUSAND OTHER PEOPLE WOULD BE EASIER THAN BEING *ALONE* WITH THE OLD MAN. AND IT'S THE ONLY PLACE HE'S EVER BEEN HAPPY.
OH SHIT. THAT'S IT!
HAPPINESS.
MOST OF WHAT I DO IS SYMPATHETIC MAGIC.
IT'S ABOUT HARNESSING WHAT'S ALREADY THERE.
VENI AD ME. ANIMUS MEAS.
WHAT ARE YOU DOING?
SHHH.
IT'S A SUMMONING SPELL.
FOR THE DEMON?
YES.
SUMMONING HIM WHERE?
WAIT...

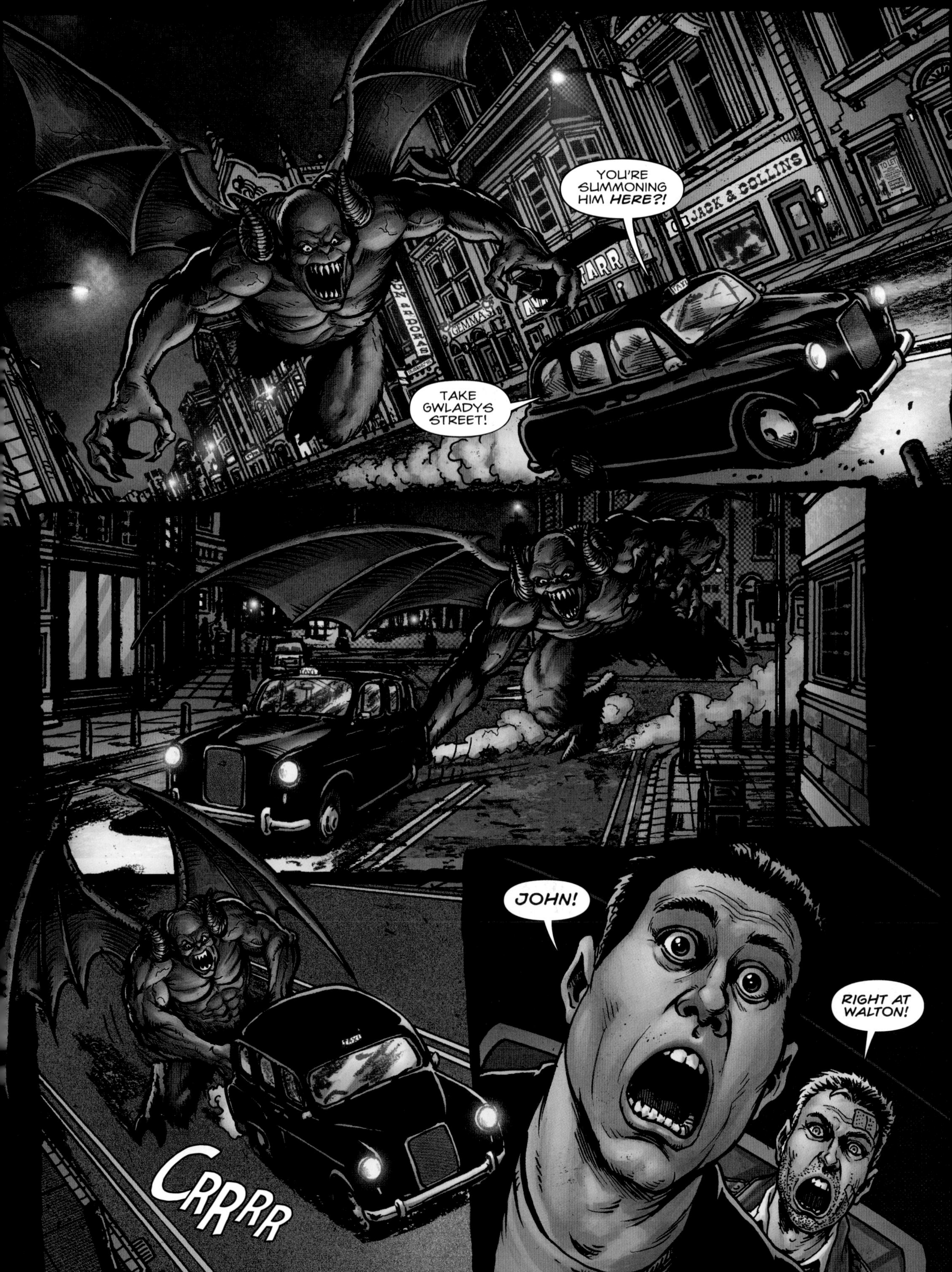

YOU'RE SUMMONING HIM HERE?!
TAKE GWLADYS STREET!
JOHN!
RIGHT AT WALTON!
CRRRR

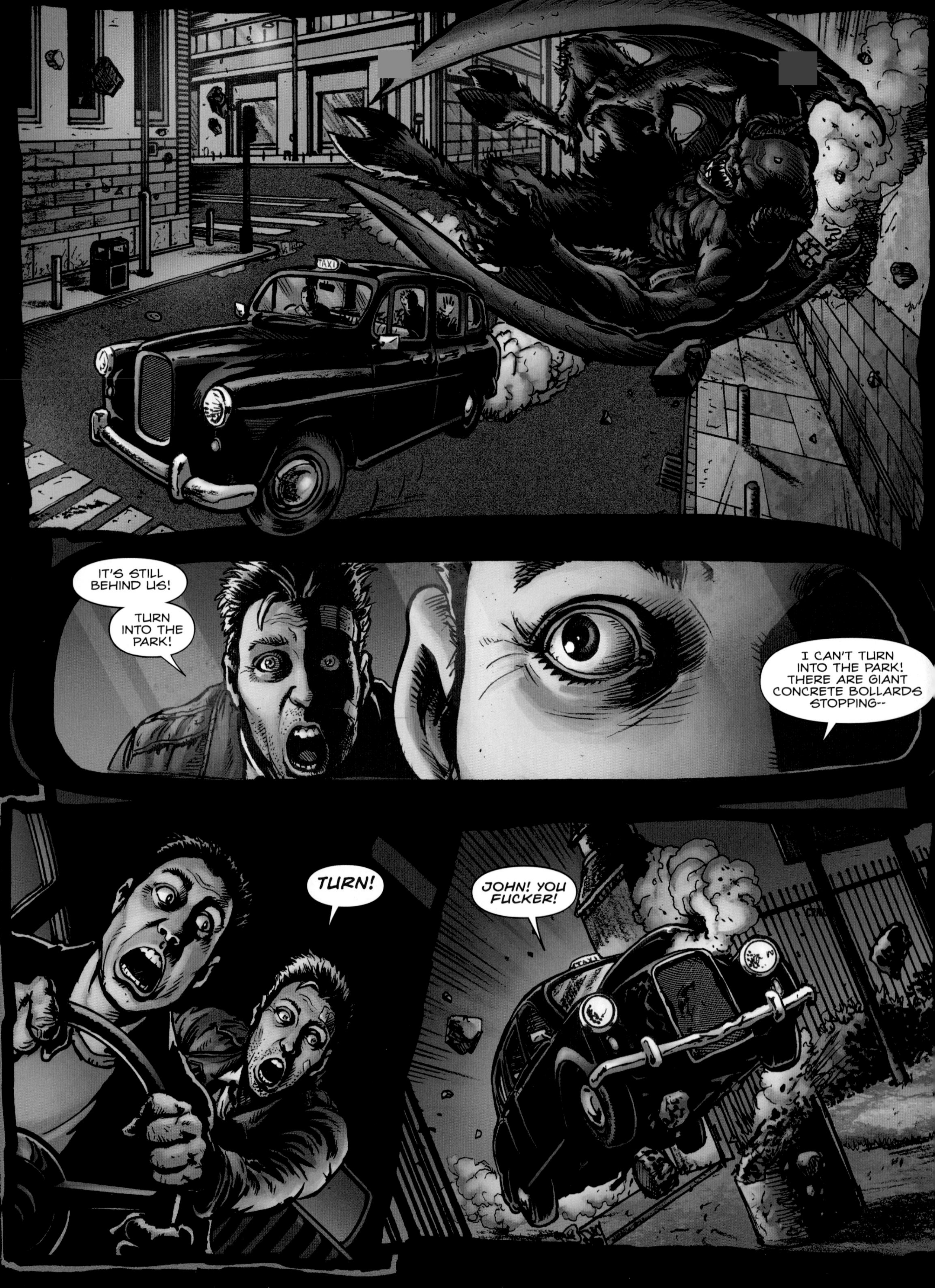
IT'S STILL BEHIND US!
TURN INTO THE PARK!
I CAN'T TURN INTO THE PARK! THERE ARE GIANT CONCRETE BOLLARDS STOPPING--
TURN!
JOHN! YOU FUCKER!

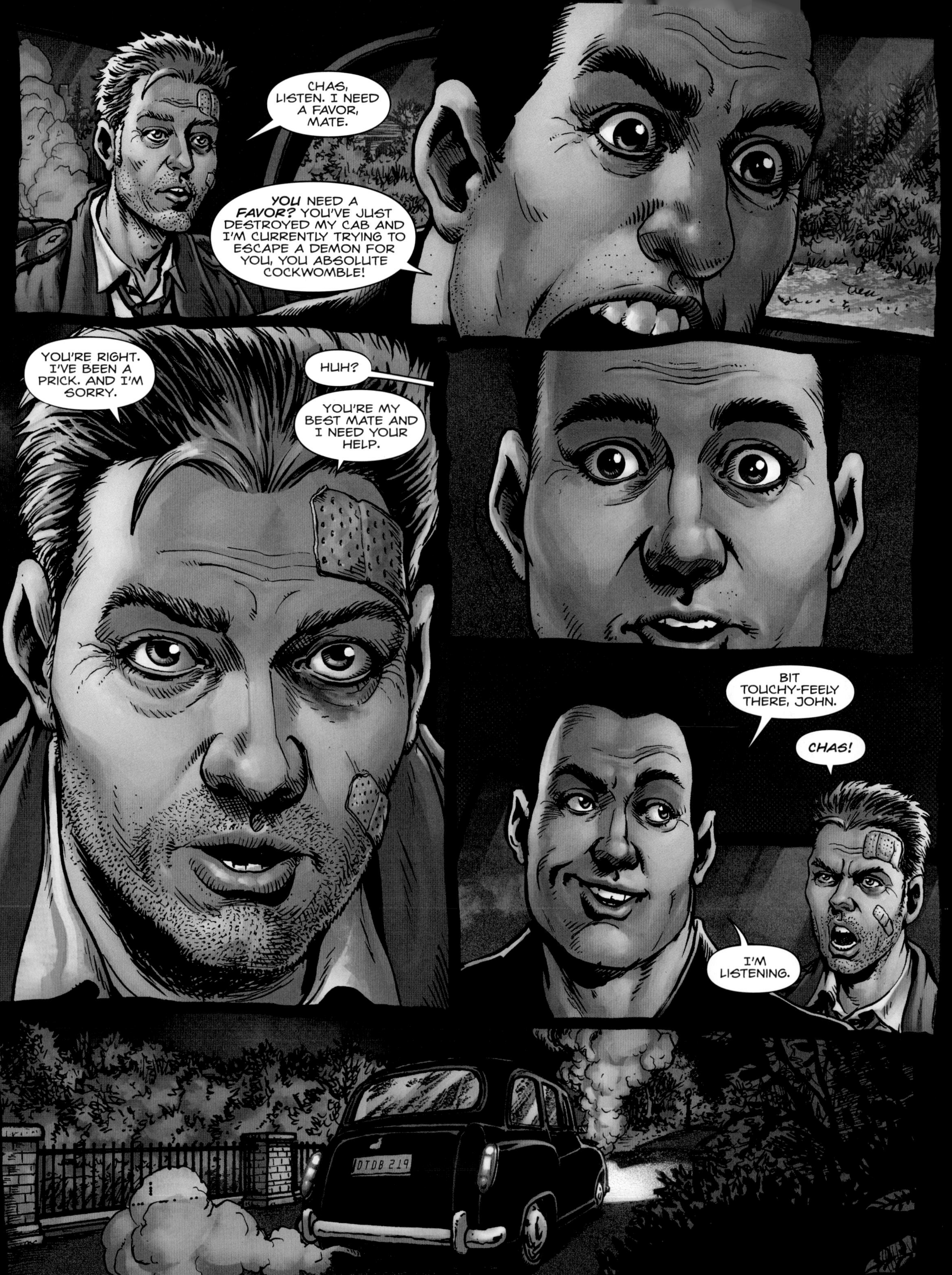
CHAS, LISTEN. I NEED A FAVOR, MATE.
YOU NEED A FAVOR? YOU'VE JUST DESTROYED MY CAB AND I'M CURRENTLY TRYING TO ESCAPE A DEMON FOR YOU, YOU ABSOLUTE COCKWOMBLE!
YOU'RE RIGHT. I'VE BEEN A PRICK. AND I'M SORRY.
HUH?
YOU'RE MY BEST MATE AND I NEED YOUR HELP.
BIT TOUCHY-FEELY THERE, JOHN.
CHAS!
I'M LISTENING.
DTDB 219

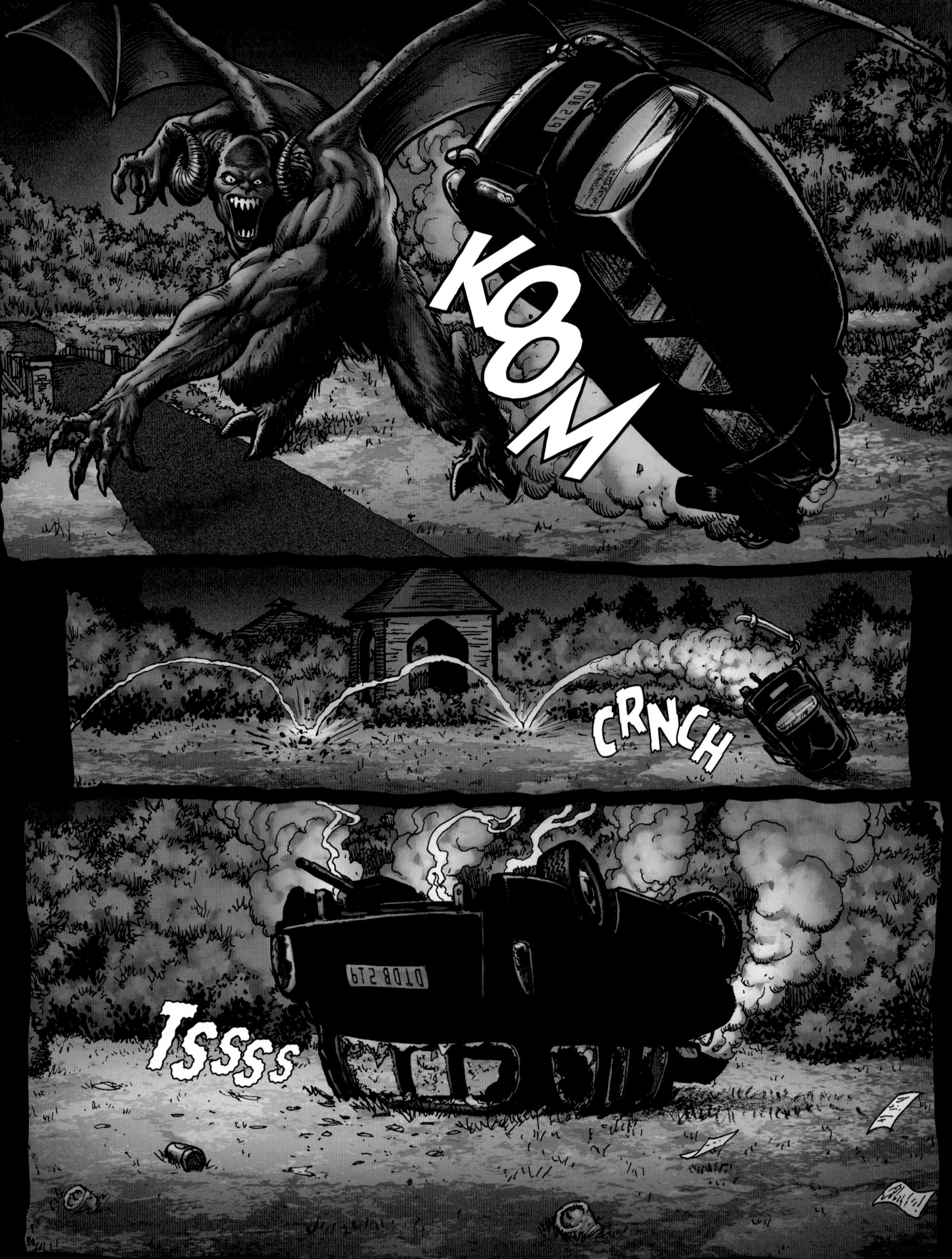
KOOM
CRNCH
TSSSS

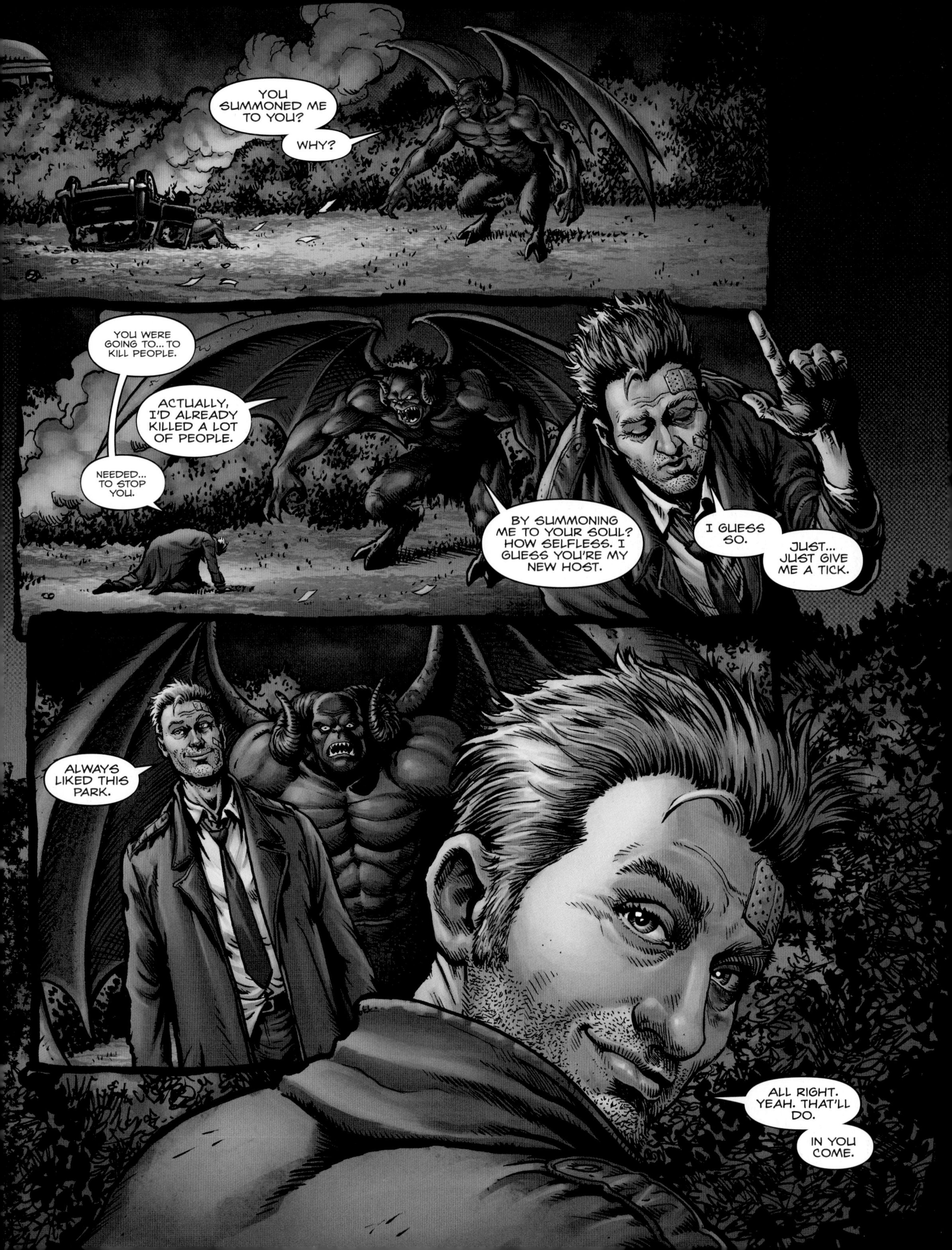

YOU SUMMONED ME TO YOU?
WHY?
YOU WERE GOING TO... TO KILL PEOPLE.
ACTUALLY, I'D ALREADY KILLED A LOT OF PEOPLE.
NEEDED... TO STOP YOU.
BY SUMMONING ME TO YOUR SOUL? HOW SELFLESS. I GUESS YOU'RE MY NEW HOST.
I GUESS SO.
JUST... JUST GIVE ME A TICK.
ALWAYS LIKED THIS PARK.
ALL RIGHT. YEAH. THAT'LL DO.
IN YOU COME.

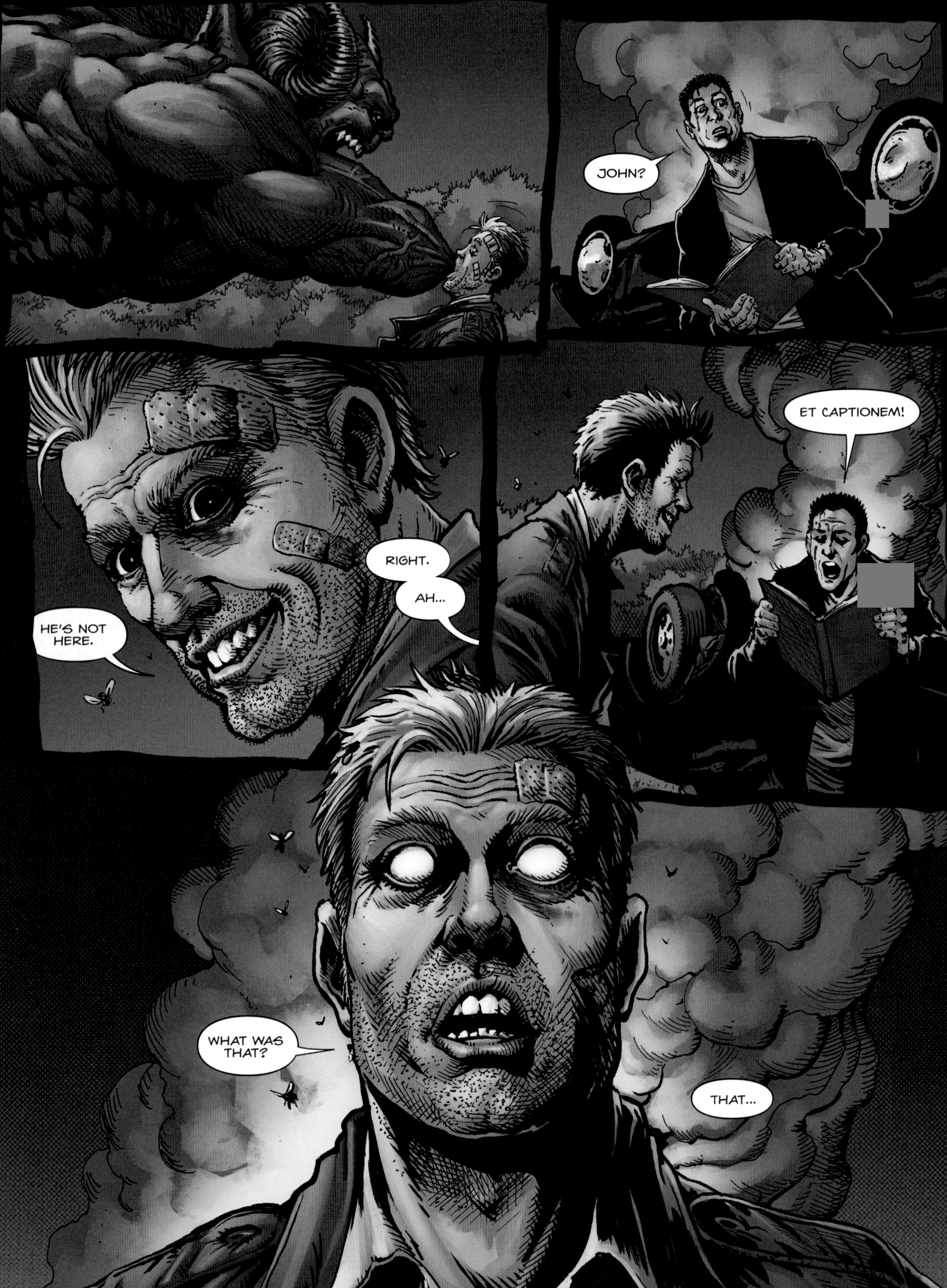
JOHN?
RIGHT.
AH...
HE'S NOT HERE.
ET CAPTIONEM!
WHAT WAS THAT?
THAT...

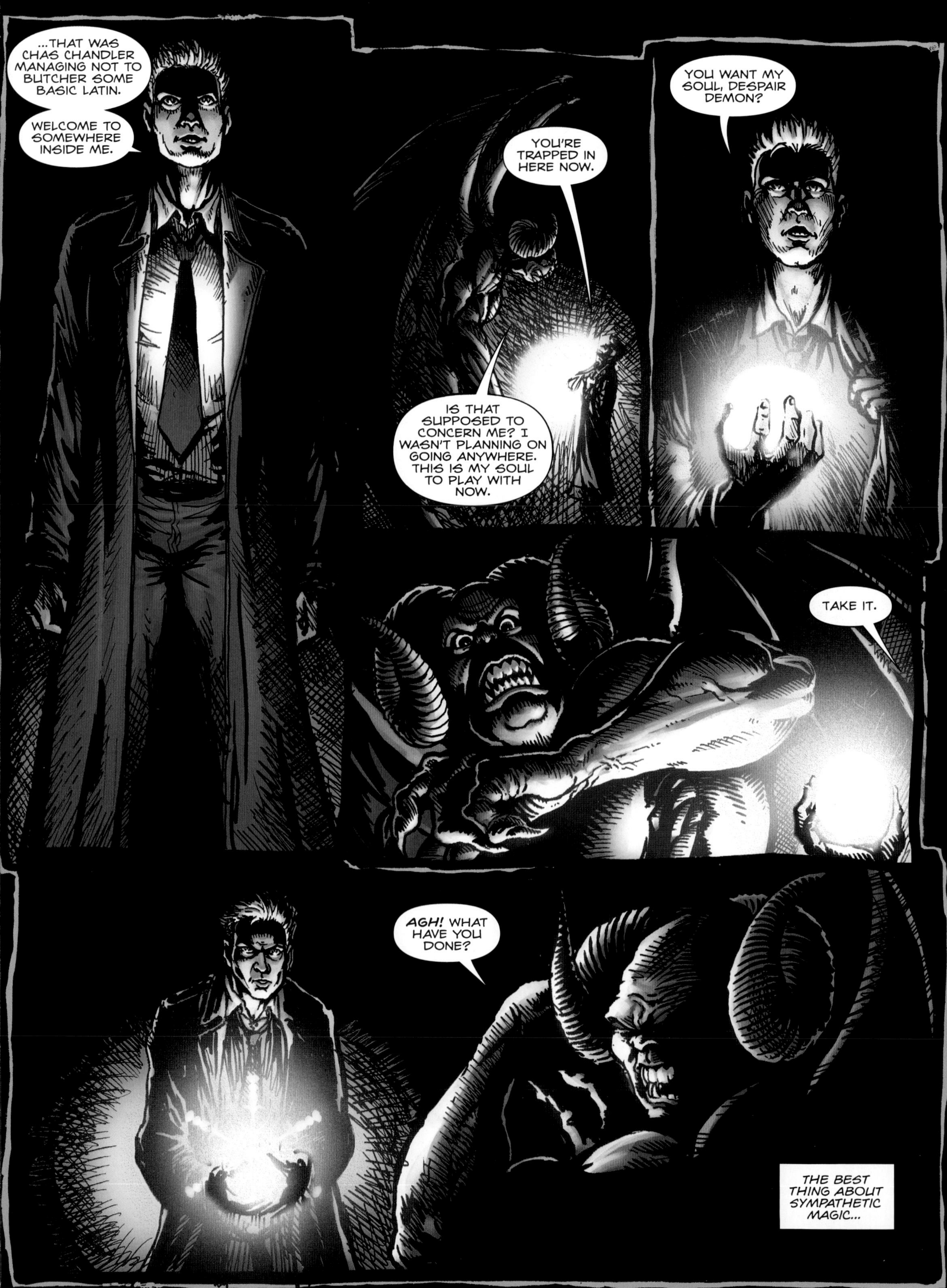
...THAT WAS CHAS CHANDLER MANAGING NOT TO BUTCHER SOME BASIC LATIN.
WELCOME TO SOMEWHERE INSIDE ME.
YOU'RE TRAPPED IN HERE NOW.
IS THAT SUPPOSED TO CONCERN ME? I WASN'T PLANNING ON GOING ANYWHERE. THIS IS MY SOUL TO PLAY WITH NOW.
YOU WANT MY SOUL, DESPAIR DEMON?
TAKE IT.
AGH! WHAT HAVE YOU DONE?
THE BEST THING ABOUT SYMPATHETIC MAGIC...

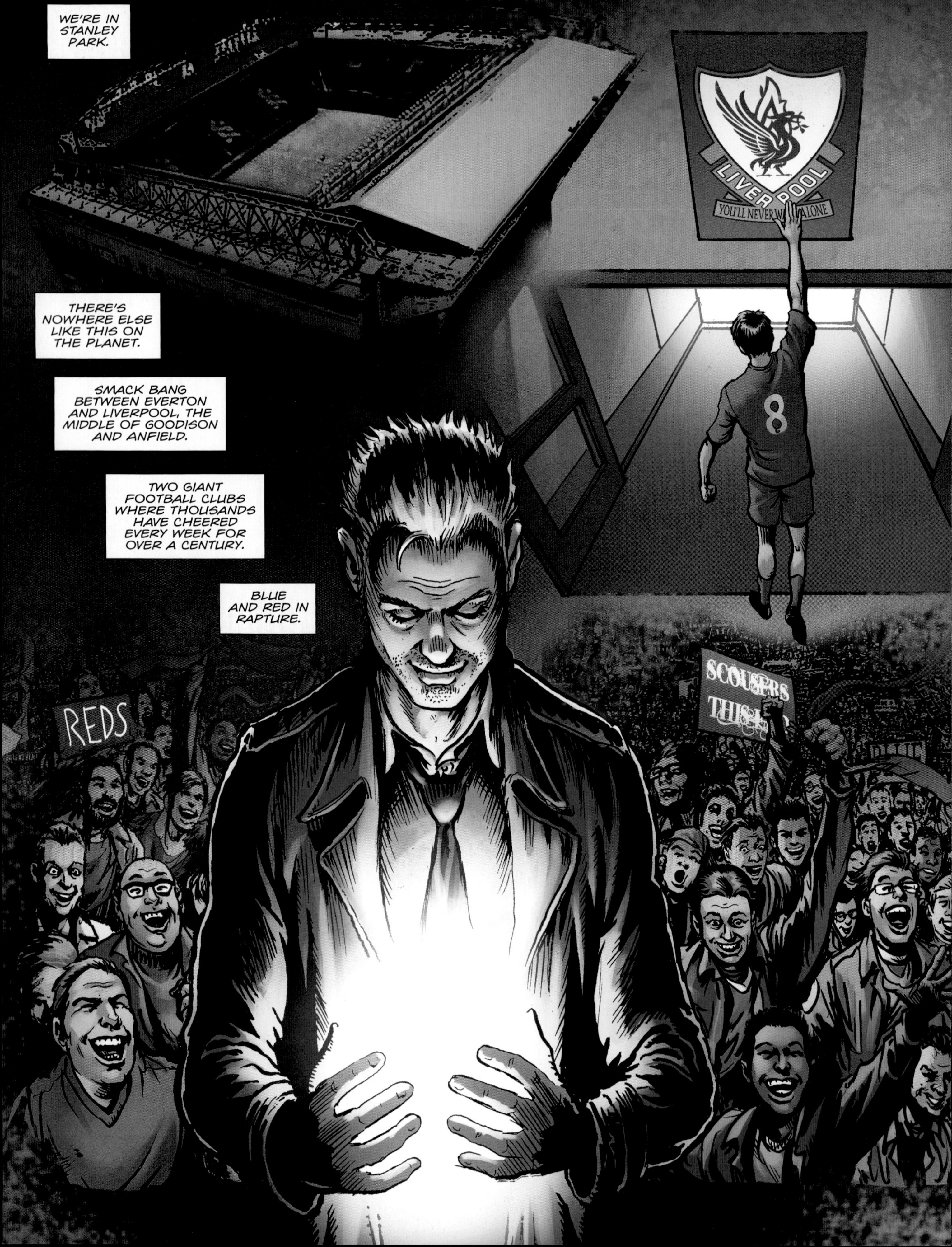
WE'RE IN STANLEY PARK.
THERE'S NOWHERE ELSE LIKE THIS ON THE PLANET.
SMACK BANG BETWEEN EVERTON AND LIVERPOOL, THE MIDDLE OF GOODISON AND ANFIELD.
TWO GIANT FOOTBALL CLUBS WHERE THOUSANDS HAVE CHEERED EVERY WEEK FOR OVER A CENTURY.
BLUE AND RED IN RAPTURE.
LIVERPOOL
8
REDS
SCOUSERS

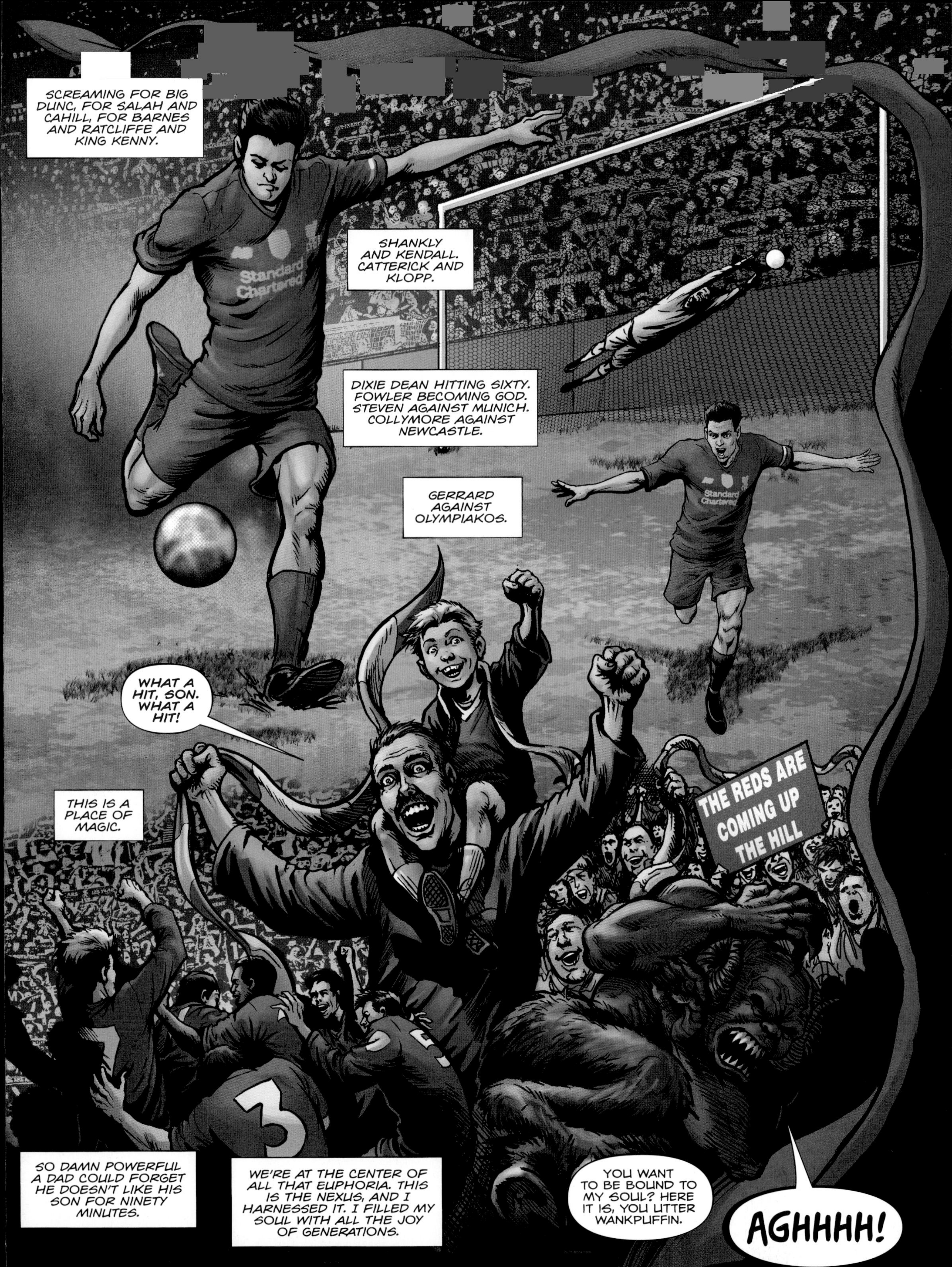
SCREAMING FOR BIG DUNC, FOR SALAH AND CAHILL, FOR BARNES AND RATCLIFFE AND KING KENNY.
SHANKLY AND KENDALL. CATTERICK AND KLOPP.
DIXIE DEAN HITTING SIXTY. FOWLER BECOMING GOD. STEVEN AGAINST MUNICH. COLLYMORE AGAINST NEWCASTLE.
GERRARD AGAINST OLYMPIAKOS.
WHAT A HIT, SON. WHAT A HIT!
THE REDS ARE COMING UP THE HILL
THIS IS A PLACE OF MAGIC.
SO DAMN POWERFUL A DAD COULD FORGET HE DOESN'T LIKE HIS SON FOR NINETY MINUTES.
WE'RE AT THE CENTER OF ALL THAT EUPHORIA. THIS IS THE NEXUS, AND I HARNESSED IT. I FILLED MY SOUL WITH ALL THE JOY OF GENERATIONS.
YOU WANT TO BE BOUND TO MY SOUL? HERE IT IS, YOU UTTER WANKPUFFIN.
AGHHHH!

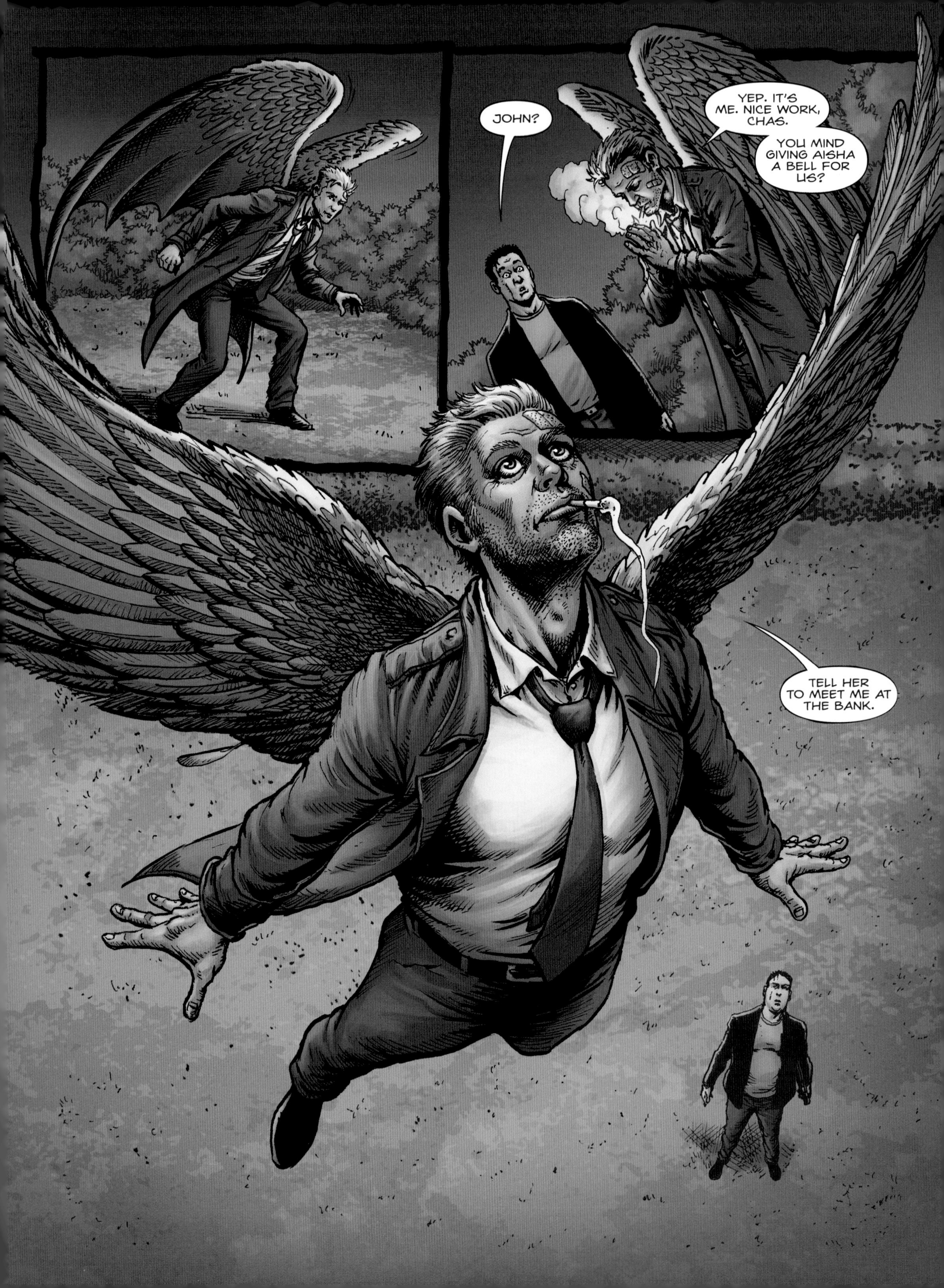
JOHN?
YEP. IT'S ME. NICE WORK, CHAS.
YOU MIND GIVING AISHA A BELL FOR US?
TELL HER TO MEET ME AT THE BANK.

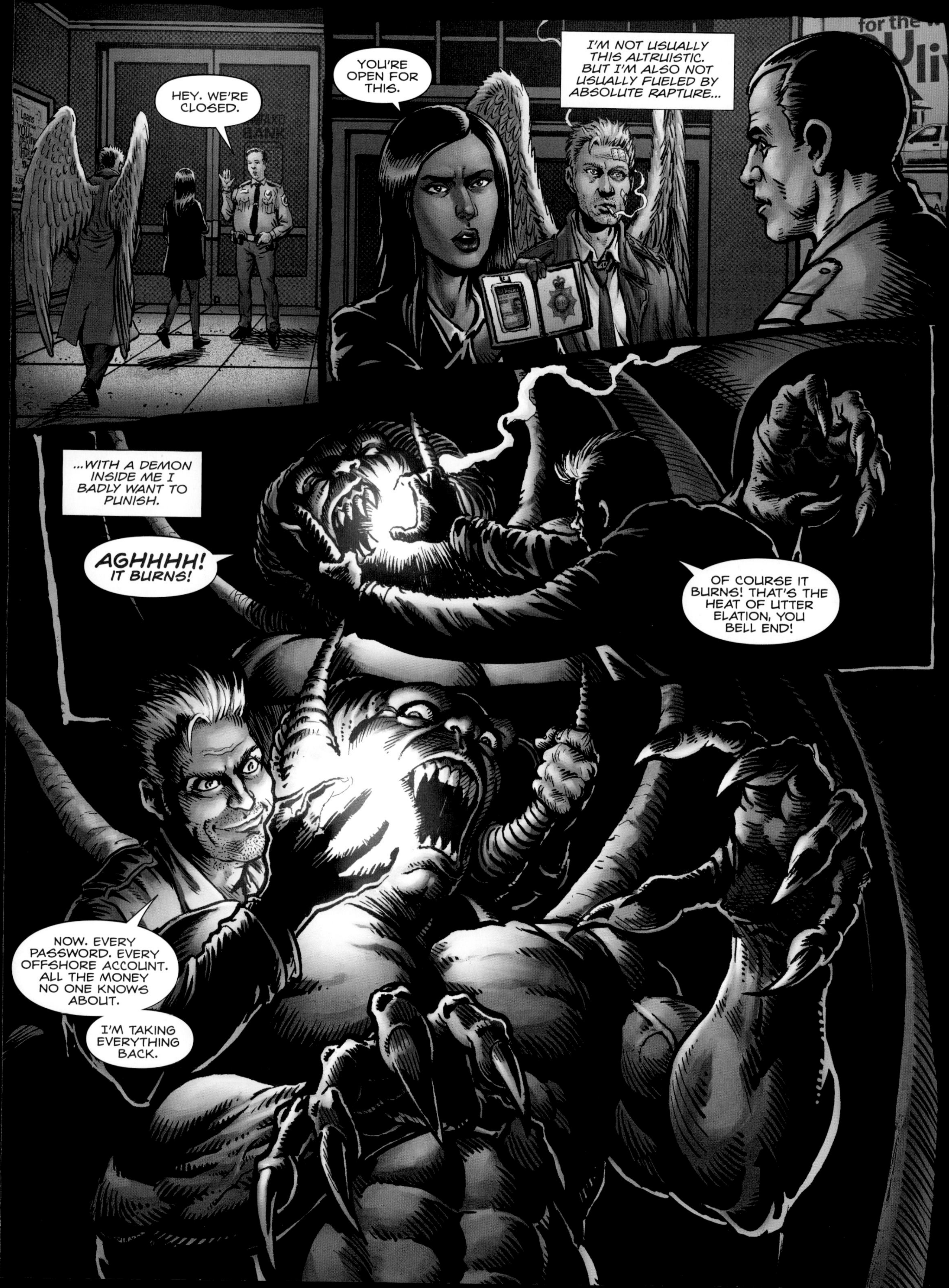
HEY. WE'RE CLOSED.
YOU'RE OPEN FOR THIS.
I'M NOT USUALLY THIS ALTRUISTIC. BUT I'M ALSO NOT USUALLY FUELED BY ABSOLUTE RAPTURE...
...WITH A DEMON INSIDE ME I BADLY WANT TO PUNISH.
AGHHHH! IT BURNS!
OF COURSE IT BURNS! THAT'S THE HEAT OF UTTER ELATION, YOU BELL END!
NOW. EVERY PASSWORD. EVERY OFFSHORE ACCOUNT. ALL THE MONEY NO ONE KNOWS ABOUT.
I'M TAKING EVERYTHING BACK.

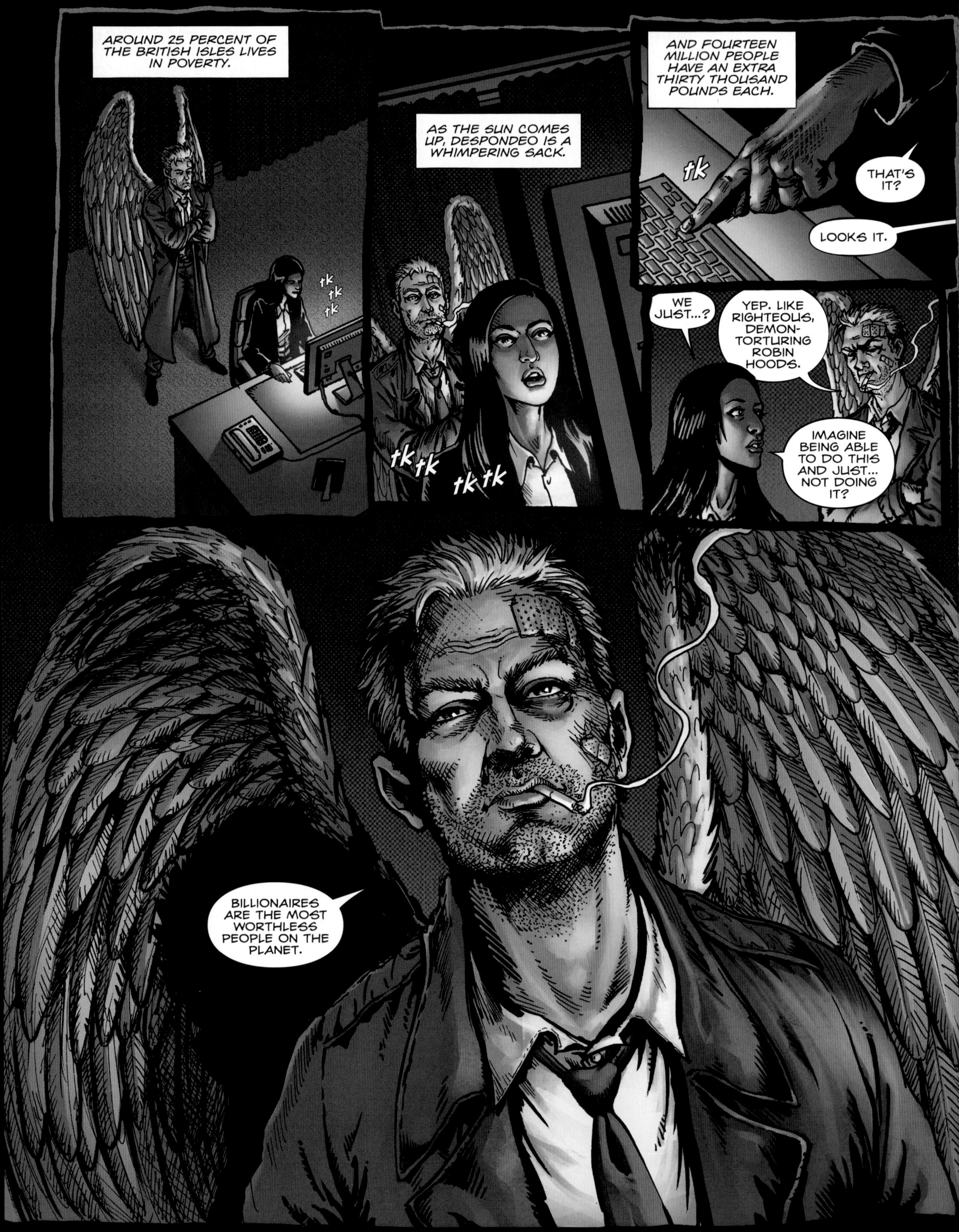
AROUND 25 PERCENT OF THE BRITISH ISLES LIVES IN POVERTY.
tk tk tk
AS THE SUN COMES UP, DESPONDEO IS A WHIMPERING SACK.
tk tk tk tk
AND FOURTEEN MILLION PEOPLE HAVE AN EXTRA THIRTY THOUSAND POUNDS EACH.
tk
THAT'S IT?
LOOKS IT.
WE JUST...?
YEP. LIKE RIGHTEOUS, DEMON-TORTURING ROBIN HOODS.
IMAGINE BEING ABLE TO DO THIS AND JUST... NOT DOING IT?
BILLIONAIRES ARE THE MOST WORTHLESS PEOPLE ON THE PLANET.

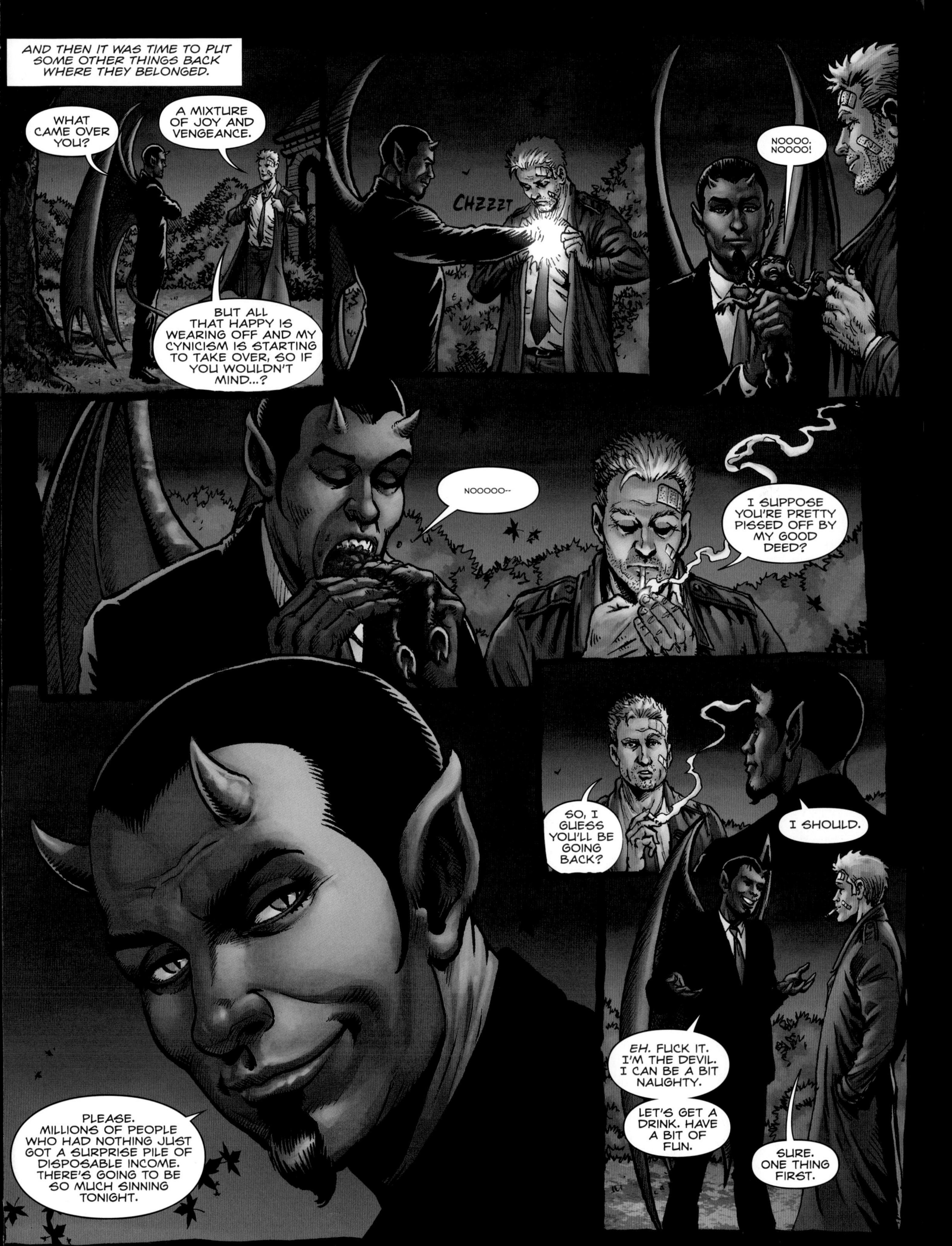
AND THEN IT WAS TIME TO PUT SOME OTHER THINGS BACK WHERE THEY BELONGED.
WHAT CAME OVER YOU?
A MIXTURE OF JOY AND VENGEANCE.
BUT ALL THAT HAPPY IS WEARING OFF AND MY CYNICISM IS STARTING TO TAKE OVER, SO IF YOU WOULDN'T MIND...?
CHZZZT
NOOOO. NOOOO!
NOOOOO--
I SUPPOSE YOU'RE PRETTY PISSED OFF BY MY GOOD DEED?
PLEASE. MILLIONS OF PEOPLE WHO HAD NOTHING JUST GOT A SURPRISE PILE OF DISPOSABLE INCOME. THERE'S GOING TO BE SO MUCH SINNING TONIGHT.
SO, I GUESS YOU'LL BE GOING BACK?
I SHOULD.
EH. FUCK IT. I'M THE DEVIL. I CAN BE A BIT NAUGHTY.
LET'S GET A DRINK. HAVE A BIT OF FUN.
SURE. ONE THING FIRST.

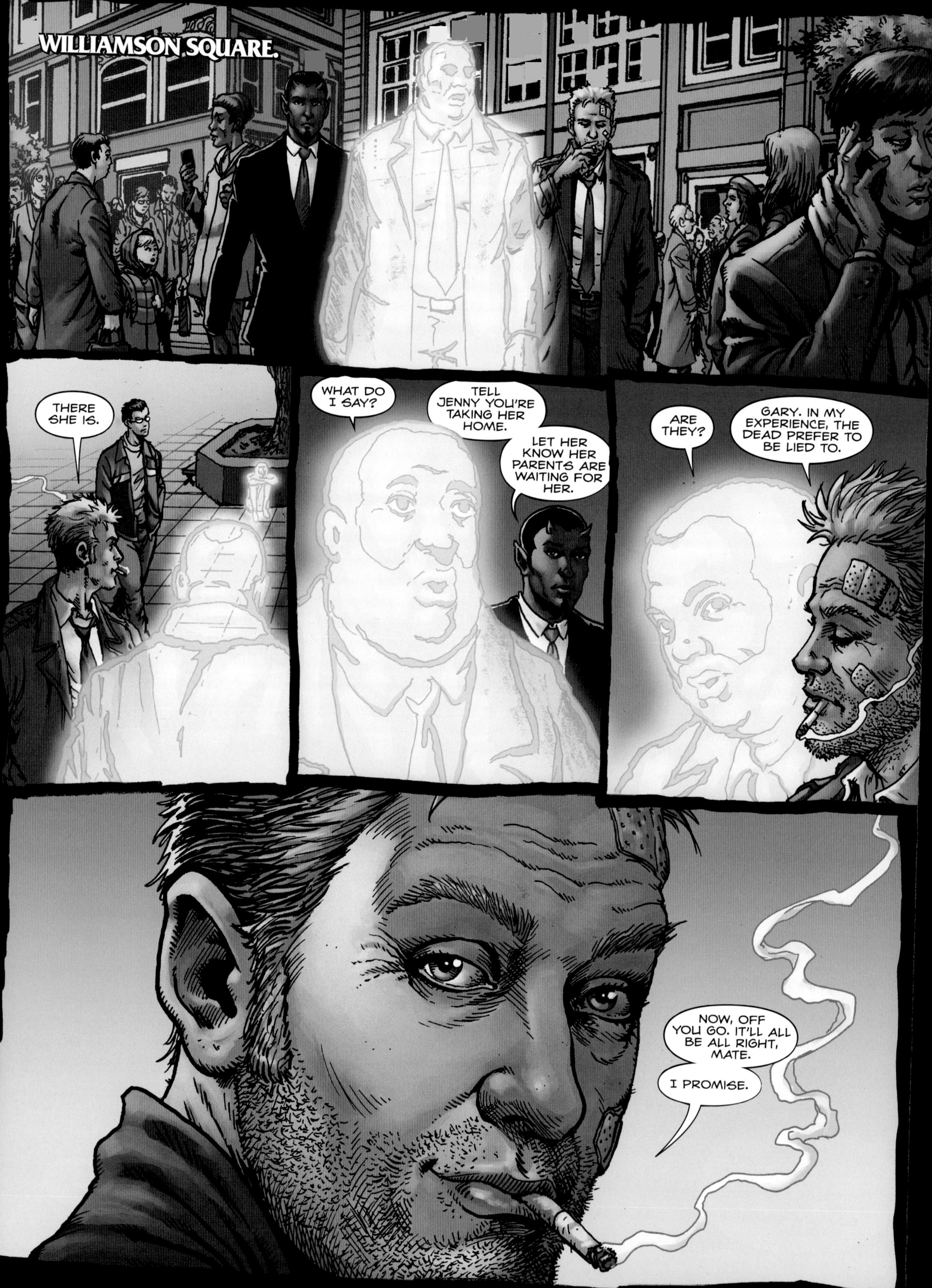
WILLIAMSON SQUARE.
THERE SHE IS.
WHAT DO I SAY?
TELL JENNY YOU'RE TAKING HER HOME.
LET HER KNOW HER PARENTS ARE WAITING FOR HER.
ARE THEY?
GARY. IN MY EXPERIENCE, THE DEAD PREFER TO BE LIED TO.
NOW, OFF YOU GO. IT'LL ALL BE ALL RIGHT, MATE.
I PROMISE.

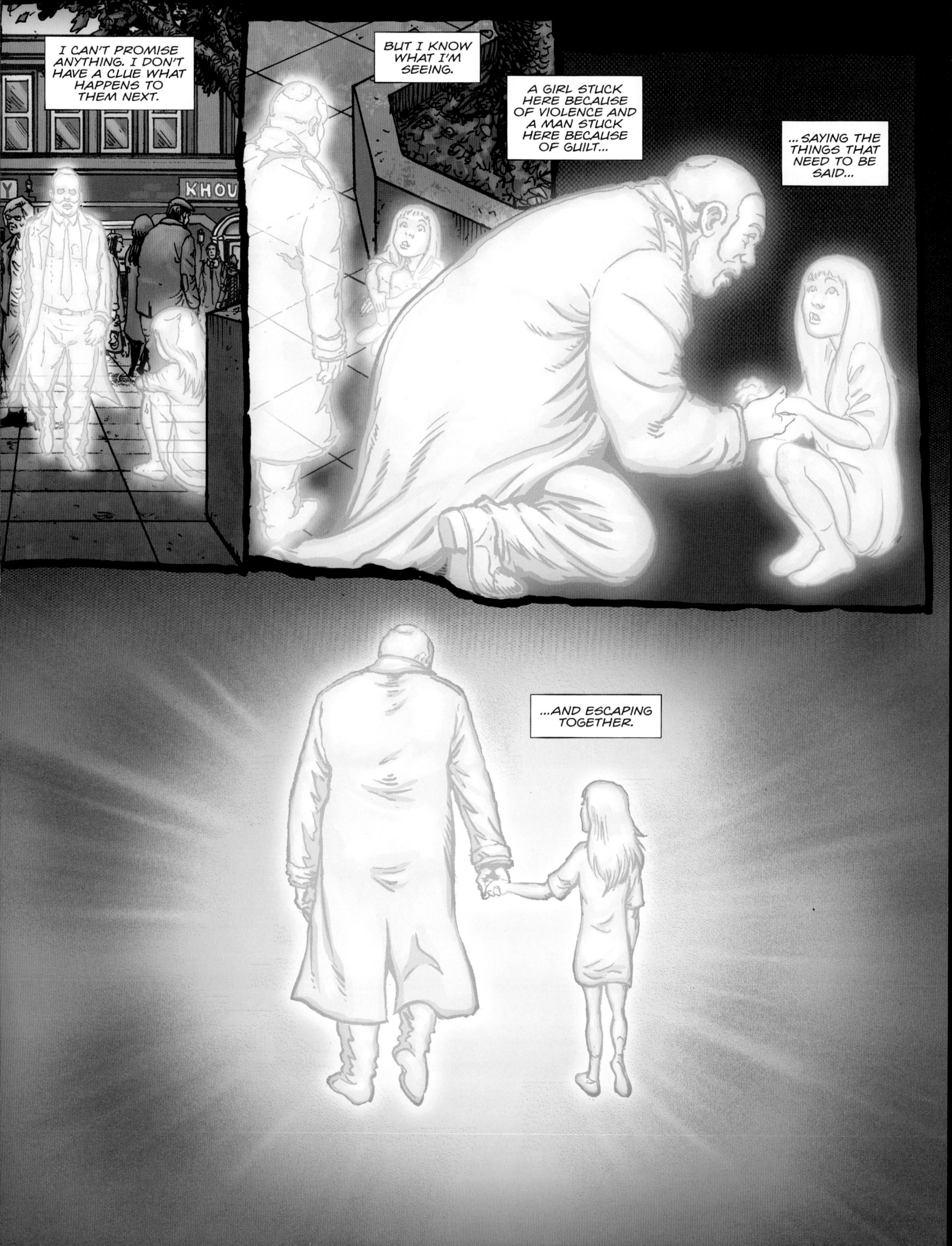
I CAN'T PROMISE ANYTHING. I DON'T HAVE A CLUE WHAT HAPPENS TO THEM NEXT.
BUT I KNOW WHAT I'M SEEING.
A GIRL STUCK HERE BECAUSE OF VIOLENCE AND A MAN STUCK HERE BECAUSE OF GUILT...
...SAYING THE THINGS THAT NEED TO BE SAID...
...AND ESCAPING TOGETHER.

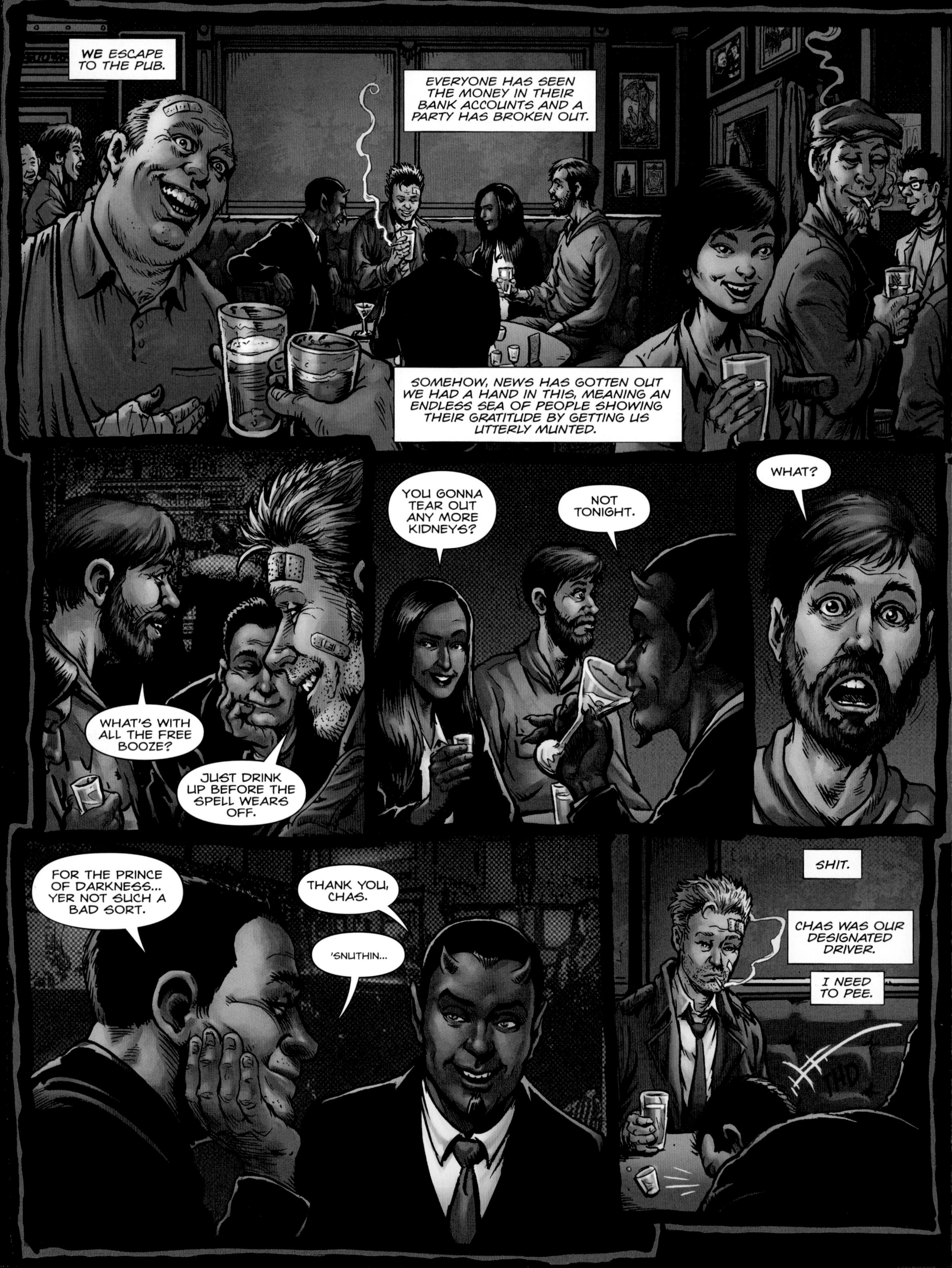
WE ESCAPE TO THE PUB.
EVERYONE HAS SEEN THE MONEY IN THEIR BANK ACCOUNTS AND A PARTY HAS BROKEN OUT.
SOMEHOW, NEWS HAS GOTTEN OUT WE HAD A HAND IN THIS, MEANING AN ENDLESS SEA OF PEOPLE SHOWING THEIR GRATITUDE BY GETTING US UTTERLY MUNTED.
WHAT'S WITH ALL THE FREE BOOZE?
JUST DRINK UP BEFORE THE SPELL WEARS OFF.
YOU GONNA TEAR OUT ANY MORE KIDNEYS?
NOT TONIGHT.
WHAT?
FOR THE PRINCE OF DARKNESS... YER NOT SUCH A BAD SORT.
THANK YOU, CHAS.
'SNUTHIN...
SHIT.
CHAS WAS OUR DESIGNATED DRIVER.
I NEED TO PEE.

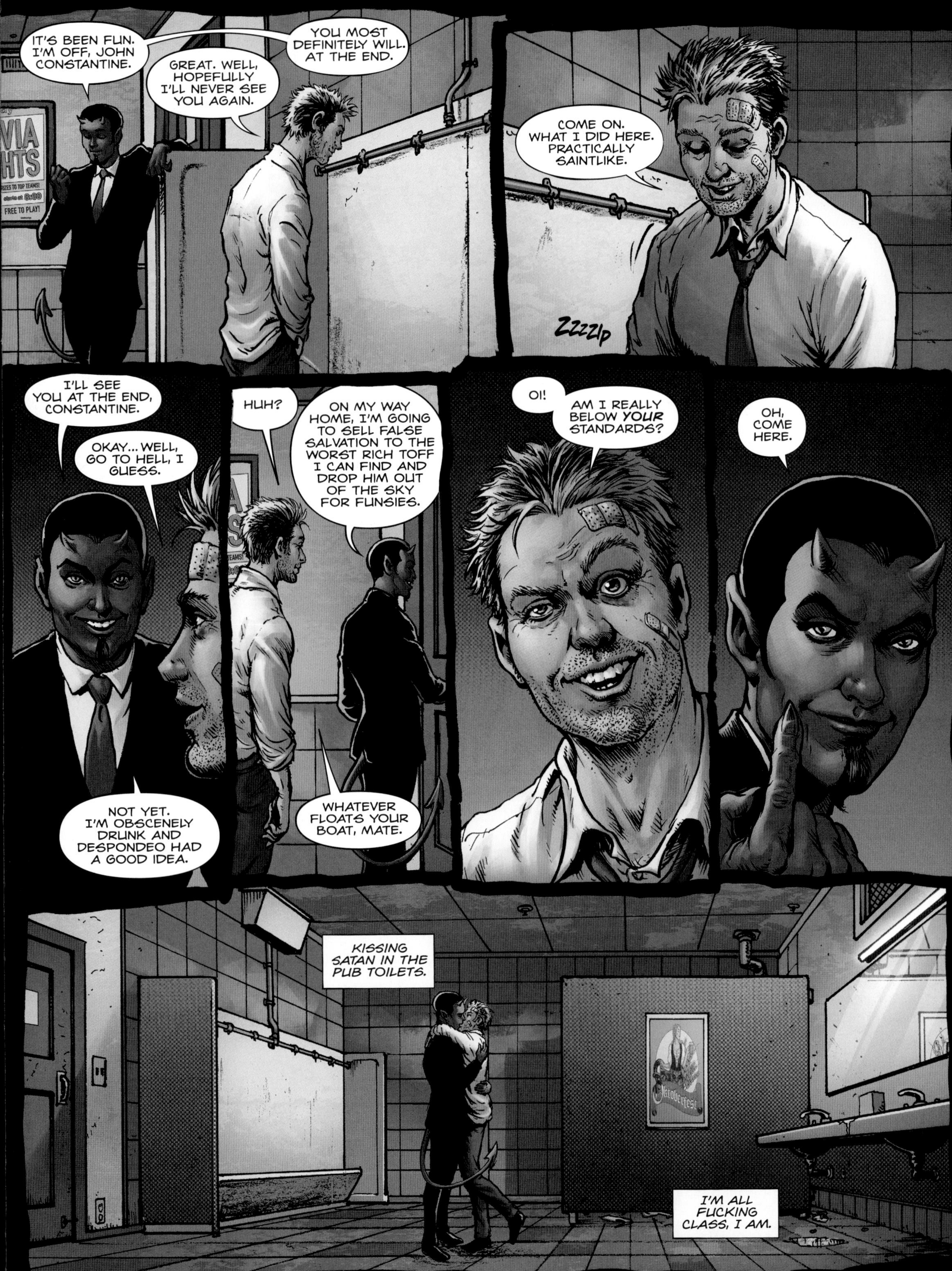
IT'S BEEN FUN. I'M OFF, JOHN CONSTANTINE.
GREAT. WELL, HOPEFULLY I'LL NEVER SEE YOU AGAIN.
YOU MOST DEFINITELY WILL. AT THE END.
COME ON. WHAT I DID HERE. PRACTICALLY SAINTLIKE.
ZZZZIP
I'LL SEE YOU AT THE END, CONSTANTINE.
OKAY... WELL, GO TO HELL, I GUESS.
NOT YET. I'M OBSCENELY DRUNK AND DESPONDEO HAD A GOOD IDEA.
HUH?
ON MY WAY HOME, I'M GOING TO SELL FALSE SALVATION TO THE WORST RICH TOFF I CAN FIND AND DROP HIM OUT OF THE SKY FOR FUNSIES.
WHATEVER FLOATS YOUR BOAT, MATE.
OI!
AM I REALLY BELOW YOUR STANDARDS?
OH, COME HERE.
KISSING SATAN IN THE PUB TOILETS.
I'M ALL FUCKING CLASS, I AM.

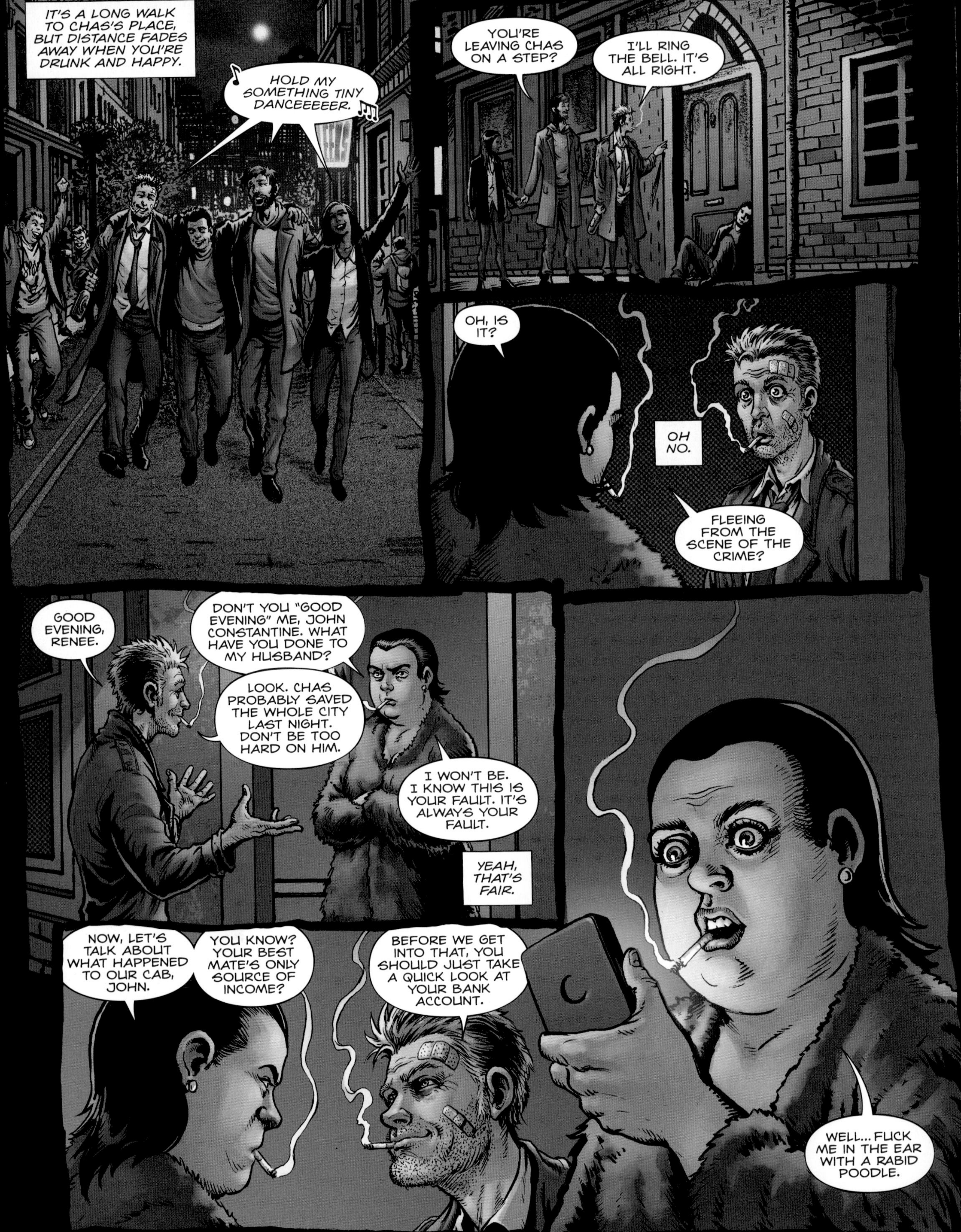
IT'S A LONG WALK TO CHAS'S PLACE, BUT DISTANCE FADES AWAY WHEN YOU'RE DRUNK AND HAPPY.
HOLD MY SOMETHING TINY DANCEEEEEER.
YOU'RE LEAVING CHAS ON A STEP?
I'LL RING THE BELL. IT'S ALL RIGHT.
OH, IS IT?
OH NO.
FLEEING FROM THE SCENE OF THE CRIME?
GOOD EVENING, RENEE.
DON'T YOU "GOOD EVENING" ME, JOHN CONSTANTINE. WHAT HAVE YOU DONE TO MY HUSBAND?
LOOK. CHAS PROBABLY SAVED THE WHOLE CITY LAST NIGHT. DON'T BE TOO HARD ON HIM.
I WON'T BE. I KNOW THIS IS YOUR FAULT. IT'S ALWAYS YOUR FAULT.
YEAH, THAT'S FAIR.
NOW, LET'S TALK ABOUT WHAT HAPPENED TO OUR CAB, JOHN.
YOU KNOW? YOUR BEST MATE'S ONLY SOURCE OF INCOME?
BEFORE WE GET INTO THAT, YOU SHOULD JUST TAKE A QUICK LOOK AT YOUR BANK ACCOUNT.
WELL... FUCK ME IN THE EAR WITH A RABID POODLE.

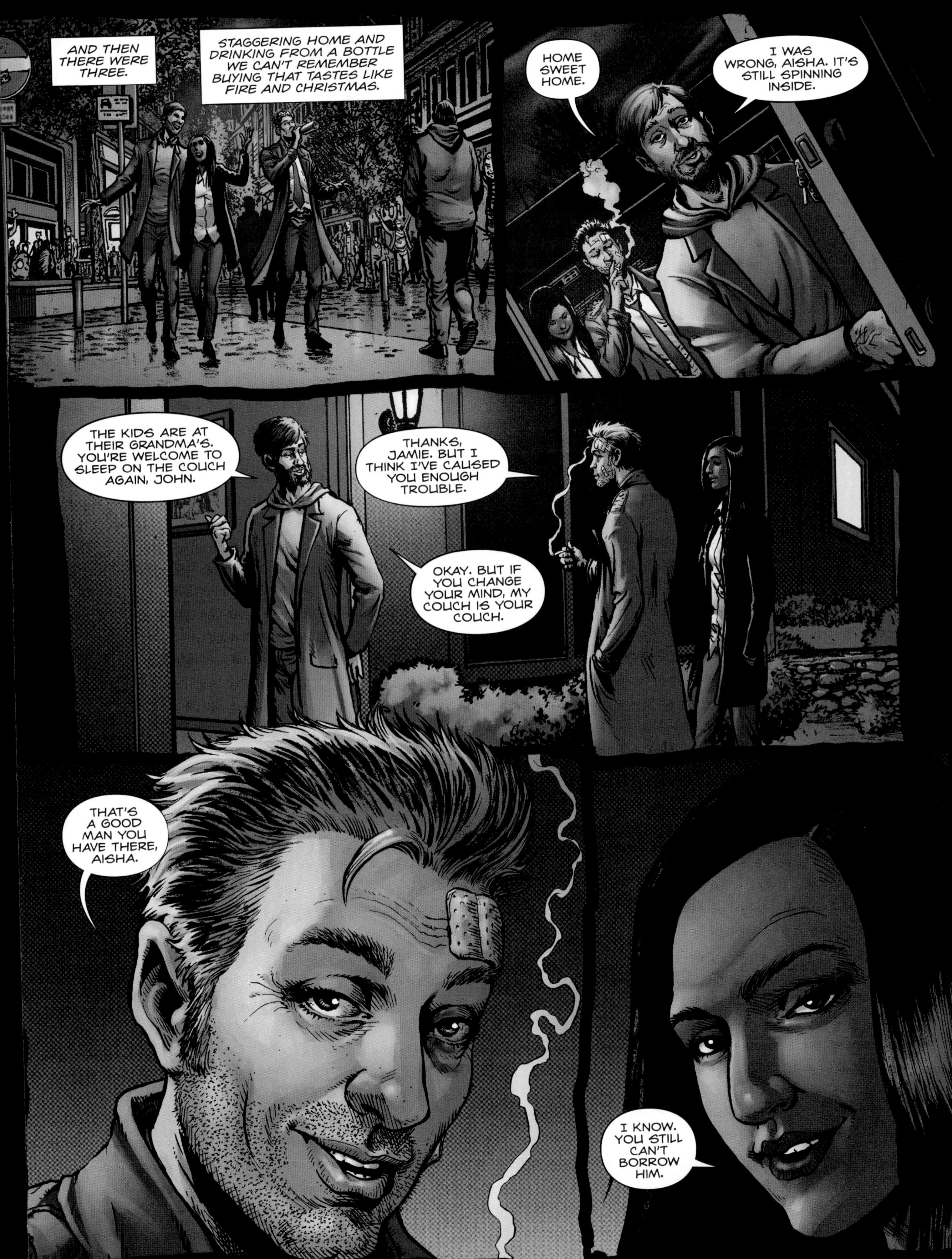
AND THEN THERE WERE THREE.
STAGGERING HOME AND DRINKING FROM A BOTTLE WE CAN'T REMEMBER BUYING THAT TASTES LIKE FIRE AND CHRISTMAS.
HOME SWEET HOME.
I WAS WRONG, AISHA. IT'S STILL SPINNING INSIDE.
THE KIDS ARE AT THEIR GRANDMA'S. YOU'RE WELCOME TO SLEEP ON THE COUCH AGAIN, JOHN.
THANKS, JAMIE. BUT I THINK I'VE CAUSED YOU ENOUGH TROUBLE.
OKAY. BUT IF YOU CHANGE YOUR MIND, MY COUCH IS YOUR COUCH.
THAT'S A GOOD MAN YOU HAVE THERE, AISHA.
I KNOW. YOU STILL CAN'T BORROW HIM.

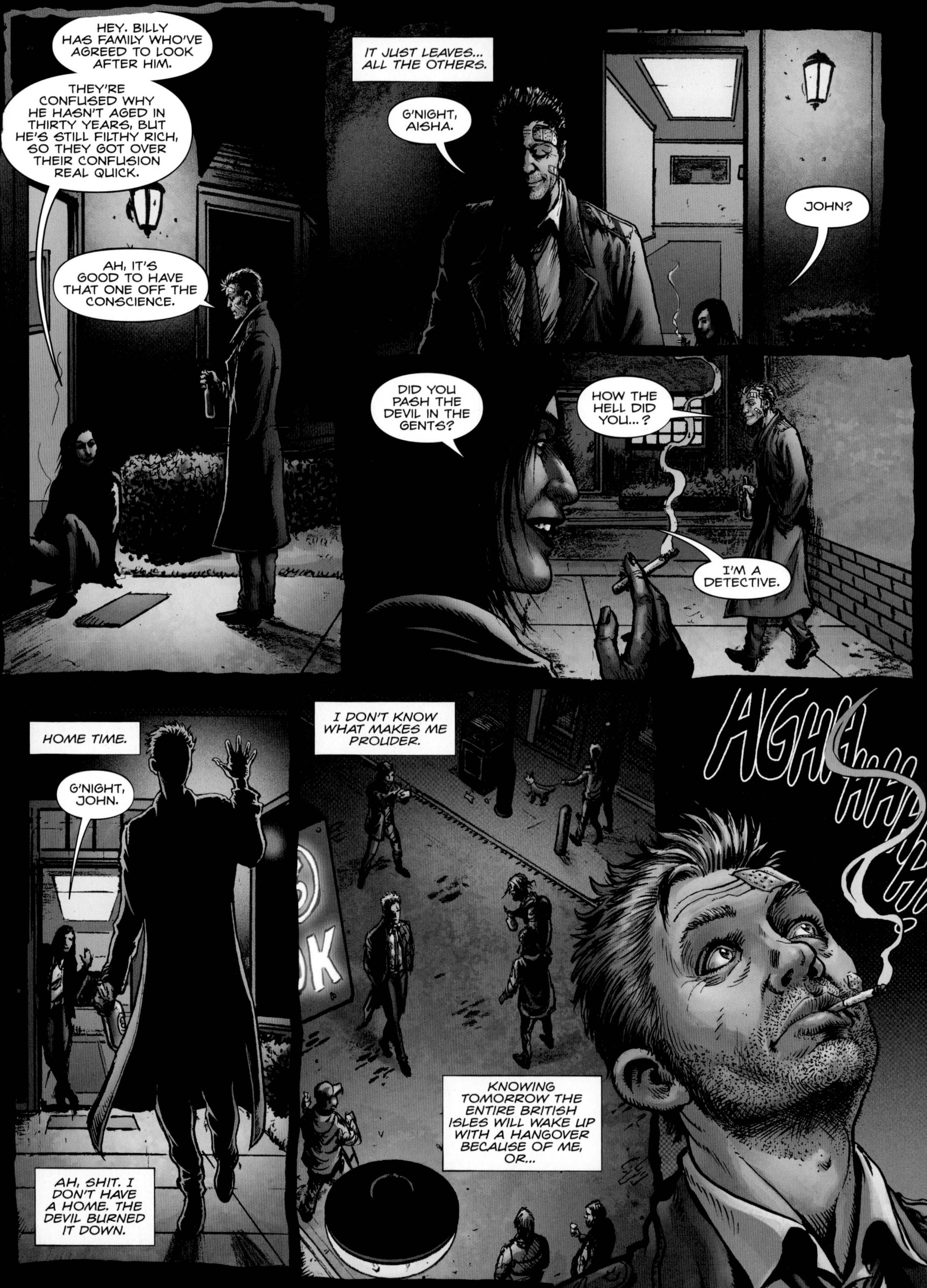
HEY. BILLY HAS FAMILY WHO'VE AGREED TO LOOK AFTER HIM.
THEY'RE CONFUSED WHY HE HASN'T AGED IN THIRTY YEARS, BUT HE'S STILL FILTHY RICH, SO THEY GOT OVER THEIR CONFUSION REAL QUICK.
AH, IT'S GOOD TO HAVE THAT ONE OFF THE CONSCIENCE.
IT JUST LEAVES... ALL THE OTHERS.
G'NIGHT, AISHA.
JOHN?
DID YOU PASH THE DEVIL IN THE GENTS?
HOW THE HELL DID YOU...?
I'M A DETECTIVE.
HOME TIME.
G'NIGHT, JOHN.
AH, SHIT. I DON'T HAVE A HOME. THE DEVIL BURNED IT DOWN.
I DON'T KNOW WHAT MAKES ME PROUDER.
KNOWING TOMORROW THE ENTIRE BRITISH ISLES WILL WAKE UP WITH A HANGOVER BECAUSE OF ME, OR...
AGHHHHH

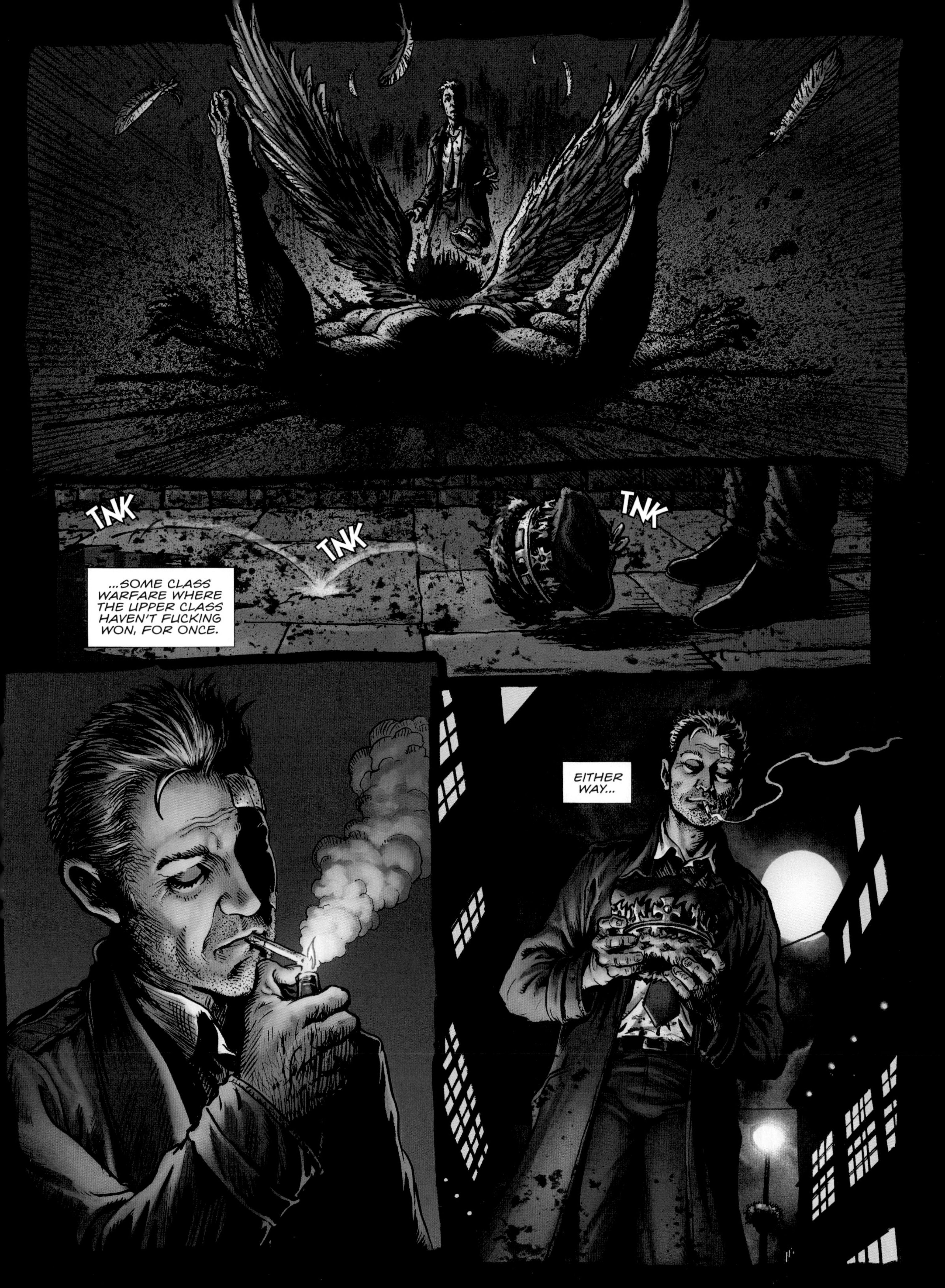
TNK
TNK
TNK
...SOME CLASS WARFARE WHERE THE UPPER CLASS HAVEN'T FUCKING WON, FOR ONCE.
EITHER WAY...

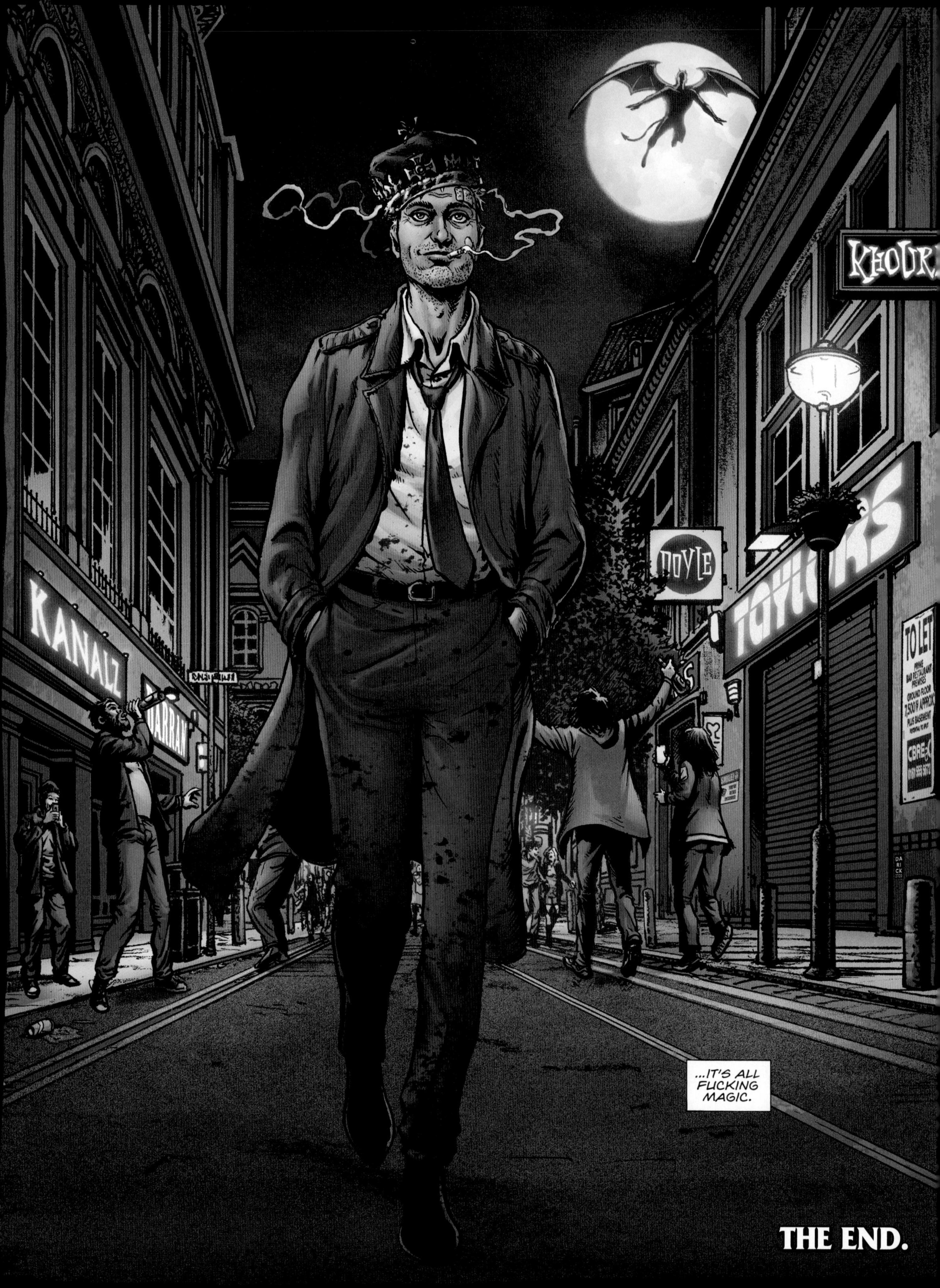
KANALZ
DOYLE
TO LET
...IT'S ALL FUCKING MAGIC.
THE END.

variant cover gallery

Hellblazer: Rise and Fall #1 variant cover by **LEE BERMEJO**

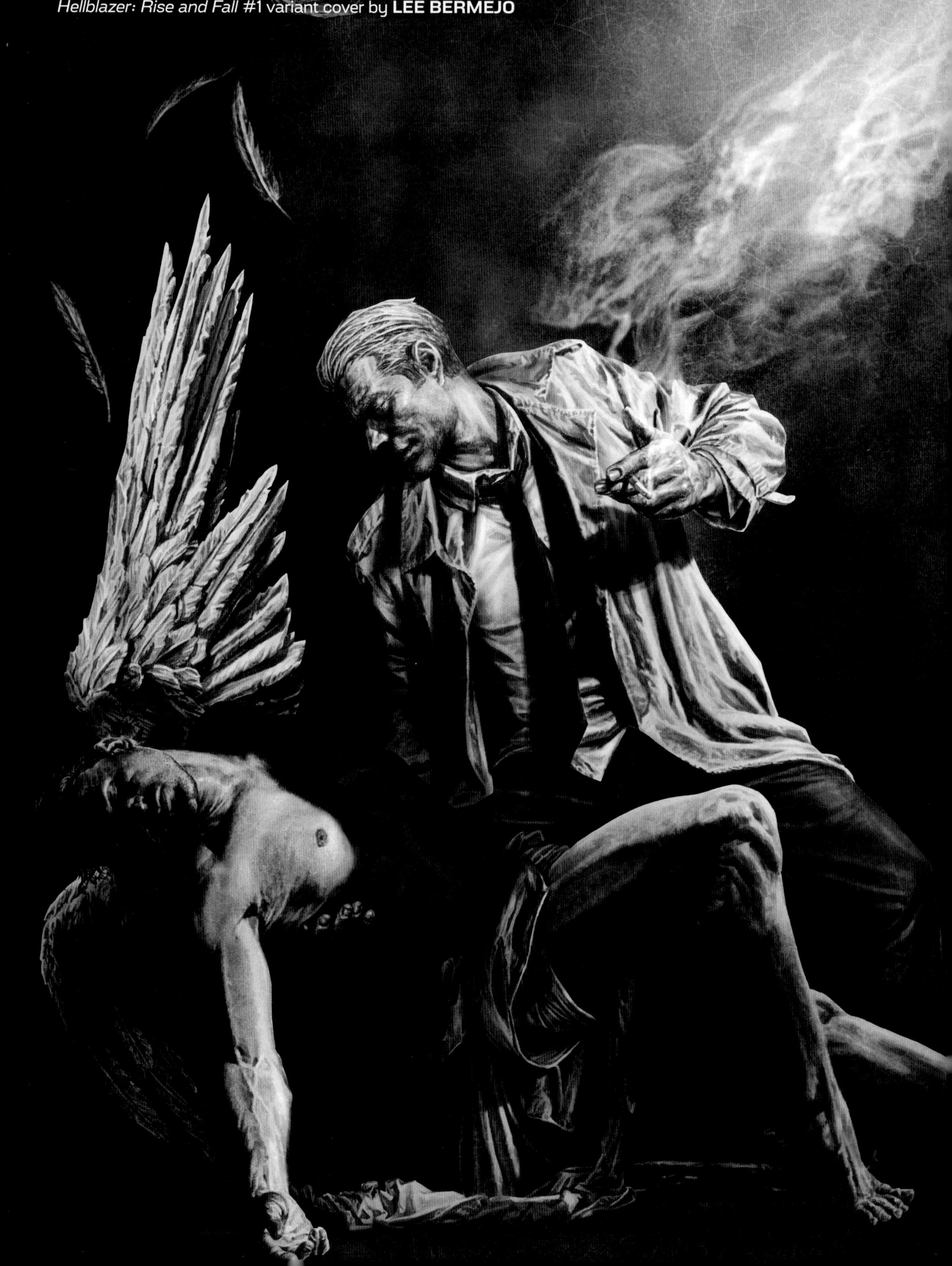

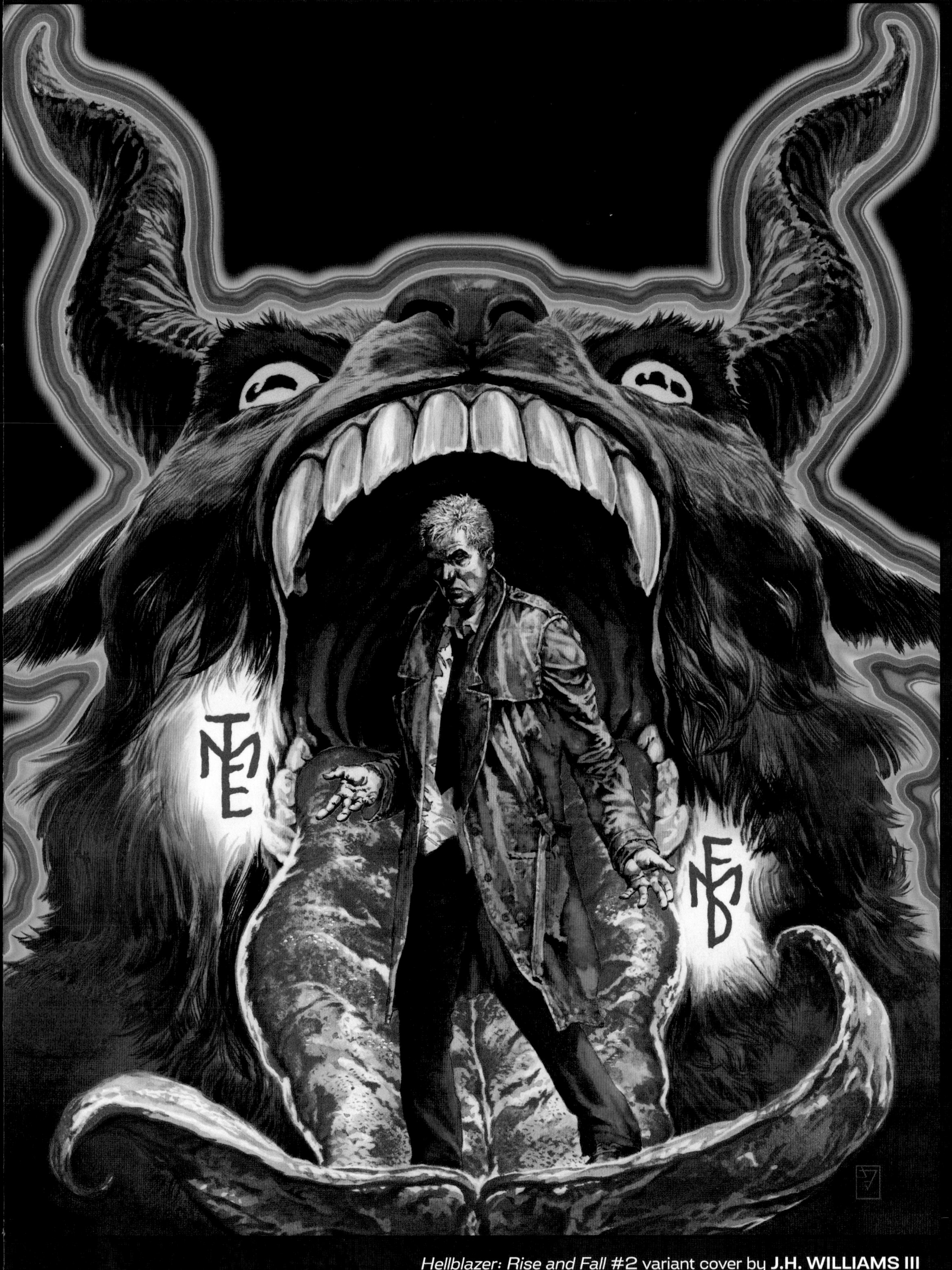

Hellblazer: Rise and Fall #2 variant cover by **J.H. WILLIAMS III**

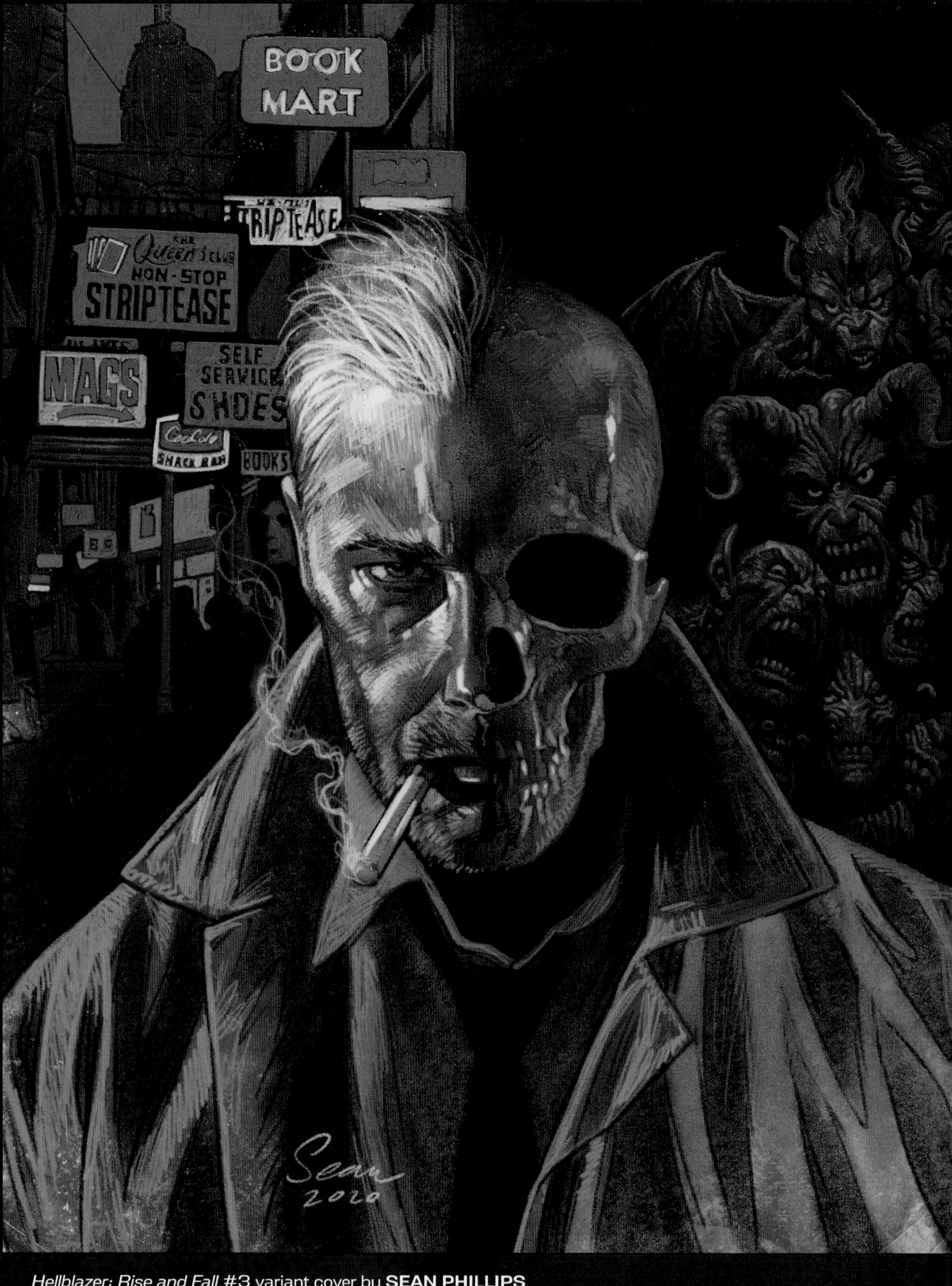
BOOK MART
STRIPTEASE
NON-STOP
STRIPTEASE
MAGS
SELF SERVICE
SHOES
BOOKS
Sean
2020

Hellblazer: Rise and Fall #3 variant cover by **SEAN PHILLIPS**

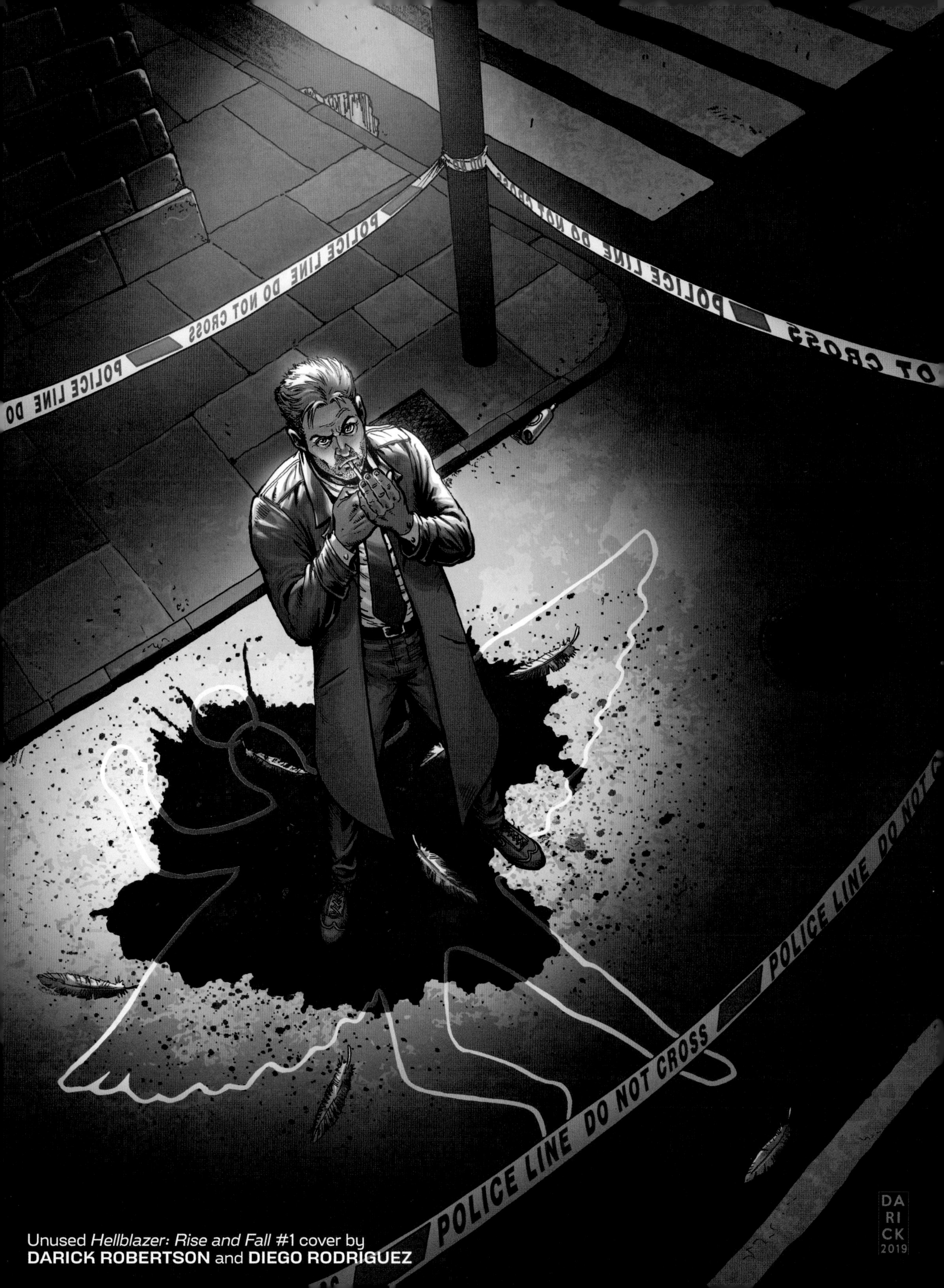
POLICE LINE DO NOT CROSS
POLICE LINE DO NOT CROSS
POLICE LINE DO NOT CROSS
DA
RI
CK
2019

Unused *Hellblazer: Rise and Fall* #1 cover by
DARICK ROBERTSON and **DIEGO RODRIGUEZ**

Unused *Hellblazer: Rise and Fall* #3 cover
line art by **DARICK ROBERTSON**

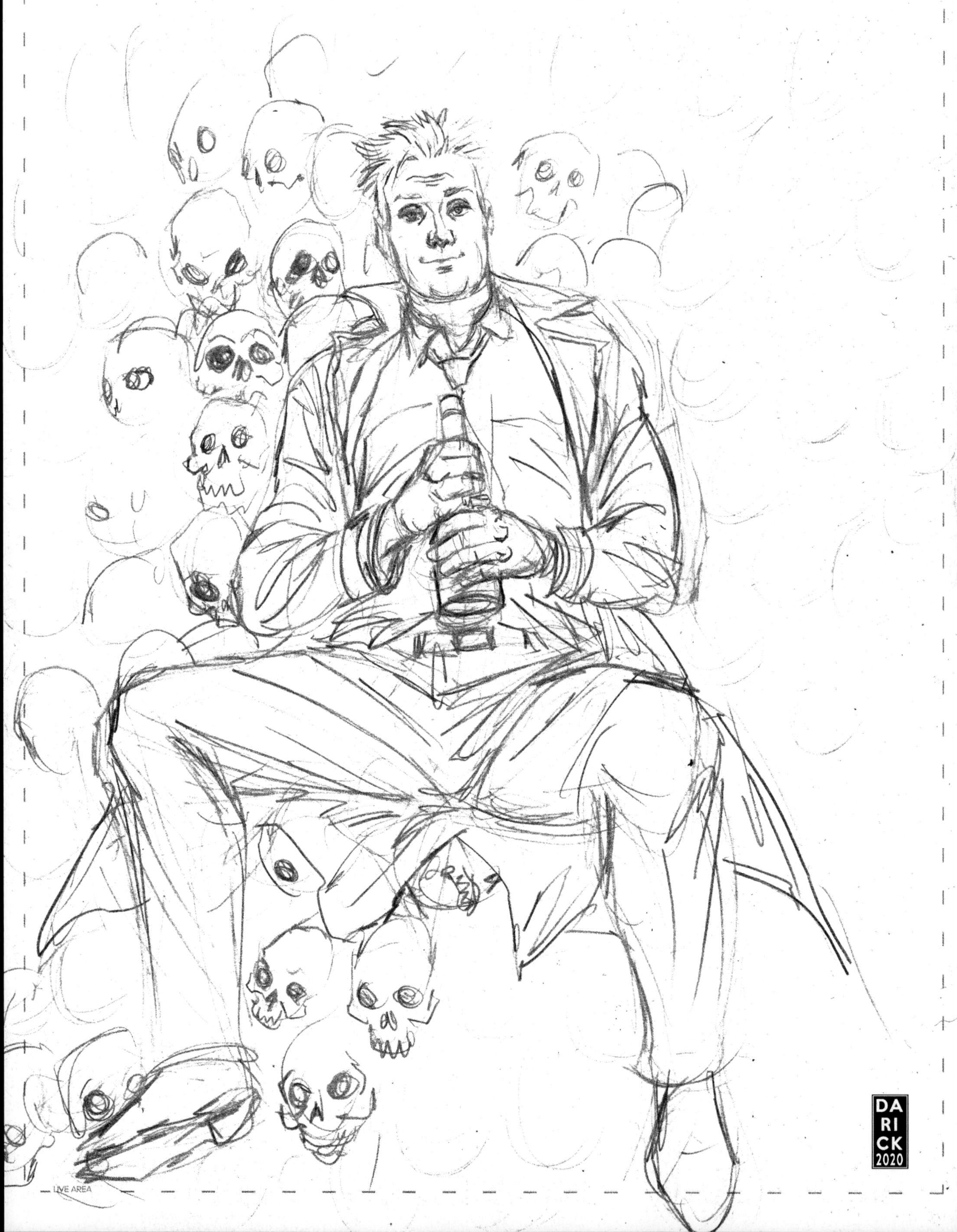

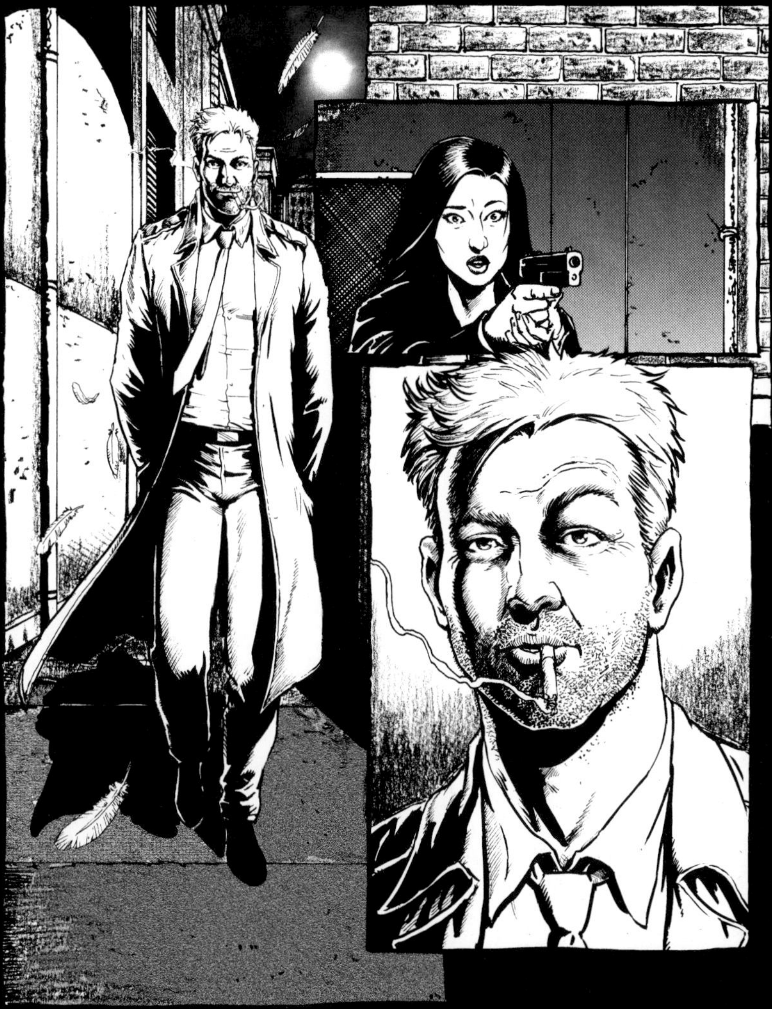

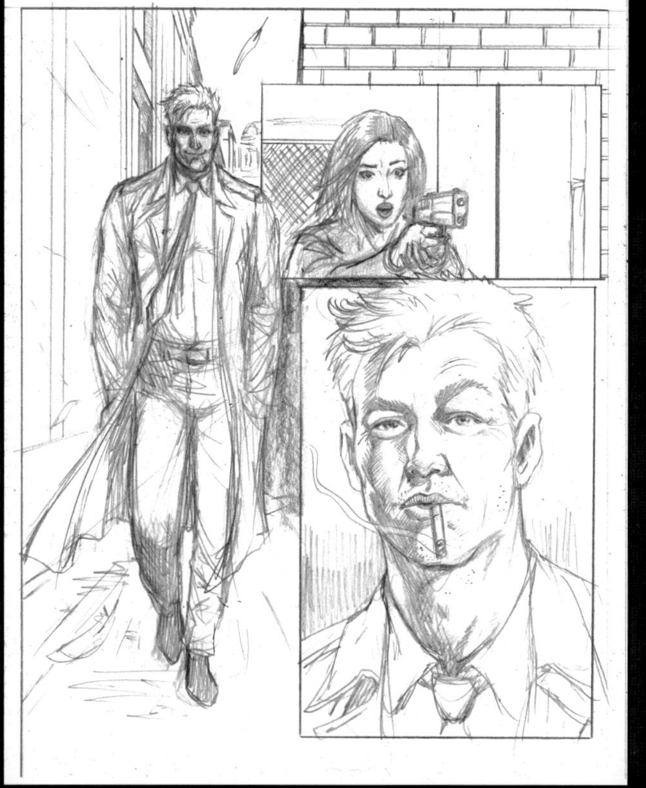

Under the skin...
of *Hellblazer: Rise and Fall!*

A look behind the scenes
with Darick Robertson

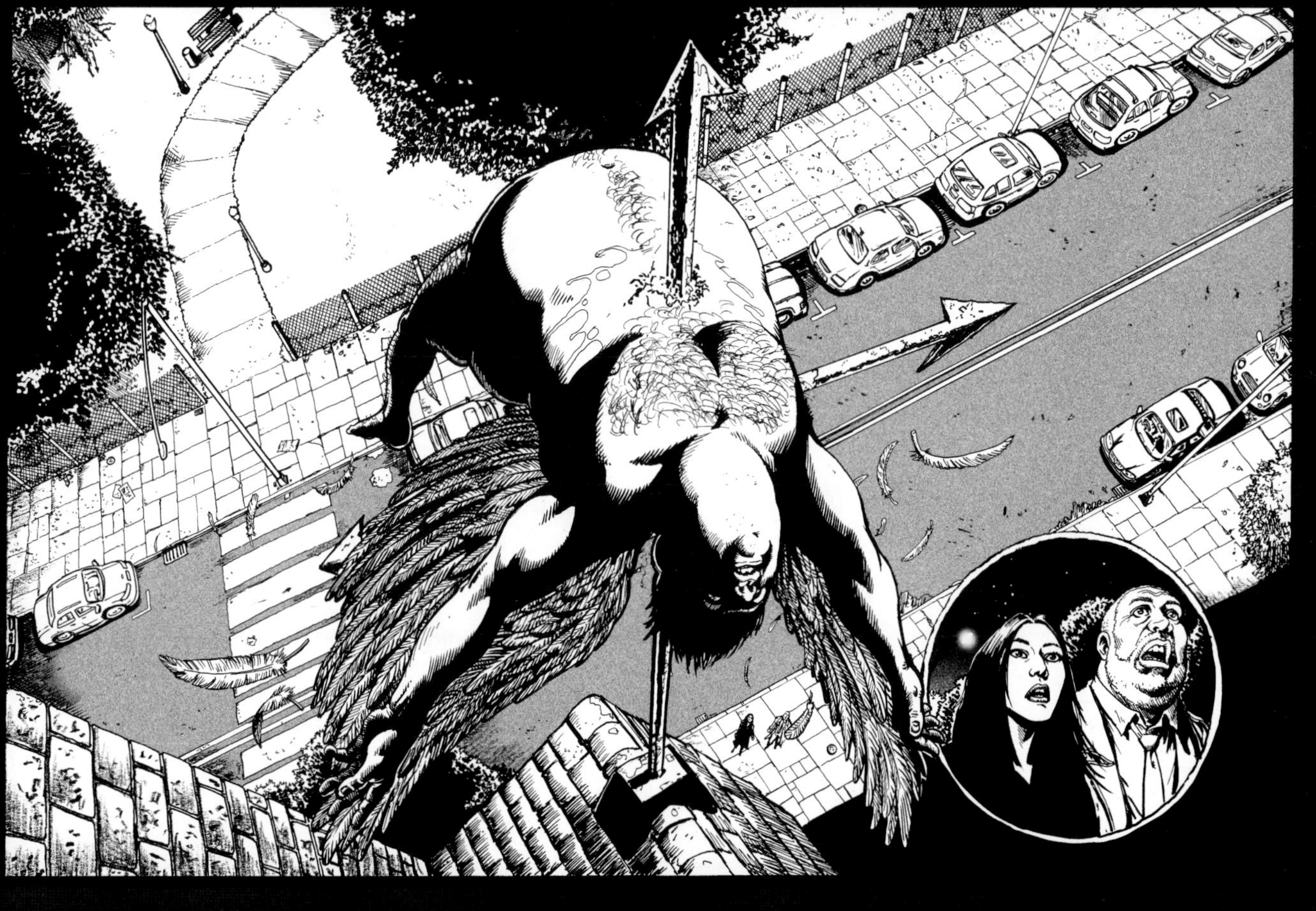

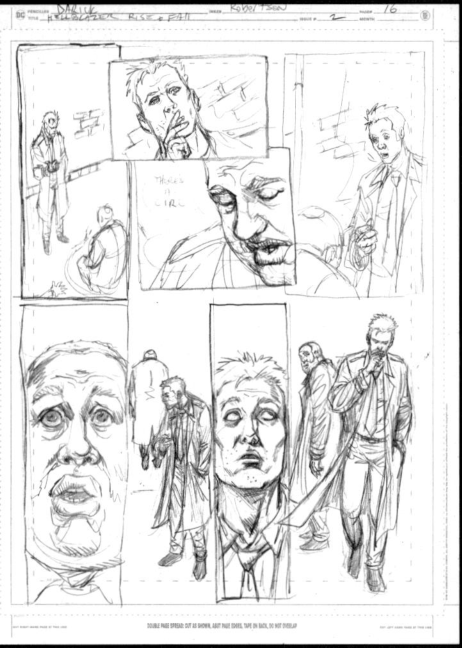
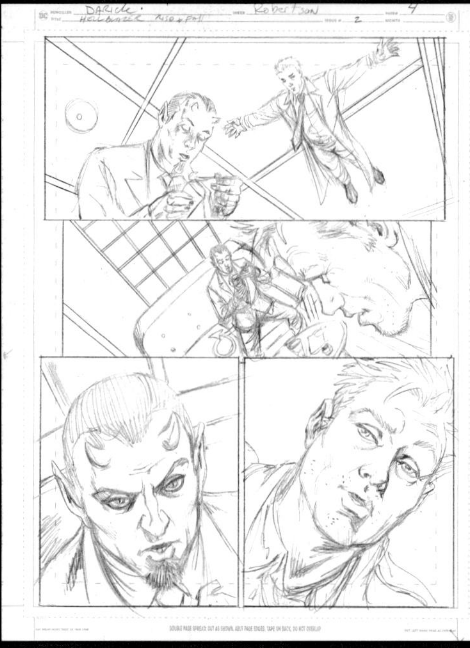
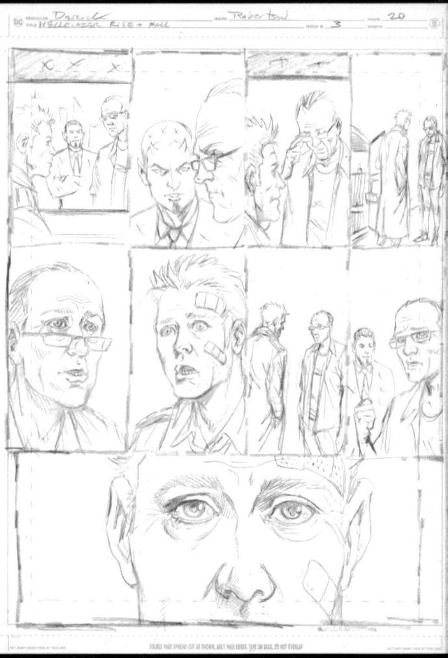
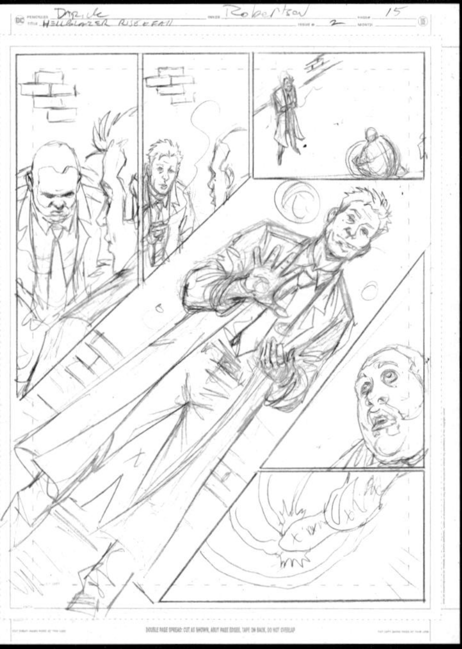
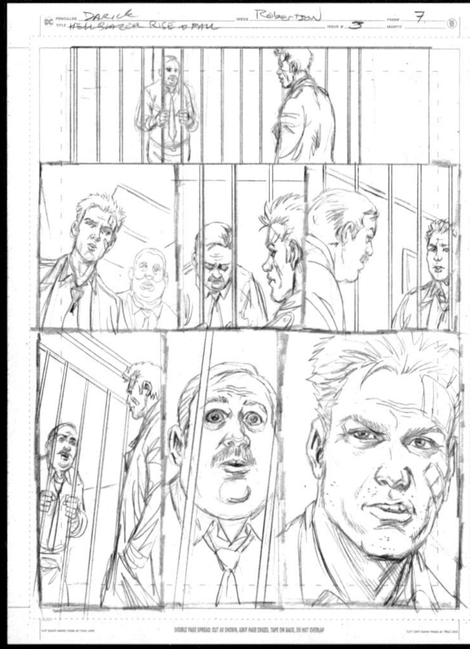
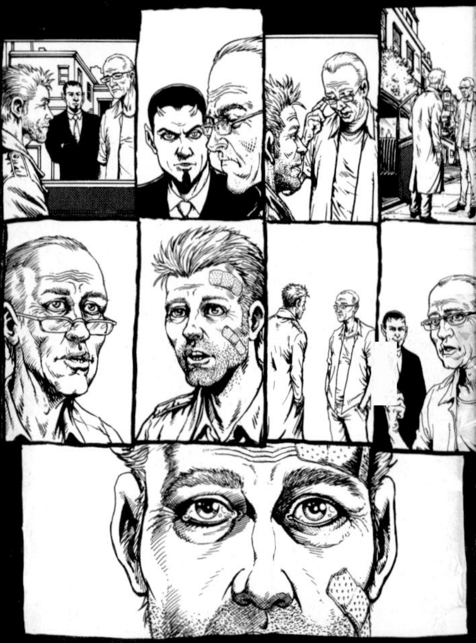
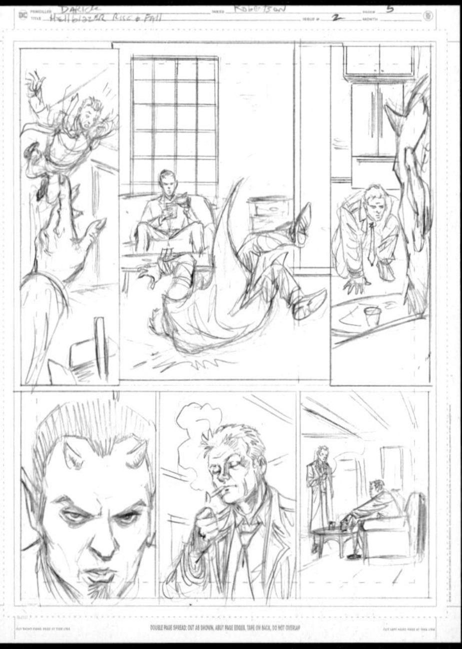
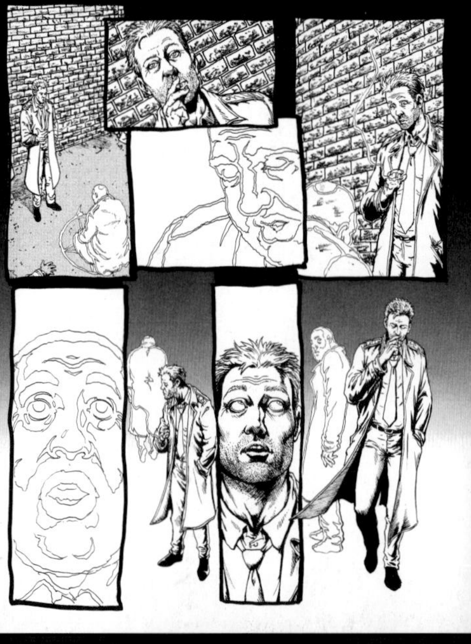
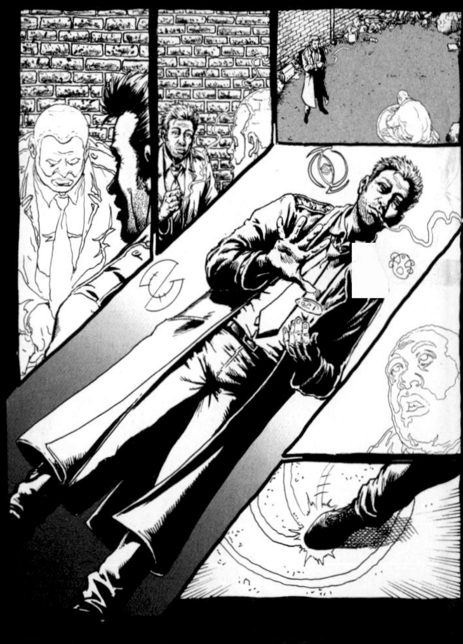

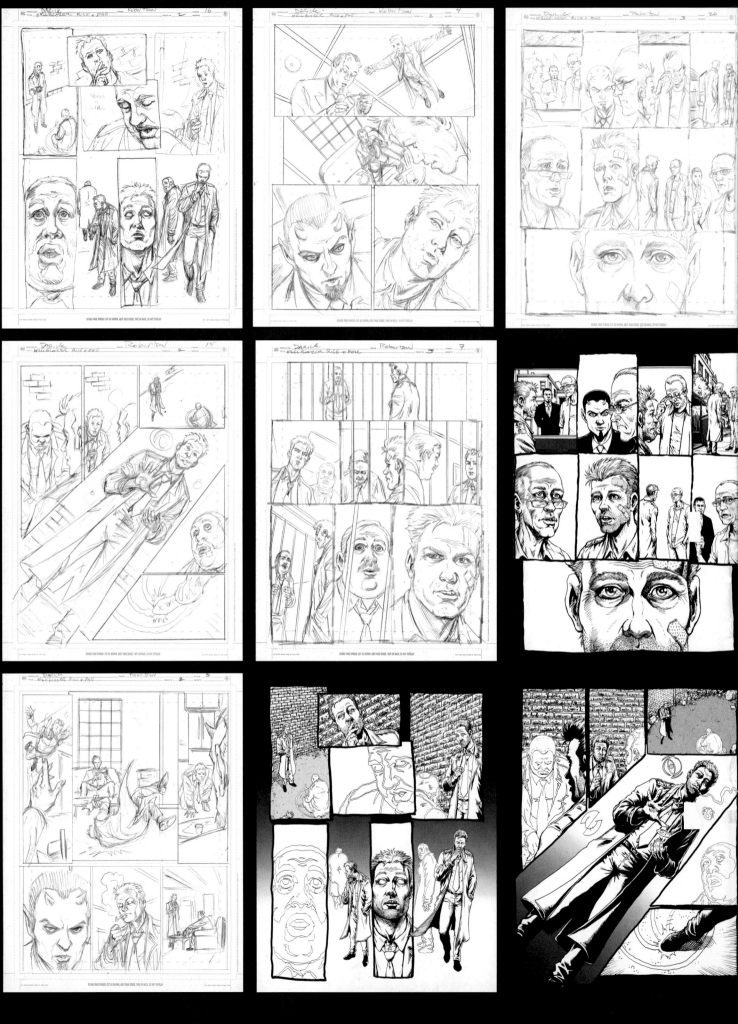

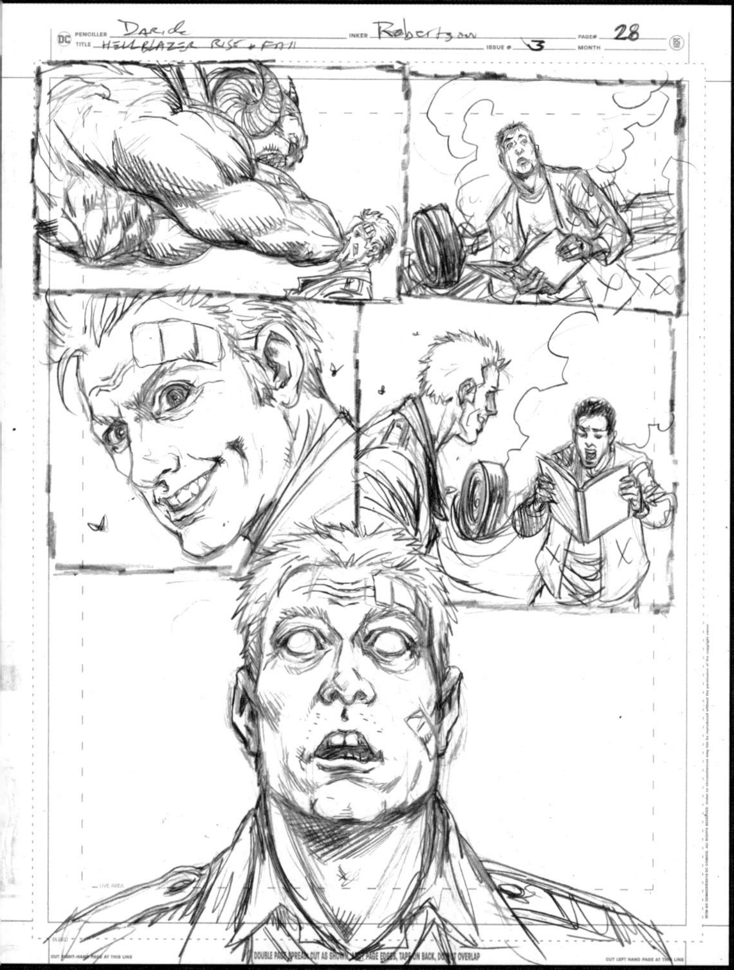
PENCILLER Darick
INKER Robertson
PAGE# 28
TITLE HELLBLAZER RISE + FALL
ISSUE # 3
MONTH
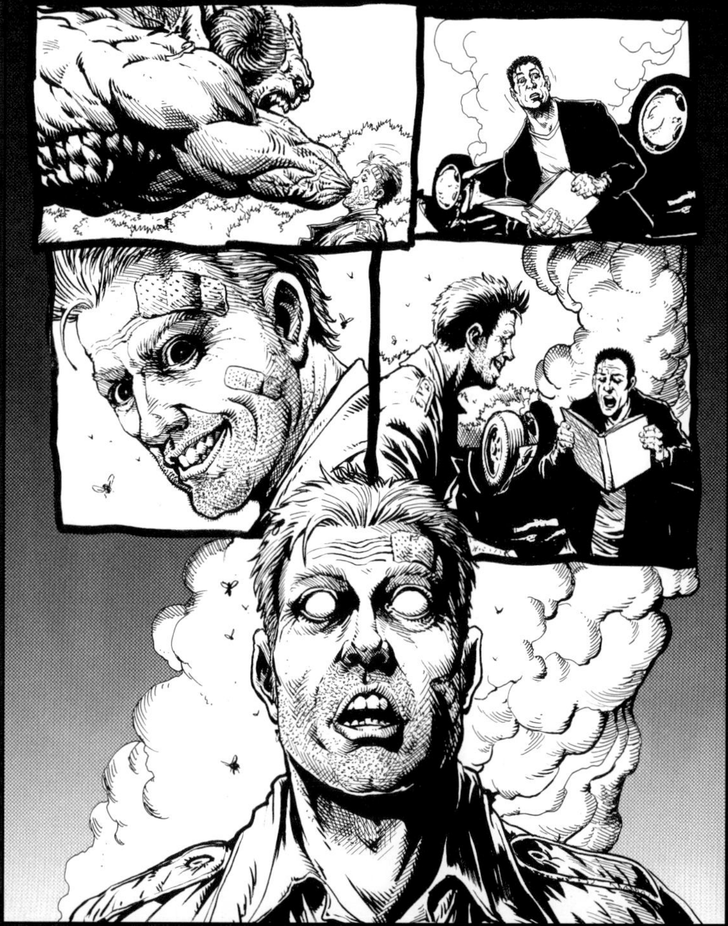
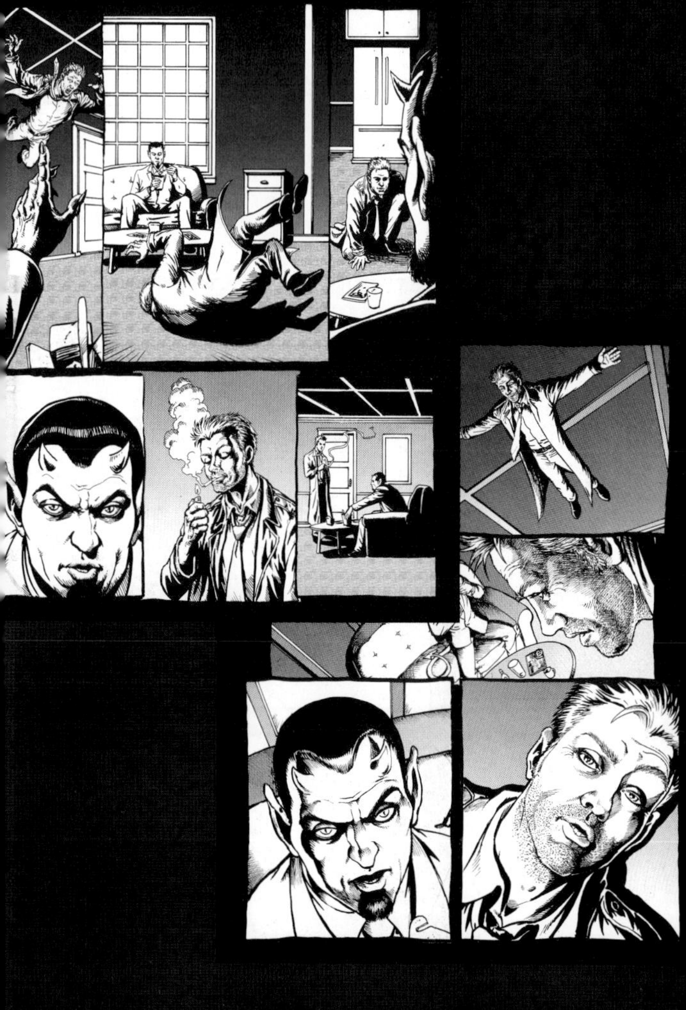
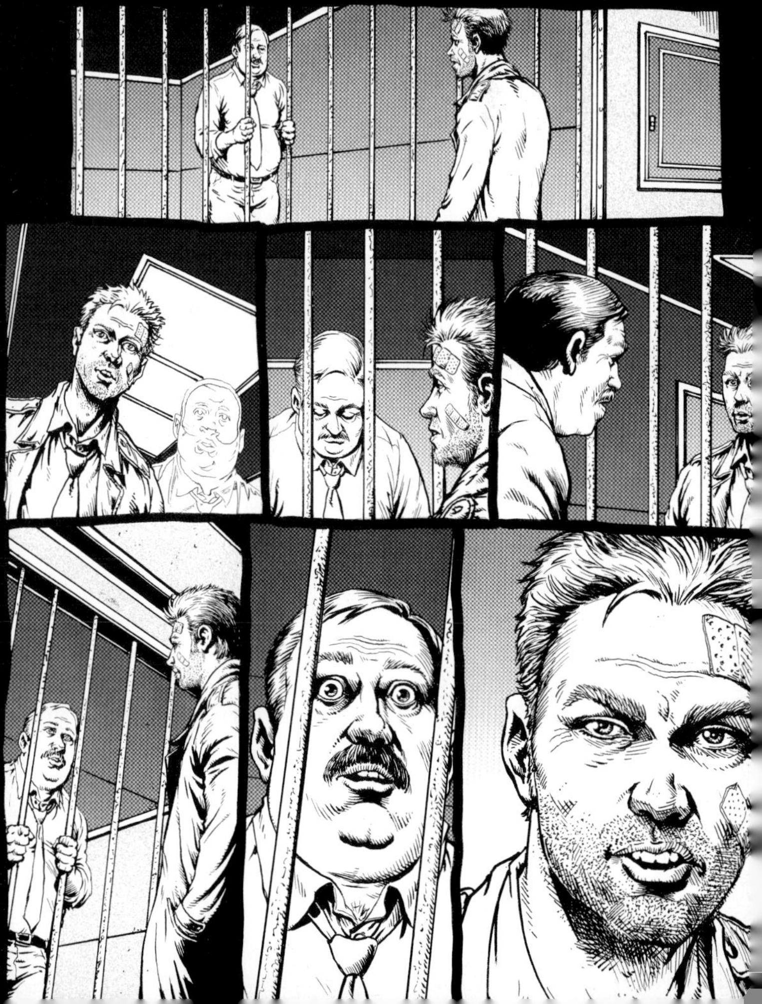

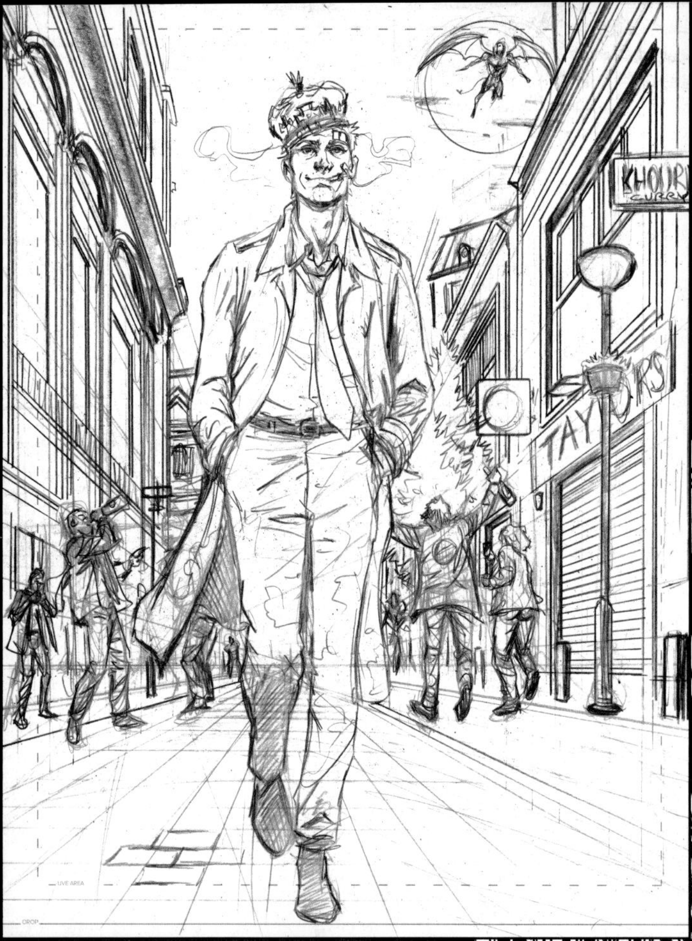
KHOURI

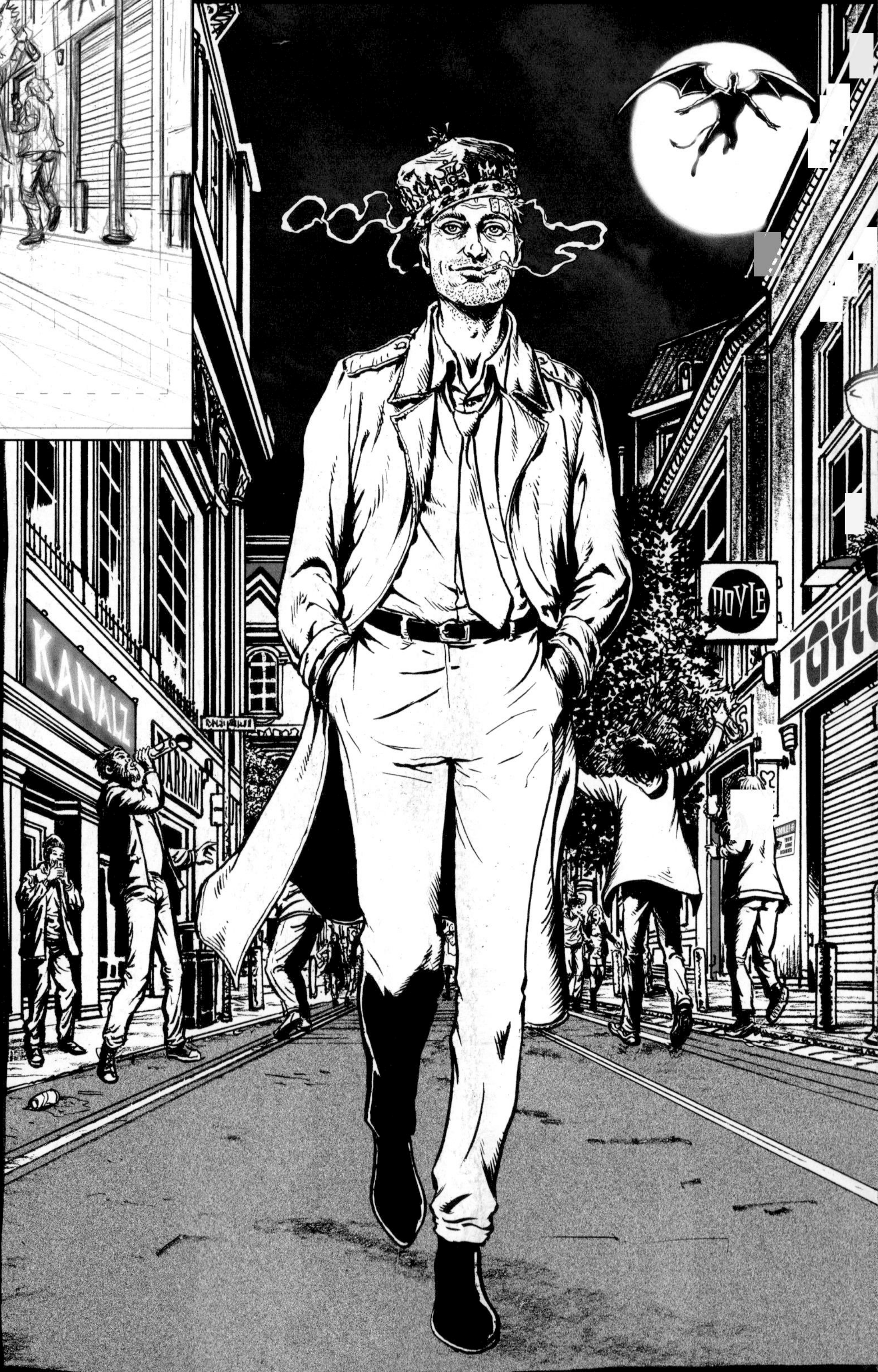
DOYLE